Be

Beau Jack

The Boxing Life of Sidney Walker,
Two-Time Lightweight Champion

ROBERT MULLINS

McFarland & Company, Inc., Publishers
Jefferson, North Carolina

ISBN (print) 978-1-4766-7906-8
ISBN (ebook) 978-1-4766-3721-1

LIBRARY OF CONGRESS AND BRITISH LIBRARY
CATALOGUING DATA ARE AVAILABLE

Front cover: Beau Jack, circa 1941 (courtesy of Bruce Kielty)

Printed in the United States of America

*McFarland & Company, Inc., Publishers
Box 611, Jefferson, North Carolina 28640
www.mcfarlandpub.com*

Table of Contents

Part V. Called to Service

Part VI. Jack Breaks His Kneecap

Part VII. Retirement from the Ring

Preface

Once a man has made a commitment to a way of life, he puts
the greatest strength in the world behind him. It's something
we call heart power. Once a man has made this commitment,
nothing will stop him short of success.
　　　　　　　　　　　—Vince Lombardi (1913–1970)

Sidney "Beau Jack" Walker was no ordinary person—much less an ordinary boxer. Born in 1921 south of Augusta, Georgia, he faced adversity with every step he took. From being abandoned by his parents to being beaten up by a gang of white boys who stole his pocket change earned from shining shoes, life was demanding for Sidney.

It was challenging for a black boy growing up in the South. The 13th Amendment banning slavery was adopted in 1865, but sadly it did little to curb tensions between whites and blacks. The "separate but equal" doctrine declared by the U.S. Supreme Court in *Plessy v. Ferguson* (1896) reinforced separation of races as a way of life. In the 1930s and 1940s, segregation and racial tensions permeated American culture. Jim Crow laws and discrimination prevailed in the South. Schools were segregated, as were passenger trains and busses. Blacks and whites drank from different water fountains, ate at separate restaurants, worshipped in separate churches, and lived in separate neighborhoods. Public cemeteries, parks, streetcars, entertainment venues, barbershops, and restaurants were all segregated.

The mean annual income for a black male was less than half of that for a white male. Blacks were also often the first to be laid off from their jobs, and they suffered from an unemployment rate two to three times that of their white counterparts. Blacks were incessantly subject to animosity and racial slurs. Moreover, in the South, blacks were threatened with lynching or being held as peons by xenophobic white landowners.

Segregation permeated all aspects of society, including the world of sports. Black people were not allowed to compete in major league sports. It was 1946 before the first black athlete, Kenny Washington, was allowed to participate in the National Football League, and 1947 when Jackie Robinson broke the race barrier in Major League baseball.

In boxing, progress was somewhat quicker, setting the stage for Jackie Robinson and Kenny Washington to break the "color" barrier in their respective sports. In 1902, Joe Gans became the first African American to win the world lightweight title. In 1908, Jack Johnson became the first black world heavyweight championship, setting off race riots across the country. Johnson's accomplishment was a victory for the black community, but his disdain for the constraints of white society made him a poor ambassador for integration.

Then there was Joe Louis, world heavyweight champion from 1937 until 1949. No one can underestimate his impact. He was not only a civil rights pioneer but also a national hero. After debuting on July 4, 1934, the "Brown Bomber" went on a tear, winning his first 24 bouts. His first loss came against former heavyweight champion Max Schmeling of Brandenburg, Germany, on June 19, 1936. Schmeling knocked Louis out in the 12th round. Two years later, on June 22, 1938, Louis avenged his loss in a rematch with Schmeling. The bout was veiled with nationalistic and racial implications, as Adolf Hitler upheld Schmeling as a specimen of Aryan supremacy. Louis inflicted immediate and brutal vengeance, knocking Schmeling out in the first round. Overnight, Louis became a hero to Americans, black and white. His popularity transcended racial boundaries.

Beau Jack built on the advancements established by those before him becoming one of the most exciting and popular boxers among both blacks and whites during the forties. On his journey to two lightweight titles, he set amazing records that still stand today. Outside the ring, Beau was humble and polite, but he was a furious mass of flying punches inside the ring. Fans loved his unorthodox style. Listeners anxiously gathered around the radio on Friday nights to hear the aggressive and colorful Beau Jack in action at Madison Square Garden.

Beau started out life in rags but through his incredible heart and determination, made it to the top of the ladder. Ironically, Jack rose out of the wealthy opulent world of the southern white man, receiving financing for his boxing career from Bobby Jones, Clifford Roberts, and other founders of the Augusta National Golf Club. When his boxing days were finally over, he went back to where he started, shining shoes. He didn't complain, but counted his blessings. Jack enjoyed his final days shining shoes, working with youngsters in the gym, and visiting with the many improbable friends he made throughout the years.

Sadly, not many people in Beau Jack's hometown would even recognize his name, much less what he accomplished. A deeply religious man with gritty fortitude and integrity, he was and still is an upstanding role model. His story is inspiring.

Remarkably, only bits and pieces of Beau's life and accomplishments have been published. Many contain factual errors. It is my intent to change that. It is my hope that through Jack's story, the reader will attain a better appreciation for the man who rose from poverty and discrimination into the limelight of Madison Square Garden. A black American hero, his story documents the tragedies he encountered and his steadfast ability to overcome such adversities. Beau's story helps one comprehend the significant changes and progress toward unity that transpired during his life. Abraham Lincoln once said, "I like to see a man proud of the place in which he lives. I like to see a man live so that his place will be proud of him." Beau Jack did just that, earning well-deserved admiration. His perseverance and love for others inspires us to never give up, but to become the best we can be through honesty, integrity, and respect for each other.

Introduction

Beau Jack holds the record for [the] most main events fought at the old Garden. And though he fought long before the age of millionaire athletes and multimillion-dollar TV revenues, no fight anywhere has ever matched his best in ticket-sale revenue.[1]

—Michael Hirsley, *Chicago Tribune*

As a young man, Sidney "Beau Jack" Walker took the nation by storm, boxing his way to two world lightweight titles during the forties. Born into poverty, Sidney was virtually orphaned by his parents and given to his grandmother for raising. As a young boy, he shined shoes on the streets of Augusta, Georgia, to help support his household. It was his grandmother that gave Sidney his notorious name, "Beau Jack," after he stood up to a gang of toughs who earlier that day forcefully bullied him and stole his shoeshine money. Short in stature, Beau Jack only stood 5'5½" tall and weighed 135 pounds as an adult. Irrespective of his size, Beau realized that he could reap additional money fighting in battles royal, where he displayed an uncanny talent.

Growing up a black teenager in a segregated South, Beau found an inexplicable route out of poverty. With the assistance of golf legend, Bobby Jones, and other founders of the Augusta National Golf Club, the Georgia bootblack embarked on a tremendous record-setting boxing career. Boxing in five title bouts during the 1940s, Beau Jack won the world lightweight title twice. He earned his first title at the fledgling age of twenty-one. Boxing during boxing's golden years, in 1943, Beau was the sole fighter to yield a $100,000 gate at boxing's mecca, Madison Square Garden. Then, in March 1944, he became the only boxer to fight in three main events at the Garden in one month, producing a combined gate of $332,579.

Five months later, Jack set the record for the highest priced sports ticket—$100,000 for a ringside seat when he fought Bob Montgomery in the illustrious "War Bonds Fight" of 1944. Yes, that number is correct. Accounting for inflation and cost of living increases, $100,000 in 1944 has the equivalent buying power of $1,416,804.60 in 2018. The fight itself raised $35,864,900 in war bonds to aid the U.S. effort in World War II. Several months later, he was honored as "Fighter of the Year" by *The Ring* magazine, boxing's foremost authority of the day.

During his 15-year professional career, Jack fought in a record 27 main events at the Garden and yielded gross gates exceeding $2.2 million. In 1944, he set the record for the largest non-heavyweight purse, producing a gate of $132,823. Then, he broke his own record in 1946, with fans paying $148,152 to witness his slugfest with Canadian Johnny Greco. Two years later, Jack also established the mark for the all-time high gate in Canada, generating $51,832.

In addition to those who had the pleasure of witnessing Beau's prowess in person, millions gathered around the radio on fight night, listening to blow-by-blow commentary of his ring battles. He knew how to please the crowds, fighting with an exciting, unorthodox swarming "all out" style. Revered by both black and white fans, Beau was one of the best-known American athletes during the forties.

Jack's story is one of perseverance, hard work, and humility. Bits and pieces of his narrative, accurate or inaccurate, are virtually forgotten. Mystery shrouds many events in his life. Most people in his hometown have never even heard of him. Cast from the grounds of the world's most prestigious "whites only" golf club into the prime time of New York, Jack's success came through sheer heart and gritty determination.

Respectful and polite, Beau Jack was a heartwarming ray of light and innocence in a sport infiltrated by the mob. Beau did not submit to the racket. His honor and soul could not be sold. The bull-shouldered battler, whether he won or lost, always gave his best. He rose from poverty to riches in a white man's world and helped to break down the walls of segregation and hate. Regrettably, by the time he finished his ring career, ostensibly he was penniless, the money set aside for him by his handlers mysteriously depleted. He went back to shining shoes on his knees once again.

PART I

The Early Days

Some folks now say they were bad, but for me it was that or pickin' cotton. Back then the money from Battle Royals bought me clothes, shoes and food. So if that's what you call bad, well, keep it comin'.

—Sidney "Beau Jack" Walker

1

Roaring Twenties, Racial Tension and Segregation

Although racial tensions and segregation prevailed throughout the country during the early 1920s, times were good for many people in the United States. World War I had ended a couple of years earlier. Women had obtained the right to vote through the 19th Amendment. Americans were moving into the cities, and personal wealth was dramatically increasing. It was the "Roaring Twenties."

The American consumer was born. Families were buying electric washing machines and refrigerators. With rising wages, the automobile, such as Ford's Model T, became more accessible. Telephones were connecting people across the country. The radio industry was growing, bringing with it a fresh source of entertainment and the transmission of information. The film industry was booming as Americans flocked to movie theaters. The first Miss America pageant was held in Atlantic City, New Jersey.

It was also an emergent time for the African American community. Jazz and blues music became prominent and cardinal elements of black culture. It was the time of the Harlem Renaissance as African American art, literature, and music flourished. The famed Cotton Club in Harlem was in full swing with musicians such as Duke Ellington and Louis Armstrong performing in front of the soulful sounds of their jazz orchestras. In sports, the Negro National Baseball League was established, incorporating eight teams.

Social conflicts and unrest, however, accompanied prosperity. With the 18th Amendment becoming effective on January 16, 1920, the U.S. entered the prohibition period. Manufacturing, transporting, and the sale of intoxicating liquors was prohibited. Coinciding with prohibition came the increasing impact of Organized Crime or the Mafia. Its network was infamous for running illegal alcohol. It was also the time of Chicago gangster, Al Capone.

Segregation

With the progress of the black American came a sinister counter movement. The Ku Klux Klan (KKK) was in resurgence, using intimidation and violence to assert white supremacy. In 1921, approximately 300 people died in the Tulsa Race Riot, as 35 city blocks lay in ruin after being blazed by white rioters. Lynching of blacks by white posses were regular occurrences. In Georgia alone, there were over 450 lynching fatalities between 1882 and 1930. Blacks were incessantly subject to hatred and racial slurs.

Jim Crow laws and segregation prevailed in the South. The "separate but equal" doctrine declared by the U.S. Supreme Court in *Plessy v. Ferguson* reinforced segregation as a way of life. Debuting in 1915, the racist film, *The Birth of a Nation*, directed and co-produced by D.W. Griffith, portrayed black men as dimwitted and physically bellicose towards white women. It glorified the KKK and abetted its second formation at Stone Mountain, Georgia, during the same year.

Incredibly, it was the first film screened at the White House during Woodrow Wilson's presidency. The 28th president of the United States, Woodrow Wilson (1856–1924), served from 1913 to 1921. Only recently have Wilson's racial undertones been openly discussed. Quotes from Wilson's book, *A History of the American People*, were actually utilized in *The Birth of a Nation*. For instance, the following "toned-down" language from Wilson's book served as one of the silent film's quote cards. "The white men of the South were roused by the mere instinct of self-preservation … until at last there had sprung into existence a great Ku Klux Klan, a veritable empire of the South, to protect the Southern country."[1] After screening the movie, President Wilson reportedly said to D.W. Griffith that the film could "teach history with lightning."

It is very arduous to understand contradictions between Woodrow Wilson's words and actions. He was extraordinarily progressive and led the fight for idealism in international relations during and after World War I. Although instrumental in the formation of the League of Nations, when it came to race issues in the U.S., his Southern upbringing clouded his judgment. The son of a Presbyterian minister, Wilson spent time as a child in Augusta, Georgia, and Columbia, South Carolina, where racism was prevalent.

Soon after his inauguration on March 4, 1913, Wilson allowed Jim Crow laws to be enacted and carried out in Washington, D.C. When his postmaster general, Albert S. Burleson, argued that the railway mail service should be re-segregated, he did not object but permitted its segregation. He did the same when William G. McAdoo, secretary of the treasury, requested to segregate his department. Reportedly, during World War I, he was appalled that the French Army allowed black men to serve next to whites.

Schools were segregated, as were passenger trains and busses. Miscegenation was a felony in many states including Georgia. There were separate parks and even separate eating and sleeping accommodations for white and black prisoners. Blacks and whites drank from different water fountains, ate at separate restaurants, worshipped in separate churches, and lived in separate neighborhoods. Lillian Smith, in her book *Killers of the Dream*, describes segregation as a dance.

"Colored" sign outside of Greyhound bus station in Rome, Georgia, c. 1943 (Library of Congress).

From the time little southern children take their first step they learn their ritual, for Southern Tradition leads them through its intricate movements. And some, if their faces are dark, learn to bend, hat in hand; and some, if their faces are white, learn to hold their heads up high. Some step off the sidewalk while others pass by in arrogance. Bending, shoving, genuflecting, ignoring, stepping off, demanding, giving in, avoiding…. So we learned the dance that cripples the human spirit, step by step by step, we who were white and we who were colored, day by day, hour by hour, year by year until the movements were reflexes and made for the rest of our lives without thinking.[2]

Racial separation was a pervasive rule of life. The color of a person's skin was judged on a racial hierarchy with blacks being thrown to the bottom. The lighter your skin, the better. Mulattos were perceived better than dark black. White was the preferred color.

Racism in Sports

Racism and segregation permeated the sports world. The top three spectator sports at the time were baseball, college football, and boxing. Baseball, of course, reigned as the favorite national pastime. Blacks, however, were not allowed to play Major League baseball. They were relegated to play in their own leagues, known as the Negro Leagues. Only in 1947, when the Brooklyn Dodgers signed Jackie Robinson (1919–1972), did baseball's racial barrier break. Schools in the South were segregated; therefore, there were no black football players at white schools. Blacks were not even allowed in college stadiums. Only where colleges were integrated up North and out West, were blacks allowed to play football. It would not be until 1970, when Bear Bryant, the legendary head coach of the University of Alabama, invited the University of Southern California Trojans, which had black running backs and a black quarterback, to play in Tuscaloosa, that the route to desegregation in college football was paved. In the fledgling National Football League, blacks were secretly banned in 1933. Thirteen years later, Kenny Washington (1918–1971), a football teammate of Jackie Robinson at UCLA, finally became the first black football player in the modern era of the NFL when the Los Angeles Rams signed him in March of 1946.

Unlike baseball and college football, boxing integrated much earlier. At the turn of the century, however, blacks were not allowed to compete in the same circuits as white boxers. When they did, they were only permitted to fight other black fighters, leading to the development of a "Negro League," as in baseball. For example, the legendary black heavyweight boxer Sam "Bone Crusher" Langford (1883–1956) was almost exclusively relegated to fight other black fighters. Therefore, many of his fights were against the same opponents. For instance, Langford fought Harry Wills 17 times, Sam McVey 16 times, Joe Jeannette 14 times, "Battling" Jim Johnson 12 times, Jeff Clark 10 times, Jack Thompson 9 times, and Bill Tate 9 times. Although Langford retired with an exceptional record of 180–29–39, he never received a title bout. At last, a year before his death, he was honored with induction into *The Ring*'s Boxing Hall of Fame and Canada's Sports Hall of Fame.

Gradually, black fighters were permitted to fight against their white counterparts in title matches. In 1902, Joe Gans (1874–1910) won the world lightweight title, defeating Frank Erne (1875–1954) of Switzerland, to become the first native-born black American to win a title. Gans finished his outstanding career with a record of 145–10–16 and was posthumously honored in 1990 by induction into the International Boxing Hall of Fame.

The esteemed heavyweight division was the last to integrate. It evolved through the prowess of the Galveston Giant. John Arthur "Jack" Johnson (1878–1946), standing 6'1" tall and weighing 200 pounds, won the world colored heavyweight title in 1903. His sights were set on James J. "Boilermaker" Jeffries (1875–1953), who wore the world heavyweight title crown. Jeffries, however, refused to fight Jack during his undefeated reign. Irrespective, after Jeffries retired, Johnson finally received a chance at the undisputed title in 1908, when he faced off against Tommy Burns.

Tommy Burns (1881–1955), the only Canadian-born world heavyweight champion, held the title. Persistently an underdog, the 5'7", 175-pound Burns won the title in 1906, defeating Marvin Hart in Los Angeles. Unlike other boxers, Tommy didn't mind crossing the "color line." The fight took place in

Sydney, Australia, on December 25, 1908. Johnson destroyed Burns, to finally seize the world heavyweight title. Mocking him the whole way, Johnson insulted Burns calling him "little boy" and comparing him to a woman, saying, "Who taught you to fight? Your mother? You hit like a woman." Johnson even let Burns survive the 13th round so he could dish out more punishment. Police ultimately called a halt to the fight in the 14th round. Typical for black boxers at the time, Burns earned $30,000 for the bout, while Johnson only received $5,000.

Many viewed the bout as a fight for racial supremacy, but Burns was supposed to win. Famous journalist and novelist Jack London (1876–1916), commenting from Sydney on behalf of the *New York Herald*, wrote, "It had all the seeming of a playful Ethiopian at loggerheads with a small and futile white man."[3] Johnson's gold capped teeth and smile annoyed London. "But one thing remains," London wrote from Sydney, "Jeffries must emerge from his alfalfa farm and remove that smile from Johnson's face. Jeff, it's up to you."[4] After the fight, Jeffries was asked what he would do if Jack Johnson came to him looking for a fight. Jeffries retorted, "If that coon comes around here I will take him by the neck and throw him out."[5]

Ultimately, Johnson got his chance at undefeated heavyweight James J. Jeffries. Jeffries, christened the "Great White Hope," announced on April 19, 1909, that he would come out of his five-year retirement to fight Johnson for the heavyweight championship of the world. Initially set to take place in California, Governor James Gillett (1860–1937) refused to host the bout, so promoters Jack Gleason and Tex Rickard moved the fight to Reno, Nevada.

Johnson battered a cut and bleeding Jeffries in the 15-round fight on July 4, 1910. After knocking Jeffries down for the first time in his career, Jeffries' corner threw in the towel. The bout became known as the "Fight of the Century" and set the nation on fire. That evening a headline in the *Reno Evening Gazette* read, "Greatest Tragedy of Ring History Was Enacted in Roped Arena in Reno Today."[6] In the tone of the times, Frank Hall, a writer for the newspaper wrote, "It seems a terrible thing for a white man to go down to defeat at the hands of a black."[7]

Johnson's long-awaited victory over Jeffries set off a succession of racial instabilities. Race riots across the country immediately followed the announcement of Johnson's victory. As many as 18 casualties were reported from riots, ranging in locations from Uvaldia, Georgia, to Tallulah, Louisiana. In the small town of Uvaldia in south Georgia, three black people were killed during rioting at a cross-tie camp on the Georgia & Florida Railroad. When black men from the cross-tie camp went into town drunk the day after Johnson's victory, tensions heightened. Several white men marched to the encampment to arrest the ringleader but were met with gunfire. Posses led by bloodhounds were called in to seek out the remaining members of the camp.

Jack Johnson knocks James Jeffries down in the "Fight of the Century," c. 1910 (author's collection).

In New York, more than 100 people were wounded during riots. It was a horrible scene. In Fort Worth, Texas, it was reported that a desk sergeant asked a "dusky giant" held at the jail for drunkenness for his name and received the following reply, "My name's Jack Johnson, and I can whip any white man living." In the wake of the riots, many cities and states banned replay of the fight film. Jeffries, however, was humbled and praised Jack Johnson's ability.

Ironically, Johnson was not the most suitable ambassador for integrating the heavyweight division. He verbally abused his white opponents, and outside the ring, he had a sexual attraction to white women. In 1913, Jack Johnson was arrested for violating the Mann Act on the grounds that he had transported a white woman, his girlfriend and future wife, Lucille Cameron, across state lines for immoral purposes. He was sentenced to a year in prison. Released on bond, Johnson fled to Canada where he began a seven-year period as a fugitive. In 1920, he surrendered to U.S. Marshalls on the Mexico–U.S. border and served ten months in prison before being released. Later that year, he opened a bar named the Club Deluxe at the corner of 142 Street and Lenox Avenue in Harlem. It subsequently became the famous Cotton Club. In 2018, Johnson received a posthumous presidential pardon from President Donald Trump citing the racial injustice suffered by Johnson.

2

Beau's Early Life

On March 31, 1921, a deadly tornado ripped through Albany, Georgia, killing one person and injuring at least 60 others. The next day, Augusta merchants presented a plan to Postmaster J. C. McAuliffe to have carriers deliver all mail to intended addressees, thereby eliminating the need for independent porters and deliverymen. For the first time in the history of Augusta, baseball fans could see every game played by their beloved Tigers via tape delay. Baseball matinees of the games were shown downtown at the Federation of Trades Labor Hall. Augusta's prominence as a winter colony for wealthy northerners was in full swing and the real estate market was booming.

A campaign for Georgia Tech was underway. Education was needed so that Georgians would not have to continue shipping their valuable natural resources out of state for manufacturing. Georgia sought to transition past its reliance on cash crops. The trustees of the University of South Carolina modified entrance regulations to require students to declare allegiance to a state statute prohibiting Greek letter fraternities at the university. In Mobile, Alabama, Coach Cozy Dolan of the New York Giants and Umpire Lauzon were arrested for fighting during a baseball game after Lauzon swung on Dolan and lunged at him with a knife.

A headline on the front page of the *New York Age* read, "Georgia White Planter Holding Men in Peonage—Killed Eleven, Deaths of 11 Negroes Charged to Employer."[1] John Williams, a white plantation owner near Covington, Georgia, had enslaved twelve black men as peon workers on his plantation. Gus Chapman, one of the men held against his will and forced to work for free, escaped to Atlanta and told Bureau of Investigation agents about his indentured colleagues, terrible beatings, and whippings. Agents visited Williams' plantation but the men, frightened for their lives, denied Chapman's horrid story. After the agents departed, Williams destroyed the evidence by killing the 11 black men, demanding some of them bludgeon the others to death with axes. He hid the evidence, burying bodies on his property and chaining the bodies of others together, weighting them with rocks, and dropping them in local rivers.

Although Williams was indicted for the murder of all 11 men, he was only tried on one. At the time, white men were not usually convicted of murder for killing a black person in the Deep South. Astonishingly, a jury of 12 white men found Williams guilty of murder and he was sentenced to life in prison. As horrible as it was, the case would help pave the way to eradicate the practice of peonage and white justice.

Childhood

In Burke County, Georgia, a little baby boy was born. The date was April 1, 1921, and the infant's name was Sidney Rogers Walker (1921–2000). Family life was rough. Sidney's mother, Lilly Scott, and father, Willie Walker, split up after he was born and took Sidney to Augusta, where he was raised by his maternal grandmother, Evie Dixon,[2] on a farm a couple of miles south of town.

Sidney's mother and father formally divorced when he was six years old. His mother moved to St. Petersburg, Florida, and Sidney rarely saw his father. Willie Walker was always in and out of trouble. Although not convicted, he was twice indicted for assault with intent to murder. He was also arrested for stealing a case of cigars from a freight car. Trouble seemed to follow Walker all the way to his untimely death. Sidney's father died from a bullet wound to his abdomen in an altercation over a dollar bill. The day was Sidney's 18th birthday.

Cotton was king in Georgia, but the previous arrival of the boll weevil had taken its toll on cotton

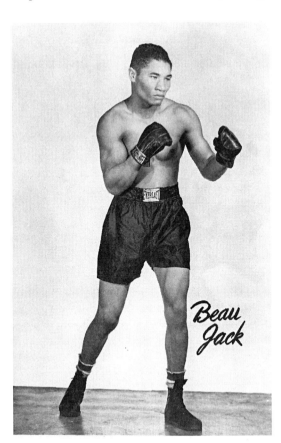

Beau Jack, c. 1941 (courtesy Bruce Kielty).

farms. Georgia also suffered a three-year drought beginning in 1925, making life even harder for small farmers. Cotton prices were falling with the introduction of man-made fabrics. In rural areas, blacks made less than half the income of their white counterparts. Many blacks were forced off their land, leading to massive migrations to urban areas or to industrial areas in the North. The forthcoming Great Depression only made daily struggles worse. Life on the farm was grueling. It was especially difficult for black families.

Not only was it hard for blacks to survive economically, but racism was rampant in Augusta. Blacks were banned from public places frequented by whites, except if they were serving on the staff. Jim Crow laws ensured separate facilities and continual segregation. The local newspaper even had a separate page for news about black people.

Sidney struggled as a child to help his grandmother with the household and farm. He spent countless hours hoeing and picking cotton in the fierce heat. During the summer, in his spare time, Sidney scoured the briars, picking blackberries. He then walked around selling quarts of blackberries to white landowners for a quarter. He also helped out on his Uncle Jesse's hog farm. Digging scraps out of garbage cans, Sidney put them on a wagon and wheeled them to his uncle's hogs.

Instead of an education, Sidney learned the art of shoe shining at an early age to help his grandmother. When he was eight years old, Sidney would wake before dawn and walk to downtown Augusta in hopes of earning money shining shoes. He gathered his rags, horsehair brush, and tins of polish, placed them in his shoeshine box, and walked three and a half miles from his grandmother's house to the corner of Ninth and Broad streets in downtown. Sidney strategically chose this specific spot, because it was on this corner that cotton farmers entered the city to sell their crop. Near the intersection, there was also a Walgreen's Drug Store, Bowen's Hardware, Green H. L. Department store, and the Quality Shop, where men shopped for clothing. It was a prime spot for shoeshines.

Sidney, short and small in stature, was a mild-mannered young boy. Not disposed to conflict, he was pressed to acquire fighting skills at an early age. Other kids resented Sidney's hardworking character and the money he made as a bootblack. Unfortunately, success made him a target of older kids. One afternoon after shining shoes, Sidney was surrounded by five older white boys who demanded his pocket change. Sidney respectfully refused, but the leader of the gang threatened to beat him up if he did not comply. Confronting five bullies, Sidney reluctantly yielded the $1.90 from his pockets.

His day's earnings gone, he was so distraught that he went home in tears. Instead of comforting Sidney when he came back, his grandmother, a harsh disciplinarian, showed him no sympathy. Determined to teach him a lesson,

Broad Street (south side), between Fifth and Eighth streets, Augusta, Georgia, c. 1936 (Library of Congress).

she made him pull up his pants legs and then beat him with a switch saying, "You better fight till the blood runs out your shoes…. No Walker is supposed to be runnin' nowhere."[3]

It was a harsh lesson, but one that Sidney would not forget. Having successfully bullied Sidney for his money, the group of boys came back a week later demanding Sidney's earnings. Instead of backing down as he had previously done, Sidney confronted the leader, sucker punched him and smashed his head against the ground. Defeated, the boys departed, and Sidney kept his money. When he returned home and told his grandmother what transpired, she declared him "'reborn,' and renamed him 'Beau Jack,'" a name that he would proudly use for the rest of his life.

Young Sidney had more obstacles to overcome. At the age of nine, Sidney's life was almost lost. On the cold winter evening of February 15, 1931, Sidney and his younger brother, John Henry Walker, were walking home on New Savannah Road in south Augusta. As they walked by a local slaughterhouse, J. Shapiro & Sons, the night watchman, Tom Burton, fired upon the boys with his shotgun. One of the shots struck Sidney, spreading birdshot in his chest. He was rushed to University Hospital where he was listed as being in "fair" condition. In his story to Sheriff L. H. Wilkins, Burton claimed that he thought the boys were stealing coal. "When I shouted at the boys, they ran, so I shot one of the pests."[4] Doubting Burton's story, the sheriff locked Burton up in the county jail and charged him with assault with intent to murder.

Years later, when Beau underwent an X-ray as part of his physical for induction into the Army, it showed "a pattern of .22 birdshot, about No. 8 spread over an area the size of your hat" in his chest.[5] Beau spun a yarn to explain the birdshot. "My daddy shot me a long time ago with a shot-gun while we were out rabbit hunting. I guess I was about eight or nine. It was a long time ago. They wanted to cut them out, but I knew that'd hurt, so I wouldn't let 'em. I don't feel them when I fight...."[6] Why Beau spun that tale, no one knows. His father was never a significant part of his life.

Sidney's grandmother, on the other hand, was an enormous influence on his life. She taught Sidney manners and how to live humbly. She instilled character into Sidney. She made him promise her that he would never smoke or drink and that he would work hard. She told him to always aim to do right and get along with everybody. Throughout his life, Sidney respectfully honored his grandmother's request.

Tragedy struck Sidney when he was nine years old. His grandmother called him to her side. Little did Sidney know the significance of what she had to say to him. He thought she needed him to do a chore. As she sat in her rickety old rocking chair, gently rocking back and forth, she said, "Sidney, don't cry, but I am going away to be with the Lord." With tears filling his eyes, Sidney recalled, "She sent me to the kitchen for a bowl of soup and when I came back the Lord had stole her away."[7]

Sidney's rock of strength had been taken home to the heavens above. It would always be a moment of misery and tragedy for Sidney. He was frustrated and lost. Sidney had grown up so fast, and now he seemed to have lost everything. Instead of self-pity, he remembered the vigor that his grandmother instilled in him and determination set in for the young lad.

Following his grandmother's death, Sidney and his brother went to live with their grandmother Lulu H. Walker in the house she shared with their Uncle David and Aunt Pearl. Not far from his grandmother's house, they also lived on a small farm in south Augusta.

3

Battles Royal
Bring Opportunity

Life was hard, and Beau needed to find additional ways to support himself. It was common at the time for teenage boys, regardless of race, to fight on the streets or in fight clubs with the winner earning at least some pocket change. Moreover, it provided bystanders a chance to possibly make money wagering on the winner. For instance, the legendary "Bronx Bull," Jake LaMotta, learned to fight on the street.

The Experience

Despite racial overtones, battles royal provided an additional opportunity for teenage boys to make extra cash. A gory tradition from years past, battles royal were common in 17th and 18th century England. Following the American Civil War and the post-war Reconstruction, they gained popularity in the United States. Usually featuring six or more black boys or men in a room or ring, the combatants were blindfolded and then obliged to battle against each other until only one victorious person was left standing. Spectators would then throw coins into the ring as a reward for the participants' efforts. In addition to blindfolds, gloves were often used and, in some cases, the combatants had one of their arms tied behind their back. Although white boys also participated in battles royal, participants were predominantly black.

Battles royal were extremely popular and customary as preliminaries to boxing and wrestling matches. They took place at both black and white venues. Ironically, battles royal furnished opportunities for black fighters to enter the realm of professional boxing. Early boxing greats Joe Gans and Jack Johnson participated in battles royal when they were teenagers. Gans became the first black man to hold the world lightweight title, whereas Johnson became the first black man to earn the world heavyweight championship.

Even the legendary soul singer James Brown (1933–2006) fought in battles royal. In his 1997 autobiography, *The Godfather of Soul*,[1] Brown states how he was used to recruit black boys for battles royal for the entertainment of white men. As he describes the battle royal, the boys were blindfolded, one hand tied behind their back, and a boxing glove tied on the other hand. Then they were pushed into a ring with five other kids. When the battle begins, you swing at anything that moves. The winner is the last one standing. Coincidently, Brown revered Beau Jack as someone to model himself after.

Battles royal were brutal. Ralph Ellison provides a vivid insight into the viciousness of battles royal in his critically acclaimed book, *The Invisible Man*.

And I heard the bell clang and the sound of feet scuffling forward. A glove smacked against my head.

Child in boxing stance, c. 1888 (Jefferson R. Burdick Collection, Metropolitan Museum of Art).

I pivoted, striking out stiffly as someone went past, and felt the jar ripple along the length of my arm to my shoulder. Then it seemed as though all nine of the boys had turned upon me at once. Blows pounded me from all sides while I struck out as best I could. So many blows landed upon me that I wondered if I were not the only blindfolded fighter in the ring.[2]

Most of the time participation was voluntary, but not always.

After the death of his grandmother, Jack began fighting in battles royal, where he developed into a warrior. Jack recollected the typical battle royal he participated in as a youth: "Five young fighters would be blindfolded and put in a ring or roped off area," said Beau. "They began swinging and trying to knock the other fighters down. When there were only two left, the two would fight a regular four-round match to determine a winner. Then all the participants would line up along the ropes as spectators tossed money into the ring. At the sound of the bell, they all fought for the coins littering the ring."[3]

Jack excelled at the brutal battles. Despite his small frame and weight, legend has it that he never lost a battle royal. Beau explained that he "would stay in the corner, real low." "People would miss me and hit the post, or just hit me in the stomach," he said. "Those other bigger fighters were busy trying to knock each other out. Whenever one of them backed up near me I slammed him good and knocked him out."[4] Beau was keen on strategy. Whatever his tactic was it worked for Beau. He even knocked out a 200-pound giant in one of his fights. Admittedly, Jack said he would sometimes peek through a sagging blindfold. Near the end of one battle, the only one standing between Beau and victory was his younger brother, John Henry. In the fierce competition for triumph, Beau knew what he had to do. Without hesitation, he knocked his brother out with a left hook to the stomach.

Around town, Beau became a repeatedly summoned participant in battles royal. When he was fifteen years old, Jack appeared at the Epicurean Hall at 1212 Ninth Street. The African American entertainment venue hosted dances, musical entertainment, and boxing. On December 10, 1936, Beau appeared on the Thursday night fight card, which billed Beau Jack as "Bo Jack, the king of the battle royals." That night the battle royal was sponsored by the Home Boys' Charity Club, an organization of prominent black citizens who banded themselves together for charity work to help the city's less fortunate. Tickets cost 25¢ for general admission and 35¢ for ringside. There was also a reserved section for white people.

When Beau was up in years, he looked back on his battle royal days with pride, discounting the savagery of the contests and racial overtones.

> You know, those Battle Royal days were fun. They were better than when I had the title. Everything was simple.
> Some folks now say they were bad, but for me it was that or pickin' cotton. Back then the money from Battle Royals bought me clothes, shoes and food. So if that's what you call bad, well keep it comin'. … I wanted to give the people a good show and I did…. I was a champion.[5]

With a twinkle in his eye, he recalled the time legendary golfer Bobby Jones gave him a $100 bill. "I remember the great Mr. Bobby Jones, called me over one time and said, 'Here kid.' He stuck a $100 bill in my hand. I said, 'I ain't got no change,' but he said, 'Keep it!' But just then this boy snatched it outta my hand. I run after him, hit him a shot on the chin and knocked him out to get that money back. After that everybody at the golf club wanted to see me fight."[6]

Opportunity Knocks Through Bowman Milligan and the Augusta National Golf Club

Beau's victorious style and reputation in battles royal landed him into some of the most prominent battles royal in town and ultimately a boxing world title. Jack often fought at the prestigious Bon Air Vanderbilt Hotel, entertaining members and guests of the Augusta National Golf Club.

One of the finest hotels in the South, the Bon Air was renowned for its gourmet food, golf, tennis, and horseback riding. After the original hotel burned down, it was rebuilt as the Bon Air-Vanderbilt Hotel at the cost of over $1,000,000. Opened on January 8, 1921, the Italian Spanish renaissance hotel was equipped with more than 300 guest rooms. Some of America's most elite dignitaries visited the esteemed hotel, including American novelist and author of *The Great Gatsby*, F. Scott Fitzgerald (1896–1940); industrialist, philanthropist, and founder of the Standard Oil Company, John D. Rockefeller (1839–1937); U.S. president and subsequent Supreme Court chief justice William H. Taft (1857–1930); U.S. President Warren G. Harding (1865–1923); British prime minister Sir Winston Churchill (1874–1965); Judge Kenesaw Mountain Landis (1866–1944), the first commissioner of Major League baseball; Canadian prime minister Robert Borden (1854–1937); Nobel Prize winner Nicholas Murray Butler (1862–1947); and Harvey Samuel Firestone (1868–1938), the founder of the Firestone Tire & Rubber Co.

The Bon Air also served as the spawning ground for the world-famous Augusta National Golf Club which traces its roots to the Bon Air's lawyer, Bobby Tyre Jones, Jr. (1902–1971). Bobby Jones, a lawyer by profession, was one of the world's most influential amateur golfers, having won the four major golf tournaments known as the Grand Slam in the same year. Remarkably, he never turned professional. His entire career in competitive golf was as an amateur.

In 1931, Jones announced the development of the Augusta National Golf Club. Other notable and wealthy people participating in the venture included: Clifford Roberts, New York investment banker; Fielding Wallace, president of the Augusta Country Club; Alfred Bourne, winter resident of Augusta and millionaire sportsman; Tom Barrett, Jr., mayor of Augusta; Kent Cooper, famous journalist and executive director of the Associated Press; President M. H. Aylesworth, of the National Broadcasting Company; Grantland Rice, the world's premier newspaper golf authority; William C. Breed, president of the New York State Bar Association; and Eugene G. Grace, president of the Bethlehem Steel Company.

Formal opening ceremonies for the golf course were held on December 24, 1932. A couple of days later, the first official rounds took place with Bobby Jones and well-known sportswriter Grantland Rice greeting players at the first tee. More than 18,000 prominent governors, golf stars, USGA members, newspapermen, bankers, and others were invited for the occasion. Clifford Roberts, chairman of the Augusta National Golf Club from 1931 until 1976, and Grantland Rice went so far as to charter a train from New York to Augusta to recruit members for the Augusta National.

The first Masters Tournament, at that time known as the Augusta National Invitation Tournament, was held in March 1934. Five years later, the tournament officially became known as the Masters. Today, the Masters Tournament is one of the most renowned and famous tournaments in professional golf.

Oddly, it was the Augusta National's first clubhouse employee, Bowman Milligan (1899–1984), who is credited with discovering Beau Jack. Bowman was a large, attractive black man, articulate and well-versed. He also was reportedly a great southern cook. Years later, President Eisenhower's wife Mamie raved about the crisp southern-style fried chicken Bowman prepared for her.

Bowman made his living serving the elite. At age twenty, he was a bellboy at the esteemed Bon Air-Vanderbilt Hotel. Through connections he made at the Bon Air, Bowman obtained employment as the porter at the prestigious Flint County Country Club in Flint, Michigan.

It just so happens, he left his service there quite abruptly to come back to Augusta. It was during the summer of 1926 and the height of Prohibition. As part of his duties, Milligan was tasked with acquiring liquor for the club during its summer invitational tournament. After receiving tips about the prohibition violations, federal revenuers raided the club, discovering more than 100 bottles of bonded liquor. As club rules prohibited the presence of alcohol, everyone pointed the finger at Milligan. A warrant was subsequently issued for his arrest, but he was long gone. Years later, Clifford Roberts recalled the story as he was told. Apparently, to escape jail, Bowman tricked the officials when they arrived at the club to arrest him.

"May I help you?" Bowman politely asked.

"We're looking for Bowman Milligan," the magistrate demanded. "Do you know which one he is?"

"Yes, sir!" said Bowman. "I know right where he is and I'll go get him for you." With that, Bowman left by the back door and has never been seen since in the state of Michigan.[7]

Bowman got out of "Dodge" as quick as he could. Subsequently, a federal grand jury indicted Frank D. Buckingham, club president, and Lucien Eck, the general manager, on violations of the Prohibition Act.

Back in Augusta, the Augusta National Golf Club hired Bowman to serve as the club steward. As such, Bowman was responsible for organizing entertainment for the club members and guests. Frequently, Bowman arranged boxing matches and battles royal at the Bon Air Hotel where many of the members and guests stayed. After roping off a section of the dining room, five or six black boys wearing boxing gloves would enter the ring, where they would duke it out until only one remained standing. Then the spectators would shower the ring with coins.

Given his reputation, one of the boys that Bowman summoned to participate in the battles royal was Beau Jack. Recalling those days, Beau said his most significant battle came during one of the first Masters Tournaments. "All those rich people who'd come to Augusta to see the tournament had to be entertained at night," Jack explained. "So the club put on this big battle royal in the dining room of the Bon-Air Hotel."[8] One evening, the brawl came down to Jack and a "big feller." Without hesitation, Jack knocked him out with a long, looping bolo punch. In appreciation, the men around the ring threw $10, $20, and $50 bills into the ring. Beau took home $1,000 that night.

Impressed by Beau's tenacity, Bowman hired Jack as a bootblack and locker room attendant at the Augusta National. Learning that he was orphaned and couldn't read or write, Milligan took him in as a fatherly figure and became his guardian. They would have a uniquely special relationship for years. At the club, Beau shined shoes and even caddied on occasion, but Beau was undeniably a fighter.

4

Beau Begins Boxing

A natural evolution from battles royal and his passion for combat, Beau Jack began boxing when he was fourteen years old. During his time downtown shining shoes, Beau met a wrestler named Jack Ross (1891–1953). Ross operated the Coney Island Sandwich Shop on the corner of Eighth and Ellis streets. He was barrel-chested, balding, 6 feet tall, and weighed 195 pounds. Ross immigrated to the United States from Greece when he was 14 years old. At age 20, Ross became a professional wrestler. Ross, aka the "Greek Demon," wrestled from coast to coast. He was a heavyweight with ribs of steel. During his 31-year wrestling career, Ross held numerous title belts, including the Southern middleweight title, which he held for over five years, the Southern light-heavyweight title, and the Southern heavyweight title. His son, Louis Ross, Jr., played football at Richmond Academy and was also a prevalent wrestler. But Jack Ross was not just a wrestler, he was a savvy businessman. Along with wrestling, he was a restaurateur and local wrestling promoter.

Ross came across Beau one day while he was shining shoes outside his restaurant. Ross could tell that Beau was an extraordinary teenager. He was polite, ambitious, and a hard worker. Beau was eager to survive the tough times, so Ross put him to work. Beau ran errands at his restaurant and worked around some of the local pool halls. Recognizing his grit and toughness, Ross gave Beau some of his first ring experience. As Ross promoted wrestling matches, he let Beau fight in boxing preliminaries and battles royal before his events, in return for "eating" money.

It didn't take long before Beau became a dominant boxer around town, fighting in local venues, such as the Lenox Theatre, Richmond Arena, the New Coliseum, and Aiken's Municipal Auditorium. Beau's first recorded boxing match took place at the Lenox Theatre. An African American venue built in the early 1920s, the Lenox Theatre was located on the corner of Ninth Street and Gwinnett Street in Augusta's "Golden Blocks" district, where black businesses prospered. The Greco-Roman architecture was inspiring. A headline in the *Augusta Chronicle* on January 9, 1921, hailed the theatre as "Lenox

Theatre Finest Theatre Owned and Controlled by Colored People in the United States."[1] When the stage was removed, the venue had seating for 1,191 spectators.

Beau was only 15 years old when he stepped into the theatre's ring on Thursday night, October 8, 1936. Presented by the Home Boys' Charity Club, the all-star boxing card was scheduled for 37 rounds of action featuring such fighters as "Battling Puggie" of Savannah, "Fast Black," and "Battling" Beau Jack. Special seats were reserved for white people in attendance. Jack continued his winning ways and his reputation continued to grow as he defeated his foe.

Although there were undoubtedly fights in between, Beau's next recorded bout was three years later on Friday night, April 7, 1939, at the Richmond Arena in Augusta, Georgia. Richmond Arena, also known as the American Legion Arena, was located at the corner of Jones and Ninth streets. Beau opened the weekly wrestling card featuring Red Raider and Red Dugan of Chattanooga. He thrilled the battle-hungry fans by demolishing his opponent by knockout.

With the help of Jack Ross, Beau became a regular on the local boxing scene. Five days after knocking out his opponent at the Richmond Arena, Jack was back in the ring on another American Legion wrestling card. In the main event, 250 spectators witnessed veteran wrestler George Romanoff of Jacksonville lose to Red Shadow by disqualification. To open the ticket, the increasingly popular Beau Jack was featured in a six-round exhibition bout with "Battling" Henry. Needless to say, he did not disappoint the fans. Beau overwhelmed "Battling" Henry with his furious flurries, terminating the bout in the fifth round when he landed a hard punch upstairs, ending Henry's night early by way of knockout.

After Beau's victory over Henry, he fought his next nine matches at Aiken's new Municipal Auditorium. Located in Aiken, South Carolina, approximately 17 miles east of Augusta, the Municipal Auditorium had seating for 500 spectators. Fight cards were fervently presented every Thursday night. Beau began his run at the Municipal Auditorium on January 18, 1940, entering the ring not only for a four-round boxing match but also in the battle royal before the beginning of the fight card. Beau won both battles.

Jack was back two weeks later to fight a four-round preliminary contest against Jake Mosely of Aiken. Beau easily pounded out a decision victory over Mosely. The main event featured Augusta's Baxley Hardy, a talented southpaw fighting in the middleweight division. Hardy defeated Jimmy Dillon on his way to a professional record of 46–6–2. Before a packed auditorium the following Thursday, February 8th, Beau won another decision in his preliminary bout with "Battling" Burns of Warrenton, Virginia. The next week, Jack knocked Alvin Stevens out in the 3rd round of their six-round battle. It was reportedly his eighth victory in a row. On Thursday night, February 29, Beau defeated Vincent Corbett of Bath, South Carolina.

Jack was on a roll, winning his next four fights at the Municipal Auditorium between March 7 and April 4. On March 7, Beau defeated Son Jenkins of Spartanburg, South Carolina. Two weeks later, he emerged victorious on points over Silent Stafford of Pittsburgh, Pennsylvania. Then he scored a second-round knockout over Joe James of Charlotte, North Carolina. Finally, after working the first day of the Masters Tournament, Jack defeated Tommy Lee of Atlanta, Georgia, in a four-round bout.

Within three months, Beau belted out at least nine straight victories at the Municipal Auditorium, improving his record to 11–0. Other accounts have Beau winning at least two more bouts, but they are not recorded. Two months later, in a fantastic turn of events, Jack would test his boxing skills in Holyoke, Massachusetts.

5

A Syndicate Forms

Sidney had strong character and a cordial demeanor that was both humble and pleasing. A hard worker, he rapidly endeared himself to members at the Augusta National, where he worked as a bootblack and locker room attendant. As Beau served the members, they often praised his remarkable talent in the ring. Beau loved it. He took pride in boasting about his fighting skills. When he was not shining shoes, waiting tables or caddying, you could find him shadow boxing around the locker room.

Following his string of victories at Aiken's Municipal Auditorium, Jack went to work shining shoes during the seventh annual Masters Tournament held on April 4–7, 1940. Jimmy Demaret, the Houston Hurricane, won the tournament with a score of 280. On a rainy Sunday afternoon, darkened by a partial solar eclipse, Demaret made 17 pars and one birdy in the final round. A record 10,000 spectators showed up for the final day. Speaking afterward, Bobby Jones, president of the Augusta National Golf Club, expressed "gratification at what he termed 'the finest and best behaved golf gallery in the world.'"[1]

In the evenings, Jack amused the Augusta National members and guests by showing off his dominance in battles royal. Knowing of his uncanny abilities, several of the affluent members made substantial returns wagering on Beau at one of the battles. Beau's fighting skills were quickly becoming renowned.

Young Jack's success in fighting and his work ethic caught the attention of legendary golfer Bobby Jones and Augusta National co-founder and CEO Clifford Roberts. Following the conclusion of the tournament, Jones and Roberts, along with other members, discussed the proposition of providing Beau a chance to box professionally. Eagerly, they resolved to furnish Beau a chance to prove himself in the ring. As a boxer, Beau would need money for training expenses, a boxing license, a manager, a trainer, food, and housing. Funds were soon raised for Jack to embark on a professional boxing career.

There are several different versions of how the money was raised, who contributed funds, and the amount advanced. All accounts, however, refer to

Fruitland Manor, Augusta National Golf Club, c. 1933 (Library of Congress).

the contributors as the "Syndicate." According to Clifford Roberts, Bowman Milligan requested $500 to take Jack up north to test out his boxing skills. So, Clifford Roberts, an investment banker by trade, passed a hat around and 20 people contributed $25 each to raise $500. Another version states that 20 individuals, including Bobby Jones, each threw in $50, for a pot of $1,000.

Recalling later, Beau Jack gave Bobby Jones credit, praising him for helping him start his boxing career.

> It was Mr. Jones more than anyone else. He told me one day, "Hey, you're a little bitty, skinny kid and you always seem to want to fight. Would you like to try for a career in the big time?" I told him, "Yes, sir" and he said, "See me when I get in from my round today and we'll talk about it."
>
> I did and he said, "I'm going to get some of my friends to see if we can't get you the money to do it right." He did everything he said, got me money for clothes, got me a trainer and manager (Bowman Milligan, steward at the Augusta course) and sent me off to New York to train right.[2]

Beau enthusiastically acknowledged Jones as leading the effort. Reportedly, Jones put up $500 for the venture and then convinced 50 other members to contribute $50 each. Irrespective of the version, the Syndicate agreed that if Beau won the 135-pound title, members would only receive their investment back.

Who were members of the Syndicate contributing funds for Beau Jack? Unquestionably, Bobby Jones and Clifford Roberts were members of the

Bobby Jones, c. 1921 (Library of Congress).

Syndicate. Comparing the different stories, it appears the rest of the members included Frank Craven, Frank Crumit, Billy DeBeck, Henry McLemore, Distiller Ellis "Slats" Slater, and Tom Yawkey. It was indeed an outstanding and distinguished group of men.

Frank Craven (1875–1945) was a well-known actor, director, producer, and screenwriter. Craven scripted screenplays, such as *The 19th Hole* (1927), *The First Year* (1926) and *Too Many Crooks* (1931). One of his best-known screenplays was the *Sons of the Desert* (1933), a Laurel and Hardy film. Craven also acted on Broadway and in film. He appeared in *Jack London* (1943) and as the stage manager in the original 1938 Broadway production and 1940 movie version of *Our Town* (1940).

Frank Crumit (1889–1943), along with his wife, Julia Sanderson, were popular radio entertainers, known as the "singing sweethearts on the air." They engaged in comedic discourse and entertained their listeners with their singing and dialogue. Frank was also a prevalent singer, songwriter, and vaudeville star. His versions of *The Gay Caballero* and *Abdul the Bulbul Ameer* sold more than 4,000,000 records.

Billy DeBeck (1890–1942) was a famous cartoonist and the creator of the renowned and critically successful comic strips, *Barney Google* and *Snuffy*

Smith. During the 1920s and 1930s, virtually every newspaper reader knew his characters Bunky, Snuffy Smith, and Spark Plug, the racehorse. DeBeck was also a huge sports buff.

Henry McLemore (1906–1968), born in Macon, Georgia, was a United Press International (UPI) sportswriter and eminent syndicated sports columnist. He also was an actor, appearing in such films as *Swing with Bing* (1940) and *The Millionaire* (1955). Interestingly, he violated the "no women" rule in the press box at Yankee Stadium, when he brought his wife Mary with him, ignoring the howls of disapproval.[3] In his later years, he joined the publicity department for the Daytona International Speedway and was an avid NASCAR fan.

Distiller Ellis "Slats" Slater (1895–1983) was the president of Frankfort Distillers Corp., a profitable liquor company. Slater, like Clifford Roberts, was a good friend of President Eisenhower. Slats frequently played golf and bridge with Ike. Through his interactions with President Eisenhower, Slater penned the biography *The Ike I Knew*.

The final member of the Syndicate was Tom Yawkey (1903–1976). Yawkey inherited a multimillion-dollar fortune from his late uncle on his 30th birthday. Four days later he bought the Boston Red Sox. He served as the sole owner of the Red Sox for 44 seasons (1933–1976).

Other accounts often include sportswriter Grantland Rice as a Syndicate member, but Rice denied any financial interest in Beau. According to Rice, his only interest in Beau was covering him as a sportswriter. Sportswriter Richards Vidmer was also frequently mentioned but he denied any monetary interest as well.

Ironically, Beau Jack rose out of this wealthy opulent world of the white man. Like many other clubs and venues, segregation and discrimination were commonplace. In the game of golf, there were very few black golfers. Steeped with traditions that began in the thirties, the Augusta National emphasized its traditionalistic, wealthy, aristocratic atmosphere. Only white golfers adorned the fairways at the Augusta National. The first African American golfer was not allowed to participate in the Masters Tournament until Lee Elder did so in 1975. Black caddies for white golfers was the rule until 1983 when professional golfers were permitted to use their caddy of choice. It is said that Clifford Roberts once stated, "As long as I'm alive, the golfers will be white and the caddies will be black." The first African-American member was admitted in 1991.

PART II

Media Sensation at "Valley" Arena

When they learned about this little boy from Georgia named Beau Jack, they loved me, because they found out that I would fight every second of every round and never give up.
—Sidney "Beau Jack" Walker

6

Learning the Ropes

Overflowing with excitement, Beau was ready to test his boxing skills. An olive-brown bundle of muscles, Beau weighed 131 pounds and stood 5' 5½" tall. He was 19 years old and bursting with guts, determination, and perseverance. It was now time for him to learn the art of boxing. So, after the 1940 Masters Tournament concluded and with money from the Syndicate in hand, Jack and his newly proclaimed manager, Bowman Milligan, boarded a northbound train at Union Station in downtown Augusta to begin the venture of a lifetime.

In 1940, black Americans made up 9.8 percent of the national population. Sixty percent of black women employed worked as domestic maids or servants. Black Americans, however, were slowly making strides for equality. The U.S. Post Office sold the first commemorative stamp celebrating the life of a black man. The stamp honored the work of Booker T. Washington, the educational pioneer and founder of the Tuskegee Institute. The first black actor also received an Oscar. Hattie McDaniel won Best Supporting Actress in her role as "Mammy" in *Gone with the Wind*. Ironically, she had to obtain special permission to enter the "whites-only" hotel to receive her award.

Springfield

Beau Jack and Bowman departed the train at Springfield Union Station in historic Springfield, Massachusetts. Located in western New England, Springfield is situated on a steep bluff overlooking the Connecticut River. Historically noteworthy, Springfield is where Shays' Rebellion occurred in 1787. With economic depression and heavy taxes placing a grave burden on small farmers, Massachusetts' farmers rebelled against the government. Led by Revolutionary War officer Daniel Shays, 4,000 rebels marched on the federal arsenal in Springfield to gain arms and overthrow the government. Although they were defeated, Shay's Rebellion became an impetus for the Constitutional Convention. Springfield is also the birthplace of basketball, which was invented by James Naismith in 1891.

Valley Arena, Holyoke, Massachusetts, c. 1940 (Holyoke Public Library).

After arriving at the train station, Beau and Bowman caught a car to Longmeadow Country Club just outside of Springfield, where Bowman worked during the summer months thanks to club member Bobby Jones. A prestigious and esteemed golf club, Longmeadow's woodland golf course was designed by J. Donald Ross (1872–1948) and landscaped by Frederick Law Olmstead.

Valley Arena, Holyoke, Massachusetts

During the summer of 1940, Beau worked in the locker room and shined shoes during the day. In the evening, after the day's work was done, Beau received a primer on boxing. The location was idyllic. Springfield was only ten miles away from Holyoke, Massachusetts, the home of the illustrious Valley Arena (the "Valley") where numerous boxers tested their skills and launched their professional careers.

Situated on South Bridge Street in Holyoke, Valley Arena was originally an old gas house built by the Gasometer City Works in 1884. In 1926,

Homer Rainault, a boxing promoter and a leader of French-Canadian politics in Holyoke, transformed the abandoned gas house into an entertainment venue, featuring a domed roof and seating for 1,800 spectators. The Valley quickly developed into a popular entertainment venue for western Massachusetts, featuring such big bands as Lionel Hampton, Count Basie, Sammy Kaye, and the Dorsey Brothers. The forum was best known, however, for its highly anticipated Monday night boxing matches. Roaring with enthusiasm, stomping their feet, and clapping thunderously, Valley spectators had a resilient reputation.

Valley Arena was revered by the boxing community. Numerous legendary boxers in the early 20th century began their professional careers at the Valley. A partial list of world champions and boxing hall of fame members initiating or improving their professional records at the Valley include Lou Ambers, Fritzie Zivic, Rocky Marciano, Jimmy Carter, and Tony Demarco.

Two-time lightweight champion Lou Ambers (1913–1995), the "Herkimer Hurricane," fought at Valley Arena five times between 1933 and 1934, winning all five matches. Ambers went on to acquire the lightweight title on September 3, 1936, when he defeated Tony Canzoneri. Ambers held the title until August 17, 1938, when he lost to Henry Armstrong. A year later, on August 22, 1939, Ambers won the title a second time, this time defeating Henry Armstrong. He held his second title until May 10, 1940, when Lew Jenkins defeated him.

On March 4, 1935, the lightning-fast Fritzie Zivic (1913–1984) scored a unanimous decision over "KO" Castillo in the Valley's main event. Zivic went on to hold the welterweight title from October 4, 1940 until July 29, 1941. He acquired the title in Madison Square Garden when he defeated the great Henry Armstrong, then holder of the featherweight, lightweight, and welterweight titles, knocking Armstrong face down on the canvas in the last second of their 15-round bout.

The legendary Rocky Marciano (1923–1969) debuted his undefeated heavyweight career at Valley Arena, knocking Lee Epperson out in the third round on March 17, 1947. It was the first of 43 consecutive knockouts on Rocky's way to an undefeated professional career record of 49–0. Marciano ruled as the world's heavyweight champion from 1952–1956.

On December 6, 1948, Jimmy Carter (1923–1994) from Aiken, South Carolina, conquered Louis Joyce by unanimous decision at the Valley Arena. Carter subsequently won the world lightweight championship three times. His first title came on May 25, 1951, when he defeated Ike Williams. A year later, he lost the title to Lauro Salas before recovering it from Salas five months later. Carter then lost the title to Paddy DeMarco on February 6, 1954, only to regain it from him on November 17, 1954. Carter's third reign as lightweight champion ended on June 29, 1955, when he was defeated by Wallace "Bud" Smith.

Finally, the "Boston Bomber," Tony Demarco (1932–) started his career and path to the welterweight world title at the Valley, knocking out Bobby Weaver and earning a unanimous decision over Dee Shanley in the fall of 1950. Demarco won the welterweight title on April 1, 1955, defeating Johnny Saxton. He lost it in his next fight on June 10, 1955, against Carmen Basilio.

Within a month after his arrival in Springfield, Beau Jack was prepared to make his first professional appearance at Valley Arena. It was time to resolve whether the Valley would be a launching pad for Jack, as it had been for other legendary boxers. Although Beau had won all of his previous contests, the competition at the Valley was going to be much tougher.

First things first, Beau had to decide in which weight class to compete. Exploring his best fighting weight, Beau fought in both the lightweight (130–135 lbs.) and featherweight divisions (125–130 lbs.) during his first eight months, before settling down in the lightweight division. At the time, the lightweight division was one of boxing's deepest and most competitive divisions. Legendary boxers such as Henry Armstrong, Lou Ambers, Allie Stolz, Sugar Ray Robinson, Ike Williams, Kid Gavilan, Fritzie Zivic, Bob Montgomery and Lew Jenkins all fought in the lightweight division during the forties.

Jack Debuts

Beau debuted on the Valley's Monday night fight card on May 20, 1940, the same day the U.S. Navy launched the destroyer Niblack, a 1,600-ton Warcraft costing $5 million. He faced Frankie Allen, a local Holyoke fighter with two years of experience and an impressive record of 18–4. The contest was a four-round bout in the featherweight division. Beau scaled 131 pounds to Allen's 127¾ pounds. Anxiously, the former Georgia bootblack entered the ring and awaited the sounding of the opening bell. In his first significant test, Beau performed well. He held the impressive veteran in check. After four competitive rounds, Referee Jack Dekkers and the two judges declared the contest a draw.

A week later, Beau faced an equally young lightweight boxer, Billy Bannick of Pittsfield, Massachusetts, in a four-round lightweight bout. Debuting a week earlier on the same card as Beau, Bannick belted out a victory over Eddie Micatka. Beau weighed 132¾ pounds to Bannick's 134½ pounds. At the opening bell, the "Georgia Wildcat" swarmed Bannick with flurries of punches. Billy hardly had time to catch his breath. By the third round, Beau had Bannick where he wanted him. Jack connected with a barrage of hard punches and down went Bannick. Unable to continue, Bannick suffered his first defeat. Beau, on the other hand, notched not only his first victory but a technical knockout ("TKO"). Bannick subsequently proved to be a talented fighter. After losing to Jack, he went on to have a career of 41–1 while fighting in the African and European campaigns during World War II.

Beau quickly became familiar fixture on the Valley's Monday night fight card, fighting 25 of his first 28 bouts at the Valley. With his relentless punching, swarming style, and never-dying energy, the press soon began referring to him as a miniature Henry Armstrong. That was quite the compliment, as Armstrong had already won world championships in three different weight divisions.

Still green, Beau had a lot to learn as a boxer. He had an all-out offensive attack but needed to gain experience to refine his boxing skills and improve his defense, such as how to utilize an effective counter-attack. Almost all of Beau's early training came through self-experience in the ring. As a result, Beau lost three of his next four contests before going on an encouraging 10-bout win streak.

In his third bout, Beau met Jackie Parker, a southpaw from Worcester, Massachusetts. Jackie's brother also boxed, but under the name Al Scully to avoid confusion. Parker came into the June 17 match with five victories and two defeats. He left with six wins, earning a split decision over Beau in their four-round lightweight battle. Beau, on the other hand, suffered his first defeat.

Ten days later, Beau traveled to West Haven, Connecticut, 75 miles south of Holyoke, for his next two contests, both against lightweight Joe Polowitzer, a hard-punching southpaw from East Hartford, Connecticut. It was Jack's first bout in the passionate boxing state of Connecticut and an excellent opportunity to gain exposure. Connecticut produced numerous world-class boxers during boxing's golden years, including Boxing Hall of Famers Jack Delaney (1900–1948), Gene Tunney (1897–1978), Louis "Kid" Kaplan (1901–1970), Lou Brouillard (1911–1984), and Willie Pep (1922–2006). Jack Delaney (77–12–2) won the world light heavyweight title in 1926. Gene Tunney (80–1–3) won the American light heavyweight title twice in the early 20s, before acquiring the world heavyweight title in 1926. Louis "Kid" Kaplan (108–23–13) held the world featherweight title from 1925–26. Winning the world welterweight title in 1931, Lou Brouillard (100–31–2) also won the middleweight title in 1933. Finally, Willie Pep (229–11–1) won the world featherweight title twice in the late 40s.

West Haven's White City Stadium was the venue for Beau's upcoming bouts. Incorporated within the Savin Rock amusement park, the multipurpose stadium was located on the shores of the Atlantic Ocean. Originally a popular seaside resort, Savin Rock ran along the west side of New Haven Harbor. Over the years, it developed into a full-scale entertainment venue, featuring amusement rides, baseball games, stock car races, theaters, restaurants, and hotels. Within Savin Rock, White City Stadium was in its 13th year promoting open-air boxing cards.

Sky Blazer, White City, Savin Rock, Conn.

Postcard of the Sky Blazer roller coaster at White City, Savin Rock, c. 1930–1945 (Boston Public Library, Tichnor Brothers Collection).

It was steamy hot when Beau arrived. A heat wave had blasted the northeast for two weeks with the mercury rising into the 90s and 100s. On Tuesday, July 30, the date of the first bout, temporary relief was provided when a dangerous summer storm blew through producing massive lightning, wind, and hail, forcing a three-day postponement.

Contrary to the hot weather earlier in the week, it was remarkably mild and cloudy on August 2. Jack squared off in a preliminary six-round bout against Joe Polowitzer before the main event featuring two New Haven lightweight rivals, Julie Kogon and Willie Andrews. Polowitzer came into the ring with a professional record of 3–2 but had enjoyed an outstanding amateur career culminating with the Connecticut lightweight title. Even though Jack had suffered defeat in his last battle against a southpaw, he still came in as the favorite with a record of 1–1–1. Unfortunately, the oddsmakers were wrong. Beau lost his second fight in a row to a southpaw, dropping the contest on points.

An enthusiastic crowd of 3,300 spectators gathered at White City Stadium ten days later for the evenings' boxing card featuring a rematch between Beau and Polowitzer and the main event between promising Connecticut heavyweight prospects George "Dick" Fuller and Henry Morez. The large crowd multiplied due to the celebrity referee on hand. The fans wanted to catch a glimpse of Joe Louis (1914–1981), the world's heavyweight champion and referee for the main event.

Joe Louis

Joe Louis (1914–1981) reigned as the world's heavyweight champion for twelve years, from 1937 until 1949. After debuting on July 4, 1934, the "Brown Bomber" went on a tear, winning his first 24 bouts. He wasn't only winning, he was knocking his opponents out. He knocked out 20 of his first 24 foes. His first loss came against former heavyweight champion Max Schmeling of Brandenburg, Germany on June 19, 1936. Schmeling used an effective jab and right cross, knocking Louis down in the fourth and finally knocking him out in the 12th round.

Louis became an American hero two years later, however, when he attained a chance for revenge in a rematch with Schmeling on June 22, 1938. As Adolf Hitler upheld Schmeling as a specimen of Aryan supremacy, the bout was shrouded with patriotic and racial implications. Louis inflicted immediate vengeance, knocking Schmeling out in the first round. Overnight, Louis became a hero to black and white Americans.

Louis ended his career after suffering an eighth-round knockout by Rocky Marciano in 1951 and retired at age 37 with a record of 66–3 (52 knockouts). He was inducted into *The Ring* Boxing Hall of Fame in 1954 and the International Boxing Hall of Fame in 1990. Following his death, he was awarded a Congressional Gold Medal and was the first boxer, black or white, to appear on a commemorative postage stamp.

The ten days between bouts seemed like an eternity to Beau as he eagerly awaited his rematch with Joe Polowitzer. Jack intended to

Joe Louis training for his fight with Lou Nova at Greenwood Lake, New York, c. 1941 (Library of Congress).

beat the southpaw curse that painfully bested him in his last two bouts and he certainly didn't want to lose twice to the same opponent. Relentlessly, Beau reversed the tide in his second contest against Joe, exacting vengeance, this time defeating Polowitzer on points.

The main event had a whimsical conclusion. After refereeing the Fuller–Morez bout, Joe Louis, amidst the enthusiasm of the crowd, stepped out of the ring without announcing the decision. Louis began walking through the throng of fans before someone reminded him that he forgot to declare the winner. So, Louis animatedly climbed back into the ring and raised both fighters' hands declaring the fight a draw.

Conquest over the southpaw curse did not last long. On August 19, Beau was back at the Valley to face his fourth consecutive southpaw. He was once again paired with Jackie Parker in a four-round rematch. Just two months earlier, Parker had defeated Beau by split decision. As in their first match, Parker entered the ring with a three-and-a-half-pound weight advantage, tipping the scale at 137½ pounds, while Beau came in at 134 pounds. The southpaw curse rose its ugly head once again. Somewhat muddled, Beau did not fare well. Parker defeated Beau, this time receiving a unanimous decision over the Georgia bootblack.

Having lost three of his last four bouts, Beau's record was 2–3–1. Downhearted, Jack knew he had to get on track. Fortunately, his fate was about to improve. Between August 26 and December 30, 1940, Beau won ten fights in a row. Impressively, seven of those victories came by way of knockout and three by unanimous decision. Beau was learning the ropes.

The winning streak began on the mild Monday night of August 26, 1940, at the Valley. Beau faced Carlo DaPonde, a Springfield welterweight, in the third preliminary match of the evening. Even though Beau's opponent had a dismal record of 10–23–3, DaPonde was a seven-year ring veteran, easily the most seasoned opponent Beau had yet faced. Youth got the better of experience. Throwing non-stop flurries of punches from all angles, Beau overwhelmed Carlo. Carlo was brutalized as Beau swarmed him like a Tasmanian devil. At the end of four rounds, Beau was awarded a clear-cut unanimous decision. The press took note. The next day the *Hartford Courant* reported, "Beau Jack, who pours on the leather faster than any boxer in these parts, handed Carlo DaPonde of Springfield, one of the fiercest defeats ever handed out in the glorified gas-house."[1]

With his easy victory, Jack continued to gain prominence among young boxers, fight fans and the media. He didn't possess dominant power and his boxing skills were mediocre, but Beau electrified the fans with the sheer volume of his punches, aggressiveness and astonishing energy. In just five bouts at the Valley, Beau had already become a fan favorite. Fans began flocking to see Beau box and his fierce reputation continued to gain momentum.

Seven days after his victory over Carlo DaPonde, Jack returned to the Valley to battle Boston boxer Jackie Small in a four-round lightweight bout. After losing his first four matches, Jackie had won his last two, defeating Charley Gilman and Oliver Barbour. Beau was not impressed. Not wasting any time, he dispensed of Jackie halfway through the second round, landing a fatal blow that sent Small to the canvas, earning Jack another TKO victory. For the first time, Beau had won two consecutive bouts, improving his record to 4–3–1. It was a good feeling.

Burke-Wadsworth Act

On the same day Beau knocked out Jackie Small, September 2, 1940, Congress passed the Burke-Wadsworth Act imposing the first peacetime draft in the history of the United States. The registration of men between the ages of 21 and 36 began one month later. The draft age would be expanded in November 1942, a little less than a year after the U.S. entered World War II.

With renewed confidence, Beau entered the ring against lightweight Oliver Barbour (7–7–5) of Warwick, Rhode Island on Monday, September 16. Barbour had a victory and a loss over Beau's last opponent, Jackie Small, but had lost his last four contests. Jack smothered Barbour, winning a TKO victory two minutes into the third round.

Next, Beau entered the ring for the second time as a featherweight to face another ring veteran. Although he had lost his last six fights, 25-year-old Tony DuPre of Manchester, New Hampshire came into the September 30 fight with six years of experience and a 33–15–9 record. He was also a former contender for the world featherweight title and a former New England featherweight champion. DuPre had a three-pound weight advantage, weighing in at 129 pounds to Jack's 126 pounds and stood a half-inch shorter than Jack. A formidable overhand left highlighted his arsenal of punches. Beau wasn't fazed by DuPre's experience or resume. Jack knocked DuPre down five times before polishing him off in the second round, collecting his third consecutive TKO and fourth victory in a row.

7

A Featured Attraction

Four months after his debut, Beau boasted a 6–3–1 record with four knockouts. With his exciting leather throwing style and improving record, Beau was moved to the top of the fight card. Starring in his first main event on the Valley's October 14 fight card, Beau faced Abe Cohen of New York in a six-round lightweight contest. Cohen had five years of professional experience, a 9–4–2 record, but had lost his last three matches.

The Valley was electrified. Graciously greeting Beau was an overflow crowd. More than 2,100 passionate fight fans crammed into the 1,800-seat Valley Arena to see Beau in his first feature event. Cohen and Jack weighed in at almost identical weights. Jack weighed 129¾ pounds to Cohen's 130 pounds. From the opening bell, Beau captivated the crowd with his dynamic flurries, hurling punches from all conceivable directions. As the rowdy Valley fans stomped their feet, Beau swarmed Cohen. Jack took to Cohen like bees to honey. It seemed like the louder the fans cheered, the more punches Beau threw. Fifty seconds into the third round, Beau connected a hard right to Cohen's chest, driving him dejectedly to the canvass for the fatal count. Beau scored his fourth consecutive knockout. Everyone likes an exciting boxer, especially a knockout artist. Sportswriters took notice, raising Beau's status to an "up and coming" Springfield lightweight.

A week later, on a clear cool Monday night, Beau Jack met Ritchie Jones, an inexperienced fighter from Saratoga, New York. Jones had yet to win in four previous outings. Beau had no sympathy for him. Ritchie's losing streak was quickly extended to five, as Beau knocked him out in the third round. Admirers were now turning out in droves to witness Beau Jack's furiously exciting style of boxing.

An even larger overflow crowd of 2,300 fans crammed into the Valley to witness Jack's next headline fight on November 4. Beau was matched with Joey Stack of Philadelphia in a six-round bout. The Philadelphian had a record of 22–25–9 and a ferocious reputation for a featherweight but had lost four of his last 10 fights. Irrespective, Stack was esteemed by his supporters. Even though he lost his previous contest against Johnny Compo by a slim margin, his fans cheered him after the final round, showing appreciation for their warrior. Jack balanced the scales at 128 pounds to Stack's 125 pounds.

The four-year veteran came to fight, providing a stiff test for Beau. Joey fought tough, punching and countering Beau the whole six rounds. When Stack boxed in tight, he created problems for Beau. On the other hand, once Beau distanced himself, he made Stack pay, blistering the Philadelphian with his rabid attack and stamina. After six rounds of action, Beau gained a unanimous decision. Beau had now won seven bouts in a row and his record was beginning to look much more imposing at 9–3–1. Stack, on the other hand, retired after losing 27 of his next 30 matches.

Twins

Following his bout with Joey Stack, Beau was in a hurry to get back home to Augusta and join his wife Josephine Jones Walker (1923–1994), who was expecting their first child. Much to their surprise, Josephine had twin boys. Donald Joseph Walker (1940–2004) and Ronald Sidney Walker (1940–1998) were born at University Hospital on November 7, 1940. The proud new father spent a couple of weeks with his wife and twins before returning to Springfield.

Beau and Irish Jimmy Fox squared off in the main event at Valley Arena on Monday, December 2, 1940. Fox, an 11-year veteran, possessed a 40–25–13 record. Experience must have aided him. Beau threw his whole repertoire of punches at the boxer from Nashville, Tennessee, but Fox didn't go down. To Jimmy's credit, he made Beau go the full six rounds in their featherweight bout, but in the end, Beau earned a unanimous decision.

Fourteen days later, Beau appeared on the December 16 fight card paired against featherweight Young Johnny Buff, "Newark's latest ring sensation," in a six-round bout. Who knows why Buff was touted as a "ring sensation." In his last 22 bouts, he was 2–19–1. Beau didn't waste any time with Young Johnny, knocking him out 2:20 minutes in the first round.

On December 30, 1940, Beau belted his way to another TKO victory at the Valley. His inexperienced opponent, Mel Neary of Harrisburg, Pennsylvania, was undefeated with a 3–0 record since debuting earlier in the month. Beau ruined Mel's perfect record. The referee called a halt to the fight 2:04 minutes into the fifth round. Neary was in no shape to continue.

With his victory over Mel Neary, Jack closed out the year with 10 consecutive victories, improving his record to 12–3–1. Within eight months of his first contest at the Valley, Beau had emerged as the top boxer and a fan-favorite featured event. Moreover, Beau had knocked out eight of his sixteen opponents, earning him a "KO artist" tag.

Learning from Henry Armstrong

In early January 1941, Beau spent a couple weeks in Florida, fishing, relaxing, and visiting family. He had fought 16 bouts in the last seven months and needed a break from Springfield and Holyoke. While Beau was vacationing, Bowman Milligan visited with his brother Lawson Bowman, Jr., in New York. Lawson had moved to New York in 1935, where he quickly worked his way up from bartender to a successful restaurant/bar entrepreneur in Harlem. Located at 92 St. Nicholas Avenue, Lawson's Melody Room and Cocktail Lounge provided swanky entertainment during the late 40s and early 50s. With his charming demeanor, Bowman built an exceptionally strong clientele. There was no telling who you might see at his place, but you were almost guaranteed to see a local celebrity. One day you might see Jackie Robinson or Ella Fitzgerald. Another day you might run into Henry Armstrong, Joe Louis, or Jersey Joe Walcott.

While in New York, Milligan and Lawson caught up with an old acquaintance, the legendary boxer Henry Armstrong (1912–1988). Born in Columbus, Mississippi, Armstrong's father was a mixed-race sharecropper, and his mother was a full-blooded Indian. "Homicide Hank," as he was often

called, began his boxing career in 1931 and had previously won simultaneous world titles in three different weight classes—featherweight, lightweight, and welterweight. A couple of months earlier, however, Henry lost his welterweight title in a bloody ring war with Pittsburg boxer Fritzie Zivic and was currently training hard for his title rematch on January 17. Having finished his preliminary conditioning at Hot Springs, Arkansas, Armstrong was entering final preparations at Stillman's Gym in New York. His professional record at the time was 112–13–7.

Bragging about his

Henry Armstrong, c. 1937 (Library of Congress).

young boxer to Armstrong, Bowman asked Henry if he could impart some of his ring wisdom on Beau Jack and help him tighten up his boxing skills. The apprenticeship was a natural fit. Armstrong, "perpetual motion machine of boxing,"[1] came at his opponents like a relentless buzz saw with a persistent windmill style, similar to the style that Beau employed. In need of another sparring partner, Armstrong agreed. When Beau learned of his new temporary boxing coach, he was ecstatic. Henry Armstrong was his idol. He was even more surprised when Armstrong invited him to stay in his apartment while he taught him the ropes.

As Armstrong and Beau sparred, young Jack eagerly soaked up his advice, as well as his bobbing and weaving style. Henry instructed Beau to shorten up his punches and taught him how to defend himself from being crowded in close. Coaching by example, Henry made it look easy by coming in close and putting his shoulder into Beau's chest, jamming him. He taught Beau rhythm and style. Following his tutelage of Jack, Henry exclaimed to Milligan, "The kid's strong as a bull, and if he ever learns to box, he can be a champion."[2]

Beau had another stellar year in 1941, improving his overall record to 29–6–1. Nonetheless, the year did not start off or end well for him. He opened the year with a loss and finished with two losses. In between those losses, however, Jack scored 17 commanding victories.

Beau's first bout of 1941 was on January 27 at the Valley. His opponent scheduled in the six-round main event was Paul "Tennessee" Lee. However, on the day of the fight, Joey Silva was substituted for Lee.

Silva had an enthralling background. His father was a prosperous silver mine operator working outside of Mexico City, Mexico. One day, when Joey was still a young boy, the notorious Mexican bandit, Pancho Villa, and his gang descended upon the home of Joey and his 44-year-old father. They kidnapped both of them and demanded a vast ransom for their return. Desperately, Silva's family and acquaintances raised the ransom for their return. They were then directed to a specific site to retrieve Joey and his father. When they arrived, Joey was tied to a tree with a note pinned to his clothing leading them to another location where Mr. Silva could be found. When the Silvas reached the next spot, they were greeted by the ghastly sight of Mr. Silva's dead body dangling from a tree with a noose around his neck. Following this horrific experience, Joey's mother hastily moved the family to Los Angeles, where Joey spent the rest of his childhood.

In his early career, Silva was a featherweight title contender but was now largely an experienced journeyman boxer with a record of 11–26–6. With his slightly cross-eyed stare, he looked quite threatening in the ring. An aggressive fighter similar in style to Beau, he loved to heave windmill punches. Silva weighed in at 131 pounds to Beau's 130½ pounds.

Silva and Beau came out of the starting gate swinging, both men trying to knock out the other. Unexpectedly, Silva weathered Beau's perpetual storm and landed ample punches of his own to notch the victory. When the scorecards came in, Silva was victorious, winning by a close split decision. It was Beau's fourth loss in 17 bouts.

Having lost to Silva, Beau needed to dish out some therapeutic punishment. Mexican Joe Rivers made a good target. The two met at the Valley on February 10, the 15-year anniversary of Valley Arena. A frustrated Beau came out steaming. Striking Rivers repeatedly with leather, Jack knocked Rivers down twice in the second round and twice in the third, before finishing him off 2:45 minutes into the fourth round. Lenny "Lefty" Isrow, Beau's next opponent on February 24, didn't last that long. Beau knocked Isrow out 2:40 minutes into the third round. He did the same to Nicky Jerome in their March 10 bout, knocking Jerome out in the third round. Beau was on fire, producing TKOs over Mexican Joe Rivers, Lenny Isrow, and Nicky Jerome.

Securing three straight victories, Beau procured a chance to redeem himself against Joey Silva. Beau had only suffered two defeats to the same opponent once in his young career. Jackie Parker pulled off that feat. Beau's only other losses had come at the hands of Joe Polowitzer and Joey Silva.

The rematch was billed as the main event at Valley Arena on March 24, 1941. Beau came in weighing 135 pounds, four-and-a-half pounds heavier than their earlier fight. Silva weighed 133 pounds. Since they last met, Silva had only won one of his four contests; whereas Jack had won four in a row. Zealous Holyoke fight fans came out in throngs for the highly anticipated rematch. More than 3,300 frenzied fans crammed into the Valley Arena, making it the largest Valley crowd to witness Beau in combat.

Contrary to the oddsmakers who had Silva a 6 to 5 favorite, many of the loyal fans predicted Beau to emerge the victor. The fans were right. Jack avenged his loss to Silva, prevailing with a six-round unanimous decision.

Jack was rapidly adding to his win column. By March 1941, Beau had amassed a 16–4–1 record, with 11 victories coming by knockout. *The Ring* magazine featured a picture of Jack and hyped him as one of the most popular fighters in New England. In his syndicated column "Breezy Sports Briefs," sportswriter Eddie Brietz began to depict Beau as an up-and-coming 135-pound contender for the lightweight title that hits like a middleweight.

With his improving record, Beau was sought after, not only by enthusiastic supporters enthralled by his swarming style but also by other fighters wanting to burst his bubble. Future Hall of Famer Willie Pep, an undefeated featherweight, announced to the world that he was gunning for a match with Beau. Pep had appeared on the same card with Jack at the Valley a month earlier and watched Beau knock out Joe Rivers. Pep would never get the opportunity he desired. Seeking to take advantage of Beau's popularity, matchmaker

Joe DeMaria prematurely announced a four-man elimination tournament to determine which fighter might get a shot at the sky-rocketing Beau Jack. De-Maria, however, did not have the needed endorsement from Jack's camp.

Two weeks later, six days after celebrating his 20th birthday, Beau was ready for his next battle at the Valley. It was a mild night with temperatures in the low 50s. Hailing from Los Angeles, California, Henry LaBarba, fighting under the name Tony Iacovacci, was Beau's next adversary. It was Tony's 12th fight of his fledgling career. To date, his record was 5–4–2. Beau evened out Iacovacci's won-loss column, ending the bout via knockout in the final round. Iacovacci's boxing career only lasted four more months before he bowed to working in the war effort as a checker in a tank production plant. His final record was 6–10–4.

Although Beau had fought two contests in Connecticut, he had not yet made it to the capital city of Hartford. Hartford boxing fans were itching to witness Jack in action and he was ready for a formal introduction. The *Hartford Daily Courant* touted Beau as sensational. "Sensational is an overworked adjective as applied to fighters, but it can be attached to Beau Jack without fear of being extravagant. The Holyoke colored boy, a terrific puncher, has been flattening one opponent after another."[3]

Beau's Hartford debut came on April 22, 1941, at historic Foot Guard Hall. Constructed in 1888 as an armory and drill hall, the red brick building served as the home of Connecticut's Foot Guard First Company, the United States' oldest continuous military organization. Founded in 1771, the Foot Guard's First Company was charged with escorting the newly elected Colonial governors on election days. The red-coated Foot Guard still occupies the Hall which is protected under historical certification.

Not much was known about Beau's opponent, Bob Reilly. Reilly, an Irish boxer from Cliffside, New Jersey, had 14 professional fights but had never fought an eight-round battle; much less a fighter like Beau Jack. To make matters more interesting, it was also Jack's first eight-round bout.

The night's fight card featured an electrifying twin headliner. Italian-American boxer Guglielmo Papaleo, aka Willie Pep, who had just recently called out Beau, faced Mexican Joey Silva in the first contest of the twin bill. Pep dominated Silva, continuing his winning streak by earning a unanimous decision. Pep would maintain his unbeaten streak for 62 fights before suffering his first defeat. Twice Pep would hold the world's featherweight crown before finishing his 26-year career with an astonishing 241 contests and a record of 229–11–1. He earned *The Ring's* 1945 Fighter of the Year award and was inducted into the International Boxing Hall of Fame in 1990. Willie Pep is considered by many to have been the number one featherweight of the 20th century.

The final ring-war of the evening was between Beau and Bob Reilly.

Roaring with fervor, the crowd acknowledged Beau's unofficial trainer and tutor, Henry Armstrong, who was spotted along with his trainer Pee Wee Beale, giving Beau some pre-fight instructions. One couldn't ask for a better mentor.

As the opening bell rang, Jack rushed out looking to land punches rapidly on the Irish boxer. Reilly, as Beau soon discovered, was not a push-over. Dancing around in the ring, the clowning Reilly made Beau look foolish at times as Jack threw punches in the air, failing to connect with the cunning Reilly. It seemed like the jester from Cliffside was going to go the distance in their eight-round bout until Beau floored him in the seventh round for a nine count. Although Reilly raised himself off the canvas, Beau quickly dropped him again with a flurry of punches. Having seen enough, referee Frankie Portelle stopped the fight, awarding Beau a TKO victory.

Another fight, however, was only just beginning. A group of Hartford gamblers mistakenly placed bets on Reilly going the distance with Beau. When Portelle halted the fight in the seventh round, they became irate and nonsensical. As Portelle stepped out of the ring to make his way to the dressing room, one of the upset gamblers punched him. Immediately, a ringside ruckus erupted with more spectators jumping into the fray. Portelle suffered several blows before police could escort him to the dressing room. Police soon subdued the instigators, ending the last fight of the night.

Ben "Evil Eye" Finkle

After the fight, W. J. Lee, the sports editor for the *Hartford Daily Courant*, received a steamy letter from Lew Diamond, Justice of the Peace of Fairview, New Jersey, a self-proclaimed fistic authority and boxing manager. Diamond, who dubbed himself as the "honest brakeman," felt the need to respond to Lee's prefight assertions that Reilly was virtually unknown as a boxer. Diamond's letter was quite amusing.

> In order to bring peace to the House of Reilly, the fighting son of the family, Bob, would like another shot at the supposed killer from Holyoke, Beau Jack. I would appreciate the same referee, Frank Portelle. I will bring Ben (Evil Eye) Finkle with me to demonstrate the power of his eye and he will hit Beau Jack and the referee with Slodobka Stare, the Whammy, the Zaza and the Zinger all at one and the same time.[4]

Reilly would never get a second chance at Beau Jack. Who knows if a rematch would have ended differently for Reilly with the presence of the "Evil Eye" and his curses?

Brooklyn native Benjamin David "Evil Eye" Finkle (1899–1978) was a legendary figure in boxing. He boxed for a short period before managing Patsy Flanagan. As a manager, Finkle discovered a new trick. He began giving

Flanagan's opponents the "Evil Eye" hex with his somewhat bloodshot left eye. Many fighters became troubled by it and refused to look at Finkle in fear of the impending spell.

Telling sportswriters that his eyes had "evil" powers, Finkle quickly grew his "Evil Eye" legend. The effectiveness of the hex was so powerful, many well-known managers and boxers would call on his services to hex their adversaries with his "Evil Eye." Depending on the price, Finkle would put spells on opponents such as the "Slobodka Stare" or the "Warsaw Wink." Joey Archibald, a featherweight from Providence, Rhode Island, discovered the power of Finkle's "Evil Eye" the hard way. After Finkle assisted Archibald in notching victories for several years, including the world featherweight title, Joey failed to retain his services when he battled Petey Scalzo. Spitefully, Finkle went to Scalzo's team. With the "Evil Eye" in his corner, Scalzo knocked Archibald out in the second round. It was Archibald's first loss in 16 contests.

There are numerous other examples of Finkle's "Evil Eye" hexing opponents. In 1938, Finkle put the "Slobodka Stare" on Lew Jenkins when he lost in a huge upset to Chino Alvarez. Finkle also put his hex on Billy Conn, a future light heavyweight champion and an 8 to 1 favorite, when he lost in an upset to Solly Krieger. Astonishingly, he had a notable list of clients including Doc Kearns, Angelo Dundee, Honest Bill Daly, Sugar Ray Robinson, Carmen Basilio, Gus Lesnevich, Floyd Patterson, and Rocky Marciano.

"Evil Eye" Finkle, however, didn't limit himself to prize-fighters. He would use his "Evil Eye" to hex racehorses, baseball and football teams, and even Adolf Hitler. In the famous 1938 horse race between War Admiral and Sea Biscuit, Finkle cast a spell on War Admiral, resulting in Sea Biscuit's victory. In 1949, he hexed the University of Georgia football team, which subsequently lost in a huge upset to the Miami Hurricanes. During World War II, two weeks after Finkle started casting his hex toward Germany, Hitler killed himself.

Less than a week after defeating Reilly, Beau was back at the Valley to confront a veteran boxer from Hartford, Connecticut, Harry Gentile (1916–1997). Gentile was a "club-fighting Hartford lightweight" with six years of ring experience, despite a bleak record of 13–47–3. "Handsome Harry," as Gentile was often called, came into the bout desperate for a win, having lost his last five matches, two of which were by knockout.

A full house was on hand as Beau entered the ring, hoping for another knockout. Beau had knocked out seven of his last nine opponents and was primed to add another KO to his list. The match was scheduled for six rounds, but like five of Beau's last six fights, it did not go the distance. It didn't even make it to the second round. At the opening bell Beau came out of his corner and quickly closed in on Gentile, attacking his head with power punches. Gentile tried to clinch, but as he did, the two pugilists got tangled up inside and bumped heads, opening a severe gash on Gentile's head. With blood flowing down Gentile's face, Referee Billy Lieberman called the fight 1:44 minutes into the first round.

According to the State Physician Dr. Edward D. Warren, Gentile received a deep laceration over his left eye measuring one and one-quarter inches long from a head-butt. Beau notched up yet another easy TKO victory. In awe of his featured attraction, Homer Rainault, the owner of the Valley Arena and long-time fight promoter, ecstatically exclaimed Beau Jack to be "the greatest fighter for his experience that I've ever seen."[5]

Beau was rolling. Eight of his last ten adversaries tasted defeat via knockout. With his overall record improving to 19–4–1, Beau was eager to add more wins to his win column, but he hit a minor bump in the road. On May 5, 1941, Beau faced a hungry 5'8" tall New York fighter from Puerto Rico, Chester Rico (1917–1981). The dark-haired, 24-year-old Puerto Rican welterweight carried his respectable record of 21 victories, three losses, and one draw into the ring. Rico also brought renowned power into the battle. He had knocked out his last opponent, Marty Shapiro, 2:24 minutes into the second round. Moreover, Rico brought his fervent determination. Both fighters weighed in at 136 pounds. Eagerly awaiting the impending slugfest was another full-capacity crowd filling the seats at the Valley.

At the opening bell, Rico came out tough, giving Beau a boxing lesson for the first half of the fight utilizing his speed and skills. Then Rico thumped Beau around the ring for the second half, mixing in two-fisted body punches with jabs and hooks. It looked like Rico would snag the victory, but Beau did just enough to save himself from defeat. The fight ended in a draw. It was Jack's second draw.

Notwithstanding Beau's second draw, his stock was still rising. Jack was fighting at a blistering pace. In one year, he had fought an astonishing 26 bouts, averaging over two contests a month. That pace doesn't provide much time for bruises and wounds to heal.

Two weeks later, on May 19, Jack was back in the Holyoke ring for his 13th main event appearance. He faced Boston boxer George Salamone. Salamone had a respectful record of 27–8–4, had never been knocked out, and recently had been hailed as an up-and-coming young lightweight. Beau wasted no time asserting his control early in the bout. He battered the Bostonian so hard with a vicious fifth round attack, most fans didn't think Salamone would survive till the bell. But Salamone, with gritty fortitude, weathered the storm. Tenacity, however, would not save Salamone in the end. In the final minute of the eighth and final round, Beau persistently bombarded punches off Salamone's head until he dropped to the canvas. For the first time in Salamone's 48-bout career, he fell victim to a knockout.

The Stork Club Adopts Beau

As Beau continued progressing toward a possible shot at the lightweight title, news stories began appearing regarding Beau's financial backers and prefight routines. Two respected journalists in particular, Jack Cuddy and Bob Considine, began writing about the up-and-coming Beau Jack in their sports columns.

Jack Cuddy (1898–1975) was the dean of boxing writers during the '30s through the early '60s. Writing for United Press International and its successor, UPI, Cuddy covered nearly every major fight. The UPI boxing editor for 24 years, Cuddy's knowledge of boxing was legendary, as was his consideration for others and his willingness to help his colleagues in need. In 1965, Cuddy was honored as the recipient of the James J. Walker Award from the International Boxing Hall of Fame and the Boxing Writers' Association for long and meritorious service to boxing.

Robert "Bob" Considine (1906–1975), grew up in Washington, D.C. In 1930, he began work at the *Washington Herald*, a newspaper owned by William Randolph Hearst. A correspondent for the International News Service, his syndicated column, "On the Line," was extremely popular. A prolific writer, Considine wrote numerous books in addition to his news stories. It is said that he often used two typewriters at one time, writing his "On the Line" column on one and a book on the other. Considine also served as a war correspondent during World War II and travelled all over the world.

Jack Cuddy described Beau as a "syndicate" fighter backed by more money and publicity than anybody in the game. "He has a manager, trainer, rubber, cook and a lot of people making sure he gets the choicest steaks for his meals."[6] Moreover, before each fight, Clifford Roberts, CEO of the Augusta National Golf Club, would write the Syndicate stockholders a letter touting their rising stock in Beau and his climb toward the top.

On fight night, many of Beau's millionaire Syndicate supporters gathered at the swanky Park Lane Hotel or Stork Club in Manhattan for food, drink, and fellowship. Then they would saunter over to Madison Square Garden to witness the battle and cheer for their little muscle-bound "Georgia Bootblack." Following the fight, they would often retire to the Chatham Hotel to engage in a few rounds of bridge.

They were anxious to furnish Beau the opportunity to show the world his boxing ability. Bob Considine explained. "Under the terms of their contract with Beau Jack," wrote Considine, "all they'll get back is their grand, plus the fun of giving an orphaned bootblack a chance to show that the talents he was wasting shining shoes and participating in battle royals at the club functions, would be appreciated by the most sophisticated boxing audience in the country."[7] Financial gain didn't motivate the Syndicate members. They just wanted their "Georgia Bootblack" to rise to the top of the lightweight ranks.

The famed Stork Club, where many of the Syndicate members patronized, also adopted Beau as its prizefighter. The epitome of American charm, intricacy, and elegance, the Stork Club operated in Manhattan from 1929 until 1965. Originally located on West 58th Street, the club moved to 3 East 53rd Street after it was raided by Prohibition agents in 1931. The best and brightest of American personalities frequented Sherman Billingsley's Stork Club, from the wealthy elite and movie stars to showgirls. You would always see celebrities at the Stork Club. Frequent guests included such prominent people as J. Edgar Hoover, Ernest Hemingway, John F. Kennedy and his wife Jackie, Irving Berlin, Carl Sandberg, Marilyn Monroe, Joe DiMaggio, the Duke and Duchess of Windsor, Lucille Ball, Desi Arnaz, and Frank Sinatra. An iconic symbol of 20th century American culture, the Stork Club has been featured in numerous films, such as *The Stork Club* (1945), *All About Eve* (1950), and *Executive Suite* (1954).

More Peonage

The week before Jack's next bout, more horrific news of racial discord came out of the state of Georgia. On Thursday, May 29, 1941, William T. Cunningham, an Oglethorpe County plantation owner, and Hamilton McWhorter of Lexington, Georgia, a lawyer and former president of the Georgia Senate, were named in federal indictments in Chicago and charged with conspiracy to enslave six "Negroes in a condition of peonage and slavery"[8] contrary to their civil rights under the 13th Amendment guaranteeing freedom from slavery. The maximum penalty for the crimes was 14 years' imprisonment and a $25,000 fine.

For many years, Cunningham had induced scores of black men to work on his plantations by promising wages or getting them out of jail or off chain gangs. When they came, he enslaved them, making them work 14- to 17-hour days for no pay. Cunningham restrained them by instilling fear through lashings with straps and imprisonment if they attempted to run away. A federal judge in Georgia, however, refused to extradite Cunningham and McWhorter to Chicago for trial. Progress was sluggish in the South.

Crossroads

Beau's biggest fight to date came on June 2, 1941, when he faced 27-year-old Tommy Speigal (1913–1945). The media hyped the event as a critical test for Jack and his future. "Up to the cross-roads of boxing moves Beau Jack ... next

Monday night when he meets 10th ranking lightweight Tommy Speigal."[9] Holy-oke boxing fans were also restless to see if Beau could stand up to one of the superior lightweights. Hailing from Uniontown, Pennsylvania, Speigal was a veteran boxer, having lost only 33 of 117 contests and enjoying a top ten ranking among lightweights. As an amateur, he had won titles in Pennsylvania, Ohio, and Michigan. Tommy may have been a little weathered, but his record and victories over Sammy Angott, NBA world lightweight champ; Bob Montgomery, Pennsylvania State lightweight champion; and Dave Castilloux, made him a significant threat.

Speigal also possessed remarkable character and grit. In high school, Tommy suffered an injury playing sandlot football, leaving him with a stiff right knee. Despite suffering a handicap, Tommy hit hard, had a formidable looping right punch and an exceptional inside game. Due to his inability to back up quickly, he was forced to bore in on his opponent. Instead of viewing it as a disability, Tommy used his stiff knee to his advantage as he bored in on his adversaries.

Both fighters weighed in at 136½ pounds, but Speigal had a significant

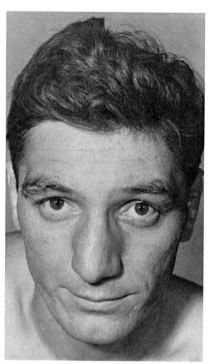

Tommy Speigal, c. early 1940s (courtesy Philly Boxing History Collection).

height advantage at 5'8". The oddsmakers also listed Speigal as their favorite. With the Syndicate on hand for the bout, Beau was bent on beating the odds, and he did just that. Beau won every round of the contest, earning a unanimous decision over the Uniontown fighter. The next day's sports headline stated, "Beau Jack Wins in Fistic Upset."[10]

In his twelfth bout of the year, Beau met George Zengaras, the Greek Adonis, in an eight-rounder at the Valley on Monday night, June 16, 1941. Zengaras, at 25 years of age, was a nationally recognized lightweight with a record of 55–20–7. The muscular, dark-haired Zengaras won his previous fight, knocking out Tony Saraullo in the seventh round. He was clever and ingenious. George was also known for boring his way into his opponent as he threw punches. Beau was not daunted. In a tough, well-fought battle, Beau emerged with a unanimous decision over George Zengaras.

Roosevelt Seeks to End Discrimination in Defense Industry

Earlier in the day on June 16, 1941, President Franklin D. Roosevelt (1882–1945) made emphatic statements to the American public and the Office of Production Management to end discrimination in the defense industry plants throughout the United States. Acknowledging nationwide discrimination against black people in the defense industry, President Roosevelt declared that it was of utmost importance "for us to strengthen our unity and morale by refuting at home the very theories which we are fighting abroad."[11] The president emphasized,

> Our government cannot countenance continued discrimination against American citizens in defense production. Industry must take the initiative in opening the doors of employment to all loyal and qualified workers regardless of race, national origin, religion or color. American workers, both organized and unorganized, must be prepared to welcome the general and much-needed employment of fellow workers of all racial and nationality origins in defense industries.[12]

Too many qualified workers were being sent away because of their race or color. Especially in light of the ongoing world conflict, there was a needed effort to alleviate discrimination.

Part III

Beau Bounces to New York

You know, if you didn't get your ticket before Friday when I fought, forget about it. They was none left. I had 2,000 ladies came to see me. They'd yell, "Uh-oh, here comes that tiger again."[1]

—Beau Jack

8

Publicity and Training

Beau Jack was moving up in the boxing ranks and rapidly entering the title hunt. During his first 13 months of professional fighting, he racked up 22 victories, four losses, and two draws. Now an earnest contender to be reckoned with in the lightweight division, it was time for Beau to depart Springfield and Valley Arena and move to the boxing capital of the world, New York City. Beau's Holyoke days were over. He would only make one return trip to the Valley.

The Syndicate enthusiastically embraced Beau's rising stock. In an aggressive move to ensure Beau's success and a shot at the title, they hired famed New York publicity guru Chick Wergeles and well-known trainer Sid Bell. They even acquired a private dressing room for Beau at the legendary Stillman's Gym, located a couple of blocks from Madison Square Garden.

Charles "Chick" Wergeles (1893–1972), lightheartedly referred to as "Hercules" because of his short height, immigrated to the United States from Russia as a toddler with his mother and siblings in 1894. He grew up in an Irish neighborhood on the lower East Side of New York, the sixth of seven children. "As a Jewish boy in an Irish neighborhood, Chick had to fight his way to fame—and did."[1]

Chick was small in stature, standing 5'4" tall, with dark hair and brown eyes, and he almost always wore a smile on his face. He married Charlotte "Nettie" Sigel in 1918 and they parented three boys and three girls. His upscale office at 9 Rockefeller Plaza in Rockefeller Center was located in Midtown Manhattan between 48th and 51st streets and 5th and 6th avenues. Chick, however, was rarely there. He was always on the go. At 48 years of age, Wergeles was not your ordinary publicity man. The little man never slowed down. He trotted rather than walked, and continually promoted his projects. Chick bubbled with gusto for any venture he embraced to ensure its success.

Chick comprehended the challenges of promoting sports. His publicity ventures encompassed football, basketball, auto racing, golf, and boxing. Ironically, his knowledge of sports was rather feeble. Chick seldom knew much about a sport beforehand. It was often said that Wergeles, "has as much knowledge of athletics as a hog does about mathematics."[2] In fact, Chick habitually used ghostwriters. Wergeles explained, "I had to have ghostwriters because I did not know which end of a football you sat on, or ate."[3]

National Associated Press Sports Editor Dillon Graham[4] said it right when speaking of Chick. "Perhaps the best known purveyor of publicity in New York," Graham wrote, "he distributes ballyhoo that other fellows write, hopping from one sport to another as the seasons roll around."[5] Like the boxer he was hired to promote, Chick was a man of perpetual motion. He had "more irons in the fire than a village blacksmith."[6] John Kieran, a journalist for the *New York Times*, depicted Wergeles, the publicity man:

> For untold years Mr. Wergeles, happy as a lark, has been trotting in and out of newspaper offices, leaving in his wake vast bundles of publicity for sports events of an amazing variety—boxing, wrestling, football, basketball, golf, skating, or name your poison. He chats cheerfully and fluently and he slaughters the English language with gusto, but his heart is in the right place even if his adjectives are not.[7]

Cheerfully promoting his sports, Wergeles could also massacre the English language.

Chick's publicity resume included his role in making professional football successful in New York. In 1925, he muscled his way into the New York Giants of the American Professional Football Association (APFA), the predecessor to the National Football League (NFL), as their publicity man. When Wergeles first started, he was given 5,000 tickets to give away for every home game. It was a struggle promoting professional football. Chick avowed, "We used to have to take a suitcase full of tickets and scatter them around to get people to pro games."[8] Not anymore!

For many years, Chick worked publicity for Edward "Ned" S. Irish. Irish (1905–1982), a former sportswriter and prominent figure in collegiate basketball during the 1930s, was convinced that basketball would flourish at Madison Square Garden. So, in 1934, he began renting out the Garden for the duration of the college basketball season. With Chick's assistance, Irish's college basketball program at the Garden averaged an attendance of 18,196 by 1946.

Wergeles also served as the publicity agent for the $100,000 Roosevelt Raceway located in Westbury, Long Island, New York. Built in 1936, the speedway was situated on Roosevelt Field, the same field from which Charles Lindburg (1902–1974) departed on his 1927 historic plane trip across the Atlantic to Paris. In plugging the speedway, Chick worked closely with George Washington Vanderbilt, III, George Preston Marshall, and Eddie Rickenbacker, the raceway's chief financiers. Featuring four miles of winding, twisting track, the racetrack was surrounded with enormous grandstands for nearly 100,000 spectators. The inaugural race took place on October 12, 1936, in front of roughly 50,000 spectators—the 300-mile George Vanderbilt Cup.

Regrettably, the racetrack proved too twisty and curvy for racecars of the day, so it was converted to a half-mile harness track in 1940.

In 1939, Wergeles commenced working with the Goodall Round Robin Golf Tournament. At the time, he didn't know which end of a golf club to use, but he did so well, the tournament retained his services for the next two years. An unusual event, only fifteen professional golfers received invitations to participate in the Goodall tournament. Held at Fresh Meadows Country Club between 1939–1941, players vied for a $5,000 purse. Sam Snead collected the purse in 1939. Ben Hogan won the tournament in 1940, and Paul Runyan earned the prize money in 1941.

Out of all the sports he publicized, Chick was best known for his connection with boxing. Chick always had an interest in boxing. When he was 16, he already had his own stable of fighters. Subsequently, the *New York Morning World* hired Wergeles to conduct publicity for its boxing interests "and out of that grew a career."[9] Chick also began to manage fighters and operate a fight club. Later, he would obtain a ten percent interest in Rocky Marciano and serve as his co-manager along with Al Weill.

Through his work, Chick developed a close relationship with the *Herald Tribune's* sportswriter, Richards Vidmer, an avid golfer. When Vidmer was in Augusta covering the 1941 Masters Tournament, he recommended Wergeles' services as a second manager and publicity man for Beau Jack. The Syndicate thoughtfully approved.

Chick initially learned that he was being retained as Beau's manager by telegraph. For his services, he would receive 25 percent of the net gate for Beau's fights. Chick immediately began touting his new fighter and "had the big columnists doing pieces about this boy before he even got a prelim bout."[10] The press began buzzing. "Chick is bringing in a new face in Beau Jack, a hard-hitting lightweight, who has been making a name for himself the hard way," wrote Harold Conrad (1910–1991),[11] sportswriter for the *Brooklyn Daily Eagle* and one of the founding members of the Boxing Writers' Association, "by eliminating the toughest men in his division."[12]

Wergeles was adamant that Beau reside in New York. New York City was the central hub of professional boxing. At the time, the New York State Athletic Commission (NYSAC) and National Boxing Association (NBA) championship titles were considered analogous to a world championship. Under Chick's guidance, Beau swiftly moved to New York. "I got him livin' wit' a nice Negro family in that Kingsboro Housin' Objeck in Brooklyn," commented Wergeles. "Cost 14 bucks a week. Plus his allowance, of courst. I make up a bill each week an' give it to the sportsmen an' they pay me."[13] By September 1941, Beau was living in the newly opened Kingsboro Housing Project on Albany Avenue in the Bedford-Stuyvesant neighborhood of Brooklyn and ready to embark on the championship path.

Importance of Image

Wergeles also knew the importance of image for Beau Jack. As a black man in a segregated world, Beau needed to present an acceptable appearance if he wanted to be embraced as a champion among both black and white fans. Jack had to keep his violence inside the ring and be careful not to upset anyone outside of the ring.

Years earlier, Jack Johnson had fought the powers that were. Revered among the African American community, Johnson became the first black American to earn the world heavyweight title. Ironically, Johnson was not the best representative for integrating the heavyweight division. He verbally abused his white opponents and outside the ring and had a passion for white women, both of which were taboo at the time. Johnson didn't care what white people thought and was consequently despised by many whites.

The world heavyweight champion, Joe Louis, and his manager, John Roxborough, knew the importance of image for the black boxer. Joe Louis, determined to avoid Johnson's disdain, took great strides to not come across offensively to white fans. His manager John Roxborough stressed to Joe that if he wanted to be embraced by the public, he had to live and fight clean. He needed to have a positive image and a pleasant demeanor. As Anthony O. Edmonds wrote in his article, "Joe Louis, Boxing, and American Culture," there were two dominant images that whites used to define blacks—"the 'angry bestial' and the 'docile childlike,' or, more bluntly, the 'bad nigger' and the 'good Negro.'"[14] Louis mastered the second image with his modest and unassuming character.

Integration was a psychological challenge in all sports. Years later a similar tact was taken in baseball by Branch Ricky. Rickey, the president, general manager, and part owner of the Brooklyn Dodgers, laid the groundwork for integrating Major League Baseball. In exchange for an opportunity to break the color barrier in professional baseball, Jackie Robinson had an agreement with Branch Rickey that he would hold his tongue and fists. Also aiding Rickey in his selection of Robinson was the fact that Robinson was educated, a nondrinker, didn't smoke, and had competed with and against white athletes. Moreover, he was not a womanizer.

Sid Bell Joins Beau's Team

A talented group of trainers was retained by the Syndicate to guide and instruct Beau. Sid Bell, well known for his conditioning expertise and his brash, demeaning motivational style, was Beau's head trainer. When Sid first saw Beau fight, he proclaimed, "You are a natural-born murderer. You are a natural fighter. Any boxer who can outfight you, he is a champion." To motivate Beau, Bell would scream at him, "You bum, you're nothing, you'll never be nothing. Don't give a man a chance to do nothing. Just rip him all the time you're in there and you'll come out all right."[15] Years later, Jack recalled Bell's training style. "He kept riding me, riding me, riding me," said Beau. "He would make me spar 10 rounds straight, with no rest between rounds. He was a mean man, sir. He's gone now, but I'm so thankful he was mean, because he got me in shape. If you don't train, you get hurt upstairs."[16] Sid Bell was not only a master conditioner, but he was also the first trainer to utilize the concept of punching in numbered sequences.

Bill "Pop" Miller (1925–2012) served as Beau's assistant trainer. Pop was a little black man with a loud voice. He had been a successful welterweight boxer, soldier, trainer, and manager. Miller was race-conscious and didn't like the way black boxers were treated. Vividly, he could remember when integrated matches were not allowed, as well as when "Negroes" were dressed up in colors and paraded in front of the public as untamed cannibals in Madison Square Garden. Pop's experience included working with such boxers as Panama Al Brown, Eugene Burton, Tiger Flowers, "Sugar" Ray Robinson, Coley Wallace, and Johnny Saxton. Unpretentiously, Miller never took credit for making anybody a fighter. "A youngster who has ambition to become something in the ring will succeed if he is given a little constructive advice," explained Miller. "No one can make a fighter."[17]

Rounding out his stable of trainers were Carmine Maurone and Larry Kent. Carmine, a former flyweight boxer from Philadelphia, worked part-time in Jack's corner. He also worked with Ike Williams, Bob Montgomery and Pete Logue. Kent was green at the time but was a great motivator known for encouraging his fighters to box aggressively while still utilizing their best skills. He also trained numerous world champions, such as "Sugar" Ray Robinson, Georgie Pace, and Jimmy Carter.

Legendary Stillman's Gym

In addition to hiring Chick Wergeles and Beau's trainers, the Syndicate retained a private dressing room for Beau at Stillman's Gym. Located on 8th Street in New York City, a couple of blocks away from Madison Square Garden, Stillman's was legendary. If you wanted to fight in Madison Square Garden in the '40s, you trained at Stillman's Gym. It was the holy grail of boxing gyms. Among the many great champions which trained there were Jack Dempsey, Joe Louis, Rocky Marciano, Rocky Graziano, Sandy Saddler, Paddy DeMarco, Willie Pep, Terry Young, Ike Williams, Bob Murphy, Jimmy Bivens, Jimmy Carter, Johnny Bratton, Jersey Joe Walcott, Bob Montgomery, and Max Baer. Sportswriter W. C. Heinz once declared that thousands of boxers from every continent but Antarctica came to Stillman's to train. Other people like Frank Sinatra, Dean Martin, Jerry Lewis, Buddy Hackett, and Tony Bennett would drop by just to watch the boxers work out.

The gym itself, like many boxing gyms during those days, was a dive. It was proudly heralded as one of the filthiest gyms in New York, smelling of cigar smoke and sweat. "The floor was one gigantic spittoon; the windows were dark with grime and never opened," recalled author Jeffrey Sussman. "Stillman claimed that fresh air was bad for fighters."[18] The first floored housed the shower for the entire gym. It was a single open stall, "with a concrete floor and drain and a rusted-solid shower head."[19] The heavy bags and speed bags were located on the second tier of the loft. Journalist Irving Rudd described Stillman's as a "narrow, dirty, airless three-story structure and ruled by a tough-talking, harsh-faced, constantly spitting martinet named Lou Stillman."[20]

Initially started by Marshall Stillman, the gym was envisioned as a way to give kids an alternative to crime. Stillman hired Lou Ingber (1887–1969), a former policeman, to run the gym. Before long, boxers training at the gym began to refer to Ingber as Mr. Stillman. So, Ingber changed his name to Lou Stillman. A rough character, Ingber sat at his desk near the entrance with his big, ugly cigar that smelled like rotten cabbage stuffed into his face. Hair billowed out from the sides of his head, and he wore a shoulder holster containing a snub-nosed .38 pistol.

Beau's first visit to Stillman's Gym was a flamboyant affair. He showed up with his entourage of trainers and manager Chick Wergeles, creating quite the excitement. "The heavyweights peered over each other's shoulders, the shadow boxers stopped dancing, the managers and matchmakers turned to stare," wrote sportswriter Richards Vidmer. "The parade passed through the room and on to a private dressing room."[21]

Beau loved the place. He would get to the gym at 10 a.m. and stay until late in the afternoon. Sometimes you would find him with his chin propped on the ring apron watching other fighters work in the ring. Harold Parrott, sportswriter for the *Brooklyn Daily Eagle*, one day asked Beau, "Learning all the time, Beau Jack," [Parrott] asked. "Yassah," he said, flashing a chinaware grin, "Learnin' what-all not to do as much as what to do."[22] The former lightweight king, Benny Leonard, trained alongside Beau at Stillman's Gym. When asked about Beau Jack, Leonard said, "He loves to fight, he loves to work. He is full of fire and ginger. He is going to go a long way."[23] Lou Stillman saw firsthand Beau's commitment to training. "That Beau," Lou grinned. "He used to wait for me when I opened at 10 in the morning and then I'd have to kick him out to close up the gym at 3:30. Always wanting to train."[24] Chuckling, he often teased Chick Wergeles that he should pay double the fees because Beau spent more time in the gym than any other two fighters combined.

9

Fistic Debut in New York

Beau's success in the ring, coupled with his move to New York and the hiring of Chick Wergeles, made him a sensational topic among sportswriters. Beau was climbing the lightweight ladder and a match in Madison Square Garden was inevitable. Before entering the Garden ring, however, Beau had to make it through two fights at historic Ebbets Field in the Crown Heights section of Brooklyn, his first bouts in the state of New York.

Home to the Brooklyn Dodgers, Ebbets Field was built by Charlie Ebbets. It opened on April 9, 1913, when the Dodgers hosted the Philadelphia Phillies. Ebbets Field was also home to one of the most momentous sporting events in professional baseball. Jackie Robinson (1919–1972) broke the color

Ebbets Field, c. 1913 (Library of Congress).

barrier in baseball when he debuted at Ebbets Field as the first black major league baseball player on April 15, 1947. Marking an early footstep in the Civil Rights movement and changing baseball forever, the Dodgers won the game with Robinson's assistance. Subsequently, the Dodgers moved to California changing their name to the Los Angeles Dodgers and, unfortunately, the stadium was demolished.

On a warm August evening, Beau made his metropolitan fistic debut. Having lost only one of his last 22 bouts, Beau Jack rode into Ebbets Field to battle Minnie DeMore of Trenton, New Jersey. DeMore had credentials. He won the Tri-State Amateur Boxing Tournament in 1934 for the 112-pound class. After debuting as a professional on January 27, 1938, DeMore went 11–3–1 in his first two years. Following his quick success, however, he had begun to wane. When he faced Jack, Minnie's professional record was 13–13–1, having lost 10 of his last 12 fights.

The two faced off on August 5, 1941, in a six-round preliminary bout before the main event between welterweight titleholder Freddy "Red" Cochrane and his challenger Izzy Jannazzo. Beau didn't waste any time in adding another victory to his record. Jack floored DeMore three times in the first round. Picking up where he left off, Beau floored DeMore again in the second round. When the bell sounded for round three, Beau rushed Minnie, throwing deluges of punches, knocking him down for the fifth time in the fight. Referee Jimmy Crowley called an end to DeMore's night, one minute and seven seconds into the third round. With the TKO victory, Beau improved his overall record to 23–4–2, with 16 wins coming by way of knockout.

A wave of encouraging press followed Beau's annihilation of Minnie DeMore. Sportswriter Harold Conrad boldly opined that Beau was in route to the lightweight championship. He was not the only one. Raymond Johnson of *The Tennessean* avowed that Jack would rule the lightweight title throne in a short time. Grantland Rice made the same prediction. "I don't see how he can miss," wrote Rice. "He's got the greatest pair of arms I believe I've ever seen. They look like Wolgast's. He has powerful shoulders and can hit as hard as anyone I've ever seen for his size, much harder than most of them."[1] Rice unapologetically recognized that Beau knew little about boxing, but that didn't affect his appraisal of Beau. "He just hits them and watches the other fellow fall," Rice explained. "When they get up, if they do, he hits them again and turns his back, for he knows they'll not get up again."[2] It seemed the lightweight title was Beau's destiny. Moreover, Beau's popularity was rapidly rising. Reportedly, Chick Wergeles received over 90 requests from local Brooklyn fans to bring Beau back to Ebbets field after his spectacular knockout of Minnie DeMore.

As requested, Beau was back at Ebbets Field within two weeks. On Thursday night, August 14, 1941, Jack faced Al Roth (1913–1982) in an eight-round preliminary fight. Roth hailed from the Bronx and sported a 47–29–13 record. Only once in 89 professional bouts had Roth tasted the canvas. He was a short 5'4" tall dynamo who got off to a brilliant professional career going 22–0–5, but like Minnie DeMore, had faded since becoming a top-ranked lightweight, winning only one of his last ten bouts.

For the second time in a row, Beau stole the show at Ebbets Field, demolishing Al Roth in five rounds. In the second round, Beau stung Roth under his left eye and then peppered the spot with punches, opening a gash over the same eye by the next round. Beau was pounding Roth's face with thunderous punches. By the fifth round, the referee stopped the fight upon the ring doctor's advice, as "both eyes were merely slits in Al's puffed, grotesque face."[3] Harold Conrad remarked, "Beau did a job on Roth that would have been the envy of a Washington Market butcher."[4] Roth retired from boxing after the fight. When asked what he aimed to do when he was finished boxing, Beau said, "I would like to be a bouncer in a saloon!"[5]

A week after demolishing Al Roth, the headline of Jack Cuddy's article in the *Danville Morning News* read "Beau Jack Latest Sensation along Cauliflower Row."[6] In fact, the article was in newspapers throughout the country, thanks to Jack Cuddy, a United Press Correspondent. "Cauliflower row" was a term often used to refer to boxing experts and those intimately involved in the sport.

Two months later, Ebbets Field went on to host three games of the 1941 World Series between the Brooklyn Dodgers and the New York Yankees. The Brooklyn Dodgers finished first in the National League with a record of 100–51. They faced their cross-town rivals the New York Yankees, who had finished on top of the American League with a record of 101–53. Regrettably, for the Dodgers, Joe DiMaggio and the Yankees took the World Series four games to one.

It was an anxious time in the States, as Americans sensed that the U.S. would soon enter World War II. Private land was being usurped by the government to make way for ammunition plants and workers. The American Federation of Teachers adopted an amendment barring Communists, Fascists and Nazis from membership as teachers were being fired as city school systems tried to purge themselves of "Reds."

Madison Square Garden and Tex Rickard

For over a century, New York's Madison Square Garden was the ultimate boxing venue. Beau Jack would fight in the third version of the Garden.

Adjacent to Madison Square Park, the original Garden was a converted railroad station, located at 26th Street and Madison Avenue in Manhattan. After Commodore William Vanderbilt acquired the lease in the 1870s, he named the venue Madison Square Garden. Vanderbilt couldn't make the Garden lucrative, so he closed shop and had the building demolished.

The second Madison Square Garden was built in 1890 at the same location by a consortium led by J. P. Morgan and the Madison Square Garden Company. Not profitable, they sold it to another company that likewise failed to make it gainful. The New York Life Insurance Company, which held a $2.3 million mortgage, called for the Garden to be flattened like the original Garden.

In the darkness of impending doom, George Lewis "Tex" Rickard (1870–1929) came riding in to save the day. An avid boxing fan, Rickard grew up orphaned but turned into an extremely successful boxing promoter. He promoted Joe Gans when he defeated Oscar "Battling" Nelson in 1906, and Jack Johnson when he defended his title against James J. Jeffries in the "Fight of the Century" in 1910.

In 1916, Rickard rented the Garden with funds loaned to him by his friend Mike Jacobs and staged a fight between Jess Willard, the "Kansas Giant," and Frank Moran. Willard wore the heavyweight belt that he acquired by defeating Jack Johnson in 1915. Over 13,000 spectators filled the Garden, providing a gate of $151,254 to see Willard, standing 6'6½" tall and weighing 235 pounds, defend his title against Moran.

Three years later, Tex brought Jess Willard to the Bay View Park Arena in Toledo, Ohio to face heavy-

George Lewis "Tex" Rickard, c. 1919 (Library of Congress).

weight champion Jack Dempsey. Dempsey demolished the "Kansas Giant" who outweighed him by more than 40 pounds. Willard went down for the seventh time in the third round. With his right eye closed shut, his right cheek swollen and blue, and blood covering his body, Willard threw in the towel. Thereafter, Rickard entered a financially prosperous relationship promoting Jack Dempsey.

In the early 20th century, boxing was difficult to promote in New York. Legalized boxing was a subject of intense debate in New York at the time. The Frawley Law, passed in 1911, sanctioned boxing but limited the number of rounds to ten. Ringside decisions were not permitted. Instead, sportswriters would provide their verdict in the next day's paper. In 1917, the Slater Law repealed the Frawley Law, and once again, boxing was not legal in New York. However, in 1920, the Walker Law was passed, ending a three-year ban.

Named after its advocate, former New York senator and mayor James J. Walker, the law created the New York State Athletic Commission and provided much-needed regulations for boxing. Two judges would now render decisions on all bouts. If the judges disagreed, the referee would make the decision. All clubs, physicians, referees, judges, timekeepers, professional boxers, managers and trainers were required to be licensed with the Commission. Five-ounce gloves were mandatory for fighters up to and including the lightweight class. Six-ounce gloves would be used for the heavier divisions. With the passing of the Walker Law, Rickard quickly signed a 10-year lease on the Garden. Despite the lease, New York Life foreclosed on the Garden in 1925 to erect an office building.

Given the second Garden's demise, Tex Rickard decided to construct the third version. Built in 1925, the third version of the Garden was located in Manhattan on Eighth Avenue between 49th and 50th streets. The indoor venue was a triple-decked arena with a seating capacity for boxing of 18,500. The first event at the "new" Garden featured light heavyweight champion Paul Berlenbach as he defeated Jack Delaney. In addition to numerous boxing matches, concerts, and other events, the Garden was also home to the New York Rangers of the National Hockey League and the New York Knicks of the National Basketball Association. It survived 43 years before closing in 1968, shortly before the opening of the fourth Madison Square Garden.

Beau Enters the Ring at Madison Square Garden

The evening of Tuesday, August 26, 1941, was a momentous occasion at Madison Square Garden. Beau made his historic debut in a six-round preliminary battle to the Gus Lesnevich–Tami Mauriello light heavyweight

Madison Square Garden III, c. 1940 (author's collection).

championship fight. Little did anyone know, but Beau was embarking on a record-breaking historical journey at the Garden.

In his first encounter inside the Garden ring, Beau met Columbian Guillermo Puentes, the lightweight champion of South America. Puentes had earned the nickname "macieste," or "strong man," after knocking out Oliver White and defeating Julie Kogon. He had a hard right hook and carried "dynamite in both hands." Although Puentes had lost three bouts in a row, resulting in a professional record of 7–6–1, his style was similar to Beau's. He was aggressive and threw flurries of punches. Both fighters stood at a comparable height, but Beau had a five-pound weight advantage at 136 pounds.

Jack and Puentes came out slinging at the opening bell. It was a hectic and frenzied slugfest. Puentes aggressively pushed the action and hurt Jack three or four times. Resiliently, Jack survived, earning an unpopular six-round victory. A chorus of boos greeted Beau when renowned announcer Harry Balogh (1891–1961) raised his hand in victory. The win was great, but it wasn't the debut Beau sought. He was a crowd pleaser, and the booing saddened him.

Between 1933 and 1957, Harry Balogh reigned as the most famous boxing announcer in the world. It was Harry who initiated the tuxedo and stiff front shirt, making it the standard uniform for announcers. After introducing the combatants, Balogh would always exclaim, "And may the better boxer emerge victorious." An advocate for unity, he also used his platform in the center of the ring to fight racial prejudice. He even learned enough Spanish to introduce Spanish boxers in their native language.

The disappointing boos did not last long for Beau. He fought 11 of his next 21 contests at Madison Square Garden, winning each one. Beau later admitted that at 20 years of age, those big lights at Madison Square Garden scared him to death.

Beau had three weeks to prepare for his next fight. Movies and arcade shooting galleries were Jack's choice for relaxation. He would walk to the 50th Street shooting gallery, where he would shoot pigeons and ducks as they traveled across the backdrop. Taking in a movie was also a favorite pastime of Beau's. Movies playing at the time included Orson Welles' *Citizen Kane*, John Wayne in *Shepherd of the Hills*, Bob Hope and Dorothy Lamour in *Caught in the Draft* and showing for the 45th consecutive week, Walt Disney's *Fantasia*.

In front of a crowd of 11,945 spectators, Jack was set to enter his second duel at Madison Square Garden on September 19. The main event featured a lightweight battle between "up and coming" Sugar Ray Robinson and Maxie Shapiro. Robinson won by TKO in the third round after knocking Shapiro to the canvas four times, improving his undefeated streak to 24 victories.

Featured in an eight-round preliminary match, Beau was scheduled for a rematch with Guillermo Puentes. Puentes, however, fell ill before the fight. Veteran 26-year-old Jewish boxer Al Reid agreed to substitute for Puentes. A natural featherweight, Reid, whose birth name was Abe Reibman, had six years of boxing under his belt and a respectable record of 56–29–13. Possessing uncanny speed and finesse, Al's resume included victories over Joey Fontana (47–7–5), Bernie Friedkin (47–6–10), and Joey Iannotti (29–2–3). Moreover, a year prior, he handed undefeated top lightweight contender Maxie Shapiro his first loss in 39 contests.

At the opening bell, Reid came out throwing leather. As he kept Jack at bay, it became obvious that a fierce battle had erupted. Nonetheless, the tide turned in the seventh round. Beau landed two consecutive uppercuts to Reid's chin, dropping him hard to the canvas. As Reid sluggishly made it to his feet, Jack landed a vicious body hook, dumping him right back on the canvas. Reid was done and Referee Arthur Donovan had seen enough. Donovan stopped the fight 1:31 minutes into the seventh round, awarding Beau victory by technical knockout. Harry Balogh again raised Jack's hand in victory. Beau reveled in his victory on the big stage of the Garden.

Reid's next fight on November 18, 1941, would be his last. The next day he joined the U.S. Coast Guard. Reid finished his career with a 60–28–12 record and was inducted into the New Jersey Boxing Hall of Fame in 1996.

Beau's success did not sit well with Bobby Ruffin, a young white fighter from Astoria, Queens, New York, sporting a record of 35–13–6. On September 22, 1941, Maurie Waxman, Bobby Ruffin's mouthpiece, issued a challenge to Jack, claiming that Beau had only fought pushovers and nobody the likes of his fighter. Both Ruffin and Jack had victories over Young Johnny Buff, Minnie DeMore, Al Reid and Tommy Speigal. A fight with Ruffin, however, would not happen for several years.

It was a windy evening outside the Broadway Arena on October 14. Broadway Arena was referred to as a "Brooklyn Institution, second only to the Dodgers."[7] A couple of blocks off Broadway, the arena backed up next to Halsey Street near Saratoga Avenue. Although it was home to the Gothams, a professional basketball team, and wrestling was often on the card, the beloved arena was most treasured as the oldest neighborhood fight club in Brooklyn, drawing fans from Coney Island to New York's Lower East Side. The 4,500-seat venue featured a much-anticipated weekly Tuesday night fight card.

Jack appeared in the main event on October 14. For the second time, he was matched against Tommy Speigal, in what was again declared a bout of "nationwide fistic significance." Five months earlier, Beau had belted out a unanimous decision over Tommy in Holyoke. Even though Beau had not lost in his last 15 bouts, the feisty, unorthodox, 5'8" Uniontown fighter came into the match as a six to five favorite. Speigal was out to halt Beau's winning streak and get revenge for his previous loss. He trained rigorously for the rematch. Speigal's training showed at the weigh-in. Tommy had lost over five pounds since their last fight, standing 131 pounds on the scale to Beau's 135½ pounds.

From the ringing of the opening bell to the clanging of the closing bell, both fighters brawled at a blistering pace. Much of the bout was fought inside, as the combatants stood next to each other swapping blows. Speigal threw nasty punches, but when they closed in on each other, the shorter Beau landed the better blows. Effectively offsetting his shorter reach, Beau stuck close to Speigal and pounded away. Jack consistently connected with ripping right uppercuts, repeatedly snapping his foe's head back in pain. Speigal's left jabs were his most effective offense, opening a small cut next to Beau's left eye. It was a close fight, especially after Beau was penalized for a low blow in the fifth round, but Beau once again emerged victorious on the scorecards. The next day the headline in the *Brooklyn Daily Eagle* read, "Beau Jack Now Ready for Big Time."[8]

Tommy only fought four more bouts before retiring due to health issues. Problems with his stiff leg had progressed into bone tuberculosis. Unfortunately, Speigal spent his last years in the Sunny Acres Sanitarium and Cleveland Hospital before passing away on November 9, 1945, at the young age of 32. His record was 76–42–9.

Sinking Ships

While Beau was immersed in boxing, the United States was getting closer and closer to entering World War II. Axis powers[9] had sunk their eighth American ship, the tanker *I. C. White*, between Brazil and the western bulge of Africa. On October 4, Secretary of State Cordell Hull emphatically denounced the torpedoing and sinking of the tanker, strengthening President Roosevelt's hand in seeking any potential revision of the Neutrality Act, which limited U.S. involvement in the war. Two weeks later, a German U-boat torpedoed the *Kearny*, a U.S. destroyer, near Iceland. To make matters worse, a German U-boat sank the destroyer *Reuben James* on October 30, killing almost 100 men.

Moving Up the Lightweight Ladder

Madison Square Garden was bursting with a sellout crowd of 20,551 rowdy spectators on Halloween night, October 31, 1941, to witness the main event. Featured sensational lightweights were unbeaten Sugar Ray Robinson and ex-champion Fritzie Zivic. It was the year's second-largest crowd, providing Beau a great occasion to cultivate more supporters. Beau appeared in a preliminary eight-round rematch with Guillermo Puentes. Two months earlier, Jack had defeated Puentes in a controversial decision. Sitting ringside to assess the boxers was lightweight boxing sensation Allie Stolz. Stolz, the former New Jersey featherweight titleholder, boasted an impressive 46–4–2 record. The winner of the contest between Jack and Puentes was contracted to be his next opponent.

The booing of the fans following his previous victory over Puentes troubled Jack. Beau loved to please the fans. The more they clapped, the better he fought. He wasn't going to give them a reason to jeer again. Coming into the match, Jack had a 4¾ pound advantage over Puentes, who weighed in at 130¼ pounds.

Unlike their first contest, much to Beau's liking, the rematch produced a decisive winner. Jack came out fast and furious. Even though he began to dawdle in the middle rounds, Beau accelerated the pace in the final two rounds, punishing Puentes with destructive left jabs and right uppercuts to the head. Beau painlessly scored a unanimous decision over Puentes. In the main event, Robinson extended his undefeated streak to 27, by taking a 10-round unanimous decision over Zivic. As customary, Chick gave Beau Jack $1 for spending money after the fight, so Beau could unwind by taking in a couple of dime movies.

Along with his success, Beau developed one weakness. Sharp dressing became an obsession. He loved buying new clothes. His wardrobe featured fawn-colored sports jackets, tailored pants, pork-pie hats, and even silk underwear. One of Beau's favorite outfits was a green pork-pie hat, peg-top pants, and a yellow checkered jacket with a purple tie and yellow shoes. Colorful is an understatement.

As Beau moved up the lightweight ladder and began to fight for larger purses, sportswriter Bob Considine reported that Jack had become the ward of Lansing B. Lee, Jr., of Augusta, one of Augusta's most distinguished lawyers. Considine explained that half of Beau's earnings, or $850 from the Puentes fight, was sent to Lansing for safe keeping in a trust account for Beau.[10] Jack's training expenses, room and board and clothes were paid for out of the remaining $425. Interestingly, less than a year later, in May 1942, Lansing Lee filed for Dismission as Guardian of Beau Jack's property.

Following several weeks in Augusta, Beau soon returned to New York to begin training for his upcoming bout. Although he was supposed to meet Allie Stolz, it didn't happen. Instead, he would battle Sammy Rivers, aka Santiago Rivera, on December 1, 1941. Sammy was a robust two-fisted body puncher but had a dismal professional record winning only one of his 45 fights. With Madison Square Garden not available due to the Ice Follies performances, smaller venues were thrust into the boxing limelight. Ridgewood Grove Arena, located at Palmetto Street and St. Nicholas Avenue in Queens, New York, was the venue for Beau's contest against Rivers. Seating 5,000 spectators, Ridgewood Grove Arena was a boxing mecca between 1926 and 1956.

The loyal Ridgewood fans were eagerly anticipating the Tuesday night fight card featuring the main event between Beau Jack and Sammy Rivers. As expected, Beau did not need eight rounds to finish off his prey. Beau swarmed Rivers at the opening bell, unleashing flurries of punches. All Sammy could do was to hold on to Beau for dear life. On occasion, the taller Rivers futilely struggled to force Beau out of his rhythm by slugging long range but his efforts were to no avail. The harm done by Beau in the third round proved to be fatal for Rivers. Beau's furious series of stiff punches created a deep cut under Rivers' left eye. Sammy, with blood running down his face, tried to carry on, but Referee Joe Vaccarella prevented Rivers from answering the bell in the fourth. Damage to Rivers' eye was too severe. With the stoppage, Beau earned a trouble-free victory via technical knockout. The next day's headline in the *Brooklyn Daily Eagle* read, "Rivers Doesn't Even Make Beau Breathe Hard."[11]

Pearl Harbor and James Wergeles

Horror struck the morning before Beau's next fight. At 7:35 a.m. Hawaiian time on December 7, 1941, hundreds of Japanese fighter planes attacked

Three civilians were killed in this shrapnel-riddled car by a bomb dropped from a Japanese plane eight miles from Pearl Harbor, December 7, 1941 (Library of Congress).

the U.S. naval base at Pearl Harbor, near Honolulu, Hawaii, killing more than 2,000 American soldiers and sailors and wounding more than 1,000 more. In what the United States "officially and unequivocally described as treacherous and utterly unprovoked," the Japanese destroyed more than 20 naval vessels, including eight battleships and more than 300 fighter planes.

Among those injured was Chick Wergeles' 19-year-old son, Marine Private First-Class James Arthur Wergeles (1922–2013). The noise of anti-aircraft guns awoke his company on the morning of December 7. Accounting the events of the day, James expressed, "we couldn't believe it was an attack—so the men in my tent rolled over and went back to sleep."[12] The delayed reaction was experienced by many of the servicemen at Pearl Harbor. Despite their disbelief, the men in James' outfit were quickly awakened again by an exploding piece of shrapnel that tore through their tent. "I was bending over to pick up some gear," gasped Wergeles, "when a piece of shell whistled over my head and hit a buddy in the neck."[13]

Wergeles jumped in a jeep and headed toward the waterfront. Unfortunately, in the shock of the moment, the vehicle crashed, breaking James' back in three places. He was subsequently transported to the St. Albans Naval Hospital on Long Island for treatment.

Remarkably, James would heal quickly enough to be in the first wave of invading Marines in the Guadalcanal Campaign. During the battle that waged from August 7, 1942, through February 9, 1943, he was injured again, this time hit with shrapnel in his back. Doctors thought he might be crippled for life, but James rebounded once again. Following his service in World War II, James Wergeles became the Publicity Director for the New York Knicks of the National Basketball Association.

Jack Stumbles Against Freddie Archer

A day after Pearl Harbor and hours after President Roosevelt and Congress declared war on Japan, Beau squared off with Newark, New Jersey's crack 19-year-old lightweight, Freddie Archer (1922–1985). Archer was on a tear, winning his last 8 bouts and only suffering two defeats in his previous 20 matches. Archer had already defeated future titleholder Ike Williams and former Beau Jack opponents George Zengarass, Tommy Speigal, Joe Rivers, and Bob Reilly. He was not unstoppable though. Twenty-four-year-old Tippy Larkin knocked Archer out in the first round of their fight six months earlier. George Zengaras, whom Beau defeated several months earlier, had put Archer on the canvas as well. Still, Archer was considered one of the top 135-pounders.

The contest took place at the 4,000-seat St. Nicholas Arena located at Columbus Avenue and West 66th Street in Manhattan on December 8. It was about eight miles away from Beau's last fight venue, Ridgewood Grove Arena. The arena previously operated as a skating rink known as St. Nicholas Rink. In the early 1900s, the skating rink was overhauled and renamed St. Nicholas Arena, and began hosting boxing matches and other entertainment. Known as the "Bucket of Blood," the arena was filled with cigar smoke on fight nights. It was demolished in 1962 to make way for an office building.

At the pre-fight weigh-in, Archer weighed 137½ pounds to Beau's 136¼ pounds and stood 5'7" tall. Even though Archer had an outstanding record, the oddsmakers favored Beau three to one over Freddie. It was a close, tough-fought battle. After eight rounds of action, the decision went to the scorecards. In one of the year's largest upsets, Archer was awarded the decision on points, thanks in part to Jack losing the sixth round because of a low blow. Beau later recalled his loss to Freddie Archer as one of his biggest disappointments. Not only did he lose to Archer, but it was also the day after Pearl Harbor.

Freddie Archer had Beau's number. They fought for the second straight time at St. Nicholas Arena in an eight-round feature on December 29, 1941. The Newark fighter used his powerful left hook, dropping Beau for a 2-count

ST. NICHOLAS SKATING RINK, NEW YORK CITY.

St. Nicholas Skating Rink, New York City, c. 1901 (Wikimedia Commons).

in the second round, recording Beau's first taste of the canvas. Throughout the bout, Archer continually caught Beau with his left hook when Beau tried to come inside. After eight rounds, Archer was again victorious on points. Who knows how it affected the outcome, but after the fight, it was learned that Beau was suffering from a high fever and pneumonia.

Archer finished his professional career with a remarkable 88–24–3 record. In 1945, *The Ring* magazine ranked Freddie Archer as the number four welterweight in the world. Archer was inducted into the New Jersey Boxing Hall of Fame on November 1, 1981.

War Rationing

Because of World War II, there were severe shortages of materials, fuel, and foods. In 1941, President Roosevelt created the Office of Price Administration (OPA) to place price ceilings on most goods and implement a system of rationing. The OPA established nationwide rationing through War Ration Books containing removable stamps good for specific rationed items.

The initial War Ration Books designated for sugar were issued to Americans on May 5, 1942. Some of the other items rationed during the war included cheese, canned food, meat, coffee, butter, jams, jellies, cooking oil, gasoline, fuel oil, coal, nylon, silk, and tires. Much of the processed and canned foods were shipped overseas to U.S. and Allied troops, creating a high demand for food items. Citizens were also requested to return tin cans and waste fat to the local Salvage Committee after the ration was used to make munitions for the military.

Beginning on May 15, 1942, gasoline was rationed in the Eastern United States. Within the next four months, gas was limited across the entire nation. Even whiskey was restricted. According to a city jailer in Roanoke, North Carolina, it decreased the Monday morning drunks' population in his jail from 180 to 76 guests.

The government underscored the patriotic fervor in supporting the war cause and our troops overseas. The War Ration Books contained language such as, "rationing is a vital part of your country's war effort." By rationing, the everyday American could contribute to the war effort. The ration stamps themselves often featured drawings of airplanes, guns, tanks, and aircraft. Violation of the rationing rules was equated to "treason," subjecting one to punishments ranging as high as ten years' imprisonment or a $10,000 fine, or both. Needless to say, fake cards were commonplace, and a black market developed for rationed items, but overall the rationing process worked reasonably well.

Sports were also affected by World War II. For example, there was a shortage of available wood, making baseball bats and bowling pins hard to find. Having had professional baseball discontinued during World War I, baseball officials didn't know whether to plan for a 1942 season. Executives requested Commissioner Kenesaw M. Landis to question the president. President Roosevelt responded swiftly and decisively, signing what became known as the "Green Light Letter" that signaled baseball to keep going. President Roosevelt stated, "I honestly feel that it would be best for the country to keep baseball going."[14] Baseball provided relaxation and low-cost entertainment to hard-working Americans whose work was desperately required for the U.S. war effort.

10

Eleven Straight Wins
and a Title Fight

The year 1942 was the year of the "Jack Rabbit." To launch the year, Beau reeled off eleven straight victories, including seven by way of knockout, on his way to a lightweight championship bout against Tippy Larkin on December 18. His competitors were determined and experienced. The first six fighters he faced had a combined record of 192–84–30. The last five opponents had an even more daunting collective record of 231–30–13.

In his first bout of 1942, Beau returned to his old stomping grounds, the Valley Arena in Holyoke, Massachusetts. Although it was his 38th bout since arriving in Massachusetts, it was Beau's first 10-round bout. More than 2,000 fans filed into the arena eager to see their "hometown" boy in action once again. It had been seven months since Jack last fought in the Valley.

Beau was paired with Spaniard Carmelo Fenoy, aka Carmello Fenoy Garrido, of New York, for the January 5 bout. A previous South American lightweight champion, Fenoy had a professional record of 48–14–4. On the other hand, Fenoy's stock was deteriorating, as he had lost his last four bouts. Although 2¼ pounds heavier than Jack, Carmelo was an inch shorter.

Beau did not disappoint his "hometown" fans. From the opening to the closing bell, Beau drove the Spaniard around the ring, throwing flurries of punches and keeping Fenoy off balance. Even though Carmelo managed to survive Beau's onslaught, the decision was never in question. At the end of ten rounds, Beau was awarded a unanimous decision over Fenoy.

Tonsillectomy

A week later, Jack was scheduled to meet Guillermo Puentes for the third time at Madison Square Garden, this time as a preliminary to the rematch between Sugar Ray Robinson and Fritzie Zivic. Before the fight, however, Beau developed a nasty cold and had to back out. Beau was also scheduled to meet Terry Young at the Garden on January 30 but had to cancel that match as well. Reportedly, he was suffering from pneumonia.

It turns out that Beau suffered from more than a simple cold or pneumonia. On February 11, 1942, Beau boarded the train with Bowman Milligan and headed for home. Beau's illness had advanced to the point that a tonsillectomy was necessary. Following surgery, newspapers carried a picture of Beau lying in his hospital bed at University Hospital with Bowman standing next to him. Beau rested in Augusta for several months before stepping back into the ring.

While in town, Beau registered for the draft. On his registration card, he identified himself as a "prizefighter" with a cut over his left eye, standing 5'4½" tall, and weighing 135 pounds. He listed his Uncle Jesse as his contact person. Interestingly, contrary to popular belief, Beau was not only capable of signing his name but did sign his name on his registration card.

As usual, while he was recuperating in Augusta, Beau waited tables at the Augusta National clubhouse during the ninth annual Masters Tournament in April. After the first round, Ben Hogan came in with a score of 73, six shots behind the leader. One of the members asked Beau if he knew what might be wrong with Hogan's golf game. "Overtrained," responded Beau. "Once I overtrained. All during the fight I knew what I wanted to do, I saw the chance to do it. But could I make my hands move? No sir, I just couldn't get them to work. I think maybe the same thing happens to Mr. Hogan. He works too hard."[1] Ben Hogan finished second that year, falling to Byron Nelson after an 18-hole playoff round.

Dim-Out

Within a month after Pearl Harbor, German U-boats began terrorizing the U.S. coastline, sinking fuel tankers, cargo ships, etc. Therefore, in April of 1942, a government-mandated "dim-out" was instituted along the East Coast. The regulations were enacted to protect U.S. ships from potential submarine attacks by reducing "shore glow" which aided the enemy in locating ships at sea.

New York had stringent dim-out restrictions. Regulations required elimination of all interior window lighting projecting above the horizontal, or screening of such lights to project their rays downward, blackout of all external lighting for advertising, elimination of all exterior lighting on theaters and concert halls, blackout of all lights above the 15th floor, elimination of all lights visible from the sea and reduction of lighting on all streets, parkways, parks, highways and racetracks.

Beau Returns from Layoff

Following a four-and-a-half-month layoff, Beau returned to the Garden ring on May 22, 1942, to tackle Bobby "Poison" Ivy (1915–1984) of Hartford, Connecticut. The "Hartford Bludgeon" had a record of 47–14–9 and previously contended for the featherweight title only to lose to Pete Scalzo. Ivy possessed a powerful short hook and a ripping right uppercut. In his last fight, Ivy scored an enormous upset by winning a unanimous decision over a heavily favored Jackie Callura. Coincidently, six months later Callura was crowned the world featherweight champion, defeating titleholder Jackie Wilson.

It was a bizarre bout. In the first round, Beau hit Ivy with a hard right to his head. Ivy was hurt and appeared as if he wouldn't make it to the bell. Although groggy, Bobby not only survived the round, he managed to come back and take a turbulent second round. The third was equally rough after Beau shoved Ivy down for a two count. From the fourth round on, however, Beau got on track and simply took advantage of his weight, keeping pressure on Ivy and continuously attacking him with punches. After the final bell, Jack was declared the victor on points.

The next day, Ivy's manager, Pete Reilly, was heavily criticized for taking the fight and failing to insist on the contracted 135-pound weight limit. Ivy, a natural featherweight, came in about six to eight pounds over his optimal fighting weight. Beau, on the other hand, weighed in above weight at 137½ pounds and boosted up over 140 pounds by fight time. Five months after his bout with Jack, Ivy, the winner of only one of his last six matches, hung up the gloves. Ivy finished his four-year career with a record of 48–18–10 and went to work for United Aircraft.

After defeating Bobby Ivy, Beau went on a remarkable knockout streak, knocking out his next five opponents. The streak began on a mild summer evening in June at MacArthur Stadium and ended back at MacArthur Stadium two months later. Located in Syracuse, New York, the 10,000-seat MacArthur Stadium was initially named Municipal Stadium or Bay Area Stadium but was subsequently renamed in honor of General Douglas MacArthur.

Beau's first three knockouts occurred within 14 days. His opening victim was Guillermo Puentes, who Beau was meeting for the third time. Beau had won the previous two bouts on points and three of his last five matches since he last met Puentes. Guillermo, on the other hand, had lost his last five bouts.

Beau was undeniably ready for Puentes for their main event match at MacArthur Stadium on June 23, 1942. Four thousand avid fight fans were on hand for the eight-round main event. The mighty bull-shouldered Beau Jack didn't take long to show Puentes who was boss of the ring, knocking him out with a right uppercut 2:52 minutes into the first round. Referee Jed Gahan gave Puentes the 10-count and Jack gave Puentes his first career knockout. After one more fight and 12 consecutive defeats, Puentes hung up his boxing gloves. He finished his career with an unremarkable record of 7–15–1.

Eyeing a title fight, Jack's team began calling out the lightweight champion Sammy Angott. Angott had taken the NBA lightweight title from Davey Day on the eve of the Kentucky Derby in Louisville on May 3, 1940, and defeated Lew Jenkins on December 19, 1941, to acquire the NYSAC's lightweight title. Chick Wergeles telegraphed Angott's manager, Charlie Jones, offering a $10,000 guarantee for an Angott title bout. Wergeles even offered to let Angott pick the place and date. Sammy's camp, however, did not accept the challenge.

A week after his first-round knockout of Puentes, Beau faced Detroit veteran Bobby McIntire. McIntire had recent victories over tough opponents including Carmine Fatta, Julie Kogon, and Billy Marquart, but had suffered knockouts in his last two outings. Jackie Wilson knocked Bobby out on May 29, and Chalky Wright knocked McIntire out in the fifth round on June 24 on his way to the featherweight title three months later. McIntire's overall record was 45–22–5.

The bout, scheduled for Thursday night, July 2, 1942, was heralded as the main event on historic Fort Hamilton's weekly fight card. Named after Alexander Hamilton, Fort Hamilton, located in the southwestern corner of Brooklyn, is the fourth oldest military installation in the United States. Unfortunately, heavy rain on the day of the fight forced a one-day postponement. It didn't hurt attendance. The next night, with Beau Jack, the hard-hitting sensation of New York in the main event, Harlem's army crowd turned out in hordes.

McIntire held a slight weight and height advantage over Beau, but that was the only benefit he had. Beau took McIntire to school and had him lumbering in distress the whole fight. Finally, in the sixth round, Beau mercifully ended Bobby McIntire's night, flattening him 2:20 minutes into the 6th round. McIntire was Beau's second opponent in 10 days to suffer defeat via knockout.

With no time to rest, Beau quickly prepared for his next match on July 7. He faced Danny McMillan (1921–1977), who fought under the name Cosby Linson, of New Orleans, Louisiana in the main event at Queensboro Arena. Located in Long Island, New York, Queensboro Arena was an open-air arena built in the early twenties, capable of seating 25,000 spectators.

Cosby was rapidly rising in the lightweight ranks with recent upsets over Vinnie Rossano and Chief Crazy Horse. Moreover, he had won his last four fights, improving his record to 26–3–5. Cosby stood 5'7" tall and weighed 141 pounds, four pounds heavier than Jack for their welterweight clash.

Beau busted out of the gates against the boxer from the "Big Easy," flooring Linson in the first round for a nine-count. Beau continued the assault, opening up deep gashes over both of Linson's eyes. Using his signature bolo punch, Beau easily won five of the first seven rounds. By the eighth round, Linson was a bloody mess. Blood was flowing from cuts above his eyes, nose, and mouth when referee Johnny MacAvoy stopped the fight 2 minutes and 17 seconds into the eighth round. Linson was Jack's third knockout victim in two weeks. After losing to Beau, Linson went on a seven-bout win streak. He finished his career with a record of 49–19–8.

Beau Jack's stock was swiftly rising. He had finally earned a spot in line for a crack at Sammy Angott and the lightweight title, joining contenders Allie Stolz and Chalky Wright. With Uncle Sam's continuing call to service during World War II, the Syndicate behind Beau wanted to ensure that he would get a title bout before he was called into service. Chick Wergeles again offered Angott a $10,000 guarantee to fight Beau. Angott again turned down the offer. Beau would have to wait.

Puerto Rican fighter Ruby Garcia was Beau's next adversary. They met in an eight-round featured bout on August 1, 1942, at the Twin City Bowl, an open-air arena located on the Newark-Elizabeth City line. Boxing fans were excited, as this was the first Saturday night boxing match in the Newark area in years. On paper, it looked to be a tremendous matchup. Garcia was fighting in the best form of his professional career, having lost only one of his last eight contests. Jack weighed in at 138 pounds; Garcia at 140 pounds.

Beau did not disappoint the boisterous fans. With thunderous applause from the crowd, Beau scored a sixth-round knockout over the Puerto Rican, flooring him 1:59 minutes into the round. It was Jack's fourth consecutive knockout. International News Service sports editor and acclaimed sportswriter Lawton Carver (1903–1973) described Beau's fanatic style. Jack "simply wore his foes down, then popped them over when they were softened up. He's like a swarm of gnats. While you brush him off here, you get stung in six other places."[2] Garcia only won seven of his next 62 bouts, finishing his career with a 25–71–8 record.

Beau next stepped into the ring on August 18, 1942, to face Carmine Fatta (1919–2008). It was billed as a battle between knockout artists. Beau had won his last four bouts by way of knockout, whereas Fatta had knocked out half of his 56 opponents and had a 45–9–3 record. The 23-year-old Italian American from Bensonhurst, Brooklyn had two more years of ring experience than Beau and was passionately referred to by his fans as "135 pounds of fighting fury." Both men were gunning for a title fight and planned to file a challenge to lightweight champ Sammy Angott with the NYSAC. Odds were almost even going into the eight-round main event.

Many of Fatta's "hometown" fans were among the 5,200 enthusiastic spectators gathered in anticipation of a Carmelo victory and Fatta's entry into a top-five ranking in the lightweight class. Needless to say, they were utterly disappointed. At the opening bell, both warriors stood toe to toe, slamming each other with punches. Right before the end of the first round, however, Beau connected a vicious left to Fatta's head, sending him to the canvas for the count. The KO was Beau's fifth in a row. Carmine Fatta went on to end his professional career with a record of 70–19–7 and was inducted into the New Jersey Boxing Hall of Fame in 1991.

Beau was quickly progressing towards the top of the lightweight ranks, winning all seven of his bouts so far in 1942. Moreover, he had knocked out his last five opponents. Nonetheless, before he would gain a shot at the title, Jack had four more grueling opponents to conquer. Meanwhile, Chick Wergeles, the little man of perpetual motion, was doing all he could to hype Beau up for a title bout.

For the first time in Madison Square Garden's history, four 10-round main events were scheduled for Friday night, August 28, 1942. Cleo Shans (37–20–17) and Maxie Shapiro (60–8–3) were re-matched in the top main event. They had fought a couple of weeks earlier in what was deemed the "fight of the year." Shans edged out a slim victory in that bout. In the second 10-round main event, Beau Jack was scheduled to meet Chester Rico for the second time, but Rico cancelled due to a back injury suffered in training. Billy Murray, a 21-year-old out of Bellaire, Ohio, was substituted for Rico. In the other 10-round events, Jake LaMotta faced Jimmy Edgar, and Carmine Fatta met Carmelo Fenoy.

A crowd of 10,021 was on hand for the exciting night of boxing at the Garden. A dazzling display of diamonds and emeralds surrounded the ring, many of which were worn by wives of Beau's Syndicate members and millionaire supporters hoping to see Beau score his sixth knockout in a row. Murray was an up-and-coming fighter and a terrific puncher, having won 59 of his 61 professional bouts and reeling off 19 straight victories.

Murray was ready for the contest, putting up a good fight, using his height and reach advantage to make Beau miss countless punches as he rushed in. Murray just couldn't connect enough to earn points. Beau easily outpointed Murray on the scorecard but was not exceptionally impressive. Even though Beau managed to cut Murray above his eye in the last 14 seconds of the fight, his knockout streak was halted. After one more fight, Murray was ready to call an end to his short 33-month boxing career, retiring with a record of 59–4–0. Meanwhile, Beau was tentatively promised a title fight with Sammy Angott, the current lightweight champion, but the matchup would have to wait.

Chick Hypes Jack

Chick Wergeles ardently plugged Beau Jack whenever he had a chance. He wanted to pave the shortest road possible to the title for Beau. Madison

Square Garden promoter Mike Jacobs' publicity man Harry Markson[3] commented: "Wergeles had the big columnists doing pieces about this boy before he even got a prelim bout. The ballyhoo that kid was getting I'd have bet a thousand to one that he could never live up to it."[4] Wergeles was doing his job promoting Beau.

A perfect example of Wergeles' tact was displayed in his August interview with Harold Parrott, sportswriter for the *Brooklyn Daily Eagle*. Chick scolded Parrott over not providing adequate coverage of his fistic Georgia bootblack.

> "You don't never write nothing," he [Chick] complained, "about my fighter. Wotta kid that is—."
>
> "I am a nursemaid to the kid," laughs Chick, "name's Beau Jack. You know him. He fought in the Garden last Friday and win, and now they are goin' to trun him in ther wit' Sammy Ingott [Angott]. 'Git me champeens,' the kid allus says to me. 'I kin fight better against the champeens.' He is a nice colored boy, 21, but he never knows who he's fightin'. By name, I mean. So I tell him, 'This guy you're fightin' tonight is almost a champeen.' That keeps him happy—."
>
> "The kid he don't care who it is out there. He goes through a coupla fast rounds shadow-boxin' in his dressin' room before the fight, an' then he says, 'Leave me at dat man' an' when we do, it is usually too bad. He belted that Billy Murray last week, an' they bin sayin' that guy ain't lose a fight since he was in knee pants—"[5]

Wergeles knew how to spin his fighter in the eyes of the public, ensuring Jack received the best coverage conceivable and that his image was clean, unlike many of the colorful boxers of the day.

Curiously, Parrott questioned Wergeles if Beau enjoyed the nightlife of Harlem. What does Beau do after his fights? Chick responded: "You cannot get him near that Harlem. He thinks it is too tough for him. Imagine—a kid like him who will tackle anything on two legs. But it is a good thing anyway and he spends his allowance in them shootin' galleries at Coney Island. Spent his whole $2 there last time."[6] Chick always gave Beau a dollar or two after he fought, so he could relax at the shooting gallery or take in a dime movie. Beau was a simple young lad that didn't care about the bright lights of Harlem. "It's too gay out there,"[7] said Beau. He preferred shooting galleries and movies.

In his subsequent column, "Both Sides," Parrott humorously mocked Wergeles' grammar and language. "Now ... here is a character who can't pilot a short sentence unharmed through the perils of grammar and syntax ... and he's guiding a fighter! ... All Mr. Wergeles needs is the right literary jockey and he will be laughing at them there college perfessers."[8] A master at his profession, Chick Wergeles drew attention to himself and his clients, even if it meant butchering the English language.

In a contest long in the making, Beau received a chance to alleviate his previous draw against Chester Rico. The two were scheduled to meet in an eight-round preliminary bout to the contest between Sugar Ray Robinson and Jake LaMotta at Madison Square Garden on October 2. Since their last fight, Rico had excelled, racking up sixteen victories, two draws, and only one loss. Meanwhile, Jack had won eighteen of his previous 20 bouts. A crowd of 12,784 eager spectators anxiously awaited the evening's combat.

At the opening bell, Beau rushed Chester, pounding him with sharp uppercuts and right crosses. The two battled a bruising eight rounds. Jack, however, put the fight in his corner in the fifth round when he landed a thunderous right uppercut to Rico's left eye, opening a deep gash on his forehead. Chester retaliated by trying to tire Beau with powerful body punches, but it didn't deter Beau's fortitude or stamina. With blood pouring from the laceration above his eye and nose, Rico's best punches were dismissed without difficulty. Beau coasted through eight rounds, easily outpointing Chester on the scorecards. In the main event, Ray Robinson (35–0) made his successful middleweight debut, defeating the "Bronx Bull" by a unanimous decision. The fight card grossed $29,434.

On Monday, October 12, 1942, ten days after defeating Rico, Beau met Angelo DeSanza, aka Terry Young (1921–1967), a welterweight from New York's East Side. Young was trained by legendary trainer Ray Arcel (1899–1994). Arcel had already worked with 16 world champions, including Benny Leonard (1917 lightweight), Frankie Genaro (1928 flyweight), Abe Goldstein (1924 welterweight), Charley Phil Rosenberg (1925 bantamweight), Jackie "Kid" Berg (1930 light welterweight), Lou Brouillard (1931 welterweight), Barney Ross (1933 lightweight & junior welterweight, 1934 welterweight), Bob Olin (1934 light heavyweight), Teddy Yarosz (1934 middleweight), James J. Braddock (1935 heavyweight), Sixto Escobar (1936 bantamweight), Tony Marino (1936 bantamweight), Freddie Steele (1936 middleweight), Ceferino Garcia (1939 middleweight), Billy Soose (1940 middleweight), and Tony Zale (1941 middleweight).[9]

Arcel would later run afoul of the mafia by competing with the International Boxing Club (IBC) for televised bouts. In 1953, Ray was targeted by the mob, which delivered a stiff warning to get out of boxing, when an assailant bashed Arcel's head in with a lead pipe. Fortunately, he survived the warning. Despite his trouble with the mafia, in the early seventies, Arcel returned to boxing to train Alfonso "Peppermint" Frazer (1972 light welterweight champion), Roberto Duran (1980 welterweight champion), and Larry Holmes (1978 heavyweight champion).

Arcel's current pupil, Terry Young, was a formidable adversary with a respectable 45–10–4 record. Possessing dynamite in both hands, Young had knocked out three of his last four opponents. In his previous bout, he knocked Tony Costa out in the second round. Young was blossoming as a boxer, producing two of the biggest fistic upsets of 1942, defeating NBA featherweight champion Jackie Wilson (89–21–7) and Cleo Shans (34–18–7). Augmenting his tough image, Young brutally fractured Wilson's left forearm through a series of ripping lefts and a powerful left uppercut in the third round of their battle.

The venue for the featured 10-round bout was St. Nicholas Arena. Jack had not fared well in his previous visits to St. Nicholas Arena, losing both matches to Freddie Archer. Young, on the other hand, had performed well. Beginning with his professional debut on October 9, 1939, Young fought his first four professional matches at St. Nicholas Arena. Since then, he had appeared in eleven more bouts at the Arena, winning all but two. A crowd of 4,500 gathered in the arena, principally to see their hometown favorite, Terry Young.

Young was no patsy, but Beau was a slight favorite going into the fight. As expected, the two warriors produced an exciting battle, entertaining the enthusiastic crowd. From the opening bell throughout most of the contest, Jack and Young fought toe to toe. Trading punches, they both rocked each other with brutal blows. In the later rounds, Young attempted to wear Beau down, persistently pounding his midsection, but Beau just kept advancing, striking Young with a plethora of punches. Although Young managed to bruise Beau's eye and Beau suffered a point deduction for a low blow in the eighth round, Terry couldn't overcome Beau's tenacity. After 10 fierce rounds of action, Beau was awarded a unanimous decision.

PART IV

Claiming the Lightweight Title

They loved me, because they found out I would fight every second of every round and never give up.

—Beau Jack

11

Stolz Stands Between
Beau and a Title Bout

Beau Jack was rapidly approaching his first title fight, but the rugged, heavily favored Allie Stolz (1918–2000) stood in his way. Stolz was ranked as the number one lightweight contender by both the New York State Athletic Commission (NYSAC) and the National Boxing Association (NBA). The winner would be in line for a title match against the champ, Sammy Angott. Seeking a title bout for Beau, Chick Wergeles pulled some strings to bring Stolz's camp on board for the contest. Chick had to guarantee Stolz $10,000, and a $2,000 forfeit should Beau not come in under 135 pounds. In essence, Beau would be fighting for free. Although he would get 50 percent of the gate, he had to pay Stolz and his camp out of that amount. If the amount fell short of $10,000, Beau's camp would have to come out of pocket to pay the difference.

Stolz's manager, Willie Ketchum, was unyielding on the terms. Ketchum sternly expressed to Chick, "Not an ounce over 135, Wergeles, or the dough is mine. The Boxing Commission allows a pound leeway, but not me. And no sweatin' in phone booths or running around the block. If your man don't weigh under 135, I collect."[1] Unfaltering, Wergeles agreed to Ketchum's demands, optimistically hoping to assure Jack a title fight with the lightweight champion Sammy Angott. On October 16, with the concessions agreed to by Beau's team, promoter Mike Jacobs announced that Jack and Stolz had agreed to terms and signed to meet each other on November 13, 1942, at Madison Square Garden with the winner assured a title fight with Sammy Angott.

Mike Jacobs

New Yorker Mike Jacobs (1880–1953), often referred to as "Uncle Mike," was the predominant boxing promoter of the 1930s and 40s. At a young age, he started scalping tickets for Coney Island boat excursions. Along with three newspaper reporters, Jacobs organized the Twentieth Century Sporting Club ("Twentieth Century SC") to promote boxing matches in the New York area. In 1935, Jacobs also signed Joe Louis to an exclusive contract which would prove to be a financial gold mine. On September 24, 1935, in Joe's first fight at Yankee Stadium, two hours after he was married, Louis defeated former heavyweight champion Max Baer in front of 84,831 paid spectators, grossing $932,944. Even when Joe lost to Max Schmeling at Yankee Stadium on June 19, 1936, the 39,878 fans produced a gate of $547,531. Jacobs was well on his way.

In 1937, the Twentieth Century SC secured a lease for Madison Square Garden. To ensure a title match for Joe Louis, Jacobs matched him with heavyweight champion James Braddock in a title fight on June 22, 1937. Allegedly, Braddock was contractually promised a percentage of Joe Louis' earnings for the next 10 years if he lost the fight. Louis emerged victorious and crowned the new heavyweight champion.

In 1938, Mike Jacobs became the sole owner of the Twentieth Century SC and entered into a partnership with Madison Square Garden. In an incredible money-making contest between Joe Louis and Billy Conn at Yankee Stadium on June 19, 1946, Jacobs raked in a gate of nearly $2 million. Over the years Jacobs promoted boxing matches, it is estimated that he made over $25 million in gates.

Jacob's fame was so prominent that the block on West 49th Street between Broadway and Eighth Avenue in New York became known as "Jacobs Beach." It was there that Jacobs' ticket office was located and the biggest boxing deals negotiated. The boundaries were somewhat fluid depending on where Mike Jacobs was on any given day. Generally, Madison Square Garden anchored one corner

Mike Jacobs with Joe Louis, c. 1941 (author's collection).

of Jacobs Beach with the other corners being defined by other pugilist hangouts, such as Stillman's Gym, Lindy's restaurant, Jack Dempsey's restaurant, and the Forrest Hotel. Jacobs Beach is where the managers, trainers, and boxers hung out, as well as sportswriters and bookies. Jacobs ruled boxing during the forties, promoting three matches grossing over $1 million each. Acknowledged for his contributions, Mike Jacobs was inducted into the World Boxing Hall of Fame in 1982 and the International Boxing Hall of Fame in 1990.

Grantland Rice, c. 1920 (Library of Congress).

Grantland Rice

In addition to the publicity guru, Chick Wergeles, Beau had an admirer and friend in renowned sportswriter Grantland Rice (1880–1954). They had met several years earlier when Beau began working at the Augusta National Golf Club. Grantland was one of the Club's original members and a close friend of Bobby Jones. Rice admired Beau's work ethic and referred to the "Augusta Ambuscade," as Rice frequently called Beau, as a "quiet, simple, modest kid willing to work and work hard."[2]

Grantland Rice's columns and writings were legendary. After graduating from Vanderbilt University in 1901, Rice worked as a sportswriter for several Southern newspapers including the *Atlanta Journal* and the *Nashville Daily News*. As his career progressed, he worked for the *New York Evening Mail*, the *New York Tribune*, and the *Herald Tribune*. His sports columns, especially "The Sportlight," became immensely popular. One on the most famous sportswriters in America during the thirties and forties, Rice's columns became nationally syndicated in 1930. Referred to as the "Dean of American Sportswriters," Rice mastered the "Gee-Whizzers," a breed of sportswriters that wrote in "the most florid and exciting prose." He was relentless in his use of metaphors to depict athletes and sporting events.

Some of Rice's well-known works will live forever. Following the Notre Dame–Army football game on October 18, 1924, Rice referred to Notre Dame's offensive backfield as the "Four Horsemen."

> Outlined against a blue, gray October sky, the Four Horsemen rode again. In dramatic lore, they were known as Famine, Pestilence, Destruction, and Death. These are only aliases. Their real names are Stuhldreher, Miller, Crowley, and Layden. They formed the crest of the South Bend cyclone before which another fighting Army team was swept over the precipice of the Polo Grounds this afternoon.[3]

Today, the "Four Horsemen" term remains a storied tradition at Notre Dame University.

The week before Jack was scheduled to enter the ring against Allie Stolz, Grantland Rice set forth the tenacious allure of Beau Jack in his column "The Sportlight." "He is a fast-moving, rough-and-ready kid who can take and give his full share of punishment," wrote Rice. "He also is one of the few who actually likes to fight."[4] Rice knew Beau was a fighter and possessed the fortitude to make it to the top. "If Beau defeats Allie Stolz," Rice declared, "he should earn a shot at the lightweight title."[5] Moreover, Georgia was used to champions and was home to two of the greatest, Ty Cobb and Bobby Jones, penned Rice. "If Beau Jack can slug his way by Stolz and Sammy Angott before the army calls him in … it will add another chapter to Georgia sporting history."[6] Rice was confident that if Beau could make it past Stolz, Georgia might possibly end up with another great champion.

Allie Stolz (1918–2000), a 24-year-old blond, curly haired New Jersey boxer, was the fighting pride of his hometown Hoboken, New Jersey, with a record of 49–5–2. After winning New Jersey's 112-pound championship as an amateur, he debuted his professional career on November 12, 1937, reeling off twenty victories and two draws before his first loss. Stolz was proud of his Jewish heritage and turned his head to anti–Semitism. In his last twelve fights, he had only lost one split decision, and that was against the lightweight champion "Slammin" Sammy Angott in their May 5 title bout. According to the scorecards, Stolz would have won the title, but for penalties, received for low blows in two rounds. The decision was highly controversial as most people witnessing the fight, as well as boxing commentators, thought Stolz should have been awarded the decision and crowned the new lightweight king. Regardless, Allie Stolz took Sammy Angott to task, flooring the champ for a nine-count in the third round.

After Stolz and Angott's first match, Mike Jacobs quickly arranged for a rematch, but Stolz backed out due to an injury to his right hand suffered in his July 7 victory over Bob Montgomery. The two top contenders to take Angott's crown were Allie Stolz and Tippy Larkin. With a win over Stolz, Beau Jack would emerge as the top contender.

Making for a title mess, on the day of the Jack–Stolz bout, Abe Greene, president of the National Boxing Association, announced that he had received a wire from Sammy Angott's manager Charley Jones declaring that Angott had retired from boxing. "Sammy Angott has decided to retire from the ring and plans to take a job in a defense plant and therefore announces his retirement. Thanks for everything the NBA has done for him in the past." Angott further explained, "I got all I could from the game and now I feel like doing something for my country." He planned to start work in a steel mill in his hometown.[7]

Sammy underscored that his injured hand figured in his decision to retire. In his first fight with Montgomery, Angott suffered a partial bone dislocation in his right hand when he landed a hard uppercut on Montgomery in the eighth round of the bout. "It's never been right after I hurt it fighting Bob Montgomery nearly two years ago," he said. "And I hurt it again fighting Montgomery in Philadelphia a few months ago."[8] With Angott's retirement, the lightweight title was now vacant. Interestingly, others speculated that he had been forced to retire because he wouldn't "do business" with gangsters in the ring.

As fight night approached, weight became a concern for Beau's camp. Stolz's manager Ketchum was unwavering that Beau not weigh "an ounce over 135 pounds." The day before the match, however, Beau weighed 137 pounds, two pounds overweight. Chick Wergeles had a lot of work to do to ensure that Jack came in at the proper weight. He put Beau through an arduous routine, which included "drying out, no food, extra road work, shadow boxing, and hard and heavy rubbing." Surprisingly, Beau not only reduced his weight to the contracted fight weight, but he came in lighter than expected at 132¾ pounds. With this news, the odds grew in Stolz's favor, 18 to 5, on the belief that Beau had weakened himself by making weight for the fight. The oddsmakers appeared to be right. Beau barely had enough energy to walk to the scales for the weigh-in.

Based on his punching power and unorthodox style, the skeptics rallied for Beau. "He weaves, bobs and jumps and is liable to throw a punch from any angle."[9] Some of the gym followers also opined that Beau was by far the heavier puncher as well. Beau was respectfully confident before the fight. "All I know is this," said Jack. "He can't hurt me and I can hurt him a lot."[10]

A boisterous crowd of 14,249, producing a gate of $34,786, waited with zealous anticipation and excitement for the clash to begin, as did people all across the country, who were gathered around the radio to listen to the match broadcast on the Mutual Broadcasting System. As the opening bell sounded, the two men stormed out from their corners. Wildly rushing at Stolz, Jack almost wrestled him down and nearly lunged through the ropes himself. As the oddsmakers predicted, Stolz gave Beau a boxing lesson in the first round with some shrewd boxing, walloping Beau's body and head with vicious left hooks and keeping Beau at a distance. Beau again dashed out at the sound of the bell in the second round, but Stolz had a left waiting for him which he dug into Beau's body. As if Stolz's punch hadn't fazed him, Beau bounced back, landing a stunning wild right bolo punch to Stolz's head. Jack pugnaciously swarmed and charged the dazed Stolz, evening the bout at one round apiece. Although Stolz fought back and won the third round, that shatteringly painful punch Beau landed to Stolz's head in the second weakened him and took the wind out of his sail.

In the fourth, Jack opened a bloody cut on Stolz's left eyebrow and eyelid with a sharp overhand right. The cut would prove to be Stolz's downfall. Jack continued to reopen and lengthen the wound until it became virtually impossible for Stolz to see. In distress, Stolz tried to counter Jack's attack with left hooks and right crosses to no avail. His fate was sealed "because he had nothing with which to stem the tide of piston-like punches from the tireless Negro lad from Georgia."[11] At the end of the seventh round, Beau caught Stolz on the left eyebrow once again with a stiff right, further damaging Allie's wound. With blood streaming from the cut, the NYSAC's physician, Dr. William H. Walker, immediately went to Stolz's corner to examine his eye. After a swift evaluation, Dr. Walker stopped the fight. Stolz's manager, Willie Ketchum, was furious, adamantly contesting that he could close the cut on Stolz's left brow, but Walker refused to listen. With Dr. Walker's stoppage, Beau was conferred a TKO victory.

In what was one of the largest gambling fights of the year for the New York metropolitan area, the Associated Press scorecard had the fight even before Beau gashed open Stolz's eyebrow in the seventh round. With his thrilling TKO victory, Beau enlarged his fan base, captivating the 14,249 fans with "his hell-for-leather primitive pummeling"[12] of Stolz. The win over Stolz was enormous. Beau was now the number one lightweight contender.

Following the fight, Jack shared his post-weigh-in strategy. After making weight, he "put away something like a gallon of soup, chops, a steak and a few potatoes."[13] The oddsmakers simply overlooked "the native, raw ability of a fighter having a fighting heart."[14] United Press correspondent Jack Cuddy depicted Beau's tenacious fighting ability: "Beau Jack, his body hardened by toil since his orphan days, treated the fans to a night of savage and primitive lambasting," wrote Cuddy. "He threw punches from all angles.... He missed a lot of them, but he kept coming in—swinging—as Stolz melted before him."[15] James P. Dawson of the *New York Times* described Jack's as "[a] rushing, tearing type of fighter, making up in punching quantity what he lacks in quality."[16] Like many opponents before, Beau simply overwhelmed Stolz with his never-ending flow of punches.

As usual, following his incredible victory over Stolz, Beau was invited to spend time with his Syndicate supporters, sip lemonade, and converse with some of his millionaire patrons. After dropping in to visit with the Syndicate, Beau engaged in his customary post-fight routine with the $5 (increased from $1) he received from his fight purse. He went to a Broadway shooting gallery. On this occasion, following his defeat of Stolz, Beau was also able to buy a watch because a supporter who had gambled correctly on him awarded Beau $40 to buy a watch.

Within the next couple of days, Bowman and Beau headed back home to Augusta for some rest. While in Augusta, Beau jubilantly worked at the Augusta National. When he made tip money working at the club, he got to keep it all. At night, he enjoyed hanging with his friends and fans at his favorite nightclub, the Palmetto Pond. Playing tunes on the jukebox, Beau proudly showed his friends the latest newspaper clippings chronicling his defeat of Allie Stolz and the latest fashion in zoot suits.

12

Beau Crowned Lightweight Champion

Who would Beau fight next? Lightweight champion Sammy Angott had agreed to give the winner of the contest between Jack and Stolz a title match, but he retired the day of the contest between the two challengers. His departure threw a monkey wrench into the title picture. Time was running out. Beau was bound to be drafted into the military soon.

Chick Wergeles vehemently argued that Beau should be crowned as the lightweight champ. The champion had retired, and Beau had defeated the number one contender, Allie Stolz. The NYSAC and NBA, however, disagreed. Along with promoter Mike Jacobs, they wanted to have an elimination tournament to determine the championship. Abe Greene, Chairman of the NBA, explained that Stolz was number one on its list before his loss to Beau. Afterward, Greene stated, "This looks like a Chinese omelet now. We'll have to drop Stolz a peg and move Tippy Larkin of New Jersey and Beau Jack up to share the No. 1 spot on our ratings. The only way the title question can be settled, I guess, is by having an elimination."[1]

Mike Jacobs suggested a fight between Beau and the new top contender, Tippy Larkin, to take place on December 18, 1942. Wergeles, however, was not ready to accept the fight. "Beau needs a rest," he explained. "He's licked everyone around. Let Larkin go out and lick the same guys."[2] Regardless, on November 25, it was announced that Beau would meet Tippy Larkin on December 18 at Madison Square Garden in the main bout of the lightweight elimination tournament. As for the elimination tournament, nine boxers—Allie Stolz, Juan Zurita, Cleo Shans, Willie Joyce, Chester Rico, Luther "Slugger" White, Maxie Shapiro, Bob Montgomery, and Joey Peralta—would vie to take on the winner of the Beau Jack versus Tippy Larkin contest.

Unexpectedly, however, in a bold announcement on December 3, the NYSAC proclaimed that the winner of the upcoming match between Jack and Larkin would be crowned as the 135-pound world lightweight champion.

The NBA was furious, accusing the NYSAC of "double-crossing" the NBA. Their accusation was merely ignored.

Golden Years and Radio

Beau Jack fought during the golden age of boxing. Between 1920 and 1946, boxing evolved into an entertaining and profitable sport, producing some of the best boxers and largest gates. Championship boxers were idolized and viewed as the strongest men in the world.

It was also the radio age. Almost every household in America had a radio. A leader in sponsoring radio broadcasts of sporting events was the Gillette Razor Company. Beginning around 1939, it underwrote sporting events under the banner of Gillette's Cavalcade of Sports. Gillette quickly developed promotional deals with Major League Baseball for the World Series and All-Star Game, the Kentucky Derby, and several college football bowl games.

One of Gillette's most popular shows, however, was its Friday Night Fights broadcast from Madison Square Garden. Fathers and sons assembled around the radio to listen to blow by blow commentary from ringside broadcasters Don Dunphy and Bill Corum. The two broadcasters were a dynamic pair, portraying the combat so well that the listener actually imagined they were seeing the fight live at the Garden.

Born in New York, Don Dunphy (1908–1998) was a radio announcer renowned for his objective, no-nonsense delivery and nasal-sounding voice. He began covering boxing in 1939 after auditioning for the Gus Lesnevich-Anton Chrisoforidis bout. Whereas other candidates had trouble pronouncing the fighters' last names, Don merely called the fighters Gus and Anton. So successful was Dunphy, that Gillette retained him to broadcast boxing matches for the next nineteen years. During his broadcasting career lasting from 1939 to 1981, Dunphy called the action for over 2,000 fights, including at least 50 championship fights. His vivid description of the fighters' body movements, footwork, and punches provided the eyes for the thousands of people listening to the radio.

Sports columnist and radio sportscaster Bill Corum (1895–1958) joined Don Dunphy on June 18, 1941, for the Joe Louis-Billy Conn fight. For the next twelve years, he worked alongside Dunphy, providing color commentary between rounds. Although a central figure in sports broadcasting, Corum was best known as one of the most recognizable and respected sportswriters of the times, working as a sports columnist for the *New York Journal-American*. Also a horse enthusiast, Corum served as president of the Churchill Downs racetrack for numerous years and was instrumental in the development of the Kentucky Derby.

Dunphy and Corum quickly became known for their ability to portray a fight as it was happening. They didn't sugarcoat their words. If the fight was not measuring up to expectations, they said so. If one fighter won a round, they explained not only why, but what it meant for the remaining rounds.

Beau Fights for the Lightweight Title

Astonishingly, two years and seven months after his first fight at Valley Arena, Beau Jack had ascended the lightweight ranks all the way to a title fight. He had fought at a blistering pace. In 1941 alone, he averaged almost two bouts a month. Now 21 years old and sporting a 41–6–1 record, Beau was appearing in the lightweight championship on December 18, 1942. It was his destiny.

Tippy Larkin (1917–1991), born Anthony Pilleteri, was of Italian heritage but fought under the Irish banner. The handsome, curly-haired, sharp-shooting 25-year-old "Garfield Gunner" of Garfield, New Jersey, had a devastating right hand. Ranking at the top of the lightweight division, Larkin had a stellar record of 86 victories against 7 losses. Moreover, he had won twenty-three straight bouts and hadn't lost a contest since March 8, 1940, a couple of months before Beau even debuted in Holyoke. There was one small question mark. Tippy had accidentally shot himself in the shoulder while cleaning his .22-caliber rifle five months earlier. However, skeptics were silenced when he continued his winning streak and emerged victorious in his next four fights.

On paper, Larkin had the advantage. He was four inches taller than Beau at 5'10" and had a three-inch edge in arm reach. Larkin had beaten Beau's nemesis, Freddie Archer, twice; whereas Beau had two back to back losses to Archer. In Larkin's first bout against Freddie Archer on June 16, 1941, Tippy literally destroyed him, scoring a devastating knockout one minute and twenty-two seconds in the first round. Archer was out for more than 15 minutes while the fight physician worked on him. In his last match, Larkin had faced Archer again. Though not a knockout victory, Tippy scored an impressive decision. On the other hand, Jack had won his last 12 fights and was an 8–5 favorite due to his youth and perpetual motion style, as well as his impressive victory over Allie Stoltz.

Larkin exuded confidence going into the title bout. Tippy was seeking to uphold the promise he made to 150 of his loyal supporters two years ago when he told them he would win the world lightweight championship. Larkin wasn't the only one that was confident. Beau declared, "I just know I'm gonna be the champion. I just know because I feel it inside."[3]

It was a rough evening for boxing fans voyaging to Madison Square

Garden for the title bout. World War II was adversely affecting the states, creating hardships for everyday life. Earlier in the day, the government halted the sale of gasoline to all private motorist in 17 states along the Atlantic coast. It was essential that all available fuel go to military efforts in North Africa. President Roosevelt explained that the U.S. Air Force and armored units were in dire need of gasoline and it was quicker to ship motor fuel directly from the East coast than from Texas. Furthermore, meat consumption was rationed to 35 ounces a week, and a new blackout plan resulted in 7,500,000 New York City residents' lights being turned off for 15 minutes. On top of the war-related issues, Mother Nature brought in a severe winter blizzard with temperatures hovering in the twenties.

Despite the gasoline ban and the horrible travel conditions, a crowd of 18,817 spectators packed Madison Square Garden to cheer on their favorite boxer. Tippy Larkin weighed 134¼ pounds to Beau's 132¾ pounds. As usual before the opening bell, Beau, a profoundly religious man, said a quick prayer in his corner, praying that it would be a good fight and nobody would get hurt. Humbly, Beau never prayed for triumph, as he left that in the hands of his Lord. When questioned why he didn't pray for victory, Beau said, "Oh no. suppose the other guy prayed that, too. Then what's the Lord going to do?"[4]

As the opening bell rang, Beau bounced off his stool "as if somebody had applied a blowtorch to the seat of his pants" and immediately swarmed Larkin.[5] Sitting ringside sportswriter Dick McCann described the wild first seconds of the action.

> [Beau Jack] flailed away at Larkin's head, body, arms, shoulders—scattering punches like a tipsy spendthrift tosses dollars around. He didn't care where they landed. Some of them hit the air, some of them merely hit Larkin's defensive elbows—but some of them found their marks and raised welts on Larkin's ribs and reddened the Jersey jolter's cheeks.[6]

After Beau's onslaught, Tippy tried to trade punches with him. That is when Beau dropped Larkin with a left hook to the body and a stiff right under the heart. Just 30 seconds into the skirmish, Larkin tasted the canvas, bringing the frenzied crowd to its feet. When Tippy jumped back up, Beau shook him again with a hard right hook to the head. Late in the round, Larkin finally began to settle down and landed several short right hands as Beau barreled in on him.

Larkin had a better showing in the second round, winning the stanza with shrewd boxing and connecting with at least fifty clobbering punches to Beau's head. Undeterred, Beau just kept marching forward, throwing flurries of punches. Although Larkin had established his dominant punching power by knocking out 41 previous opponents, he was not in the ring with just any fighter. "Larkin's hardest blows" wrote Jack Cuddy, "bounced off [Beau] like rain drops."[7]

As in the first round, Beau assertively bounded off his stool and charged Larkin when the bell sounded starting the third round. This time, however, Larkin was waiting for him. As Beau rushed in, Larkin snapped him back with a hard right to the schnozzle. No matter what tactic Larkin employed, Beau fought with reckless abandonment. Bouncing like a kangaroo, Jack just kept coming forward. Jack strategically moved in close on Larkin and waited for him to lean forward to block his flying punches. Once Larkin took the bait, Beau fainted a left hook and threw a sensational right uppercut that landed perfectly on Larkin's chin "with a jaw-breaking crack."[8]

The violent uppercut knocked Larkin out cold one minute and nineteen seconds into the third round. "It dropped Larkin as if he had been shot," penned sportswriter Bob Considine. "He fell flat on the back of his head and was still stone-cold when Referee Arthur Susskind, aka Young Otto, counted ten over him."[9] Tippy's body stood motionless for a moment before it came crashing down. Larkin was badly hurt. Joining Larkin's trainers, Beau helped carry the prostrate Larkin to his corner. Then Announcer Harry Balogh raised Beau's hand and introduced him "as the winner and new lightweight champion."

Standing proudly at the microphone, Beau praised Augusta and the people who assisted him in becoming the world champion. The first words he spoke were, "Hello Mayor Woodall, hello Mr. McAuliffe."[10] Whenever he could, Beau always gave a shout out to his supporters and friends in Augusta. He also sent best wishes to his wife and three children. Summing up his victory, Beau exclaimed, "I'll be a fighting champion, because I love to fight, and don't know anything else."[11]

In his post-fight interview with Harold Parrott of the *Brooklyn Daily Eagle,* Beau grinned as he confessed, "Ah never dreamed it would come so easy."[12] Beau gave credit for his victory to his trainer Sid Bell. "Sidney Bell, my trainer, had studied Larkin's style, and he had me shortening up those uppercuts all through my training," Beau revealed. "It was my best punch all right."[13]

It was as if Beau could have beaten any lightweight that night. He displayed quickness, power and "slightly aboriginal, aggressiveness." Jack Cuddy labeled Beau's perpetual motion style as a "blitz attack."[14] Sportswriter Lawton Carver of the International News Service remarked on the simplicity of Jack's fan-pleasing style. Carver explained that Jack was the "most inept and unlearned fighter ever to have a crown thrust upon his benumbed head."[15] He then equated Beau to his battle royal days. "The only preparation Beau had for the ring," explained Carver "was the removal of the blindfold." He described his fight style as "swing, advance, swing, lurch, swing, turn and swing some more." What got Beau to the top was that he was a "humming dynamo of energy, sending power flowing through this kid's legs and arms which sent him to the top…."[16]

Fewer than three years after inaugurating his professional career, 21-year-old Beau Jack was crowned the lightweight champion of the world. "Through sheer application of bull-like strength and a tigerish will to destroy," Carver wrote, "he became ... champion and public idol of the lightweight class, which, with the heavyweight division, ranks as the toughest of the seven weight divisions now recognized."[17] Undoubtedly, Beau Jack's accomplishment is one of the most sensational in the history of boxing.

The fight attracted a gate of $58,468, from which Beau received approximately $17,000. Of course, Beau himself was rewarded with $5. The Syndicate "post-fight soiree was extremely joyous that night as Beau was christened 'The Stork Club Champion' in honor of the home bistro of most of the Syndicate members."[18]

Jack's hometown supporters were ecstatic. Admirably, the story in the local paper concentrated more on Beau's modesty than his accomplishments.

> It is important to Augustans that they can boast of having a world's champion boxer from their community, but it is a greater source of pride to them that this champion turns out to be a modest person who has not let his fistic fame go to his head.
>
> It is not as important that this young Negro today is a world's champion fighter as it is that he remains a modest man, who accepts his honors becomingly, and does not forget his first supporters and well-wishers in an atmosphere where champions' heads are easily turned and modestly still more easily forgotten.[19]

Augustans were proud. Beau was not only a champion but an unpretentious champ. Beau would now be hailed as one of the greatest lightweights in ring history, joining the ranks of Benny Leonard, Sammy Angott, and Henry Armstrong. What a way to finish the year. Not only had Jack won the lightweight title, but he also won all 13 of his fights in 1942.

Over the next several weeks, commentators humorously described Jack's unique, unorthodox style of boxing. Beau was styled as an aggressive volume puncher who didn't mind throwing 100 punches, just to land 20. Sportswriter Whitney Martin went so far as to say Beau really didn't have a style at all, comparing his style to that of a burlap bag.

> His legs below the knee are about as big as a cornstalk, but they seem to prop up a husky torso without trouble. His handlers wind him up in his corner between rounds and point him in the right direction as he sits with a worried expression on his face.
>
> At the bell he jumps up, takes a deep breath, drops his hands to his sides and starts toward his opponent with long, bent-kneed strides. Then he goes to work and is just so darned persevering he discourages his rival. It's just wham, wham, wham, and when you've seen one of his rounds you've seen them all.[20]

Endurance and endless punching were Beau's trademarks. In addition to his swarming offense, Beau had an excellent chin. Jack Cuddy explained, "Beau Jack is so tough—has such a thick skin and bull-like reactions to a blow on the 'button'—that his attack cannot be halted."[21] He had animal-like grace and nifty ring craft.

Tippy Larkin went on to win the world light-welterweight title on April 29, 1946, and finished his career with a record of 138–13, selling out Madison Square Garden in each of his 17 main event appearances. He was subsequently inducted into the World Boxing Hall of Fame and the New Jersey Boxing Hall of Fame.

Referee Arthur Susskind

Arthur Susskind (1886–1967), or "Young Otto" as he was often called, refereed Beau's championship bout against Tippy Larkin and numerous other contests in which Beau competed. Before becoming a referee, Susskind boxed in the lightweight division under the name "Young Otto" between 1903 and 1923. Standing 5'6" tall, Otto established an incredible record for first round knock-

Arthur Susskind, a.k.a. "Young Otto," c. 1904 (author's collection).

outs. Of the 60 knockouts he produced in his career, 44 came in the first round. Moreover, he reportedly knocked out 16 consecutive opponent within the first minute of the first round. During his 20 years of boxing he compiled a record of 71–13–3.

13

Beau's First Reign

Having climbed to the top of the lightweight division, Beau now had to defend his title. Since beginning his boxing career at Valley Arena, Beau had averaged over nineteen fights a year. In 1943, with the title in hand, he scaled back his incredible fight volume to eight bouts.

Notwithstanding Beau's demolition of the top lightweight, the NBA was still reluctant to acknowledge Beau's title. To clear up the dispute between the NBA and the NYSAC, the NBA proposed another tournament to crown an undisputed champion. Although the NYSAC and the New Jersey Athletic Commission had already crowned Beau the lightweight champion (collectively referred to as the "New York championship"), to appease the NBA, the NYSAC sanctioned a tournament to establish Beau's next contender with the victor being crowned the undisputed lightweight king.

Little did anyone know, but the following week would be yet another tumultuous week for the lightweight division. On January 8, 1943, Sammy Angott declared that his hands had healed, and he was coming out of retirement. So much for his job in the defense industry. The announcement threw the NBA's elimination tournament into chaos. In response, the NBA chunked the tournament idea and set forth a new proposal to clear up the muddled lightweight championship—a title bout between Sammy Angott and Beau Jack. With dollar signs in his head, promoter Mike Jacobs jumped on the opportunity to sign the battle for the undisputed 135-pound champion.

Angott was also eager to take the fight, volunteering to fight the Georgia shoeshine boy "anytime and anywhere." The only catch was how the purse would be divided. Chick Wergeles was adamant that his man should get the champion's percentage. The money had to be right. The two warring camps, however, could not come to terms. The title match between Jack and Angott would have to wait.

With the Angott bout on hold, Mike Jacobs arranged Henry Armstrong to be Beau's next foe. The matchup between teacher and pupil was bound to be a big-ticket seller. Armstrong had won three different titles and was boxing well, and Beau had just won the lightweight title in spectacular fashion.

The highly anticipated bout was scheduled for January 29, 1943, at the Garden. Unfortunately, Armstrong began having trouble with his tonsils. In the first week of January, Henry's manager, Eddie Mead, announced that all of Armstrong's upcoming bouts were being postponed so he could undergo a tonsillectomy.

Beau Jack Battles Fritzie Zivic

Mike Jacobs quickly found a new opponent for Jack, former welterweight champion Fritzie Zivic. Jacobs scheduled the two men for a 10-round non-title bout at Madison Square Garden on February 5. Fritzie Zivic (1913–1984), a 29-year-old Pittsburg resident, was a seasoned fighter with a record of 126–33–6. The pug-nosed boxer was relished among boxing enthusiasts. Zivic's style in closing rounds, by throwing blistering flurries during the last 20 to 30 seconds, was always electrifying to witness.

Born to an immigrant family, Zivic's father was Croatian and his mother Slovinian. A ring veteran, Fritzie learned to box at an early age to avoid becoming a punching bag for his older brothers, as three of his older brothers had already blazed a trail in boxing. His brothers Pete (1901–1987) and Jack (1903–1973) fought on the 1920 U.S. Olympic team competing in Antwerp, Belgium. After the Olympics, both brothers turned professional. Pete fought in the featherweight division earning a 40–35–11 record over ten years. Jack competed in the welterweight division between 1921 and 1930, ending his career with a record of 40–28–4. Fritzie's older brother Eddie (1910–1996), on the other hand, fought nine years in the lightweight division, retiring with a record of 39–40–6.

Tragically, Fritzie's own career almost ended at Conneaut Lake in 1937. While training for a bout with Vince Dundee, he developed potentially deadly pneumonia. Fritzie was hospitalized and underwent numerous blood transfusions. He eventually improved several weeks later but was told his fighting days were over. They were far from over.

On October 4, 1940, in his 116th professional bout, Zivic defeated Henry Armstrong to claim the welterweight title, a title he held until July 21, 1941. Recently, he had beaten five world champion boxers: Sammy Angott, Henry Armstrong, Lew Jenkins, Maxie Berger, and Freddie Cochrane. It was certain to be a tough match for Beau, who was stepping up into the welterweight division (140 lbs.–147 lbs.) to meet his adversary.

Chick did his job well in publicizing his fighter's prowess and the aftermath experienced by his foes. "Look at Tippy Larkin," said Wergeles. "He hasn't even had a fight since Beau knocked him out. How about Chester Rico? He's no longer in the lightweight picture. After Beau knocked out Cosby Linson, he hasn't been heard from again. Terry Young? He hasn't even won a fight since Beau took him to task."[1]

Promoter Mike Jacobs was exuberant as the year's record crowd of 21,240 crammed the Garden to capacity, producing a gate of $70,291. It was the third largest crowd in Garden history and the warmest day of the year so far, as temperatures reached 50 degrees. In addition to the huge assembly on hand, the 10 p.m. fight was broadcast on radio from coast to coast and in Beau's hometown of Augusta, Georgia on WGAC. It was Jack's first match as the lightweight champion.

At twenty-one years of age, Beau had the advantage of youth, but Zivic had an eight-pound weight advantage, weighing 145¼ pounds to Beau's 137¼ pounds and towered over Beau by four and a half inches. Moreover, Fritzie had a tremendous edge in experience against top-notch opponents. Nevertheless, the oddsmakers favored youth, with the odds set at 11–5 in favor of Beau.

The odds didn't faze Zivic. Zivic beamed with confidence and determination as he entered the ring. He boasted to his acquaintances, "I'll win," Zivic arrogantly bragged. "I'll lick Beau Jack like he was nothing,"[2] Beau, on the other hand, was eager to extend his 13-fight win streak, the streak that took him from virtual anonymity to the top of the lightweight division.

As the fight got underway, Jack rushed Zivic but lost his footing and slipped to the canvas. He immediately hopped back up and went right back on the pursuit. Trying to chop his foe into pieces, the younger "bull-shouldered" Beau threw wild punches from long range and bombarded Zivic with inside uppercuts at close quarters. Jack took the first round, violently landing uppercuts to Zivic's head each time Zivic tied him up in clinches.

Zivic picked up the pace in the second round but still didn't look like he had landed enough punches to win the round, until seconds before the bell rang when Fritzie, in his customary style, opened up on Beau with furious rights and lefts to the head. Beau didn't take it sitting down, instead answering back with a wrath of his own. Thrilled, the crowd was on its feet and yelling with deafening applause. The noise was so thunderous that no one heard the closing bell. Oblivious to the bell, the two warriors continued to fight at a blistering pace, trading hammering punches as they stood toe to toe for almost 30 seconds after the round ended. Finally, Referee Young Otto realized the stanza was over and separated the two men.

Jack seized the third round and started the fourth fiercely rocking Fritzie again and again with inside uppercuts. Zivic, however, countered with right uppercuts to the chin, damaging body punches, and at least three flagrant low blows that Referee Young Otto failed to see. For his part, Beau also got away with a couple of hard shots to Fritzie's left kidney. All said, Zivic did enough to win the round. Fritzie also took the fifth round, but then his tank ran out

Beau Jack (right) and Fritzie Zivic tangle it up, 1943 (courtesy ACME and Bruce Kielty).

of gas in the sixth. Resting during the first part of the seventh to regain some needed energy, Zivic came alive in the last minute. Once again, the two boxers stood toe to toe banging away at each other. Before the round was over, Fritzie slammed a vicious right to Beau's jaw, knocking his mouthpiece out.

The eighth round was intensely fierce. Zivic belligerently pushed Beau into the ropes and readied himself to throw a stinging left uppercut. Reacting quickly, Beau recoiled off the ropes as Zivic started his punch. Instead of landing an uppercut, Fritzie's glove caught Beau below the belt for a heavily disputed low blow. Sitting ringside, Joe Williams of the *Pittsburgh Press* declared the punch Zivic's best of the fight, "[a] belly-whopping, back-bending, breath-taking wallop to the midriff that was as fair as fair could be."[3] Regardless, Referee Young Otto immediately cautioned Zivic to keep his punches up. At the round's conclusion, Otto instructed the judges to deduct a point from Fritzie, penalizing him for the low blow.

Zivic fans boisterously disputed Otto's deduction. Boos came down from the top of the Garden for more than five minutes. So enraged were the fans that it appeared a riot was inevitable. In a drastic move, promoter Mike Jacobs quickly had the lights, which were kept low due to the ongoing war dim-out in effect, turned on throughout the arena and police swiftly positioned themselves around the ring to prevent any impending rampage.

Once the tension subsided, the fight continued. Fritzie staggered Beau with a powerful right hook near the end of the ninth, but his pace slowed considerably in the tenth. At the end of ten rounds, the decision went to the scorecards. The two judges, Sam Robinson, and Artie Monroe, scored the bout six rounds for Beau to four for Zivic. Referee Otto gave Beau six rounds, Zivic three rounds, and scored one round even. Beau earned a unanimous decision against the former welterweight king, extending his winning streak to 14. For their efforts, Zivic earned nearly $28,000 (65 percent), while Beau received 35 percent or $15,000.

Although Fritzie subsequently admitted that he had landed several low blows that the referee missed, his fans persisted in their frustration throughout the next week. They flung accusations of connections between the press and Beau Jack and Chick Wergeles. Zivic's supporters asserted that Jack had been made a champion and granted many favors because numerous sportswriters owned a piece of Jack's ring career. The *Brooklyn Daily Eagle* defended Wergeles and the press. "Wergeles is a popular fellow in every newspaper office in town, and it may be that Jack has gained a [lot] of yardage in newspaper columns that other fellows never got. But the connection goes no further, and the most a reporter ever got out of boosting the Beau was a few Georgia pecans, or maybe a smoked ham."[4]

Several days after the bout, sportswriter Harold Parrott met with Mike Jacobs, who had become the focal point of aggravated fans. Jacobs showed Harold a few of the letters he had received from angry fans. "'Phooey on you,' one fight bug wrote Mike, 'If Beau Jack licked Zivic then I can lick Louis, and I weigh 137. Why don't you get wise to yourself and see that the right decisions are made at the Garden? You sure can louse up boxing....'"[5] Jacobs didn't mind. The turmoil set the stage for a rematch. On February 11, after Wergeles insisted that his fighter receive an equal split of the purse, Jacobs announced that the rematch had been scheduled for March 5.

Years later, Beau recalled how much he learned from Fritzie Zivic. In an interview with Joe Falls, Beau explained, "He taught me more than any other fighter. He was a great fighter, Fritzie Zivic. A smart fighter."[6] Fritzie was a great boxer, but a dirty fighter in the ring. Known for head-butting his opponents, he likewise had a reputation for using his elbows and thumbing his foes in the eye when he could get away with it. Beau, himself, had been victimized by Zivic's dirty tactics. "See this," he said, pointing to his left eye which looked off in a crazy direction, "Fritzie Zivic did that to me. He took me inside and landed two left uppercuts," he said. "I held on because I didn't know what to do. He put his right hand like this...." Cupping his right hand behind his head, Beau exclaimed, "…and pulled me down and brought his thumb up into my eye."[7]

The lessons you acquire from an unclean fighter can be invaluable. Beau was not the only fighter to hold Fritzie in high regard. Sugar Ray Robinson also touted the examples he learned in two contests with Zivic, declaring that he learned more in his two fights with Zivic than in all his other fights put together.

Zivic conveyed contempt for Beau. "Just like I said before the fight, he's an imitation Armstrong," boasted Fritzie. "He couldn't carry Armstrong's trunks into the ring. There's no comparison. The guy is just a wild swinger and nothing else. He throws them from all angles and some are bound to land."[8] Zivic admitted that his strategy was to pace himself through the fight and throw flurries during the last 30 seconds of each round. Conversely, Jack's continued aggressiveness offset Zivic's plan.

After his victory over Zivic, Beau and Bowman Milligan departed for Augusta to rest before the rematch. While in town, Beau made an appearance on behalf of his friend and former supporter, Jack Ross, at the Augusta Municipal Auditorium for a middleweight contest between Augusta boxer Baxley Hardy and Leroy Huffstickler on Monday night, February 15. Three days later, Beau and Milligan boarded the train to head back north to prepare for his return engagement with Fritzie Zivic.

Back in New York, Chick arranged a press conference for Beau at Stillman's Gym, Beau's home away from home. Beau displayed a new sense of confidence and an exuberant spirit. Wearing a blue bathrobe over his ring togs, he danced around gleefully. When asked if he felt more self-confident, Jack modestly responded:

> "No, I don't see no difference. I wuz always confident of my strength becuz I always trained so hard. But I never go cocky becuz I licked anybody. Zivic gave me my hardest fight, but I expected that." He grinned and added, "but I'll have to admit I felt pretty good after I licked him. I hope it'll be easier this time."[9]

It was an incredible feeling. Beau had defeated the former world welterweight champion. The exuberant Beau was now carrying himself as a titleholder.

Going into the rematch, Beau was again the press favorite. He was eager to defend his disputed victory over Zivic. Pugilists were also ready. Although the temperature never made it out of the twenties, fans upward of 18,818 flocked to see the March 5 rematch at Madison Square Garden, producing the largest gate of the year, $71,346. The fans got their money's worth.

At the opening bell, Fritzie, this time sporting a 10½-pound weight advantage, stormed out banging away at Beau to keep his pre-fight promise of a knockout. By the end of the first stanza, he had Beau bleeding from the mouth and nose, but moments before the bell, Beau stunned him with a round-house right to his chin. Turning the tide, Beau became the aggressor. With his hooking attack to Fritzie's head and body, coupled with a plethora of thunderous uppercuts, Beau coasted through the next four rounds. Fritzie came back to life in the sixth round, bombarding Beau with powerful head shots. The momentum changed again in the next stanza. Not to be deterred, Beau came out strong in the seventh, knocking Zivic groggy, but Zivic finished with a flurry, as both boxers stood punching toe to toe as the bell sounded, ending the round.

In a seesaw battle, Jack came back in the eighth, knocking Fritzie across the ring, but lost the round due to a foul called for a low blow. The ninth round was a complete opposite. Fritzie pummeled Beau, but this time he lost the stanza on a low blow. Connecting with a hard right to Beau's face right before the end of the round, Fritzie stole the tenth. By the end of the brutal battle, both men were physically exhausted. With wobbly legs, the fatigued warriors stumbled to their corners.

It was a menacing brawl. Although there were no knockdowns, Beau's face was evidence of the mauling combat. He had mouses under his eyes and was bleeding from the nose and mouth. Zivic didn't look quite as bad but suffered a gash above his left eyebrow. It was an excellent match, however, the winner was not disputed. Beau pounded out a unanimous decision over the future Boxing Hall of Famer. As agreed to by the opponents before the match, a portion of the gate was set aside for the National Infantile Paralysis Fund to help those afflicted by the poliovirus and to continue research in search of a cure.

The National Infantile Paralysis Fund and Jonas Salk

Feared polio outbreaks were raging in the United States. A potentially fatal infectious disease, polio is caused by the poliovirus. The virus spreads from person to person and often attacks an infected person's brain and spinal cord resulting in paralysis. If it affects the muscles used for breathing, it can lead to death. In fact, there were more than 1,000 polio-related deaths in the U.S. in 1940.

Suffering from polio himself, President Franklin D. Roosevelt formed the National Infantile Paralysis Fund, now known as the March of Dimes, on the eve of World War II. Its purpose was to help those afflicted by the poliovirus and to research a cure. The grassroots movement was instrumental during the polio outbreak in 1949.

In the early 1950s, the average number of people affected by polio was over 45,000, with more than 15,000 cases of paralysis each year. Jonas E. Salk (1914–1995), a Russian-Jewish immigrant, would change that. After receiving his medical degree from the New York University School of Medicine in 1939, Salk ended up at the University of Pittsburgh's School of Medicine. Through research funded by the National Foundation for Infantile Paralysis, he developed a vaccine composed of "killed" poliovirus. When administered, the vaccine would immunize the patient without the risk of infection.

National testing began in 1954 on one million children, who became known as the Polio Pioneers. On April 12, 1955, it was announced that the vaccine was safe and effective. Within seven years, the number of people contracting polio had dropped to 910. Affably, Jonas Salk wanted the vaccine to be distributed quickly, and as widely as possible, so he never patented the vaccine or benefited financially from it. Thanks to widespread vaccination, polio has not been a viable threat in the U.S. since 1979.[10]

Years later in an interview with Bob Drum of the *Pittsburgh Press*, Fritzie Zivic humorously told his story of meeting Beau Jack for the first time.

> "I didn't even know who he was," Fritzie reports. "But I got hanging around Stillman's gym and got someone to point him out to me. The first thing I noticed about him was that he had one of those great big turkey necks. I walked up to him and introduced myself and then asked him if his neck always stood that far away from the rest of his body. He looked at me kinda funny, then told me not to get any ideas. Well, in the first round of the fight, I grabbed his neck—one of those long skinny ones—just to check it for size. He leaped about six feet off the ground and made a noise like a hurt chicken. I couldn't get close to him after that but still wound up with the decision."[11]

Who knows the truth of Fritzie's story, because he never beat Beau.

Jack Faces His Idol—Henry Armstrong

Less than a month after his second victory over Zivic, Jack returned to the Garden ring to meet his mentor, the legendary Henry "Homicide Hank" Armstrong (1912–1988). The non-title affair, initially scheduled for January 29, had been rescheduled for April 2, 1943, due to Armstrong's tonsillectomy. It was a curious matchup. Beau and Henry were more than mere acquaintances. They were friends. Beau lived with Henry in late 1940, while Armstrong prepared for his upcoming fight against Fritzie Zivic. Henry trained and helped Beau develop some of his early boxing skills, while Jack served as his sparring partner. They both had kept in touch ever since.

At first, Beau was reluctant to fight Armstrong. "Henry is my friend,"[12] expressed Beau. Chick Wergeles was not keen on the idea either. He worried that Armstrong might get hurt because he was getting older and his eyes were not as sharp as they once were. Speaking on behalf of Beau and himself, Chick said, "Well you've seen Beau fight and they don't come much tougher. And I don't know who it would affect more—me or my fighter—if anything happened to Armstrong."[13] Only after Armstrong received a thorough physical exam by the NYSAC, did Wergeles agree to the fight. Henry, himself, convinced Beau to commit to the match. "When Henry learned I was against the fight," Beau explained, "he sent me a long telegram stating that fighting was a business. As such we were two businessmen trying to make the most money from the best possible matches ... it was our duty to give the fans what they want."[14]

Henry Armstrong was already a legend, holding simultaneous titles in three different weight classes. In 1937, he won the world featherweight championship when he knocked out Petey Sarron. Then in 1938, Armstrong defeated Barney Ross for the world welterweight title and Lou Ambers for the world lightweight championship. He was also *The Ring's* Fighter of the Year in 1937. In January 1941, having fought for 10 years and losing two consecutive bouts to Fritzie Zivic, he retired his gloves for a little over a year. In his last loss to Zivic, he suffered an embarrassing beating before 22,190 fans at Madison Square Garden.

On June 1, 1942, Henry reentered boxing on the comeback trail, defeating Johnny Taylor. Jack was the 19th fight of his comeback tour. Thriving since his return, Armstrong had won 16 of his 18 comeback bouts, including impressive victories over the future lightweight champion, Juan Zurita; former welterweight champion, Fritzie Zivic; and former lightweight champion, Lew Jenkins. He also had 11 knockouts. In his last fight, he whipped a tough Al Tribuani before a wailing crowd of 12,633, throwing a fantastic average of 100 punches in each round of the 10-round bout.

Sportswriter Harold Parrott of the *Brooklyn Daily Eagle* asked Chick Wergeles before the Armstrong bout, "Does the Beau mind fighting other Negros, like Armstrong?" Did Jack feel timid about clobbering a member of his own race? "It ain't that," Chick scoffed. "It's because he said there wasn't enough glory in it. The guys he wanted to beat were the white guys with the reputations: Angott, Stolz, Zivic, Pep--."[15]

To prepare for their upcoming bout, Beau, as well as Henry, checked into Stillman's Gym before a capacity gathering of viewers to begin final training. Armstrong recalled, "I can't forget the look of ... adoration in his eyes when he [first] saw me.... Just like my little daughter...."[16] Meanwhile, a transition was made in Beau's team. Bill "Pop" Miller, who had served as Sid Bell's assistant for several years, moved on to other opportunities. With Pop's departure, George Gainsford was hired as Beau's new assistant trainer. Gainsford, a future hall of fame trainer, was best known as the manager of the welterweight champ and five-time middleweight champion, Sugar Ray Robinson.

It was an incredible pairing of two exceedingly well-liked fighters, as proved by the sellout crowd of 19,986 paying spectators that jammed into the Garden to witness the battle. If there had been more seats in the Garden,

Beau Jack and Henry Armstrong, 1943, autographed by Jack (courtesy Bruce Kielty).

they would have been filled. In fact, over 5,000 fans had to be turned away in the frigid rain. Fans revered Armstrong for his aggressive punching and swarming style and similarly appreciated Jack's windmill style of throwing leather, which was often paralleled to Armstrong by the press. Coming into the contest, the oddsmakers had Jack an 11–5 favorite.

The air was bursting with energy and excitement as the opening bell sounded. Jack, who celebrated his 22nd birthday the day before, started strong. In the first two rounds, Beau appeared the more formidable man. Using darting left jabs and long-range uppercuts, Beau punished Henry. Landing punches to Beau's body, Armstrong made a better showing in the third round. Beau responded in the fourth, starting quickly. Like a machine gun, Jack rapidly landed about 24 short jabs. Nonetheless, just before the bell in the fifth round, however, Armstrong connected with a thunderous right hurling Beau into the ropes. Beau's best round was the sixth, as he showered Henry with a series of at least 12 bolo uppercuts to his chin.

Even though Armstrong was 10 years Beau's elder, he pushed the action in the later rounds with his bobbing and weaving attack, as Jack furiously back-peddled to stay out of his reach. When the opportunity arose, Armstrong pounded Beau's body to decelerate his backward retreat. At first, Jack seemed unfazed by Armstrong's body attack, plummeting Henry with a plethora of punches. In the ninth round, however, Armstrong's strategy seemed to be functioning as he landed powerful blows to the rapidly tiring champion and had Jack wobbly on his feet. Armstrong finished the tenth round with another strong performance, earning a thunderous ovation from the crowd.

After 10 rounds, the decision went to the scorecards. Both judges and the referee gave Beau the victory over the "Hammer." Referee Billy Cavanaugh gave five rounds to Jack, three to Armstrong, and two even. Judge Bill Healy awarded Jack eight rounds and Armstrong two. Judge George Le Cron gave Beau seven rounds, Armstrong two, and scored one round even. Beau won a unanimous decision before a disillusioned crowd. The United Press called the fight even. Jack Cuddy explained, "If we had to make a decision we would have thrown the fight to Armstrong because of his aggressiveness."[17]

The fans decried the decision, engaging in prolonged booing for their sentimental favorite. They booed so loudly that Harry Balogh could not be heard when he announced the next fight. Subsequently, the crowd gave Armstrong a thunderous ovation. Armstrong may have lost the battle, but he re-captured the affection of the Garden fans.

Following the match, Armstrong made light of the pre-fight hype and disputed the loss. "I know in my heart that I gave Beau Jack everything I had, and I feel sure he was all out to flatten me, if he could. And I want to tell my friends in St. Louis that if I ever won a fight in my life it was that one with Beau Jack."[18] As only friends can do, Armstrong complimented Beau, while at the same time discrediting his punching power. "He's a good boy, tremendously improved since I last saw him, before my retirement, and he's strictly a topnotcher," said Henry. "Frankly, I expected him to be a harder puncher. He didn't hurt me one bit."[19] If anyone was concerned about Beau hurting the older Henry, it was dismissed once they entered the ring.

The sellout crowd provided a purse of $104,976, the largest indoor gate for non-heavyweights in over a decade. A portion of the proceeds from the gate, 10 percent of net receipts or $8,947.47, went to help the Red Cross. For their efforts, each fighter received $24,158.17. As usual, after a close contest, there was the talk of a rematch. Henry wanted a chance to redeem himself against Jack, but Beau didn't seem disposed to fighting Armstrong again.

Next week there was a repeated attempt to match Beau with the former lightweight champ, Sammy Angott. After coming out of retirement, Angott's hands appeared healed as he whipped Willie Pep on March 19, ending Pep's undefeated streak of sixty-two fights. Sammy's manager, Charley Jones, called Beau out. "Sammy Angott is the lightweight champion of the world," declared Jones, "and is willing to meet to meet Beau Jack in any state in the union and any time and is entitled to the champion's percentage."[20] He even offered to donate $7,500 of Angott's purse to charity, if Beau took the fight. Chick Wergeles would have none of the match, unless Beau was promised 40 percent of the gate. His fighter was the lightweight champion now, and he needed to be compensated accordingly.

Orphaned Beau Visits Mother

Beau Jack took a much-needed break before his first title defense. For the first time in years, he did not work the Masters Tournament, as it was suspended due to World War II. Instead, in early April, Beau and his wife Josephine traveled to St. Petersburg, Florida to visit family. On Monday, April 9, while in St. Petersburg, a shocking headline in the *Tampa Bay Times* revealed his reason, "'Orphaned' Beau Jack Here to Visit Mother."[21] Until now, everybody, including the media, thought Beau's parents had deserted him and that he had no knowledge that his mother was alive or that his father had passed away years ago. Remarkably, even Beau himself never disputed such accounts.

Sandy Stiles of the *Tampa Bay Times* exposed that Beau had been writing his mother and sending her money for over a year. In fact, the April 12, 1943, *Tampa Bay Times* featured a photograph of Beau with his arm around his mother, Lillian Walker. The same photo was published in the *Pittsburgh Courier* on May 1. The associated article featured Stiles' interview with mother and son. The two revealed that Beau had been born near Waynesboro on a cotton plantation owned by E. E. Chance. According to the interview, when Beau was about five years old, his parents split up after arranging for Beau to live with his grandmother.

Beau's mother stated, "I didn't even know he was fighting 'til he wrote me two, three years ago," she said. "But he has written me often since then."[22] As an anxious mother, Mrs. Walker divulged that she never listened to Beau's fights on the radio. "I tried to listen when he fought Mistuh Tippy Larkin, but my heart wouldn't stand it," she confided. "Then when he fought Henry Armstrong I went as far away from the radio as I could get."[23]

Stiles' article was mind-blowing but was not picked up by other newspapers other than the *Pittsburgh Courier*. Beau would continue to be referred to as "orphaned," and he did not refute those accounts. Stiles concluded, "Sidney Walker, better known as Beau Jack, world lightweight champion, killed a perfectly good sports yarn during the weekend when he came here to visit his mother, Lillian Walker at 326 Tenth Street North."[24] Evidently, Beau had also visited his mother in 1941.

Beau was proud of his new role as an American champion and used his championship status to constructively influence others and support his country. While in the St. Petersburg area, Beau visited several schools to endorse the Second War Loan efforts and talk with the students. He enjoyed talking with children and promoting his country.

World War II was still raging. Although the tide had turned in favor of the Allies after the Battle of Midway, it was far from over. On April 12, 1943, the Treasury and War Finance Committee launched the Second War Bond Drive that lasted twenty days, ending on May 1, 1943. The First War Loan campaign between November 30, 1942, and December 23, 1942, had surpassed its goal of $9 billion, totaling almost $13 billion. The Second War Loan drive sought to raise $13 billion for the war efforts. It would end up raising $18.5 billion.

American citizens and corporations were eager to contribute as it was a way that they could show their willingness to sacrifice for the war effort and patriotic fervor. The Second War Bond Drive was enthusiastically discussed all over the states, including school classrooms. Pep talks were given by principals and teachers, as well as celebrities.

On Wednesday morning, April 14, Jack, along with his wife Josephine and sister Fannie Mae, also living in St. Petersburg, visited Gibbs High School, an African American high school in St. Petersburg. Before a school assembly, he told students, "if anyone wanted to become a great fighter one would have to get plenty of rest, sleep and refrain from smoking and partaking of strong drinks."[25] When asked, he acknowledged that his toughest opponent was Henry Armstrong.

The following day he visited Jordan Elementary School, another African American school, located about four miles north of Gibbs High School. As always, he was a big hit among the students and faculty. "All questions so eagerly asked by them were graciously answered by this national character," stated J. K. Neal, social science instructor at the school. "His unassuming attitude and fine manner won the hearts of pupils and teachers. This of course is a sign of true greatness."[26] That evening, Mr. and Mrs. George Ford and Mr. and Mrs. James Ford hosted a reception honoring Beau Jack and his wife. Of course, Beau's mother and sister were present as well.

Beau soon left for New York to begin training for his first title defense. But before he began training, he lent his support as a guest of honor at "Harlem on Parade" dance to benefit the Riverdale Orphan Asylum.

14

Montgomery Dethrones Beau

While in Florida, Beau contracted to battle Bob "Bobcat" Montgomery (1919–1998) in his first title defense. The 15-round title affair was scheduled for Monday night, May 21, 1943, at Madison Square Garden. Like Beau, Monty, as Montgomery was often called, hailed from the South, growing up in Sumter, South Carolina. He now lived in Philadelphia with his wife and son.

Montgomery had a fascinating journey to the title bout. In 1933, Bob was washing dishes at the Broad & Market in Philadelphia. Currently, he was working as a blacksmith's assistant at the Sun Shipyards in Chester, Pennsylvania. In his spare time, Montgomery often boxed and worked out at the Madison Athletic Club on Girard Avenue. One day when he was sparring at the Athletic Club, Bob met up and coming African American boxer Johnny Hutchinson. Hutchinson took Bob in and shared some of his ring skills with him. He also introduced him to his manager, Frankie Thomas. Thomas immediately saw boundless potential in Montgomery and quickly added him to his stable of fighters.

As a 24-year-old boxer, Montgomery had more experience than Beau. Monty debuted his career on October 13, 1938, knocking out Young Johnny Buff in Atlantic City. He already had 27 bouts under his belt before Beau even debuted at Valley Arena. Bob won the Pennsylvania State Lightweight title in 1940 and had a professional record of 50–6–3. He also had outpointed the world lightweight champion Lew Jenkins, in a nontitle fight in 1941. Monty was soft-spoken and one of the most charming fighters of the day. He had fast hands, a good chin and moved around well in the ring. Monty's weaknesses were that he tended to brawl, instead of box, and struggled with consistency.

Against common opponents, both Beau and Bob had beaten Young Johnny Buff and George Zengaras. Bob had won his one bout with Chester Rico, whereas Beau had one victory and a draw with Rico. On the other hand, Beau had won two fights with Tommy Speigal, whereas Bob had lost his match with Speigal.

To prepare for his title defense, on May 1, Beau and his entourage arrived at Joe Murchio's Cloudland Camp located in the Ramapo Mountains, a forested section of the Appalachian Mountains in southern New York. Other boxers, such as Joe Louis, frequently used the camp for training. Beau's first several days were spent gaining energy. He took in the fresh air and sunshine as he did a little fishing and hiking. Then, on May 4, Beau began training. "The 22-year-old Negro with the Indian profile jogged six miles through the rose-tinted mists beside the slumbering lake," wrote Jack Cuddy. "It was his first roadwork at Joe Murchio's Cloudland Camp—the training resort where Sgt. Joe Louis groomed for many title battles."[1] Beau trained hard during the day and relaxed in the evenings, engaging in one of his favorite pleasures, spearfishing. At night, he would head out to the lake with flashlight and spear in hand. While wading through the water, Jack looked for fish, and when spotted, he speared them with a quick thrust of his spear.

In Philadelphia, Montgomery was training hard as well and was in peak condition and full of confidence. "I can beat him. I know it," Monty said. "I figure he doesn't like good, solid body punches and I'm going to keep throwing rights to the body."[2] Beau also felt upbeat, coming into the fight riding a 15-victory streak. Although both fighters weighed 135 pounds, Montgomery was 5'8" tall and had a two-inch reach advantage. The contest marked only the second time Beau had appeared in a fifteen-round match, and his first one just went three rounds. This bout would go all fifteen rounds.

The evening proved to be another great success for Mike Jacobs. It was his 35th championship fight at Madison Square Garden. Fans poured out to see Beau defend his title. Although the paid crowd was 18,843, an over-capacity crowd of more than 20,000 boxing fans crammed into Madison Square Garden to witness Philadelphia's "Bobbing Bobcat," a 12–5 underdog, challenge Jack for the lightweight title. The stage was set for a real duel pitting Montgomery, the more experienced, sharp-hitting boxer, and Jack, a rough, mauling, light-hitting youngster. The gate of $94,500 pleasantly surpassed Jacobs' expectations.

The crowd was roaring as the fight began. Beau immediately swarmed Montgomery, throwing flurries of uppercuts to his body and head, staggering the taller man. Landing punches squarely on Monty's chin, Jack overwhelmed him. The challenger appeared as if he was going to crash to the canvas from a hard right uppercut, but Montgomery rallied in the last minute with several rights to the champ's head, opening a cut over his left eye. So furious was the battle that both combatants continued slugging each other after the bell. It took Referee Arthur Donovan to pry them apart. While Beau won the first round, Montgomery continued to settle down, taking the second and third rounds, smashing left hooks to Beau's body and landing hard rights on the champion's head. The fourth round was scored even. Beau stormed back to win the fifth and sixth rounds using daunting left jabs and uppercuts.

Beau Jack (left) and Bob Montgomery shake hands before the bout. Others pictured include fight promoters Chick Wergeles (back row, left) and Mike Jacobs (front row, left) and Frankie Thomas (front row, right), c. 1943 (courtesy John DiSanto, Philly Boxing History Collection).

In the seventh round, Beau began to slow as the effects of the Bobcat's damaging body punches took their toll. Montgomery, on the other hand, picked up his pace and continuously forced the action. The challenger was landing his straight right at will, and Jack just couldn't seem to dodge its thunderous power. With Beau's nose and mouth acutely bleeding and his temple swelling up like a tennis ball, it became apparent that Montgomery was steps away from taking the title from Beau. "Jack fought on desperately and gamely, bleeding profusely from nose and mouth and with a balcony of bruises over his left eye that almost prevented vision," wrote Jack Cuddy. "The left side of Beau's temple also swelled until it seemed that his head was lop-sided. And a large mouse rose beneath his right eye."[3]

Bobbing and weaving from his crouched position, Monty determinedly pursued Beau, admonishing him with solid left hooks to the body and rights to his head. In the eleventh round, Montgomery bashed Jack with a right to the chin that turned him sideways, dropping the champ to the canvas. Although knocked down, only Beau's gloves touched the canvas, and no count was given. Jack mounted a desperate attempt to retain his title in the twelfth and scored well with lefts to Monty's face. By the thirteenth round, however, Beau could scarcely see. Both of his eyes were nearly swollen shut from Montgomery's consistent pounding. The lump over Jack's left eye looked larger than a baseball. Monty cornered Beau against the ropes in the fourteenth round, belting him with punches. Beau wilted but refused to go down. Montgomery coasted through the last stanza.

As the two fighters stood in the center of the ring, the decision was announced. Referee Arthur Donovan gave Montgomery ten rounds, Beau three, and called two even. Judge Bill Healy gave Montgomery nine rounds to six for Beau, and Judge Marty Monroe gave Montgomery ten rounds and Beau five. By unanimous decision, Bob Montgomery captured the New York lightweight world championship. Monty was ecstatic as he rushed over to Beau and gave him a joyous hug.

Montgomery fought a smart fight and paced himself well for the 15-round bout. In just his second bout lasting more than ten rounds, Beau simply ran out of gas. In elation, Garden fans descended on the new champion in his dressing room. Just five months after being crowned the lightweight champion, Beau had been dethroned by Bob Montgomery.

Ring announcer Harry Balogh raises Bob Montgomery's arm in victory, March 5, 1943 (Associated Press).

Following the fight, the combatants conversed about their ring battle. Montgomery acknowledged Beau's gameness in the ring. "That was the toughest fight I ever had," Montgomery said. "He's a good man, but not half as tough as I expected. He hurt me in the first round, but never after that."[4] Bob also disclosed his key to victory. "He kept dropping his left and I punched right over it," declared Monty. "He's easy to hit but hard to bring down."[5] Jack likewise complimented Monty, "He's a fine fighter," Jack admitted. "Yes, he hurt me several times."

Commentators immediately began to debate the fight's outcome. Why had Beau lost his first title defense? Did he lack stamina? Was Montgomery simply the better boxer? Beau and his camp provided several explanations. First, Chick Wergeles asserted that Jack injured his hand in the third round when he landed a right to Montgomery's head. He reiterated after the fight, Beau's hand was twice its normal size and he had to cut Beau's boxing glove off his left hand. Wergeles, however, shared an additional explanation. He blamed the loss on Beau's handlers. "They kept telling the Beau to back up and stay away," said Chick. "That ain't the way he likes to fight."[6] The tactic had worked in his last fight against Henry Armstrong but not with Monty.

Chick Wergeles and Lou Stillman of Stillman's Gym furnished yet another, albeit more humorous explanation. Grinning, Stillman said it was the first time Beau did not train at his gym for a major fight. Regrettably, "Hercules" Wergeles concurred, asserting that Joe Murchio's Cloudland Camp had not been a good place for Beau to train for his contest with Montgomery. "He liked the country life so much that he rowed and fished so often it used up all his energy," explained Chick. "He stayed up nights, fishin' with a big spear and hip boots. Stabbed the fish with them, too—the spear not the boots, I mean. That learned us. No more country life for him. He needs a stuffy gym. Fresh air can kill a guy, you know, if you get too much of it."[7] No more training in the country for Jack. On top of fishing, Chick mentioned that Beau had stumbled over a rock and hurt his knee a week before the fight.

The next day, Beau dropped by the Twentieth Century SC to pick up his check for $32,076. Monty, on the other hand, received $14,033 for his efforts. Chick Wergeles had done his job as Beau's manager. Beau returned to Augusta for a much-needed breather. Before long, he would get another shot at the title. A rematch was imminent as Chick had cleverly inserted a clause into the fight contract requiring a mandatory title rematch within 60 days.

Irrespective of the loss, Beau's popularity continued to grow. Beau was handsome. His jaw was square and his smile broad and comforting. He had olive brown skin and was a flashy dresser, often wearing plaid jackets, posh ties, and fedora hats. Jack received mountains of fan mail, especially from the ladies. Random females often wrote claiming they were his sister or mother and to please send them some money. "It's funny," Chick said, "but they never forget to mention dough."[8] Several days after the loss to Montgomery, Beau received a letter from a female admirer from Christianville, Virginia. She wrote, "I prayed for you every day before the Montgomery fight, but I guess I said the wrong words."[9] Remarkably, unlike many other letters Beau received, it did not include a marriage proposal or request for money.

Larry Amadee Hired as Beau's Trainer

A month later, a determined Beau Jack started his campaign to reclaim the lightweight title. Chick Wergeles also made some changes in Beau's handlers. Wergeles hired Larry Amadee as Beau's new trainer. "After we lost to Montgomery," Wergeles said, "we fired Beau's old handlers, and the syndicate told me to go out and get the best trainer in the business. I told them we wanted Amadee, who'd worked with Joe Louis, so they said, 'Go the limit,' and we got Larry."[10]

Hailing from New Orleans, Larry Amadee (1899–1978) was a man of dignity. As a trainer, he had already worked with three world champions: Gorilla Jones, NBA middleweight champion (1925); John Henry Lewis, light heavyweight champion (1935–1938); and Joe Louis, heavyweight champion (1937–1949). Amadee would also work with Cassius Clay (Muhammad Ali) and Honey Bratton during their amateur careers.

Journalist David Condon of the *Chicago Tribune* praised Larry's skill at motivating his fighters. "When Larry was talking to the young, one-on-one, man-to-man, he had a most intent audience," insisted Condon. "He inspired by his concern, his skill, and his pride."[11] Richard Calisch, who was training with Amadee at the same time as Beau, also applauded Amadee. "Larry Amadee was a black man who took all comers for what they were worth as men and as fighters. I never heard him criticize anything about a man but his jab or his uppercut."[12] He ended every training session with the same words. "See you Thursday. Don't smoke no cigars and don't get in no fights."[13] Jimmy DeAngelo was hired as a supporting trainer.

Beau was in Washington, D.C., for his next fight, a scheduled ten-round bout with Maxie Starr on June 21, 1943. A Native American boxer from the Edgewood Arsenal, the inexperienced Starr's record was 1–2–2 in his short three-month professional career. The "stress-free" match was intended to get Beau back in the right frame of mind after losing his title crown.

The venue for the bout was Griffith Stadium. Opened in 1911 as National Park, the stadium was astonishingly constructed in three weeks to replace American League Baseball Park II, which had burned to the ground. It was renamed Griffith Stadium after the owner of the Washington Senators of the American Baseball League (ABL), Clark Griffith. With capacity seating for

Baseball game at old Griffith Stadium, Washington, D.C., c. 1909–1932 (Library of Congress).

27,410, the stadium was home to the Washington Senators of the ABL and the Washington Redskins of the NFL. Located on the campus of Howard University, the stadium was eventually demolished in 1965.

As expected, it wasn't much of a bout. Beau smothered Starr with a hard, right-hand attack, thumping Starr to the canvas twice in the first round and repeatedly driving him into the ropes. In the fifth stanza, Beau knocked Starr to the canvas twice before finishing him off in the sixth. After Beau landed a flurry of straight rights to Starr's jaw sending him once again to the canvas, Referee Eddie Lafond halted the fight one minute and 55 seconds into the sixth round.

Newspaper reports came out several days later announcing that Beau had remarkably earned $120,837 in his six months as a prizefighter. Apparently, Beau was in the money, and he proudly acknowledged it. "I have nearly $100,000 held for me by my board of directors and I haven't touched one cent of it. That's what I call my farm fund."[14] When he retired from boxing, Beau wanted to have a hog farm like his Uncle Jesse.

Beau set two main goals in July. He was not only determined to recapture the lightweight crown from Bob Montgomery, but he was also receiving tutoring so that he could pass the literacy test to enter the Army. Beau enthusiastically sought to serve his country with the same passion as he exhibited inside the ring. Reportedly, he had been rejected by the Army twice before, because he could not read or write.

Although Beau only had a second-grade education, through the years, he gained confidence. The once soft-spoken and shy bootblack became a confident and outspoken young man who knew his own mind and didn't mind speaking it. Beau had even taken a liking to playing practical jokes. One of his favorites was to sprinkle salt into his sparring partners' waters.

In late June, Beau stepped up his competition to prepare for his rematch with Montgomery. He signed to fight Johnny "Blackjack" Hutchinson of Philadelphia. Credited with finding Bob Montgomery, Johnny and Bob were stablemates. Hutchinson had a professional record of 65–20–8 and recently defeated formidable opponents Bobby Ruffin (56–16–10) and Carmine Fatta (49–11–4). Many observers proclaimed that Hutchinson packed a deadlier punch than Montgomery.

The contest was scheduled for July 19 at Shibe Park in Philadelphia. Opened in 1909, Shibe Park was home to two major league baseball teams: the Philadelphia Athletics of the American League and Philadelphia Phillies of the National League. The Philadelphia Eagles of the NFL had also recently moved to Shibe Park. Constructed by Ben Shibe, a leading owner of the Philadelphia Athletics, the 35,000-seat stadium was located in North Philadelphia.

It was a beautiful evening with temperatures in the low 80s. A large crowd of almost 17,000 fans showed up for the fistic affair between Jack and Hutchinson. Beau had a one-pound weight advantage at 135¼ pounds; whereas Hutchinson had a one-inch height advantage.

Amidst the roar of the crowd, the fight began. Jack easily won the first two rounds as he belted Johnny with windmill punches. In the third round, Johnny seized the momentum going to work on Beau's body. Then, a fight broke out in the fourth round. Both men stood toe to toe pelting each other. As the opening bell sounded for the fifth, a resolute Beau came out strong and took control of the battle, using a long-range attack and landing numerous powerful right uppercuts, leaving Hutchinson cut and bleeding. Beau came out solid again in the sixth, hitting Hutchinson's head repeatedly with his famous right-handed bolo punch.

With Hutchinson bleeding from his nose, mouth and left eye, Referee Irv Kurchner stepped in with 59 seconds left in the sixth round and halted the brutal beating. Beau scored an easy sixth-round technical knockout, as well as $18,500 from the gate of $50,057. It was the largest Philadelphia gate since Joe Louis knocked out Gus Dorazio on February 17, 1941.

Beau would not fight again until October 4. Although he was scheduled to fight Lulu Costantino in Cleveland on August 26, 1943, it was called off after Costantino suffered an ear injury during his prior bout with Chalky Wright. Meanwhile, Chick continued working with Montgomery's manager Frankie Thomas to lock down a contract and date for the rematch. Following negotiations, Beau's rematch with Montgomery was scheduled for September

10. Frankie Thomas, however, sternly insisted there would be no title fight on the 10th unless Beau signed a return match agreement. Chick and Beau agreed.

After initial training at the Christian Street Y.M.C.A., Bob left for New York to join Beau for final preparations at Stillman's Gym scheduled to begin on Labor Day. On Sunday night, however, Montgomery began to have severe pain from an impacted wisdom tooth, leading his camp to postpone the upcoming rematch. The new date was set for October 4. However, on the 17th of September, Montgomery again backed out, asserting that his jaw had taken more time than expected to heal. Therefore, Monty hadn't had adequate time to train. The fight was rescheduled for a second time, this time for November 19.

Given the delays, Chick Wergeles scheduled Beau a tune-up match on Monday, October 4 with Bobby Ruffin (1921–1996). Ruffin, of Long Island, stood 5'7" tall, had a record of 60–17–11, and had only lost one of his last eleven fights. Ruffin's father, Teddy Hubbs, a veteran of more than 200 fights, served as his manager. Expressing concern, commentators thought Beau was taking an unnecessary gamble by meeting such a formidable foe. If Jack lost, he could potentially lose his chance at the title. In a tune-up fight for his rematch with Bob Montgomery, why would you take on a significant lightweight contender? Beau had everything to lose and nothing to gain. A headline in the *Brooklyn Daily Eagle* read, "Beau Jack Gambles in Bout with Ruffin."[15] The oddsmakers, however, approved of Beau's gamble. They had little regard for Ruffin and listed him as an 8 to 1 underdog. To prepare for the bout, Beau trained at Stillman's Gym, finishing preparations with three rounds of sparring with middleweight Freddie Graham. Ruffin prepared for the fight at Bey's Camp in Summit, New Jersey.

On fight night, New York City was buzzing. Not only was Jack at Madison Square Garden, but it was the eve of the World Series in New York between the Yankees and St. Louis Cardinals. A crowd of 14,449, including actress Lana Turner and singer Frank Sinatra, were among the fans gathered at the Garden to witness the match between Jack and Ruffin. Also sitting ringside to observe Beau was the lightweight champion, Bob Montgomery. The gate was $43,429.

The night did not start out well for Jack. First, he came in overweight. Although the fight was contracted for 136 pounds, Beau weighed in at 140½ pounds, his heaviest fight weight to date, versus Ruffin's 135½ pounds. Beau blamed his failure to make weight on an injury to his right knee suffered during training that prevented him from doing sufficient road work. As a result, Ruffin's team insisted on a larger cut of the gate. Ruffin received another one and one-quarter percent of the net gate, bringing his total receipts to 22½ percent and reducing Beau's to 30 percent. Next, there was an argument over who would utilize which dressing room. The two camps settled that by flipping a coin. In a moment of success, Beau won the coin toss. As the fighters entered the ring, however, Beau wore a heavy support and bandage on his injured right knee. It had been rumored that Jack injured his right knee, but Dr. William Walker pronounced him fit and did not find a problem with Beau's knee during his pre-fight examination.

Ruffin immediately took advantage of Beau's injury, landing hard body punches within minutes after the opening bell. Throwing caution to the wind, Ruffin took charge of the fight, electing to stand toe to toe and slug it out with Beau. He piled up points by throwing jabs and effective counter punches. Ruffin's speed and flurries of left jabs and rights, as well as his defensive ability to avoid Beau's damaging blows, had the former champion bewildered. Bobby kept sticking his left jab in Beau's face and always moved to Beau's right, forcing Jack to pivot on his injured right knee. Beau attempted a late comeback, gashing Ruffin's left eyebrow in the ninth and rallying furiously in the 10th. The crowd loved the action and continued their howling appreciation after the final bell.

The decision went to the scorecards. Although the *Daily News* scorecard had Beau the winner, winning seven rounds to Ruffin's two rounds, and the Associated Press scorecard had the fight even at five rounds apiece, Referee Frankie Fullam and Judges Sam Robinson and Jim Gearns scored the contest in favor of Ruffin, seven rounds to three. In an astonishing upset, Ruffin outpointed Beau on the official scorecard to earn a unanimous decision.

After the verdict was announced, Ruffin ran over to the lone sportswriter who had picked him to win and threw kisses to him. Chick's comment after the fight summed up the evening. "We won the toss, but that's the only thing we won all day."[16] Talking to Jack Cuddy after the fight, Beau cited several reasons for his poor performance. First, his right knee injured in training and bandaged for the bout had prevented proper training for months. Evidently, Beau suffered a twisted tendon in his right knee during training. Second, he came in overweight at 140½ pounds, the heaviest of his career. Finally, he was rusty from the lack of competition.

Irrespective of his defeat, Beau's title rematch with Bob Montgomery was still on go. Promoter Mike Jacobs explained that the title bout between Beau and Montgomery had been under contract for months and both fighters had posted $1,500 forfeits. Moreover, but for Montgomery's postponements, Beau would not have fought Ruffin and suffered defeat.

Before resuming his training for his upcoming rematch with Bob Montgomery, Beau went home to Augusta for a couple of weeks. He needed to get mentally prepared for the title match. Beau also received treatments for his injured right knee. Ruffin had taken advantage of his injury and Beau wanted to be at his physical best for Montgomery.

15

Beau Regains the Title

Despite delays, the rematch between Jack and Montgomery was destined to occur. It finally transpired at Madison Square Garden on November 19, 1943. There was no training camp in the mountains this time for Beau. Chick made sure Beau trained at his usual spot, Stillman's Gym. Following preliminary training in Philadelphia, Bob Montgomery completed his fight preparations alongside Beau at Stillman's.

Pugilists appeared perplexed as to Beau's chances. In his last fight, he was upset by Bobby Ruffin. Was Beau's mysteriously injured knee to blame? Had Beau just been the recipient of good fortune in their first match? Time would tell. Recent X-rays of Beau's right knee suggested that his knee was fully recovered. Three days before the fight, Chick Wergeles announced that Beau was doing road work for the first time in seven months. He also boasted, "The kid's never been in better shape ... a 'horstopath' has fixed his knee."[1]

Sportswriter Wendell Smith was invited to ride around with Jack and Larry Amadee in their taxi following Beau's official weigh-in the morning of the fight. Both Beau and Amadee were in excellent spirits. Smith wrote of his conversation with boxer and trainer.

> "Beau will win back his title tonight," Larry assured me. "He's in great shape. His bad knee is all right and you'll see a different Beau Jack in there tonight."
>
> The challenger was sitting beside Larry munching on a big apple. In his lap was a bag full of pears. He offered me one and I took it.
>
> "They say an apple a day will keep the doctor away," Beau Jack said. "So I'm gonna' eat a lot of 'em today."
>
> "If apples keep the doctor away," I asked, "what will the pears do?"
>
> "They'll keep Bob Montgomery away," Beau said with a hearty laugh.[2]

Amadee then pulled out a thermos full of beef broth. He explained that he gave it to Beau to drink about every half hour. Beau took it all in stride. His mind wandered from the fight as he looked out the window up at a cloudless sky, remarking that it was a beautiful day to play golf.

Several hours before the rematch, Chick took Beau to dinner in Manhattan. Chick ordered them both two rare steaks. After they finished the steaks, he asked Beau what he would like for dessert. Beau said ice cream. Beau humorously described what happened next.

> "You're fighting tonight," Chick said, "so you can have only a dish of ice cream." Then he turned to the waiter, "Don't bring him nothin' fancy, just plain vanilla ice cream."
> "Yes, sir," said the waiter, "and what are you having, sir?"
> My eyes popped out when Chick replied:
> "Bring me a double order of ice cream and two hunks of apple pie—I ain't fightin'."[3]

Chick wasn't fighting so he splurged on dessert.

For the first time, Beau came into a fight as a significant underdog. Oddsmakers had Beau as a 4–1 underdog. Bob had defeated Beau seven months ago and was riding an 11-bout victory streak. Since his last battle with Beau, Monty had defeated Al Reasoner (11–7–2) by knockout, Frankie Wills (39–17–3) by unanimous decision, former welterweight champion Fritzie Zivic (130–36–6) by unanimous decision, and Petey Scalzo (90–14–6) by technical knockout. His upcoming fight with Beau, however, was his first title defense. At the official weigh-in, Montgomery weighed in one pound heavier than Beau, 133¾ pounds to 132¾ pounds.

Temperatures were in the thirties as a crowd of 17,866 jammed into the galleries at the Garden, producing a net gate of $96,873, slightly better than their last fight. With the night's gate, Beau had now generated gates totaling near $600,000 in his previous eight Garden bouts. By the time the night's five preliminary bouts ended, the fans were frenzied and eager to witness a brawl. The match was also broadcast by British radio so that U.S. servicemen overseas could listen to the fight commentary.

As the contest began, it was apparent that Beau's new trainer Larry Amadee had him ready for the contest. Following Amadee's instructions, Beau came out as a changed fighter, catching Philadelphia Bob off guard. Unlike the previous battle, Beau stuck close to Montgomery, landing short uppercuts and slugging him with rights and lefts when Referee Young Otto separated the two from clinches. Another technique Beau employed to surprise Monty was to come in low on Bob and strike him from a crouched position.

Beau won the first two rounds over the notoriously slow-starting Montgomery, connecting with a thunderous right overhand to Bob's temple in the second. Montgomery began to warm up in the third round, staggering Beau with a right to his jaw. Beau rallied back in the fourth, slowing Montgomery down with a right to his chin followed by a stream of jabs and uppercuts.

Monty landed his best punches when Beau rose from his crouch. When Beau momentarily came out of his crouch in the fifth, Montgomery landed a magnificent right on his jaw, bludgeoning him into the ropes. Reeling from Bob's stunning blow, a bewildered and glassy-eyed Beau somehow succeeded in tying Montgomery up in a clinch to avoid additional damage.

Bob Montgomery presses Beau Jack against the ropes in their second meeting, November 19, 1943, autographed by Jack and Montgomery (courtesy Bruce Kielty).

Remarkably, Beau mounted another rally to win the sixth and seventh rounds. He bashed Montgomery with left jabs. Jack was beating Bob at his own game—inside fighting. When the two were in close, Beau utilized an imposing inside attack, throwing body punches and uppercuts to the champion's head. The "Georgia Wildcat" continued to vary his game, throwing a multitude of punches, including "over-hand punches, back-hand punches, hooks, bolo punches, chops and uppercuts."[4] Although Monty managed to rally and win the eighth, the ninth and tenth rounds belonged to Beau. In the ninth, Beau delivered the blow of the night. As the two fighters broke from a clinch, Jack cracked a thundering bolo uppercut on Montgomery's chin.

Staggering Bob, the blow bounced him into the ropes. With the deafening noise of the crowd and blood pouring from his mouth, Monty resorted to last defense, some crafty bobbing and weaving along the ropes to endure the round.

In the 10th round, Montgomery hurt Beau with a staggering right. Snatching the momentum, Bob turned up the pace, winning the next round. The 12th round was even, but Beau took the 13th, hurting the champion with a left hook to the abdomen. Bob rallied in the 14th, hammering Beau with straight rights and stunning him with a one-two combination. Then Monty hurled a savage right on the challenger's jaw, transforming Beau's legs into rubber. Bob appeared to be on the verge of a knockout victory, but Beau, with a chin of steel, refused to go down. Even though both fighters tried to close strong, the final round was scored even.

At the end of the grueling 15-round melee, both men were bloodied, bleeding from the nose and mouth. Although there were no knockdowns, each man staggered the other on several occasions with thunderous blows. The decision went to the scorecards. The two judges, Bill Healy and Joe Agnello, gave Beau 10 rounds, whereas Referee Young Otto gave Beau seven rounds, Montgomery six and called the other two even.

Six months after losing the title, Beau earned a unanimous decision regaining his crown over the man who had dethroned him. It was only the second time in history that a lightweight had taken back the title from the same man who ousted him. Lou Ambers previously accomplished the task when he defeated Henry Armstrong after Henry took the title from him.

In a colossal upset, Jack was once again the lightweight king of the world. Fans and experts were surprised by his speed, stamina, and persistent attack. The champ, now former champ, had also been baffled. Fighting a savvy fight, Jack exhibited footwork like never before. Giving his new trainer Larry Amadee the credit, Beau praised him, saying, "I did just what Larry told me."[5] Larry Amadee had now trained his fourth champion.

Throngs of newspapermen gathered in Beau's dressing room after the fight. It was a madhouse. A handsome man in a blue pinstriped suit appeared in the crowd, determined to shake the champ's hand. It was none other than movie star Humphrey Bogart, and he didn't just shake Beau's hand. He gave him a big hug. Beau also received another present—Chick Wergeles' 12-cylinder sedan with white-wall tires, worth $2,400. Chick promised Beau his car if he beat Montgomery in the rematch.

Even though Beau was once again the New York lightweight world champion, the lightweight title was still in disarray between the two major sanctioning bodies. The NYSAC recognized Beau Jack as the lightweight champion, whereas the NBA acknowledged Sammy Angott, even though Angott vacated the title when he temporarily retired.

As he did eight months earlier, Jack headed to St. Petersburg, Florida, for a weeklong vacation to visit his mother and sister. While in St. Petersburg, Beau relaxed by spearfishing in the Gulf. He also visited numerous classrooms at Davis Elementary School. Leaving Florida, he traveled to Augusta to visit other family members and friends.

Returning from vacation, Beau was tentatively scheduled to meet Bobby Ruffin again. Wergeles and Ruffin's manager, Maurie Waxman, however, could not agree on terms. Although Chick had previously agreed to 30 percent of the gate, he now insisted on 40 percent. The two sides were at an impasse, so Mike Jacobs had to find Beau a different opponent. On December 21, 1943, Jacobs announced that he had lined up Jack's next two fights. In his first match on January 7, Jack would meet Lulu Costantino in a nontitle contest. The second bout, on the other hand, would feature a January 27 non-title battle between Beau Jack and the NBA lightweight champion, Sammy Angott.

A day later, Mike Jacobs, on behalf of the Twentieth Century SC, released attendance and financial numbers for the 22 boxing shows promoted at the Garden thus far in 1943. Aggregate attendance was 322,512, with gross receipts of $1,136,228. Beau was easily the commanding box-office draw of the year. Gates from Jack's six Garden bouts in 1943 drew $481,415, with attendance totaling 111,188. In other words, Jack's bouts accounted for 35 percent of the year's attendance and 42 percent of the overall gate. Jack also received the honor for the three largest gates. Beau's bout with Henry Armstrong produced $104,976, the largest gate of the year. His November 19 bout against Bob Montgomery generated the second largest gate, $96,873, and Jack's May 21 bout with Montgomery yielded $94,500, the third largest gate. Likewise, Jack drew the five largest crowds of the year. Jack dominated the year of 1943 at Madison Square Garden, procuring the largest gates and attendance.

Beau Defeats "Lulu" Costantino

It was time to kick off another year. In his first contest of 1944, Beau was matched in a ten-round non-title fight with Charley "Lulu" Costantino (1923–1981) of Queens, New York. Costantino boasted a professional record of 89 victories and only 6 losses. At 22 years of age, Lulu was quick, agile, had a good left hand, and was clever inside the ring. Although a light puncher, his speed and footwork made it difficult for his opponents to catch him. Costantino was a good scrapper but probably could have been even better if he hadn't fought such a demanding schedule, averaging one match every two weeks for the last two years. To prepare for the bout, both athletes trained alongside each other at Stillman's Gym. Standing at the same height, Beau had a three-pound weight advantage at 139 pounds. On fight night the odds-makers had Beau as a 3–1 favorite.

Entering the Garden ring on January 7, the boxers were greeted by 14,878 thunderous fans who paid a gate of $43,161 to witness the contest. In the early rounds, Costantino, using his speed and agility, danced around Beau, landing left jabs while evading most of Beau's punches. In the fifth round, Jack threw a wild right that missed Costantino and left Beau standing at the ropes, "looking dopily over the heads [of] the spectators with the grinning Lulu patiently waiting behind him."[6]

Continuing to dance in reverse, Lulu avoided many of Beau's punches. However, in the eighth round, Beau leaped in and connected a smashing hook to Costantino's head. Then in the tenth round, when LuLu made the mistake of standing toe to toe with the champion, Beau landed a booming right to his jaw, knocking out a tooth.

At the end of the match, Referee Eddie Joseph implausibly scored the bout eight rounds to two for Costantino. Judges Marty Monroe and Bob Cunningham scored the fight five rounds for Beau, four rounds for Costantino, and one even. By a slim margin, Beau won a split decision. Most sportswriters present, on the other hand, thought Beau had won by a decisive margin. The United Press scorecard gave seven rounds to Beau, two for Costantino and one even. Chick Wergeles was so upset, he was screaming at Eddie Joseph, "we wuz robbed." Enraged, Chick threatened to withdraw Beau from his upcoming bout with Sammy Angott unless the NYSAC assured Beau "protection." Later, Wergeles disclosed it wasn't Referee Joseph's honesty that he was concerned about, it was his incompetence.

Because of his disparaging outburst, the NYSAC required Chick's attendance before them on Tuesday, January 11. Somewhat surprisingly, the newest member of the three-person Commission, Dr. Clilan Powell, upheld Chick's charge that Joseph was incompetent. Following the hearing, the Commission merely reprimanded Wergeles for his initial statement about Joseph while admonishing him that they could have fined him $5,000 or suspended him.

Beau Battles NBA Lightweight Champ Sammy Angott

Several weeks later, Beau ultimately faced off in a ten-round non-title welterweight duel against the NBA lightweight champion Sammy Angott (1915–1980). Born Salvatore Engotti, Angott, at 29 years of age, had a professional record of 73–18–5, a two-inch height advantage over Jack, and the NBA championship belt. Beau, on the other hand, was seven years younger at 22 years of age, had a record of 57–8–2, and held the New York championship belt. Both Angott and Beau completed their prefight preparations at Stillman's Gym. Beau sparred six rounds with Johnny Abbott and Jackie Lemos. Angott sparred three rounds with Charley Howard. Standing on the scales at the pre-fight weigh-in, Angott weighed 140 pounds to Jack's 138 pounds.

Before the clash between titleholders, there was a consideration among various boxing commissioners to declare the winner as the undisputed lightweight champion. NBA President Abe Greene recommended that the winner of the Jack-Angott bout be declared the undisputed champion, but Major Gen. John J. Phelan, Chairman of the NYSAC, rejected the plan, explaining that unlike a title bout, this was a ten-round affair. Furthermore, both fighters weighed in over the lightweight limit of 135 pounds. The two sanctioning bodies along with the managers for Beau Jack, Bob Montgomery, and Sammy Angott did, however, devise a plan to untangle the title bedlam. They acceded that the winner of the upcoming Jack–Montgomery bout would be paired against Sammy Angott to determine the unified lightweight championship, with the match to take place on May 26.

The long-awaited battle between Jack and Angott finally occurred on January 28. Madison Square Garden was sold out with a deafening crowd of 19,113 fans on hand, producing a gate of $84,870. Excitement filled the arena as the two titleholders progressed down the aisles to the ring. The nontitle affair would determine which combatant would be crowned the unofficial, undisputed lightweight champion of the world. Featured on Gillette's Cavalcade of Sports, the match was broadcast from ringside around the country.

Beau was a 7–5 favorite, but a close fight was anticipated from the brown-haired Italian fighter from Washington, Pennsylvania. "Slammin'" Sammy possessed deceiving speed and excellent ring skills. Both men employed unorthodox styles. Beau pursued his adversaries with continuous motion, constantly throwing punches. Recently, he strengthened his cache with a deceptive right-hand bolo punch that he swung from the floor. Angott, on the other hand, plunged in at his opponents mauling at them from all angles, and using his clutch to tie them up before pounding them on the release. Much to the delight of the crowd, both set a blistering pace.

After Referee Frankie Fullam went over his final instructions, the champions went back to their respective corners for the opening bell. As the fight began, Angott moved ahead early, winning the first three rounds by out-boxing Beau. Forcing the combat, he was exceptionally productive at close quarters. Nevertheless, Beau rocked Sammy with a stunning left hook to the head in the second round and smashed some enormous right bolo uppercuts on his chin. It was a bitterly contested see-saw battle. True to form, Sammy's tactic of clutching Beau with one arm and hitting him with the other proved detrimental to Jack; whereas Beau scored by throwing right hands to Sammy's body and crown. Contrary to his critics, on several occasions, Beau displayed sharp boxing skills as he out-jabbed Angott. Beau took the fourth stanza and staggered Angott with a powerful right to his face before the bell.

The two fought evenly in the fifth round, but Beau took the sixth and seventh. Midway into the sixth, Beau crashed a right uppercut to Sammy's chin. Sammy grinned back, as he did every time he was hurt by a punch. Later in the round, Jack apparently slammed a blow on Sammy's groin, causing Sammy to agonize with pain. After the fight, Sammy disclosed that six days earlier, he injured his thigh in training when his sparring partner plunged his head into his thigh. Beau had an exhilarating ninth round when he banged seven vicious rights to Sammy's crown, leaving Angott shaken and goggle-eyed. The last round was reasonably even as both men appeared to run out of gas.

When the scorecards were tallied, the match was ultimately declared a draw. Neither fighter, however, seemed visibly upset at the decision. Referee Frankie Fullam scored the fight five rounds for each Beau and Angott. Judge Marty Monroe had Beau winning six rounds and Sammy four. Judge Charley Draycott scored the bout in favor of Sammy, with Angott winning seven rounds to Beau's three rounds. The United Press card had the fight even with four rounds going to each fighter and two rounds even.

A noteworthy aspect was the respect the fighters showed each other. During the contest, both fighters displayed virtuous sportsmanship, handshaking and bowing to each other, to the extent some people in the gallery yelled for them to kiss and make up. Interestingly, Ted Yates of the *New York Age* compared Beau to what Anthony O. Edmonds referred to as the "docile childlike" good Negro. Yates wrote that Beau, "showed signs of still being under the yoke of a southern cracker," because he bowed to Angott often during their bout.[7] Of course, the reference implied that he was still under the control of wealthy white men or former slave owners.

Beau Faces Maxie Berger in Cleveland

The draw with Angott was a disappointment for Beau, but he still wore the lightweight crown. Before facing off with Bob Montgomery for the third time, Beau had another challenger to battle. Beau faced Maxie Berger (1917–2000) in a welterweight bout at Cleveland's Public Auditorium on Tuesday, February 15. Constructed in 1922, the Public Auditorium had a seating capacity of 11,500. With significant space available for conventions, it contributed to Cleveland in becoming a preeminent national convention center.

Berger had a record of 89–16–8 and was on a 13-fight win streak. Nevertheless, he was still a two to one underdog. Maxie was a good puncher, clever boxer, and demonstrated fast footwork. Irritated with the pre-fight press, the 27-year-old Canadian welterweight grudgingly said, "It kind of looks like I'm the forgotten man here. To read all the headlines a person might think Jack was going into that ring by himself."[8] Needless to say, Chick Wergeles was a master at promoting his boxer in the press. A crowd of 8,206 boxing fans gathered for the contest, producing a gate of $30,040 with 10 percent of the gate reserved for the National Infantile Paralysis Fund.

Maxie came into the ring almost five pounds heavier than Jack, weighing 143¾ pounds, and standing two and a half inches taller at 5'8". Unfortunately for Maxie, it didn't provide him with any meaningful advantage. Jack snatched control of the fight from the opening bell, diving in with left hooks, followed by staggering rights. By the end of the first round, Beau had inflicted significant damage to his foe. He belted Berger with four solid left hooks, opening a gash over his left eye. As blood oozed out above Maxie's left eyebrow, Jack peppered his prey with stiff left hooks followed by right uppercuts. Stalking his victim around the ring, Beau bounced in, ripping left hooks bolstered by stunning right uppercuts. Berger desperately tried to slow Beau with counter punches but to no avail.

Boos rang down when Referee Joe Sedley warned Beau about low blows in the third round but didn't penalize him. Jack just kept stalking his prey, connecting with savage punches in the fourth round, pressuring Maxie into retreat. With his leaping, swinging attack, Beau continued to score but was penalized in the sixth stanza for a low blow. In the seventh round, Beau had the crowd on its feet when he knocked Berger to the canvas with a staggering right hook followed by a devastating right to the head. Berger rose up on the count of two and somehow managed to hang on until the bell sounded. In the eighth, Beau struck Berger with two hard rights followed by a left that nearly put Berger on the canvas again. In the ninth round, a hard left stunned Berger. Maxie tried to rally in the final round, but Beau simply outmaneuvered him. Beau won every round except the sixth, in which the referee deducted a point for a low blow. In an easy unanimous decision, Beau improved his record to 49–8–3, as he prepared to enter his fourth title match.

Several days before Beau's rematch with Montgomery, the fight took on more significance. The NYSAC and NBA announced an agreement, blessed by the fighters' managers, whereby the winner of the upcoming March 31 contest between Jack and Montgomery would meet Angott on May 26 for the undisputed lightweight championship. Then, Beau received the inevitable word from the Augusta Draft Board that he had been declared 1-A, ready for service. Therefore, Beau's match with Montgomery was quickly moved up to March 3, with the winner scheduled to meet Sammy Angott on March 24.

16

Beau vs. Montgomery III

The press was buzzing. There had not been a universal lightweight champion recognized by both commissions in over a year. Now, Beau Jack, the NYSAC champion, and Bob Montgomery were meeting in the Garden ring to earn the right to meet Sammy Angott, the NBA champion, for the undisputed title. In previous matches against Angott, Montgomery had suffered three defeats. Jack had fought to a draw.

Sammy Angott acquired both the NBA and NYSAC title on December 19, 1941, defeating the NYSAC champion, Lew Jenkins, by unanimous decision. He held the unified title until he retired and relinquished his titles on November 13, 1942. Just thirty-two days later, however, Sammy announced his return to boxing. During Angott's retirement, the NYSAC acknowledged Beau Jack as its lightweight champion when he defeated Tippy Larkin. The NBA title remained vacant. Subsequently, the NBA declared that the winner of Sammy Angott's bout with Luther "Slugger" White on October 27, 1943, would be proclaimed the champion of its vacant lightweight title. Angott scored a unanimous decision over White, once again becoming the NBA lightweight champ.

On March 3, 1944, for the third time in less than ten months, Beau squared off with "Bobcat" Bob Montgomery. Beau won the title on December 18, 1942, when he defeated Tippy Larkin. Montgomery took it away from him six months later when he conquered Jack on May 21, 1943, only to lose it back to Beau six months later. Quite a rivalry had erupted between the two.

Since losing the title to Beau four months earlier, Montgomery had earned victories over Joey Peralta and Ike Williams. Unexpectedly, in his last fight, two weeks earlier, he was knocked out within sixty-three seconds of the first round by welterweight Al "Bummy" Davis, a four to one underdog. It was the first time in Montgomery's career that he had been stopped. Monty assured the critics that he had learned his lesson from his last bout with Davis and was prepared to regain the lightweight title from Beau Jack.

One day last November I was lightweight champion of the world. The next day I wasn't. A few weeks ago I knocked out Ike Williams in Philadelphia and was red hot. In my very next fight, against Davis, I was caught cold. That's the way it goes.

I don't expect to make any mistakes against Beau Jack and I know my best will be good enough to win back the title. The Davis fight really taught me a lesson and I won't be caught like that again. In fact I learned a lot when I lost the title to Beau Jack last fall and I will know what to look for this time.[1]

Montgomery was anxious to meet Beau for the third time, determined to once again take Jack's title.

Since regaining the title from Montgomery, Beau won a close battle with Lulu Costantino, fought NBA champion Sammy Angott to a draw, and easily defeated Maxie Berger. Primarily due to Davis' sensational knockout of Montgomery two weeks earlier, Beau came into the fight as an eight to five favorite.

Unexpectedly, a bombshell dropped at the pre-fight weigh-in when Montgomery didn't make weight, coming in four ounces over the 135-pound limit. Adamantly, Chick Wergeles protested Monty's weight, demanding the $1,500 forfeit. William Brush, of the Department of Weights & Measures, tried to justify the discrepancy, asserting that the crowd gathered around the scales at the weigh-in could create enough pressure to explain the deviation. Chick didn't buy it. He declared that Jack would fight, but the title would not be on the line. Fortitude set in for Monty. He began running around and jumping rope. Three more times he stepped on the scales with no luck. Finally, on the fourth attempt, he took a deep breath before he stepped on the scales and somehow managed to clear the contracted weight.

Mike Jacobs was happy on fight night. Fans flocked to see Beau and Bob in their third title bout, producing the largest gate—$111,954—at Madison Square Garden since Beau fought Henry Armstrong eleven months earlier. With temperatures hovering around 40 degrees, over 19,066 fans packed the Garden to witness the third war between Jack and Montgomery.

The third contest was a vicious 15-round clash. As the opening bell sounded, Beau instantly swarmed Montgomery with left hooks and bolo uppercuts to his head, as well as looping rights to his body. A hard right to the jaw backed Monty into the ropes. After enduring Beau's onslaught, Montgomery and Jack ripped each other's heads with uppercuts. Fighting toe to toe as the bell rang, the two had to be separated by Referee Young Otto. Beau was eager to score a knockout in the first round, like the one recorded by Al "Bummy" Davis two weeks earlier. Unfortunately, his strategy did not work. Monty began to control the fight with long right crosses to Beau's temple and hard blows to his midsection, winning the second and third rounds. Beau fought back with left jabs and right crosses, but Monty backed the champion into the ropes three times in the third. With Jack on the ropes, Bob smacked him with two solid rights to the jaw, stunning the champion.

As the two traded punches in the fourth, Bob sizzled a hard right to Beau's chin, forcing him into the ropes once again. Against the ropes, Beau managed to counter Monty with body shots to even the scoring in the round. Monty won the fifth stanza by a slim margin, dazing Beau with a hard right as the round began. In the sixth round, Monty pushed Beau into the ropes once again and whaled away at his head and body for almost two minutes. Monty caught the champion with a stiff left hook and right to the chin, then pelted Jack's stomach. Bob must have thrown 100 punches in the sixth, but the punch volume left Monty sluggish at the bell. Beau fainted a grin at Bob and scampered over to his corner. Bob recovered quickly and in the seventh, again landed rights to Beau's midsection, while Beau battered Montgomery with his infighting. As the round came to a close, Bob caught Jack with a right to the jaw and then another right after the bell, staggering the champ. Viciously, Monty came out in the eighth round with a full head of steam looking for a knockout, but Beau cleverly bounced around the ring, avoiding most of Montgomery's punches. Nevertheless, Monty landed enough to win the round.

As the fight continued, Montgomery's furious pace began to take its toll on him. Taking advantage of the noticeably slower Montgomery, Beau won the next two rounds. They wrestled along the ropes in the ninth, and their heads momentarily went through the ropes. In the tenth, Beau landed a barrage of vicious left hooks to the challenger's jaw without answer, producing blood from Bob's mouth. Then Beau smashed a looping right to Montgomery's midsection, leaving Monty holding on for dear life. Beau kept up his attack in the next three rounds over a waning Montgomery. In the twelfth, Beau drove Montgomery back with a left hook to the jaw. Despite Beau's persistent aggressiveness, the eleventh and twelfth rounds were scored even. Remarkably, Montgomery somehow regained enough energy and recovered sufficiently to win the thirteenth round, but Beau belted him with several hard blows below the heart and stole the fourteenth round. Montgomery earned the final stanza with a tumultuous finishing effort, hurting Beau with two stiff rights to the body.

At the end of fifteenth rounds, the decision went to the scorecards. Anticipation filled the arena as many of the rounds were so close it was virtually impossible to score a winner. When the scorecards were announced, Referee Young Otto awarded the contest to Montgomery, scoring eight rounds for Bob, six for Jack, and one even. Judge Marty Monroe awarded the victory to Beau, giving Jack eight rounds to Montgomery's seven. Sealing a victory for Montgomery, Judge Bill Healy saw the match like Otto, scoring the bout in Montgomery's favor. By a close split decision victory, Beau lost the lightweight title to Bob Montgomery a second time.

In his dressing room after the fight, Montgomery explained his successful pre-fight strategy. "I went into the fight "'hot," not "cold"" to avoid the possibility of another knockout," explained Montgomery.[2] Shadowboxing 10 rounds in his dressing room prior to the fight ensured that he came into the ring "hot." For his efforts, Jack received $30,000 in his loss. Montgomery, on the other hand, received $25,000, the NYSAC title and the right to face Sammy Angott, the NBA lightweight champion, for the undisputed title.

The next day, Montgomery left with his wife and son for Hot Springs, Arkansas to get some much-needed rest. Although he had earned the right to meet Angott for the undisputed lightweight championship, the bout did not happen. Sammy Angott lost the NBA crown to Juan Zurita of Mexico City a week after Montgomery beat Jack. Zurita defeated Angott in a fifteen-round duel in Hollywood, California on March 8. Even though the title was no longer on the line, Angott still aspired to fight Montgomery, but Bob's manager Frankie Thomas announced that Bob was exhausted from his last three bouts and couldn't be ready for a date with Angott. After examining Montgomery, the NYSAC accepted Bob's refusal.

The week following his loss to Montgomery, Jack traveled 240 miles northwest to Utica, New York, to show his appreciation and spend time with several groups of U.S. troops. In the afternoon he visited wounded soldiers at Rhoads General Hospital. Later that evening, he put on an exhibition with his sparring partner, Baby Beau Jack, for the soldiers at Rome Army Air Field.

Hoping for a big payday, on March 10, George Parnasus, the manager of the new NBA lightweight champion, Juan Zurita, announced that Zurita would meet Beau Jack in an overweight non-title bout at Madison Square Garden on March 31. It was bound to be a highly exciting matchup with a lot of powerful slugging. Before tackling Zurita, however, Beau first had to face Al "Bummy" Davis.

On St. Patrick's Day, Beau faced Al "Bummy" Davis (1920–1945), the "Brooklyn Bomber," in a welterweight match at the Garden. Davis, whose birth name was Albert Abraham Davidoff, grew up in the Jewish ghettos of Brownsville. He was a rough southpaw boxer. When he fought welterweight champion Fritzie Zivic on July 2, 1941, he was disqualified in the second round after repeatedly landing low blows. As a result, the NYSAC fined him $2,000 of his share of the purse and revoked his boxing license. It was not reinstated until September 1943, following Al's discharge from the Army.

Grantland Rice, in his weekly column, discussed Davis' power and upcoming contest with Beau. "Davis can punch and hurt," Rice wrote. "He is one of the few left around who can punch a lick."[3] Many predicted that Davis would knock Beau out. Just several weeks earlier, Davis knocked Montgomery out in the first round and a month earlier had knocked out Buster Beaupre in 98 seconds in the first round. Davis sported an impressive record of

55–7–4, with 36 victories by way of knockout. Davis also possessed a mean left hook.

Making his fourth appearance of 1944, Jack was already the Garden's number one gate attraction of the year. "No one has made the Garden turnstiles click like that," said *Wilkes-Barre* sportswriter Fritz Howell, "since heavyweight champ Joe Louis donned his khaki uniform."[4] Eager to witness the battle, more people packed Madison Square Garden for Beau's fight with Al Davis than did for his title match with Bob Montgomery. An enormous crowd of 19,963 spectators funneled through the turnstiles to see the Brooklyn Bomber and Beau Jack in a slugfest to benefit the Red Cross. So many fistic fans turned out, mounted police had to turn more than 10,000 fans away.

At fight time the weight differential between Davis and Jack was only 4½ pounds. Davis weighed 142½ pounds to 138 pounds for Beau and was one-half inch shorter. As expected, the first four rounds produced a spectacular "barroom" style brawl. Instead of his usual crouch and weaving style, Beau thrilled the crowd when he elected to slug it out with Davis. At the opening bell, Beau came out and landed a left jab to Davis' face followed by a left hook to his head. Davis returned the favor, landing a spectacular punch to Beau's head, stunning the "Georgia Windmill." With Beau in trouble, Davis tried to finish him off, bombarding Beau with wild power punches. Beau doggedly weathered the storm and just after the bell sounded landed a hard left to Davis' head.

Agitated by the late blow, Davis came out firing in the second round, scoring with left hooks to the body. Beau recalled, "I saw it coming, but I couldn't get out of the way. I was going down. I was leaning, leaning, ready to fall, but I came back and hit him with one, two, three, four, five, six, seven left hooks in a row. I saw him go back to his corner. I remember the look in his eyes. He couldn't believe it. I knew I had him then."[5] Beau retaliated and closed the second strong.

Beau took control of the contest in the third round. He quickly landed a series of left hooks to Al's head. Then Beau fell a vicious right to Davis' temple that sent him whirling across the ring. Jack charged toward the injured Davis, pounding him with left jabs. Only the ropes prevented Davis from going down. Sensing a knockout, the fans went crazy, making so much noise that no one could hear the closing bell. Beau kept up his attack with Davis on the ropes for at least three seconds after the bell rang. Davis had run out of juice but survived the round. Al almost went down again in the sixth round. After being rocked by a powerful left hook, Davis' gloves touched the canvas.

Beau was fighting perhaps his best fight to date and continued to accurately land his punches plummeting Davis. As the final bell sounded, Davis finally went down. Jack thumped Davis with a vicious left hook, dumping him backward on the canvas. With blood streaking his face red, Davis was bleeding from a gashed left brow and cuts inside the nose and mouth. So one-sided was the affair, that one judge, Joe Agnello, gave Beau all ten rounds. The other judge, Frank Forbes, gave Beau nine rounds and scored the remaining one even, and Referee Bill Cavanaugh awarded Beau nine rounds to one for Davis. A booming ovation rang down from the Garden rafters as Jack was awarded a unanimous decision.

The sellout crowd provided an outstanding purse of $132,823 of which Mike Jacobs and each fighter agreed that 10 percent of the gate would go to benefit the Red Cross. Four days after the fight, Beau proudly returned home to Augusta to present the local Red Cross a check for $3,378, 10 percent of his purse. He also gave $1,000 to the New York chapter of the Red Cross. Beau was a box office sensation. In his twelve main events at Madison Square Garden, Beau produced an amazing gate of $947,477 or an average of $78,956 per bout.

Speaking to a young amateur years later, Beau expressed what it was like to be hit by Al Davis's power. "Son, you ever touched 'lectricity?" Beau asked. "That's what it felt like the night Al 'Bummy' Davis caught me with a left hook in the Garden. Felt like somebody just plugged me in. Saw 40 million stars. Then I shook it off. I was in shape, see. That was the key. Won the fight and had the whole Garden audience a standin' and a cheerin.'"[6]

Traumatically, Al Davis' career ended the following year. Davis was shot to death outside a Brooklyn tavern, a victim of an armed robbery. While having a beer with a couple of friends, four armed hoodlums known as "The Flatbush Cowboys" walked in to pull off a heist. Davis reacted quickly, knocking one of them down. When Davis attempted to stop the other three men, one of them pulled out a gun and fatally shot Davis in the chest. With a professional record of 65–10–4, with 46 of his victories coming by way of knockout, Davis was dead at the young age of 25.

The surprising rise of Beau Jack and the impact of his manager, Bowman Milligan, was the subject of Grantland Rice's "Sportlight" column following the Davis fight. "The former Georgia bootblack," penned Rice, "had easily surpassed the $900,000 mark as a drawing card thanks in large part to Bowman Milligan."[7] Rice described Beau's rags to riches story, comparing him to the great 19th century author Horatio Alger, Jr., who was famous for his tales of boys who rose from rags and poverty to wealth and fame. "When a ten-cents-a-shine colored kid from Georgia directed by a locker-room guardian, neither knowing anything of the fight game," Rice explained, "can move into the million dollar drawing class on short notice, we wonder how Horatio Alger ever got away with his puny 'Rags to Riches' yarns."[8] He credited Milligan with Beau's success.

> In this final summing up I must give Bowman Milligan, a quiet, honest, smart, able colored man most of the credit. Beau Jack, with all his gameness and his physical

qualities was largely physical. Bowman Milligan, through his complete honesty and his intelligence, plus his ability to handle his main job and his diplomatic capacity, was the directing force.

But back of it all there was honesty of effort, which is something the crowd sensed— plus enough ability to give honesty a chance to work.[9]

Beau Jack was a true rag to riches story. The honesty and integrity of Beau and his team were instrumental in building his enormous fan appeal.

On Friday night, March 31, the night before his 23rd birthday, Jack returned to the ring at Madison Square Garden for his third Garden contest in less than a month. History was made. It was the first time that a boxer ever appeared in three Garden main events within one month. The bout also marked Jack's 13th main event at the Garden.

In his landmark appearance, Beau confronted the switch-hitting curly, dark-haired, Juan Zurita (1917–2000), the new NBA lightweight champion, in a ten-round non-title bout. Juan won the Mexico featherweight and lightweight titles earlier in his career and touted a record of 125–21–1. Three weeks previously, Zurita captured the NBA lightweight title when he defeated Sammy Angott.

In one of the evening's preliminary bouts, Beau's stablemate from Augusta, Georgia, Frank Hardeman, aka "Baby Beau Jack," earned a decision over Bobby Henry of New York. Beau had brought Hardeman, a 17-year-old lightweight, with him when he returned from Augusta several months earlier. Hardeman, originally dubbed "Jack Rabbit," later changed his moniker to "Baby Beau Jack." During his career, he netted a record of 33–19–3.

A large crowd of 17,593, providing a gate of $87,802, greeted the warriors as they entered the ring. The bout was a thrilling skirmish with punches flying. Zurita's unorthodox southpaw style and his capacity to switch from a right to a left-hand stance seemed to trouble Beau. In fact, Juan won the first two rounds socking right jabs to Jack's bewildered face. The contest was tight, with Beau getting the better of Juan on the inside and Juan edging Beau when they punched from a distance. Beau hurt Zurita in the fourth round with right counters. When the stout Mexican threw a hard left at Beau's head, Beau bobbed to the side, causing Zurita to miss. Beau immediately seized the opening, countering back with two hard rights to Zurita's jaw.

Zurita got back on track in the fifth. He battered Beau into the ropes, forcing Beau's head through the top rope. Instead of pounding his trapped victim, Juan courteously stepped back, permitting Beau to reset himself. To complete his gesture of ring etiquette, Zurita raised his gloves together in the expectation that Beau would do the same and that they would tap gloves. Instead of tapping gloves, Beau smashed a right hook into Juan's belly. Driving Zurita across the ring, Beau thrashed him with body punches. Juan quickly faded until he got back on track in the eighth round.

JUAN ZURITA   1944   BEAU JACK

Beau Jack smashes a right on Zurita's jaw, March 31, 1944 (courtesy Bruce Kielty).

Juan was relentless in the final two rounds. His best round was in the ninth when he trapped Beau against the ropes again and landed a solid left to his midsection. Then Juan unleashed a barrage of punches at Beau's head with no return. Beau was hurt, but the tired Juan's punches didn't pack much power. Zurita outboxed Jack, handily winning the tenth round, but it was too late.

Jack won a unanimous decision. Referee Frank Fullam and both judges, Marty Monroe, and Jim Hagen, scored the bout in Beau's favor. The United Press scorecard similarly tallied Beau the winner, scoring seven rounds for Beau and three for Zurita. Hailing from Jalisco, Mexico, the birthplace of tequila and mariachi music, Zurita blamed his rowdy celebration following his victory over Sammy Angott. He admitted that he just hadn't had enough time to prepare for the fight after ten days celebrating his title victory over Angott in Mexico City.

With the evening's receipts, Beau's gates grossed over $300,000 in March alone. All in all, Beau had generated revenues totaling $1,035,279 in his 13 main event appearances at Madison Square Garden. The "Dixie Dynamo's" gates exceeded every other boxer except heavyweight champion Joe Louis.

The next day, Beau stopped by Mike Jacobs' Twentieth Century SC office to pick up his $25,000 "birthday" present. Then, he departed for his home in Augusta to unwind.

Plans were made to rematch Jack with Zurita in Mexico City, but the match was called off in the middle of April. There were also discussions about a fourth match between Beau and Montgomery, but before negotiations concluded, the draft called both men into service.

Juan Zurita held the NBA lightweight title until April of the next year when Ike Williams knocked him out in the second round before 35,000 spectators in Mexico City. Zurita finished his professional career with a record of 131–23–1.

PART V

Called to Service

"This is going to be the biggest fight of my life. I'm going to punch with both fists, just as I have in every fight."

—Beau Jack

17

Jack Selects the Army

Inevitably, Beau received his notice of selection by the Augusta Draft Board in April 1944. Fortunately, the service had not interfered with his climb to the pinnacle of the lightweight ranks. His pre-induction physical exam took place on Tuesday, April 18 at Fort Benning, Georgia. After passing his physical, Beau selected the Army as his branch of military service. Speaking passionately about the opportunity to serve his country, Beau proclaimed, "This is going to be the biggest fight of my life."[1] "I'm going to punch with both fists," Beau asserted, "just as I have in every fight."[2]

As was most of society during those days, segregation ran rampant in the Army. It was common for black men to be passed over for the draft, mainly in part of racist assumptions about their abilities. Although Congress passed an amendment to the Selective Service Act of 1940 prohibiting discrimination on account of race or color in the selection and training of men, the Army held on to its strict segregation policy. For instance, all draftees, irrespective of skin color, received notice of selection on the same day. Unlike white men, black draftees often had to wait several months before being called to report for induction, hurting those who had quit their jobs after receiving selection notices. The delay was blamed on inadequate facilities to house and train black draftees, leading to many black men being passed over for service. In an attempt to alleviate the differences, in 1943 a quota was imposed to ensure the number of black Americans drafted equaled their percentage of the population, or 10.6 percent. That helped, but the quota was never met.

While waiting to be inducted, Beau kept fit by plowing fields. Finally, on June 2, Beau was sworn into the Army. During basic training at Fort Benning, he studied education fundamentals and assisted as a physical education and boxing instructor. Interestingly, Dick Sadler, manager for George Foreman, served as an assistant boxing instructor under Jack.

After 12 weeks at Fort Benning's Special Training Unit (STU), Beau had obtained the equivalent of a fourth-grade education. Photographs of Beau writing and doing arithmetic at Fort Benning appeared in numerous newspapers around the country. Serving in the Second Company, First Battalion,

Beau Jack waiting for his pre-induction x-ray at Fort Benning, 1944 (U.S. Signal Corps and ACME Telephoto).

of the STU, Beau received high praise from his commanding officer and fellow soldiers.

Jack was just one of many American athletes that served during in World War II. Heavyweight champ Joe Louis enlisted in the Army in 1942. During his three years of service, he appeared in more than 90 boxing exhibitions and military installations around the world. For his service, he was awarded the "Legion of Merit." Allie Stolz served in the Coast Guard. Al "Bummy" Davis served in the Army. Light heavyweight champion Billy Conn, former heavyweight champion Jack Dempsey, lightweight champion Bob Montgomery, featherweight champion Willie Pep, and future middleweight/welterweight champion Sugar Ray Robinson, all served during World War II. Other athletes, such as Baseball Hall of Famers Warren Spahn, Joe DiMaggio, and Ted Williams; track and field star Archie Williams; and NFL Pro Bowler Johnny LuJack, also served their country during the war.

Calling for legislation to end Jim Crow laws, Orson Welles, the great American actor, director, and producer, was vehemently outspoken against racism.

That every man has a right to his own opinion is an American boast. But race hate isn't an opinion; it's a phobia. It isn't a viewpoint; race hate is a disease. In a people's world, the incurable racist has no rights. He must be deprived of influence in a people's government. He must be segregated as he himself would segregate the colored and Semitic peoples—as we now segregate the leprous and the insane.[3]

According to Welles, if hatred based on the color of a man's skin was not destroyed, then World War II would be meaningless.

18

The Great
"War Bonds Fight"

Not only was Beau called to service, but Bob Montgomery was sworn into the Army on the same day as Beau, June 2. While Jack was dispatched to Fort Benning, Montgomery was stationed at Keesler Field, Mississippi.

World War II was still raging since the United States joined the war following the bombing of Pearl Harbor on December 7, 1941. By 1943, the U.S. had turned Japanese forces back in the Pacific through the Battle of Midway and Guadalcanal. Germany was defeated at Stalingrad, and Allied forces took back North Africa. In early 1944, the Soviets finally broke through the 900-day Siege of Leningrad by Germany. Now, the focus was on taking back France from the Axis forces. On June 6, 1944, the Allies launched their D-Day attack on the beaches of Normandy to take back German-occupied France.

Money was needed to finance the United States' war efforts. Beginning on May 1, 1941, the U.S. government sold war bonds, or Series E bonds, to raise the necessary funds. Overseen by the War Finance Committee, the Series E bonds yielded 2.9 percent return on a ten-year maturity. Although below the market return rate, the purchase of war bonds aroused an emotional connection in American citizens, reminding them that they were helping their soldiers abroad and doing their patriotic duty by promoting democracy and liberty.

Through the War Advertising Council, a massive advertising campaign was conducted by both the government and private entities to encourage Americans to purchase bonds. Ads appeared on radio, television, and newspapers. Bond rallies were held across the country. Posters covered storefronts. Even Hollywood celebrities joined the campaign. Bette Davis, for example, sold $2,000,000 worth of bonds within a 48-hour period. Others donated memorabilia for auctions to raise funds. Movie theaters and sporting venues often offered free admission with the purchase of war bonds. Comic book heroes also joined the effort, promoting the purchase of bonds.

Sporting events were extraordinarily prolific in selling war bonds. For example, the *New York Journal-American* newspaper sponsored an All-Star War Bond game played on August 26, 1943, at the Polo Grounds in New York. The exhibition game featured members of the Baseball Hall of Fame, including Babe Ruth, Honus Wagner, and Walter Johnson. Attendance required the purchase of war bonds ranging from $18.75 to $1 million for one of the fifty front row boxes. Over 38,000 people attended, raising $800 million in war bonds.

The government was ingenious in staging events to sell war bonds. Stanley Oshan, head of the War Finance Committee, Special Events Subcommittee, was especially innovative. On June 26, 1944, the War Bonds Sports Committee presented a baseball game between the Brooklyn Dodgers, New York Yankees and New York Giants at the Polo Grounds in New York City. A brainchild of Oshan, the event was known as the tri-cornered baseball game. Each team came to bat six times in the same nine-inning game and alternated playing in the field. The Dodgers won the game with a final score of Dodgers 5, Yankees 1 and Giants 0. More importantly, the event raised $56,500,000 in war bond sales. All in all, over 85 million Americans purchased over $185.7 billion worth of war bonds during World War II.

Days after Beau and Montgomery were sworn into the Army, Stanley Oshan began floating the idea of a boxing match between Beau and Montgomery, with admission purchased through war bonds. When asked about fighting Montgomery in a war bonds bout, Beau quickly agreed. "I was so proud that I could do something for this great country," said Jack. "I said sure I'd fight Montgomery."[1] "It was for our country, the country we live in," he explained. "I felt I was doing something to help win the war."[2] Montgomery also enthusiastically agreed.

Jack and Montgomery had fought three incredible title bouts against each other within the last year. Montgomery won the first match, capturing Jack's lightweight belt. Six months later, Jack regained his crown, only to lose it again to Montgomery four months later. The paid attendance for their three fights averaged 18,592, producing total gates of $303,327. Moreover, Beau Jack had been the biggest draw at the Garden over the past year and a half with gates totaling $1,035,279. With admission to the upcoming bout requiring the purchase of war bonds, it was sure to be a triumph for the War Finance Committee. Initial estimates expected the bout to raise $50,000,000 in war bonds.

Planning for the bout began almost immediately. First, both fighters had to receive permission from their commanding officers. On Monday, July 10, Max Kase, chairman of the War Bond Sports Committee, confirmed that both Jack and Montgomery had received the necessary permissions. A week later, it was publicly announced that Beau Jack and Bob Montgomery would meet for the fourth time in a ten-round overweight bout at Madison Square Garden on August 4. "The meeting between Beau Jack and Bob Montgomery," exclaimed Stanley Osban, Treasury Department representative, "will produce a tremendous (and needed) boom in the sale of small War Bonds."[3]

The soldiers began training for the contest at their respective Army bases. Subsequently, Montgomery went to Philadelphia for intensive training and sparring, and both Bob and Beau finished their workouts at Stillman's Gym. Fort Benning's boxing instructor, Sgt. Bryant Bass, and Solomon Stewart of Providence, Rhode Island served as Beau's sparring partners to help him tune up for the fight.

On July 31, at a press conference with Nevil Ford, State Chairman of the War Finance Committee for New York, both fighters appeared in uniform to promote the bout. Four days later they would enter the ring against each other at the Garden in a ten-round exhibition sanctioned by the Army for the benefit of war bond sales. History would be made and needed funds would be raised.

In honor of their commitment to the war efforts, Jack and Montgomery agreed to fight each other for free. "While neither will get a [cent] for their labors," wrote Tommy Holmes of the *Brooklyn Daily Eagle*, "Beau and Montgomery will have one distinction—that of stuffing enough coin into Uncle Sam's Treasury—through war bonds of every denomination—to, at least, send the Nazis and the Japs into their lairs through air power."[4] Not only did Montgomery and Jack agree to contribute their efforts for the cause, but all the fighters, promoters, managers, referees and judges also acquiesced in donating their time and services. Promoter Mike Jacobs consented to handle promotional details with expenses paid by Gillette Safety Razor Co., which broadcast of the fight through the Gillette Cavalcade of Sports.

The fourth battle between former lightweight champion Beau Jack and the current lightweight champion, Bob Montgomery, was enthusiastically proclaimed the "War Bonds Fight." Fans had to purchase war bonds to gain admittance to the fight. Seats for the match ranged from $25 to $100,000. To reserve a ringside seat, fans had to purchase a $100,000 war bond. The $100,000 ticket price for one of the 72 ringside seats is the highest price ever charged for a sporting event in the United States. Today, accounting for inflation and cost of living increases, the ticket price of $100,000 is equivalent to $1,416,804.60. Sales for the event were sensational. Two days before the fight, over $13,000,000 in bonds had already been sold.

Hundreds of people purchased bonds and then nobly gave away their tickets to servicemen. The first three rows bought were turned over to wounded soldiers who had recently returned from the war. The day before the bout, the War Finance Committee made a marvelous announcement.

Officials of the War Finance Committee of the U.S. Treasury Department announced today that buyers, who had paid a total of $14,100,000 for bonds, had contributed these 260 seats to wounded veterans. There are 72 front row seats at $100,000 per

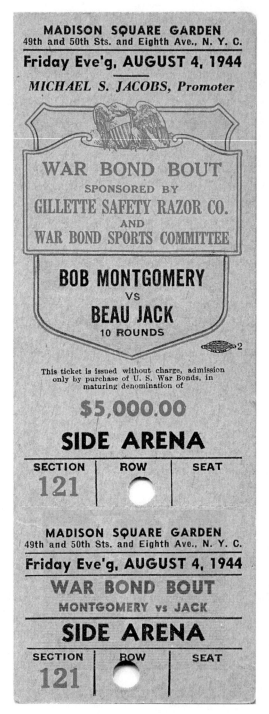

MADISON SQUARE GARDEN
49th and 50th Sts. and Eighth Ave., N. Y. C.

Friday Eve'g, AUGUST 4, 1944

MICHAEL S. JACOBS, Promoter

WAR BOND BOUT
SPONSORED BY
GILLETTE SAFETY RAZOR CO.
AND
WAR BOND SPORTS COMMITTEE

BOB MONTGOMERY
VS
BEAU JACK
10 ROUNDS

This ticket is issued without charge, admission only by purchase of U. S. War Bonds, in maturing denomination of

$5,000.00

SIDE ARENA

SECTION	ROW	SEAT
121		

MADISON SQUARE GARDEN
49th and 50th Sts. and Eighth Ave., N. Y. C.

Friday Eve'g, AUGUST 4, 1944

WAR BOND BOUT
MONTGOMERY vs JACK

SIDE ARENA

SECTION	ROW	SEAT
121		

seat; 88 second row seats at $50,000 per seat and 100 third row seats at $25,000 a piece. The men who have bought these seats, many of them famous first row "regulars" at all the fights, have consented to move back to seats from the fourth to the seventh rows so that the wounded veterans may have the foremost privileges at the fight.[5]

Practically all of the ringside seats purchased were transferred to wounded veterans. Even Bowman Milligan and Beau Jack each purchased $1,000 worth of bonds, leaving the tickets at the box office to be distributed among U.S. servicemen. Mike Jacobs also chipped in, buying forty-three bonds for distribution.

Record-breaking heat of 100 degrees and humidity greeted fans on fight day. Even though Montgomery's title was not on the line, interest in the fight was extremely high, given the tremendous battles fought between the two warriors in their previous meetings. Despite the heat, almost 16,000 patriotic spectators and wounded servicemen turned out.

Both men came in about three pounds heavier than their previous match. At the pre-fight weigh-in, Jack weighed 138¾ pounds. Montgomery weighed

War Bonds ticket for bout between Bob Montgomery and Beau Jack, 1944 (courtesy John DiSanto, Philly Boxing History Collection).

137½ pounds. Given his two previous victories, Montgomery was listed as a five to nine favorite.

With thunderous applause and enthusiasm from the animated audience, the opening bell sounded. Invigorated by the crowd, both combatants came out fighting fast and hard. Taking command quickly, Beau forced the fight over the notoriously slow-starting Montgomery. In the first round, he landed a flurry of lefts to Monty's midsection. Weaving and bobbing, Beau then mounted a left overhand attack, hammering Montgomery's head. Not to be outdone, Monty connected with a hard right to Jack's nose in the second round, producing a stream of blood. In the third stanza, Beau caught Montgomery with several looping lefts to his jaw that rattled the distressed champion. Throwing punches from all conceivable angles, Beau's blows were sharp and accurate, keeping the champion off balance for much of the night.

Soldiers filled the ringside section as well as the two rows behind it. Veterans of campaigns in Italy and Normandy, most of the honored soldiers had received Purple Hearts for their efforts. Many were even wearing their hospital robes. Sportswriter Bob Considine mingled with the injured veterans sitting ringside recording as much of their overwhelming enthusiasm as he could.

> "Yipee! What a hook!" yelled a toothless young vet with his left arm encased in a cast that bent the arm out and forward in the manner of a boxer delivering a left hook. He had forgotten all about his arm, and his shoulder, raked by machinegun fire in Italy.[6]

Repeatedly, the injured and mangled men sitting ringside told Considine that this was a night they would never forget.

In the fifth round, both fighters took a break and began clinching and wrestling on the ropes. Beau's blistering tempo began to catch up with him. As Bob came alive in the sixth, seventh, and eighth rounds, Beau began to tire from the rapid pace he established in the first five rounds. Monty's best stanza was the seventh round when he stung Beau, landing hard punches to his body after pinning him against the ropes. Sgt. Harold Hargens, one of the injured servicemen sitting ringside, exclaimed "What a punch!" after Beau landed a whistling uppercut on Monty's chin to fight his way off the ropes.

One dark night in England, planes flew over Sgt. Hargens, an Eighth Air Force engineer, and four other men from his company, dropping a 1,000-pound bomb within ten feet of them. Hargens, the recipient of a Purple Heart, painfully recalled, "Killed all the others, and I still don't know how I got off. Collapsed a lung and got my shoulder and leg, but that's all."[7]

Monty focused on Beau's body in the eighth round, giving Beau a terrible beating. After an even ninth, Beau called upon a measure of reserved energy to rebound and take the final round. When the scorecards were announced, Judge Frank Forbes scored the fight even, five rounds to five.

Judge Bill Healy scored six rounds for Beau, three for Montgomery and one even. Referee Billy Cavanaugh gave Beau six rounds, Montgomery two, and called two even. In one of his proudest moments and with fervor for his country, Beau evened his record against Montgomery with a split decision victory.

Their fourth match was the final meeting between Beau Jack and Bob Montgomery. They had now fought 55 rounds against each other. Each of their four contests went the distance, and there were no knockdowns. The total scoring tally for the 55 rounds was 78 rounds for Beau Jack, 77 for Bob Montgomery, and 10 even. Ironically, the favored fighter lost each bout.

The crowd, particularly the wounded veterans, loved the affair. In acknowledgment, the next day sportswriter Harold Conrad remarked, "[n]ever has there been, and probably never will there be as enthusiastic a fight crowd in the Garden as there was last night."[8] He also spoke about the joy it provided the veterans sitting ringside.

> One of these ringsiders was Lt. Ted Lawler, Fleet Air Arm of the British Navy. Ted lost both of his legs when his plane cracked up. One of Ted's prize moments for the rest of his life will probably be the ticket stub he clutched. "Think of it," he said as he displayed the wet, torn piece of cardboard. "Someone paid $100,000 for this seat. Just wait till I send this stub back to England and tell them I actually saw a fight in the great Madison Square Garden."[9]

It was an incredible evening, stirring the souls of those present with nationalistic pride and enthusiasm.

The "War Bonds Fight" set a monumental record, producing the richest gate in boxing history, with $35,864,900 in war bonds sold to benefit the United States' efforts in World War II. Adjusting for inflation, today that would be the equivalent of $508,135,552.16.[10] In all, over 15,822 bonds were bought. In an inspiring statement following the bout, Beau exclaimed, "That was for the country I live in. That was the proudest thing that could happen to me."[11] Montgomery said, "I'd like to fight him again—for nothing."[12]

Montgomery retired from boxing in 1950 with an overall professional record of 75–19–3. He wore the NYSAC lightweight world crown in 1943, and from 1944 to 1947. After retiring, Bob worked as a salesman and actively served his community working with street gangs in Philadelphia. Bob also managed to become Philadelphia's first black boxing promoter, staging his inaugural show at the Blue Horizon on October 5, 1971. "Bobcat" Bob Montgomery was inducted into the International Boxing Hall of Fame in 1995.

Both fighters received resounding praise for their efforts. Perhaps the most meaningful praise bestowed upon Beau came in the form of a letter from his commanding officer at Fort Benning, Brigadier General William H. Hobson.

Dear Pvt. Walker:

It has been a great source of pride for me in telling others about our fine post, to be able to mention you, a boxing champion, in our midst.

Fort Benning has long been the training center for infantry leaders—leaders of men and soldiers. Before you came to our post you had already climbed the ladder to national fame and had been known to millions as a boxing champion in your own right.

You had become a champion in the ring and have now come to our great army post to embark upon your military training and win laurels in another field—that of the soldier.

While you have been assigned to the Reception Center only about two months, your attention to duty, your interest in your fellow man, and your desire to teach many of them the fundamentals of boxing have proved a great inspiration to many of our new-born soldiers in our Special Training Unit and the Reception Center. Although, as the newspapers say, you lost the world championship several months ago to Bob Montgomery, just recently you came back and won the decision over the champion.

The nation at large is indebted to you and Montgomery for being willing to participate in that non-title bout in Madison Square Garden which netted more than $35,000,000 in the sale of war bonds for the United States Treasury.

Your success in the ring and surely your success in the army should continue to be an inspiration to your colleagues, both in and out of uniform. Congratulations to you upon your splendid contribution to the current was effort and your prowess as a fighter.

Sincerely yours,

Brigadier General, U.S.A.,
WM. H. HOBSON
Commanding[13]

Brigadier General Hobson praised Beau for being an inspiration, his heart-felt concern for his fellow man, and his desire to teach. Moreover, he thanked both Jack and Montgomery for their willingness to freely participate in the "War Bonds Fight." Beau was honored. "I was only an ordinary soldier," declared Jack, "and that night at the Garden fans had to buy war bonds to see me fight. They bought $35,864,000 worth of them bonds. That's one memory I'm going to keep."[14] Beau considered it an honor to fight for his country.

In 1982, thirty-seven years after the "War Bonds Fight," Beau received a certificate of appreciation from the Treasury Department and a $100 savings bond for his undertaking. "Mr. Walker, we recognize you not only as a great boxer but as a great American," Treasury representative Charles Crownover said.[15] It was a small token of appreciation, but one that touched Beau deeply.

Beau was on top of the world as he went back to the Army, but Chick suffered tragedy in September. His wife Charlotte had been ill for some time, but on September 25, she was found dead in the cellar of their home. Ending her own suffering, she committed suicide at the age of 44, leaving behind her husband, four sons, and two daughters.

Beau cherished his time serving his country in the Army, especially when he had the opportunity to exhibit his boxing prowess. From time to time, Beau fought in boxing exhibitions with his friend and sparring mate, Sgt. Bryant Bass. On one occasion, he boxed before five hundred paratroopers who were about to head overseas. Afterward, he remarked about how they wrote him, expressing that they would always remember what he did for them. He inspired soldiers through his boxing and his sheer determination.

In November, Col. John P. Edgerly, commanding officer of the reception center at Fort Bragg, announced that Beau's time in the Army would soon be over due to physical disqualifications. Although undergoing treatment, Beau's knee that he had injured before the Ruffin bout was not healing correctly. Col. Edgerly's comments, however, were a little premature, as Beau would serve another ten months in the Army.

19

1944 Fighter of the Year

Boxing had a banner year in 1944, attracting more fans and producing greater gates than previous years. Mike Jacobs saw gross receipts grow from $1,135,228 in 1943 to $1,400,000 in 1944. Needless to say, the top income-producing boxer for the year was Beau Jack. His three fights in March alone attracted 56,622 spectators and receipts of $332,579.[1]

The year would end in spectacular fashion for the "Georgia Windmill." When *The Ring* magazine released its annual ratings on December 27, Beau was declared the Fighter of the Year from over 4,381 active professional boxers. Nat Fleischer, owner, and editor of *The Ring*, praised Beau's impact on boxing during 1944.

> Beau Jack, Dixie's praying pugilist, did most to keep boxing interest alive during the year, Fleischer says, because he "certainly was the standout figure in New York." For five bouts at Madison Square Garden as a civilian in 1944, he attracted gates totaling $460,610. This included the year's largest gate of $132,823 for his brawl with welterweight Al Davis. In addition, after entering the Army, he donated his services for a non-title war-bond bout with Champion Bob Montgomery in August. Bond sales totaled $35,864,900.[2]

At the annual dinner of the New York Boxing Writers on Wednesday, January 24, 1945, Fleischer presented Private Jack with a medal of merit as the boxer of the year. Within the year, Beau had fought in Madison Square Garden six times, attracting 106,423 boxing fans, an average of 17,739 per bout.

Jack was also honored for making the most significant contribution to boxing during 1944 by a prominent group of Atlanta business and professional men and women at the Club Poinciana in Atlanta on Saturday, January 13, 1945. A telegram from the *Atlanta Journal* was read.

> Beau Jack is a credit to boxing, to sportsmen, and to his race. May he never detour even the slightest from the honest, sincere road he has been trodding. Thousands of children the world over look to him as a model. God grant that he continue as an inspiration to them and as a token of clean sportsmanlike living for many, many years to come. As he swings incessantly in the ring may he continue to punch his way to success.[3]

Beau was a role model and a credit to sports around the world.

In early 1945, Jack received a pass from the Army to go home and see his brother, John Henry "JuJu Jack" fight at the Augusta Municipal Auditorium. Beau was enthusiastically introduced to the crowd and gave his younger brother a little advice. Apparently, the advice worked, as "JuJu" won a decision over Battling Green. Beau also refereed a four-round match between Chuck Kinney and Bob Linardo.

World War II was coming to an end. Germany surrendered unconditionally on May 7, 1945. A couple of months later, the U.S. dropped the atomic bomb on the Japanese city of Hiroshima. Three days later, on August 9, the U.S. dropped a second atomic bomb on Nagasaki. World War II ended a couple of weeks later, on September 2, 1945, with General MacArthur accepting the formal, unconditional surrender of Japan.

On Thursday, September 28, 1945, after fifteen months of service, Jack was discharged from the Army. One of his instructors remarked, "Beau Jack is sincere and takes all of his instructions in dead earnest. There is no wonder he was champ."[4] Commenting on his fast learning, Beau emphasized that he took his education on like he did his fighting. "You can just about lick anything you train hard enough for. I learned this as a fighter.... I prepare and train for my lessons like I would for a ring fight."[5] Jack was serious about training whether it was for fighting or learning.

20

Beau's Return
as a Welterweight

A week after his discharge from the Army, Jack was back training at Stillman's Gym, firmly resolved to gain another crown. Beau, however, had to deal with the weight he gained while in the Army. He weighed 150 pounds, 15 pounds over his normal boxing weight. Should he enter the welterweight ranks or should he try to slim down and pursue another lightweight title? Ultimately, Beau decided to turn his attention to the welterweight title.

Jack's trainer, Sid Bell, was pleased with Beau's growth during his time in the service. "The Army," Sid remarked, "did something for him. He's more responsive and confident."[1] "Beau," said Bell, "runs every morning and works out tirelessly. When he was on furlough from the Army he always headed to the gym to work out with the boys."[2] Bell also divulged that Beau had developed an authoritative, looping right-hand punch.

As usual, Chick Wergeles was on top of his game, plugging publicity for Beau as soon as he was discharged. Chick dramatically boasted "the Battler is back," explaining that he called Beau the "Battler" because he was always battling when he was in the ring. "We ain't afraid of anybody," Wergeles asserted with the typical boasting of a fight manager. "We've always fought them all as they come and never asked any questions."[3] Chick was happy to have his "million dollar" prizefighter back.

Ecstatic to resume boxing, Beau pledged to box with the same high level of fervor that he had before he entered the Army. At twenty-four years of age and with a record of 52–9–3, Jack was ready to resume his boxing career. In his first contest, Mike Jacobs was exuberant to have his money-maker back as well. He scheduled Beau to battle the winner of the November 9 match between Tony Janiro and Johnny Greco. Greco defeated Janiro, winning two of their three consecutive bouts. Afterward, however, Greco announced that he would not fight again in 1945, due to tax issues with Canada and the United States.

Determined to have his "million dollar" boxer back in the ring producing fat gates as he had before entering the Army, Jacobs scrambled to find a new opponent. Jacobs completed his task quickly, signing Willie Joyce (1917–1996) to meet Jack at Madison Square Garden in a ten-round welterweight battle. Having not fought in over a year, Beau trained strenuously for six weeks to prepare for his upcoming bout. As training camp came to a close, Sid Bell assertively boasted Beau was ready to go and was up for the challenge with Joyce.

Contrary to Beau, Joyce was one of the busiest fighters of 1945, having fought fifteen contests. They weren't pushover fights, either. Joyce defeated Morris Reif, Chalky Wright, Bobby Ruffin and Ike Williams (twice). From Gary, Indiana, 28-year-old Joyce sported an impressive record of 64–15–8. He was a formidable southpaw with a great jab and was in contention for a title fight with NBA champion Ike Williams.

Regardless of his ring rust, the bull-shouldered Georgia bootblack came into the December 14 contest as a two to one favorite over his adversary. Beau had dropped six pounds during training and weighed in at 144 pounds, 7½ pounds heavier than Joyce. Nonetheless, it was the heaviest Jack had tipped the scales in his career. Joyce weighed in at 137½ pounds and stood a half inch taller. Producing a gate of $70,071, 16,231 boisterous fans assembled to see Beau's first post–Army match, expecting a thriller.

Happy to be back in Madison Square Garden's ring and before the fans, Beau came out with reckless abandon at the opening bell, throwing leather from all directions. Joyce errantly tried to out-slug the "Dixie Dynamo" but to no avail. Beau, the aggressor throughout the fight, pounded a hook on Joyce's forehead, knocking him into the ropes. Joyce wasn't done yet. He came back to win the second round on points, effectively catching Beau as he rushed in with his left jab. Joyce again made the mistake of trying to brawl with Jack in the third round. Beau won the brawl, throwing his famous bolo punch and swinging from the hips with both fists, but Joyce did manage to open a gash above Beau's right eye.

Joyce changed his strategy in the fourth and put on a boxing clinic. He landed two powerful right counters and persistently utilized Beau's gashed right eye as target practice for his left jab while tenderizing Beau's stomach with hard rights. At the end of the fifth, Willie caught Beau with another stiff right to the jaw. Jack retaliated in the eighth round, landing a hard left hook on Joyce's chin, temporarily bashing him into a groggy daze. Immediately, Joyce began retreating to survive Beau's blitzkrieg. Beau, however, was too tired to finish his man off. Joyce rallied in the ninth and then stormed through the tenth round, hammering a fatigued Beau. The aggressor throughout the contest, Beau landed the harder punches, but Joyce landed more often. Willie also did not receive the battle scars as Beau did. Jack's face was puffed and he was bleeding from his forehead and mouth as the fight ended.

It was a challenging contest to score. When the scorecards were announced, Judges Jim Hagen and Frank Forbes each gave Beau seven rounds, and Joyce three. Referee Benny Leonard gave Jack seven, Joyce two, and called one round even. Beau won an easy unanimous decision. The animated crowd, on the other hand, enthralled by Joyce's final two rounds, thought he should have been awarded the decision. Dissatisfied, they raucously booed the decision for over five minutes. Press scorecards underscored the closeness of the match. The United Press scored the fight even with each fighter winning four rounds and scoring two rounds even. James P. Dawson of the *New York Times* scored the fight eight rounds to two in favor of Jack.

While not pleased with the decision, Joyce developed a deep respect for Jack. After his painful loss, Willie proclaimed, "Beau Jack is the greatest distance fighter I ever saw. He is like an express train; keeps coming all the time and never gives one a second's rest."[4] Joyce was not alone in his praise of Jack. Virtually every fighter that faced Beau Jack developed respect for him. A couple of weeks later, Beau would earn the respect of yet another opponent, Morris Reif.

Mike Jacobs scheduled his "million dollar fighter" to open the 1946 boxing season at Madison Square Garden. Southpaw Morris Reif (1923–2013), aka Isidor Reif, was Beau's opponent on January 4, 1946. Reif, "Brownsville's Blond Bomber," was a Jewish slugger known for his punching power, knocking out 16 of his 24 opponents since leaving the Navy. His left hook was particularly destructive. In his last fight, Morris knocked Vic Costa out in the first round with a short left to the jaw and boasted a 42–8–1 record. Jack's powerful adversary had a three-pound weight advantage, weighing 146½ pounds and stood at 5'7" tall.

Irrespective of Reif's power, Beau entered the ring as a heavy favorite. Sportswriter Tommy Holmes of the *Brooklyn Daily Eagle* critically explained that although Reif was a "beautifully built welterweight who hits like a heavyweight," he disappointingly moved around the ring like a slow heavyweight.[5] Morris did not have the quick feet of a typical welterweight. The Garden's "Golden Boy" fight produced a gate of $73,280 from the 14,871 pugilists who came to witness the action. The bout was also broadcast on Gillette's Cavalcade of Sports, ABC, and WKIP.

"Georgia's brown buzz-saw" was ready for the welterweight challenge. The competitors came out like wildcats raring to go. Morris looked good for the first minute, forcing the action with brutal left hooks to Beau's body and head, but Reif made a fatal mistake. Morris landed a low blow, hurting Beau. Beau became infuriated. Before the end of the round, Beau exacted revenge, knocking Reif down with a right hook to his jaw. Reif jumped back up after a one-count and rallied in the first part of the second round, stopping Beau's attack with left hooks to the ribs and liver. While Reif landed some respectable punches and hurt Beau with a savage left body hook, he lacked the enthusiasm to do any real harm. Every time Reif landed a meaningful blow, Jack came storming after him with every punch in his cache. Beau also ducked many of Reif's notorious left hooks, making him miss repeatedly. Jack "battered and badgered" Reif through the first three rounds.

In the fourth, Beau checked Morris with an imposing right to the chin and then a fierce right to his abdomen. Unfortunately for Reif, he was not quick enough to counter Beau's swarming attack. Not giving his man any rest, Beau followed up, banging his opponent with both fists, then throwing a grazing left hook to Reif's temple and an explosive right to his solar plexus to knock Reif out two minutes and one second into the fourth round.

Commentators were critical of Reif after the fight. "Reif's wallop and gameness just aren't enough," wrote Tommy Holmes, "when he is in there with a bit of class like Beau Jack."[6] Storied ring philosopher James Johnston summed it up well. "If Reif," said Johnston, "writes down 'boxer' as his occupation in his income tax report, he is liable to Federal prosecution. If he is a boxer, I am a wooden Chinaman."[7] Reif just kept walking straight into Beau's destructive force. Beau confessed afterward that he needed to knock Reif out quickly because he felt himself rapidly tiring.

Beau had now won both of his both of his post–Army bouts. No doubt, boxing fans were just as eager to see Jack in the ring after the Army as before. The combined attendance for his two matches was 31,102. Keeping "Uncle" Mike happy was the combined purses of $143,351.

Jack's 23rd bout in Madison Square Garden was on February 8 in a highly anticipated match against the hard-hitting Montreal welterweight "Jolting" Johnny Greco (1923–1954). The muscular, dark-haired Canadian began boxing at age seven, had a professional record of 46–6–3, and had won seven of his last nine bouts. The main criticism mounted against Greco was that he had been inconsistent throughout his career, thus, reluctantly earning the nickname "the elevator." As usual, both fighters trained for the bout at Stillman's Gym. Before the ring battle, promoter Mike Jacobs sweetened the pot, announcing that the winner would get a potential match with welterweight titleholder Marty Servo. Scaling 142 pounds to 145½ for Greco, Beau was a three to one favorite.

Irrespective of his newly earned nickname, Greco was prepared. As the opening bell sounded, both men came out punching hard, hoping to score a knockout. Using a vicious body assault, Greco backed Beau up, cornering him against the ropes, where he unleashed flurries of punches. "Bouncing" Beau dished out his own style of punishment in the second with quick lefts and a series of uppercuts to Greco's jaw, leaving the Canadian with blood oozing from his mouth. Striking constant hooks to the body and right hands to the head, Greco forced Beau to cover up in the third, as the two warriors battled back and forth on the ropes. Then Johnny slammed a thunderous right-hand punch to Beau's midsection, forcing Beau to clutch. After finding his range in the fifth, Beau began setting Greco up, flicking his left jab and then reeling off bolo punches, pounding his head and bloodying his nose. Johnny's bloody nose then became target practice for Jack's jabs. Beau also earned the sixth round by landing his famous right-hand bolo punch to Greco's chin. By the seventh round, it appeared that both fighters had run out of gas. The crowd even started booing as they yelled for more action. Nevertheless, Greco's stronger physical strength and Beau's superior physical condition made for a close fight. Mauling and pounding Beau with body shots, Greco managed to take the tenth round.

After ten rounds of action, the outcome went to the scorecards. Referee Rube Goldstein scored the fight five rounds for Jack, three rounds for Greco, and two even. Judge Frank Forbes called it five rounds for Greco, four rounds for Jack, and one even. Finally, Judge Marty Monroe saw the fight dead even at five rounds apiece. Announcer Harry Balogh announced the match a draw. It was the fourth draw for both fighters.

In his post-fight comments, a demoralized Greco claimed he injured his left hand in the third round. Beau, on the other hand, praised Greco's ability and strength. "Ah always do mah best," he said, "but Greco is a strong boy. Ah'm a good spoh't and however the judges call it is all right with me. Ah only hope we can put up a good fight in a return match."[8] The rematch would not happen for several months.

It was a spectacular night for Mike Jacobs. Although the gate of $148,152 was a little less than he predicted, it was the third-highest gate in the Garden's history, and a new indoor attendance record was set with 19,941 fistic fans cramming into the seats. Moreover, it was the highest gate for a non-heavyweight contest, with only two heavyweight bouts drawing a larger gate. It broke the previous record for non-heavyweights, set in Beau's fight with Al "Bummy" Davis, which topped out at $132,823. Ringside seats went for $20 each. In less than three months since his return to boxing, Jack had attracted a total of 51,043 fans and a combined gate of $291,503. He was a box office phenomenon.

Beau's fourth draw, however, raised concern on cauliflower row and in Beau's camp. Given that Jack ran out of gas in the seventh round, apprehension was expressed about his endurance. Chick Wergeles bluntly stated: "He wasn't quite right. He needs a rest."[9] Accordingly, the following day, Beau announced that he was going take a couple of months off to rest.

Back to Georgia went Beau. He would not fight again until the end of May, almost four months later, when he met Greco in a rematch. As usual, Jack and Bowman worked at the Augusta National Golf Club for the Masters Tournament held April 4-7. It was the first tournament following a three-year hiatus due to World War II. In a shocking upset, Herman Keiser won the Green Jacket by one shot over Ben Hogan.

Happily, Beau kept busy shining shoes and waiting on golfers at the clubhouse. Beau commented, "As long as I can get around on my feet, I'll be right here. This is where I love to be."[10] Bowman estimated that Beau shined over "2,000 pairs of brogans" during the Masters Tournament, including the shoes of Lord Byron Nelson. The golfers were excited as well as they conversed with Augusta's prizefighter. When he wasn't being beckoned into service, Beau snuck in some practice chipping on the golf course.

In the clubhouse, Jack enthralled members with his boxing narratives. Sometimes, they gave Beau a little advice. One of those members was Gene Tunney, former world heavyweight champion (1926–1928). "I was shining Mr. Gene Tunney's shoes last week and he told me something about my left jab." Beau said proudly. "He told me to keep it shorter, not to reach out so far with it."[11]

Before long Beau headed back north to prepare for his rematch with Johnny Greco, scheduled for May 31, 1946. Their previous bout had ended sluggishly, disappointing the fans. Maybe that was the reason the crowd of 11,407 was much smaller than predicted, producing a gate of only $66,922. Although "Money Bags" Jack was the favorite to take Greco all week, at fight time, he was an 11–10 underdog.

Similar to their last match, both fighters came out slugging. Greco opened the first round, charging across the ring at his foe and cornering Beau. Greco then hammered Beau against the ropes and attempted to take him down with a long right-hand punch. Astonishingly, Beau took everything "Jolting" Johnny threw at him. Once Greco subsided, Beau took over the reins, charging Greco and pounding him across the ring. With his windmill attack at full speed, Beau took the early rounds. However, by the fourth, Johnny's punishing body punches slowed Jack down. Greco's strategy seemed to be working, but Greco tired himself out and began to clutch. Jack punished the retreating Greco in the fifth and sixth with hard body shots.

The Montreal mauler had a better seventh when he was again able to reach Beau's body. However, in the eighth, Jack hurt Greco with a hard left hook to the jaw. As the final bell rang, the fight went to the scorecards. Unlike their last bout, this fight produced a decisive winner. Beau earned a unanimous decision, winning eight of ten rounds and emerging as a serious contender for the welterweight crown.

As in his first meeting with Greco, Beau's camp was again worried about his stamina. This marked the second fight that Beau waned midway through the contest. Many fistic commentators began to wonder whether Beau's best days were behind him.

Irrespectively, Chick Wergeles continued his publicity blitz, touting Jack in the media. When it was announced that Sugar Ray Robinson had suffered a broken hand and could not fight in his scheduled welterweight title match with the champion Marty Servo, Chick advocated for Jack to be substituted for Robinson. "What a bout that would be," exclaimed Chick. "It would have the fans jumping and howling their heads off. It would be gigantic, a natural. The boys are the same size—the same weight and the same height and everything. It would be the perfect match."[12] Of course, this would give Beau another title bout. However, the match between Robinson and Servo was rescheduled for August 1 and Chick's request was denied.

Next, Beau entered the ring at Griffith Stadium in Washington, D.C., to earn a decisive decision against a previous adversary. He met welterweight Sammy Angott for the second time on July 8, 1946. Angott was thirty-one years old and returning from his third loss to Sugar Ray Robinson. Both men weighed in at 145 pounds. Since their last meeting, Beau was 7–1–1, while Sammy was 5–5–1. A year and a half earlier, the two boxers fought to a draw. The outcome this time would be different. Beau gave Angott a brutal whipping.

Sammy Angott rushes Beau Jack through the ropes in the first round at Griffith Stadium, July 8, 1946. The referee is Marty Gallagher (ACME Telephoto).

Beau established the tone of the fight, whacking Angott with flurries of punches that sent the former lightweight champion to the canvas in the second and third rounds. The only bright spot for Angott was in the fourth round when he thumped Beau through the ropes. Beau jumped back in so quickly, however, no count was given. Having suffered repeated punishment from Beau's right hand, Angott quickly tired and was booed by the crowd for clinging on to and clutching Beau in the sixth. Not to be deterred, Jack threw several dozen looping rights, plastering Angott. Angott's only reaction was to complain that Beau hit him with kidney punches, but his appeal was to no avail. Moreover, similar to their first fight, Angott claimed he had suffered a hip injury from Beau's low punches. Angott refused to answer the bell for the seventh round. "My hip and leg feel paralyzed," argued Angott.[13] It was the first time in Angott's storied career that he was unable to finish a fight. Beau, on the other hand, scored his second KO since being discharged from the Army.

The crowd of 10,353 produced a gate of $41,028. Due to Angott's failure to come out in the seventh round, asserting hip and back injuries, the District of Columbia Boxing Commission initiated an investigation and held up Angott's purse, pending x-rays. The next day, however, the Commission released Angott's purse of $6,987.39. For his efforts, Beau received $10,869.28.

Abravaya the "Miracle Man"

Unbeknownst to many, Beau was still having trouble with his right knee. That is until he met Asher Abravaya, the fighters' "Miracle Man." Asher was knowledgeable in physiotherapy and had mended numerous "dislocated digits, sprained hands, twisted knees, turned ankles charley horses and various other ailments that beset fighters in training or battle."[14]

Jake LaMotta was one of Abravaya's previous success stories. Following an injury to his right hand, LaMotta, a number one middleweight contender, suffered persistent pain from even light punches. He kept his injury concealed but had visited doctors and chiropractors without success. After a seven-minute session with Asher, Jake astonishingly said his hand felt brand new. Asher worked with numerous other boxers at Bobby Gleason's gym in the Bronx, "healing" such boxers as Sugar Ray Robinson and Eddie "Red" Cameron. Interestingly, Bobby Gleason's real name was Peter Gagliardi, but he changed his name to appeal to Irish boxers and fans.

Beau needed Asher's magic touch. After suffering through undisclosed pain in his right leg for over a year, Beau decided to seek help from the "Miracle Man," meeting him at Gleason's gym. Similar to LaMotta, Jack had not found adequate relief from doctors. "For more than a year, I couldn't put all my weight on my right leg," disclosed Beau. "I didn't dare let anyone know but this was worrying me plenty. Doctors couldn't seem to help. One day that skinny Turk went to work on my leg and it hasn't bothered me since."[15] Following Abravaya's treatment, Beau pronounced his leg was fully healed. Beau's right knee, however, would cause him more trouble shortly.

In July, fight promoter Goldie Ahearn offered Beau a $15,000 guarantee to tangle with Bronx welterweight Danny Kapilow (1921–2010). Kapilow, a tough southpaw boxer, came in with an impressive 46–6–6 record. Although he lost his previous fight against Willie Joyce, it was a contentious outcome. The Associated Press actually scored Kapilow the victor, six rounds to four rounds. The offer was accepted, and the ten-round bout scheduled for Tuesday, August 19 at Griffith Stadium. Jack returned to Washington, D.C. for his second consecutive bout. Danny had a two-inch height advantage and weighed 145 pounds to Jack's 143¾ pounds.

A severe rainstorm accompanied by damaging wind arrived on Monday night before the fight. The weather was so terrible in the region, baseball games in Boston and New York were canceled. Nonetheless, the Kapilow bout went forward. Even though the inclement weather limited the crowd, 10,000 rain-drenched fans braved the weather to witness the clash.

After the fighters received the referee's instructions and touched gloves, Beau bounced out of his corner ready to battle. Aggressively and consistently, he scored his bolo punch, knocking the curly haired Kapilow down for a no count at the end of the sixth round. Beau controlled the action throughout the contest and bloodied Kapilow after opening a gash above his left eye. Jack emerged from the rain-soaked stadium with a unanimous decision.

Jack was moving up in the welterweight division, having won five of his six bouts. On top of the division sat Marty Servo, who rose to the top on February 1, 1946, by knocking out Freddie "Red" Cochrane. Unfortunately, Servo's title was taken away from him when he refused to defend his title against Sugar Ray Robinson. In Servo's last fight, a nontitle bout, Rocky Graziano knocked him out after battering Servo senseless. Marty Servo subsequently retired, vacating the welterweight title.

To fill the vacant title, the NYSAC requested two of the top welterweight contenders, Tippy Larkin or Beau Jack, to meet Walker Smith, Jr., aka Sugar Ray Robinson (1921–1989) in a title bout. Hailing from Vidalia, Georgia, the 5'11" Robinson boasted a 51–1–0 record, having beaten opposition such as Sammy Angott, Fritzie Zivic, Henry Armstrong, Jake LaMotta, and California Jackie Wilson. On September 26, the NYSAC wired Beau's manager Chick Wergeles and Tippy Larkin's manager to be ready to accept terms to battle Robinson within twenty-four hours. Commission Chairman Eddie Eagan told the managers that the Commission would award the vacant title to Robinson without a fight if neither one of them took the fight. "Failure on your part" to accept the match, Eagan told the managers, would lead the Commission to "take appropriate action by bestowing the championship on Robinson."[16]

Notwithstanding his eagerness to compete for another title, Jack refused to take the fight. As Chick explained in a statement to the Commission, Beau was not primed for such a battle. "After all, Jack has had a very limited experience as a welterweight," stated Wergeles. "He needs a few more bouts under his be[l]t in this class before he challenges Ray Robinson, who is conceded by all to be the top man in the welterweight division."[17] Instead, Chick, on behalf of Beau, requested Robinson be crowned as the champion of the vacant weight class. "Robinson long has been denied what really belongs to him," stated Chick, "and should be awarded the title without any further argument."[18] Tippy Larkin, the junior welterweight king, also turned down the fight. Eventually, the Commission found a taker in Tommy Bell, also managed by Chick Wergeles. Robinson defeated Bell on December 20 to become the new welterweight king.

Beau was back in the ring on October 22, 1946, at the Armory in Elizabeth, New Jersey, where he faced 22-year-old Buster Tyler, a virtually unknown fighter. Buster was born in Miami, Florida, but called Atlanta, Georgia, home. He had a record of 27–8–0 but had lost two of his last four fights. Beau was a five to one favorite and considered a leading contender for a shot at the welterweight title. A crowd of 3,100 assembled at the Armory to witness the fight, producing a gate of $7,600. It was the smallest crowd for a Beau Jack fight since he won his first title.

In the first session of the ten-round bout, it appeared both contestants were eager to brawl. However, with seconds left in the round, Beau connected with a right-hand bolo punch, sending Tyler spinning through the ropes. The bell tolled, ending the round before the count of three. Saved by the bell, Tyler was carried to his corner, where Pete Reilly, a second in his corner, administered oxygen to him from his portable oxygen tank. Revived, Tyler won the next five rounds with masterful boxing. Beau managed to put him down for a no count in the second round, but Tyler relied on speed and resourcefulness and won the round. He was simply out-boxing Beau.

Jack got back on track in the seventh round, and in the eighth, he smacked Tyler with a bolo punch, flooring him for a nine count. Clinching and holding, Tyler weathered the storm. Buster came back to win the ninth round and hold Jack even in the tenth. By the conclusion of the fight, Beau's left eye was virtually reduced to a slit due to swelling inflicted by Tyler's tenacious and effective right jabs.

Referee Paul Cavalier scored the fight five rounds for Tyler, three for Jack and two even. Beau was simply out-boxed and couldn't handle Buster's astonishing speed. In a huge upset, Tyler became a leading welterweight contender overnight. Following the fight, Tyler's manager Sammy Aaronson admitted, "Under old methods without the oxygen, Tyler couldn't have answered the next bell" for the second round.[19]

Although the fans and commentators were pleased with the decision, Chick Wergeles was irate. The next morning, he appealed to the New Jersey State Boxing Commission, requesting that they suspend referee Paul Cavalier for incompetence and implored them to reverse the decision. The appeal was turned down.

Beau was visibly upset and anxious to overcome his distressing defeat. His next opponent, Johnny Bratton of Chicago, appeared to be a good victim. The bout was scheduled for November 15 at Chicago Stadium. It was Beau's first match in Chicago. Opened in 1929 at the cost of $7 million, Chicago Stadium was the largest indoor arena in the world with seating for 25,000 spectators. It had already hosted three Democratic National Conventions and two Republican National Conventions. Chicago Stadium was also the site of the first NFL playoff game between the Chicago Bears and the Portsmouth Spartans.

Nineteen-year-old Bratton had secured the right to fight Beau by pulling off a major lightweight upset over Willie Joyce. However, Bratton hurt his right hand during the furious action in the third round of his bout with Joyce on October 31. Doctors expected Bratton to be out of action for at least a month. Thus, Willie Joyce, who lost the split decision to Bratton, was designated as Beau's opponent for the November 15 bout. Less than a year earlier, Beau had boxed his way to a unanimous decision over Joyce.

Beau arrived in Chicago on Monday, November 11 to begin preparations for the fight. Instead of getting off of the train at Union Station where reporters and photographers were eagerly waiting for him, Beau decided to dodge the press. He departed at Englewood Station, checked into his hotel, and went to the movies. Addressing the angry crowd at Union Station, Chick Wergeles simply said, "Get all the pictures of him you want tomorrow in Ringside loop gymnasium."[20]

Both combatants completed their preparations and sparring at Ringside Loop gymnasium. Jack looked impressive and was in excellent physical condition. His speed made Joyce look slow. Johnny Bratton, Beau's original opponent, sat in on one of Beau's sparring matches and expressed no respect for the former Georgia bootblack. "He's flatfooted and too wild. Joyce will hit him and any one Joyce can hit he will beat."[21]

The next day, as Beau engaged in his last sparring session with Gene Buffalo before the fight, Jack bounced off the ring ropes, twisting his left knee. His knee buckled, and he slipped and fell. The pain was so excruciating Beau had to be carried from the ring. Following x-rays of his knee, Dr. Mitchell Corbitt, the physician for Chicago Stadium, proclaimed that Beau had fractured his left kneecap. The injury would prove to be a pivotal point in Beau's career.

Beau was flown to New York, where he was admitted to Norwalk Hospital on November 15. Norwalk physician Dr. Ralph Padula was called on to perform the surgery. Twelve days later, as Beau was being discharged from the hospital, Dr. Padula announced that the operation had been "extremely successful" due to a new treatment he utilized, eliminating the necessity of using wiring. "Beau Jack," stated Dr. Padula, "should be able to resume training in January."[22] Beau went home to Augusta to rest. Beau's upcoming fight with Tony Janiro scheduled for January 3, 1947, was also postponed.

PART VI

Jack Breaks His Kneecap

Because what I got, no one can take but one man. And that's God. I don't want people to feel sorry for me as long as I keep going.

—Beau Jack

21

Stopped for the First Time

Beau came into 1947 heralded as the "million-dollar kid." Before Beau Jack, no boxer had ever drawn $1,000,000 at Madison Square Garden. Jack exceeded that amount with the $1,393,704 he had produced at the Garden to date. The year, however, did not start well for Beau. He suffered a devastating injury that led his Syndicate of support to terminate their backing and many commentators to predict that his boxing days were over.

Following a three-month layoff for his broken kneecap, Jack faced Tony Janiro (1927–1985) in his first fight of the year. Janiro was a 20-year-old baby-faced welterweight contender from Youngstown, Ohio. Tony earned the right to face Jack by defeating Tony Pellone. It was his 14th victory in a row and boosted his professional record to 55–3–0. Janiro possessed a respectable inside game and remarkable stamina. As a 16-year-old amateur, he was crowned the featherweight champion in the Chicago Golden Gloves tournament. Currently, he was ranked ninth in the welterweight division by *The Ring* magazine, six spots below Beau, who was ranked third.

The February 21, 1947, bout was crucial for both boxers. Anxiously, Beau wanted to silence the critics who rumored his productiveness as a fighter had declined at his post–Army weight of 147. For Janiro, it was his toughest test to date and a chance to become a serious contender for the welterweight crown.

Not only were Beau's critics expressing discouraging opinions in the news, one of numerous headlines the day before the fight stated, "Beau Jack Ordered to Feed Children." A court order had been issued against Beau's upcoming purse to provide child support for his six-year-old twin boys, Donald and Ronald, and his four-year-old son, George, who lived with their grandmother in New Rochelle, New York. Appearing before the Westchester Children's Court on Wednesday, February 19, Judge George Smyth ordered that $2,500 be withheld from Beau's purse for child support.

At least Beau received a little bit of good news at his pre-fight physical. Eager to satisfy the New York State Athletic Commission's doctors that his kneecap was mended, Beau humorously performed a little tap dance. Afterward, Dr. S. Sym Newman examined Beau's knee and declared it to be in tip-top shape for the bout. Despite having not fought in four months, losing to a virtual unknown in his last contest, and having fractured his left knee-cap several months earlier, Beau was a two-to-one favorite. The oddsmakers expected Jack's "wild and persistent head-attack" to overwhelm the young Janiro.

At the weigh-in, Janiro weighed 147¾ pounds, almost seven pounds heavier than Beau at 141 pounds. He also had the advantage of height, standing two inches taller than Beau. Jack entered the Garden ring desperately seeking a victory over the curly haired youngster from Youngstown, Ohio. He left in an ambulance.

The weather on fight night was awful. New York was suffering through its worst snowstorm in six years. Snow blanketed the east coast from the Carolinas to Maine. LaGuardia airport was closed down, and most roadways were impassable. The official snowfall during the storm measured 11.6 inches, but freezing winds created snowdrifts up to six feet deep. Nearly 60 people died from the deadly storm. Irrespective of the snow and a high temperature of 25 degrees, a rugged, enthusiastic crowd of 18,062 fight fans braved a foot of snow to trudge down to the Garden to see the bout, producing a gate of $98,053.

As predicted, in the first round, Beau baffled Janiro with swift left jabs and hooks to the head. Standing toe to toe in the second round, the two gladiators brawled for nearly two minutes. Janiro emerged from the duel with the advantage. He scored with quick one-two punches to Beau's cranium, driving Beau to the ropes, where he unleashed lefts and rights to Beau's jaw and torso. Employing his vicious attack, Janiro knocked Beau halfway through the ropes as he hammered him with straight jabs and hooks. Jack retaliated in the third round, scoring equally with Tony, but Janiro's confidence continued to grow.

In the fourth round, Janiro drove Beau into the corner. Beau attempted to counter with a left hook but missed, providing Janiro the opening he needed. Janiro seized the moment and floored Jack with a hard-left hook to the head. As Beau fell to the floor, he by some means succeeded in grabbing onto the bottom ring rope. Bouncing on the rope, Beau began to pull himself up after a seven-count as Referee Eddie Joseph reached down to help him. Everyone thought Joseph had counted Beau out, and the lights were even turned on in the Garden, but after Beau regained his footing, Joseph motioned for the fight to continue.

With his wounded prey in sight, Janiro rushed in with the smell of victory. As Beau endeavored to counter with a left hook, his foot caught something loose in the canvas, causing his left knee to crumble with a terrible, deafening pop, dropping him to the canvas. Sitting in the middle of the ring, Beau tried to shove his kneecap back into place. By some miraculous means, Beau braced himself on his right foot and managed to stand upright on one leg. Exasperated, he then tried to hop by the referee, as he begged with him to let him continue. In a pain-strangled voice, Beau pleaded, "please, please" as Frank Jacobs, Janiro's manager, and Joseph tried to help Beau to his corner.[1]

Sitting ringside, sportswriter and future inductee to the International Boxing Hall of Fame, Jimmy Cannon (1909–1973) put into words Beau's undying strength and spirit. "The referee stepped in front of him," wrote Cannon. "But Beau Jack pushed at the gray shirt, trying to get at Janiro, maimed and sickened by pain, but still a fighter. The referee held him up, and Beau Jack wept, because he still had a leg to fight on, and that is all a prize fighter needs."[2] Following a quick examination, Dr. Vincent Nardiello, the NYSAC's physician, proclaimed that Beau's left kneecap was broken. Just three months after his initial injury, Jack broke his kneecap again.

For the very first time in his stellar career, Jack had been stopped. As he was carried out of the ring on a stretcher, the awestruck crowd, acknowledging Jack's incredible courage, gave him one of the greatest ovations of his career. It was a heartbreaking scene. Grown men cried at the sight of Beau being carried out on a stretcher. Larry Kent, one of Jack's trainers, was touched with admiration. "It was," Kent said, "the greatest display of courage I ever saw."[3] Even Frank Sinatra cried while visiting Beau in his dressing room.

As he lay in his dressing room waiting for the ambulance to take him to the hospital, Beau weakly grinned and held up a fist for reporters, wittily pronouncing, "The hands are good, but the knee's bad."[4]

Experts and commentators predicted that the Georgia shoeshine boy had fought his last fight. Newspaper headlines the day after the fight agreed.

"BEAU JACK BEATEN; RING CAREER ENDS"[5]
"Beau Jack Ends Fistic Career"[6]
"Beau Jack's Career Seen Ended, Knee Gives Way, TKO Loser"[7]

A return to boxing appeared extremely unlikely. Even if Beau somehow mounted a comeback, it seemed highly doubtful that he would ever be the boxer he was before the repeated injuries.

The following day, Beau underwent knee surgery at St. Clare's Hospital. Operating together, Dr. Vincent Nardiello and Dr. William Healy set the fractured kneecap in place and alleviated a ruptured muscle running near Beau's knee. Following surgery, Dr. Nardiello predicted that Beau would be out of ring action for ten months to a year.

While in the hospital, a downhearted Beau received a special visitor. "Do you remember me?" the young man asked. "I'm afraid I don't," responded Jack. It just so happened that Beau had chatted with the young lad when he was visiting a military hospital during his service with the Army. The young veteran said, "Both my legs had been shot up—they were in casts, like one of yours is now—and I told you I'd never walk again. You just laughed and said

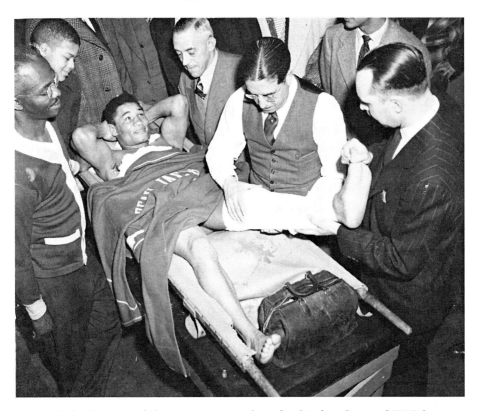

Beau Jack taken out of the ring on a stretcher after his fourth-round TKO loss to Tony Janiro, February 21, 1947 (International News).

that if I really wanted to walk, I would, and that you'd be giving me boxing lessons someday—well, I'm ready for those lessons now."[8] Beau chuckled as he responded, "Guess I can't disappoint you. So, I'll just have to get well!"[9]

Although scant words were spoken about it, it was subsequently learned that Jack entered the ring that night against doctor's orders. Evidently, his management team thought he could do quick work of Janiro before further injuring his leg, but regrettably, it didn't happen that way. A journalist for *Time* magazine critically wrote, "Had the promoters, anxious to cash in on a good thing, killed the golden goose? Oh, no, said one doctor; Beau could be patched up once more, in 'ten months to a year, if no complications develop.'"[10]

Seemingly, even the Syndicate supporting Beau Jack dissolved after the fight on the belief that his career was over. Moreover, Beau's longtime friend, manager, and former guardian, Bowman Milligan, left Beau and the boxing world behind. Bowman became a special sales promotion representative for Frankfort Distillers Corporation, handling their Four Roses, Hunter, and Paul Jones brands. Years later, Oscar Fraley, UPI sports writer, caught up with

Bowman at the 1964 Masters Tournament. Bowman, however, was reluctant to talk about his time up north with Beau Jack. "I don't know whether the club members would like it," he said. "I don't know if they figure boxing mixes with golf."[11]

Beau needed rest and time to recuperate. After spending ten days in the hospital, he headed back to Georgia. While resting in Augusta, Beau had more misfortune to handle—a family tragedy. Beau's younger brother John Henry Walker died on June 28, 1947. John Henry idolized Beau, fighting in battles royal with him and boxing under the name "JuJu" Jack. Regrettably, he was fatally shot in an exchange of gunfire with police. Police reports state that officers were answering a complaint that Walker was shooting at a woman. Officer Joe Reynolds arrived on the scene and found Walker inside a house. He shouted for him to come outside and surrender. Walker replied, "No sir, white folks,"[12] and drew his pistol. Reynolds immediately pulled his own gun, and they both fired almost simultaneously. Walker was shot and tried to run, but he fell to the ground. He died later that day on the emergency room table.

22

Comeback from a
Broken Kneecap

Astonishingly, within ten months, Beau's knee seemed ready for action. Beau resumed training in September and announced he was eager to return to boxing. Beau was optimistic about earning a chance to take Sugar Ray Robinson's welterweight title. Robinson claimed the welterweight title on December 20, 1946, when he defeated Beau's stablemate, Tommy Bell, and boasted an incredible record of 81–1–1. Moreover, Robinson hadn't lost a bout in more than five years.

First things first. Beau's knee had to pass the examination of Dr. Vincent Nardiello, the NYSAC's physician that operated on his knee. In early October, following Beau's light training at Stillman's Gym, Dr. Nardiello inspected Beau's knee. Nardiello declared Beau as ready to go on October 10. As Dr. Newman had certified before the Janiro bout, Nardiello declared that Beau had fully recovered from his kneecap operation and would be ready to enter the ring within four to six weeks. The NYSAC was not so sure. The Commission required Dr. Nardiello to continue watching Beau train for six weeks before it agreed to provide Beau the necessary license to resume his boxing career.

Even after his terrible injury and loss to Tony Janiro, the public still yearned to watch the "Georgia Windmill" in action. After announcing his comeback, Chick Wergeles commented, "I got letters and telegrams that high on my desk," he orated. "Everybody wants Beau Jack. Everybody. Everybody."[1]

Not long after that, Beau was signed to fight Humberto Zavala, a southpaw from Mexico City, Mexico. Wergeles figured Zavala would make a good tune-up opponent for Beau and test for his knee. A journeyman fighter, Zavala had a record of 13–28–4 and had suffered defeat in 17 of his last 18 fights.

Promoter Hans Bernstein set the bout for November 3 at Kiel Auditorium in St. Louis, Missouri. It was Beau's first fight west of the Mississippi River. Prior to entering the ring against Zavala, Beau needed the blessings of the Missouri Athletic Commission. Commissioners Dr. Frank Cleary and William Herring met with Beau to ensure that his knee was fit for action. First, they had Beau run up and down stairs over a dozen times. Then, they conducted a pre-fight x-ray, before declaring that Beau's knee "had healed perfectly and that there was nothing to indicate the boxer would not have full use of that left knee, in the future."[2]

Arriving at Union Station in St. Louis on Friday, October 31, Beau was walking proud when he departed the train. He sought to demonstrate to everyone that his knee had mended. "Knee feels all right," he said, explaining that he had been testing it in workouts for the last six weeks. When asked about his upcoming bout with Zavala, Beau, "smiling pleasantly from beneath his pork-pie hat" stated, "'I'm going to be doing my best."[3]

Humberto never had a chance. Jack gave the Mexican lightweight a brutal beating, knocking him down eight times. Within 35 seconds after the opening bell, Beau landed a thunderous right to Zavala's head sending him to the canvas. The embarrassed Zavala bravely jumped back up. Knocking Zavala down three more times, Jack continued his slaughter in the second stanza. In the third, Beau connected with a left to Zavala's jaw, whacking him down once again, this time for a tally of nine. Seconds later, Beau floored him for an eight count. A courageous Zavala kept getting up and coming in for more punishment. In the fourth, Zavala went down yet again. With ten seconds to go in the round, Beau finished Zavala off with a right to his jaw. Zavala laid flat on his back in the middle of the canvas as the referee counted to ten. Finally, after seven knockdowns, Humberto's punishment session was over. It was a joyful return to the ring for Jack, knocking Zavala out at the end of the fourth round.

All was not well though. Sportswriters, such as W. J. McGoogan of the *St. Louis Post-Dispatch*, noted significant concern for Beau's left knee during the fight. Even though Beau looked good with his punching, he had slipped down twice without being hit. "You could see the play of muscles in his right leg," McGoogan wrote. "They stood out like whipcord while the left looked as flat as a broomstick and Beau seemed to drag his left leg at times."[4] W. Vernon Tietjen of the *St. Louis Star and Times* expressed similar apprehension. Who could come back from a knee injury? It ruined the careers of numerous athletes.

Not your average athlete, Beau was not going to let his knee prevent him from boxing. A little over a month later, on December 16, Beau returned to action at the sold-out Hartford Auditorium in Hartford, Connecticut. His opponent was Frank Vigeant (1924–2015) of Thomaston, Connecticut. Twenty-two-year-old Vigeant had 36 professional bouts under his belt and had served 29 months on a Navy submarine in the Pacific. His record was 25–5–3. Most of his matches were in the Hartford area, so fans knew him well. He was a good fighter but suffered from a tendency to be cut around his eyes. Although he was ahead on the scorecards in his last two fights, ultimately, he lost the bouts due to blood flowing into his eyes from cuts on his forehead. He sought to ensure he was prepared for Jack and trained for three weeks, sparring with Willie Pep.

Following the best undercard in weeks, the sellout crowd of 2,530 was hollering for action. The Thomaston boxer started off well against the former champion, winning two of the first three rounds. Then Vigeant, who had a 5½ pound weight advantage, inexplicably went into a defensive back-peddling mode for the rest of the bout.

Beau, wearing an elastic support around his left knee, chased the back-peddling Vigeant from pole to pole trying to make contact and land solid punches. In fact, sportswriter Bill Lee estimated that Jack missed his target on one hundred and one of his attempts. Notwithstanding, Beau connected with several powerful windmill punches. Jack's best round was the sixth when he scored several stinging right uppercuts. He also opened up a bloody cut on Vigeant's cut-prone forehead, just above his left eye in the eighth round. Although the fight went the distance, Beau easily defeated Frank Vigeant on points, winning seven of the ten stanzas, with a final score of 47–40. Unfortunately, the gate was a miserable $427.70.

Davey Andrews of Lowell, Massachusetts was announced as Beau's next opponent, but before the fight, Billy Kearns (1926–2013) from Hartford, Connecticut was substituted. Kearns was 21 years old, five years younger than Beau, and had a record of 34–16–4. He had won six of his last nine contests. The two met in a ten-round welterweight battle at the Rhode Island Auditorium in Providence, Rhode Island on December 29, 1947. Built in 1926, the auditorium had seating for 5,300 spectators. The half-capacity crowd of 2,479 produced a gate of $4,429.

Kearns fought courageously and appeared willing to mix it up with Beau but had to struggle to stay in the fight. Beau sent Kearns to the canvas for seven counts in the third and eighth rounds. For good measure, Beau floored him two more times for nine counts in the ninth round. Kearns held on desperately in the final two rounds to endure the storm and avoid a knockout. Once again, Beau won an easy unanimous decision.

Notwithstanding his victories, Beau still seemed to have problems with his left leg. It didn't appear that it was completely healed. His thigh above his scarred left knee looked flat or thin from the lack of exercise, while his right thigh looked muscular and powerful. At times Beau would drag his limb. Other times he would slip or fall when trying to pivot on his leg.

A week after his victory over Kearns, Beau was back in the ring. Jimmy Collins (1923–1991), the "Baltimore Slugger," was the fourth straight opponent to taste defeat on Beau's comeback tour. Irishman Jimmy Collins had a record of 40–13–3 but was rapidly fading. He had lost seven of his last eight contests. The 10-round welterweight bout was held at the Arena in New Haven, Connecticut on January 5, 1948. Collins stood two inches shorter than Jack, at 5'3½" tall, but had a 3½ pound weight advantage, weighing in at 143½ pounds to Jack's 140 pounds.

If you arrived at the bout late, you missed it. In the first stanza, Beau floored the slugger to the mat for a nine count. In the second round, Beau finished him off, winning by way of knockout. It was Jack's fourth-straight victory since he broke his knee in the Janiro contest and his third victory in three weeks.

Beau was looking for his fifth straight victory when he battled Johnny "Honeyboy" Bratton (1927–1993) of Chicago at Chicago Stadium on January 23, 1948. Bratton started boxing at the age of 14 and was a flashy young fighter with a professional record of 27–10–1. At 20 years old, he stood 5'10" tall.

Opened in 1929, the "Stadium" was an all-purpose indoor venue with seating for 20,000. Events held at the "Stadium" included hockey, boxing, basketball, midget car racing, and an occasional political convention. In fact, Franklin D. Roosevelt was announced as the Democrats' nominee for president on the stadium floor at the 1932 Democratic Convention.

In his first Chicago bout, Beau was boxing before his largest crowd since losing to Tony Janiro. A group of 13,066 patrons paying a gate of $57,499 entered through the turnstiles to watch the action. In the first seven of ten rounds, Bratton controlled the "savagely fought battle" by way of his left and right crosses. The 20-year-old also took advantage of his faster speed. Johnny's best punch came in the fourth, when he smacked Beau with a hard right, sending his head through the ropes. In the eighth round, however, Beau landed a crashing punch flush on Bratton's jaw. Wrenching in pain and his lower jaw visibly sagging, Bratton appealed to Referee Johnny Behr to stop the fight. Following a quick examination, Behr ran over and raised Jack's hand in victory.

At ringside, Dr. E. C. Small, a dental surgeon, confirmed that Bratton's jaw was fractured. Subsequently, Bratton went to the hospital for x-rays, which revealed that Bratton's jaw had been broken in two places. "I felt it snap in the fifth round," Johnny said. Bratton went on to win the NBA welterweight title in 1951 and finished his career with a 60–24–3 record.

Excitement filled the air at Madison Square Garden on Friday night, February 20, 1948. Beau was making history once again. It was Jack's 26th appearance, setting an unsurpassed new record. Lightweight Tony Canzoneri (1908–1959) previously held the record, appearing at the Garden 25 times. More significant to Beau, he was returning to Madison Square Garden after a year's absence.

In his previous Garden bout, Jack suffered a broken kneecap in his battle with Tony Janiro. Originally scheduled to fight Billy Graham, a shifty New York fighter, Beau was matched with Terry Young after Graham broke his left hand in a tune-up fight with Patsy Brandino. In 1942, Beau had defeated Young in a brutal battle at St. Nicholas Arena. Since their first meeting, Young had rattled off 15 victories (nine by knockout), with four losses and one draw. Jack's record since his first encounter with Young was 23–5–2.

The stakes were high. The winner would be in line for a potential lightweight championship bout with titleholder Ike Williams. The fight contract required the contestants to weigh no more than 140 pounds. The question of the day was whether Beau would be able to make weight. To challenge Williams, he was required to come in at the agreed upon weight.

Apparently, Beau's team failed to tell him that the contract called for him to fight at 140 pounds. Even worse, Beau's trainer, Sid Bell, had also forgotten the weight limit and allowed Beau to eat a "mess of eggs and drink a quart of milk for breakfast."[5] Initially weighing in at 142 pounds, Beau tried to shed weight by shadowboxing. The best he could do was get down to 141¼ pounds. Young weighed 137½ pounds. Thus, before the fight began, Beau suffered an automatic 30-day suspension to take effect after the fight for coming in over the contracted weight. Irrespectively, the crowd of 14,923, which produced a gate of $66,317, got their money's worth.

Young jumped out to a significant advantage in the first round, dropping Beau for a two count with a sharp left hook to the jaw. In the second round, Beau, wearing an elastic support over his left knee, came blazing back against Young in what some described as the "fight of the year." It was a gruesome match with constant action and punching after the bell in three rounds. The ferocious battle had the fans roaring on their feet throughout. Even though Young injured his hand in the fifth round, he persisted to back Beau into the ropes and belt him with brutal punches. In the sixth round, Young unleashed a furious barrage of punches from both hands as he penned Beau in the corner for thirty seconds. In the final four rounds, Jack appeared to have the edge. Regardless, by the end of the duel, Beau was bleeding from his nose and mouth and his left eye was practically swollen shut. He looked the part of a beaten fighter.

In a fight that could have easily been a draw, Young won a tight split decision victory. Judge Charley Shortell scored the fight five to four in favor of Young. Judge Harold Barnes scored the fight five to four for Beau Jack. Referee Frank Fullam scored the contest in Young's favor by one point, six to five, after voting five rounds for each. By the slimmest margin of one point, victory and a chance to fight Ike Williams for the lightweight crown was received by Terry Young. Young finished his career with a record of 70–28–5. Unfortunately, Young met an early death. At age 46, Young was found shot to death with his body face down in the doorway of the 13th Street Playboy Social Club.

This was Beau's first contest in which the NYSAC's point system was utilized. In 1945, Colonel Eddie Eagan (1898–1967),[6] Chairman of the NYSAC, began requiring the use of the point system to declare winners of boxing matches. Previously, matches were scored by rounds, but that didn't take into account knockdowns, etc. Eagan also saw the point system as a way to lessen the number of draws or even decisions. According to the point system, the boxer who wins the round is given the maximum points, and the loser is given one less point. So, employing a ten-point system, the winner of the round receives ten points and the loser nine points. If a boxer wins the round by a large margin or knocks his opponent down, the loser may get less than nine. Usually, it would be scored a 10–8 round. At the time, the NYSAC required the winner to be the combatant that won the most rounds. However, if the rounds were judged even, then the point system would be used to break the tie.

Defeated, Beau appeared to be losing a little of his vigor. His previous knee injury was evidently inhibiting him from his full potential. Jack wore a basketball-type pad over his left knee when he entered the ring with Young but discarded it after the fifth round. Sportswriter Tommy Holmes opined that Jack could have won the contest, but for his previous knee injury.

> Apparently, surgery has patched up Beau Jack's knee cap which was fractured a year ago, but his knee is still stiff and the Beau couldn't get the necessary leverage to punch hard with his left hand. He fought an aggressive, boring-in battle but took considerable punishment around the face as he piled in. With his old legs he would have gotten to close quarters fast enough to have escaped a lot of Young's blows that he blocked with his classic features.[7]

Beau's knee was undeniably diminishing his effectiveness in the ring. Beau, however, wasn't going to let his trick knee hold him back. He just kept plodding along, seeking another title bout.

On March 12, promoter Raul Goddout announced that he had signed Beau to face Montreal's Johnny Greco on April 9 at the Montreal Forum. The Forum, located on the corner of Atwater and Ste-Catherine West in Montreal, Quebec, Canada, operated from 1908 until 1996. Often referred to as the "most storied building in hockey history," it had initial seating for 9,300 spectators.

It marked the third battle between Greco and Jack. They fought to a draw in their first fight, but Jack had won the second fight. With the Canadian welterweight title under his control, Greco came into the ring 6¾ pounds heavier than Beau and was also fighting before a home crowd of 10,394 fans. Excelling before a home crowd, Johnny had won fifteen of sixteen contests in the Forum, leading oddsmakers to favor Greco 7–5.

Both men came out slugging at the opening bell, throwing savage punches through the first two rounds. Greco, however, won the early rounds of the fight with his herding style and hard infighting, but Beau altered the battle in the sixth round. Beau backed up and began jabbing with light lefts until he set Greco up for a mammoth right. Using a sharp counter-punching defense, Jack hurt Greco with left crosses to the head and several wind-up bolo punches. It was a high-energy slugging match. After bouncing Beau off the ropes with a solid left in the eighth round, however, Johnny began to tire.

At the end of ten rounds, the contest went to the scorecards. Judge Johnny Gow scored the bout in Beau's favor five to four, with one round even. Judge Leo Germain gave Beau five rounds, Greco three, and two even. Finally, Judge Rene Ouimet scored the contest even, with both men winning four rounds and two even. Beau was victorious, winning on two of the three judges' scorecards. In his second fight in a row, Beau made history. The contest produced a gate of $51,832, an all-time high gate for a boxing match in Canada.

On April 26, 1948, promoter Goldie Ahearn of the Liberty Athletic Club announced that he had signed Jack and Tony Janiro to a rematch on May 17 at Griffith Stadium in Washington, D.C. Payback was on Jack's mind as he faced Janiro a second time. Janiro defeated Beau 16 months earlier in the Garden when his knee collapsed. Ahearn said the demand was so high that he turned down three impressive offers from other fight towns to relocate the bout to their venue. For instance, Madison Square Garden offered $7,000 to transfer the fight there, but Ahearn adamantly refused all offers.

Beau, along with his manager Chick Wergeles and trainer Sid Bell, arrived in Washington on Thursday, May 13th to begin final preparations for the contest. After the fighters weighed in on May 17, the District of Columbia Boxing Commission at the request of Goldie Ahearn postponed the fight for a week, due to inclement weather and rain showers. Beau stayed in Washington, while Janiro went back to New York for a couple of days. By fight time on the 24th, Beau was a seven to five favorite.

Facing off in a driving rainstorm, Beau's knee would be profoundly tested. Even with the downpour, 9,178 spectators showed up for the outdoor match, producing a gate of $27,473. Since they last met, Janiro had won nine of eleven contests and Beau had won six of seven matches.

A downpour greeted the contestants as they entered the ring. As in their first meeting, Beau started fiercely, throwing punches from all different angles, bewildering Janiro. He looked like his old self with his "jitterbug" footwork and wind-up bolo punches. With both fighters slipping on the slick canvas and falling on top of each other, at times the fight looked more like a wrestling match. The two men eventually took their socks and shoes off and kept fighting. Janiro's best round was the fourth. He shook Beau with a bombardment of punches, driving him into the ropes. Both combatants tasted the canvas in the fifth when they slipped on the wet, slick canvas after throwing simultaneous wild rights. Beau, however, was the aggressor most of the night, belting Janiro around the ring and putting him on the brink of a knockout three times after staggering him with looping rights. Revenging his previous loss, Jack won a unanimous ten-round decision over Janiro.

The next day, Beau confidently announced he was ready to drop weight and fight for another lightweight title. In a surprising turn of events, it just so happened that he would get that chance. Three years after his discharge from the Army and one and a half years after he broke his kneecap, Beau appeared in his fifth title bout against the undisputed lightweight champion, Ike Williams.

23

Third Shot
at the Lightweight Title

Philadelphia promoter Herman Taylor was determined to stage a title fight between the current lightweight champion, Ike Williams, and Beau Jack in Philadelphia. Ike acquired the NBA lightweight crown in 1945 and the New York crown in 1947. On Monday, June 7, Taylor and managers for both fighters met with Leon Rains, chairman of the Pennsylvania State Athletic Commission, to negotiate terms for the fight. Managers for Ike Williams, Frank "Blinky" Palermo and Frank Palumbo agreed to accept 37½ percent of the gate or a $30,000 guarantee, whichever was higher. Chick Wergeles, on behalf of Beau, agreed to take 22½ percent of the gate. Each side also posted $1,500 as a forfeit if their man came in over the 135-pound contracted weight. The only contingency was that Ike had to get past a rematch with Enrique Bolandos on Tuesday night, May 25th. It didn't appear to be a daunting task as Williams had previously knocked Bolandos out in the eighth round on April 30, 1946.

Bolandos, however, was ready for Williams this time, making him work extra hard. Unlike their last match, there would be no early knockout. In a bloody, action-packed fight, the contingency was eliminated as Ike defeated his Mexican challenger by split decision. With William's victory, the 15-round title fight between Beau Jack and Ike Williams was finalized. The lightweight title bout was scheduled for July 12 at Shibe Park in Philadelphia.

Born in Brunswick, Georgia, Ike Williams (1923–1994) moved to Trenton, New Jersey to pursue his boxing career. Ike stood five feet, nine inches tall and his usual fighting weight was around 135 pounds. He was an impressive lightweight boxer with remarkable hand speed and a ferocious body puncher. Williams, with fists described as "veritable blackjacks," possessed power in both of his hands, especially his right.

On April 18, 1945, at the young age of 21, Ike won the NBA's lightweight belt, knocking out Juan Zurita in Mexico City. A riot virtually erupted among the 35,000 fans after seeing their champion go down for the count in the

Promotional poster for Ike Williams and Beau Jack title fight at Shibe Park, 1948 (courtesy John DiSanto, Philly Boxing History Collection).

second round. More than a dozen policemen had to clear the area around the ring before Ike could make it to his dressing room.

Ike, the "Trenton Thunderbolt," had an outstanding year in 1947. He won the undisputed lightweight title on August 4, 1947, knocking out Bob Montgomery, the New York titleholder, in the sixth round, after spinning his head around with a thunderous right to the chin. After going nine and one in 1947, with knockout victories over Bob Montgomery and Tippy Larkin, Ike was honored as *The Ring*'s Fighter of the Year. Since he dropped a nontitle bout to Gene Burton on January 27, 1947, Williams had won 15 straight bouts. Ike boasted a record of 93–1–4, with 43 knockouts. Jack was his second title defense in seven weeks. Jack's record was 73–12–4.

Against common opponents, both Williams and Jack had defeated Juan Zurita, Johnny Hutchinson, and Tippy Larkin. Ike had knocked out Bobby Ruffin, whereas Jack had lost by unanimous decision. Jack, on the other hand, had defeated Willie Joyce, whereas Ike had lost three of four bouts with Joyce. Jack had two victories and two defeats in his matches with Bob Montgomery. Ike had been knocked out by Monty and conversely, knocked him out.

Beau prepared for his fifth title bout, conducting preliminary training in Hot Springs, Arkansas, before heading to Stillman's Gym. He finished his pre-fight training in Philadelphia at the Christian Street YMCA, while Ike trained in Grenloch, New Jersey, at Jersey Joe Walcott's training site, outbidding Beau for the same location.

Beau's trainer, Sid Bell, prepared Jack well, perfecting his techniques and endurance necessary for the fifteen-round title bout. Bell also added an effective left jab to Beau's arsenal of punches. "He's been using his left that way more and more since returning to the ring last November," said Bell. "But notice he hasn't lost any of his power. If anything he's hitting harder than ever."[1]

Confidence was abundant in Beau's camp. Chick Wergeles, Sid Bell, and Beau's sparring partners were confident Beau would claim his third lightweight title. So did the future Hall of Fame manager Al Weill, who had been added to Beau's team as an advisor for the bout. Beau was exceptionally motivated. He wanted to become the first man to hold the lightweight title three times. Revenge for a fellow boxer and friend was also on his mind. He wanted to avenge the knockout Bob Montgomery suffered to Ike Williams eleven months earlier.

The man who stole Beau's two titles, Bob Montgomery, also predicted Beau to be victorious. Montgomery had retired following his sixth-round knockout loss to Ike Williams on August 4, 1947. "Beau Jack has too much moxie for Ike," said Montgomery. "He hits too often and keeps pressing all the time. I wouldn't be surprised to see Beau Jack win by knockout."[2] Willie Joyce expressed a similar opinion. "If it goes more than five rounds," declared Joyce, "Beau Jack will whip him. Beau Jack is the greatest distance fighter I ever saw," said Joyce. "He is like an express train; keeps coming all the time and never gives one a second's rest."[3] Jack's aggressive style was bound to create trouble for Williams.

Confidence was plentiful in Ike Williams' camp as well. During his training camp, future heavyweight champion "Jersey Joe" Walcott questioned Ike about his chances against Beau. "Beat him, I hope," said Ike. "He's a pretty tough customer, but I'll be in shape for him. I saw him fight Montgomery three times and Johnny Hutchinson once. He was pretty good all four times. But I think I'll beat him."[4] Jimmy Wilson, Ike's trainer, expected Williams to win via knockout. "The way I see it, Jack is too wide open for a sharp shooter like Ike," exclaimed Wilson. "He has no defense and Williams will cut him to pieces."[5]

Philadelphia was hopping with activity during fight week. Along with the upcoming title bout, it was hosting the Democratic National Convention, which was ongoing at Convention Hall from July 12 through July 14. President Harry S. Truman, who succeeded Roosevelt after he suffered a fatal heart attack just 82 days after being sworn into his fourth presidential term, emerged as the Democratic presidential candidate. Promoter Herman Taylor ensured tickets were conveniently made accessible for the convention delegates and predicted an attendance of 35,000 and gate of $150,000.

For a while, it looked as if neither fighter would make weight. Several days before the official weigh-in, both men were over the 135-pound weight limit and chose not to weigh in the day before the fight. Instead, they waited to stand on the scales the day of the battle. Fortunately, both fighters emerged from the weigh-in at 134 pounds.

On the warm and humid evening of July 12, a throng of 12,952 enthusiastic fight fans went through the turnstiles at Shibe Park. The crowd and gate fell woefully short of Taylor's predictions, but still produced a respectable gate of $83,787. As fight time got closer, the odds in favor of Williams defeating Jack had decreased to 7–5.

The opening bell for the championship bout sounded at 10:15 p.m. Beau began strong, throwing barrages of punches and pinning the champion against the ropes. Exuding confidence, Beau fought furiously in the first three rounds, electrifying the fans with his savage hell-for-leather style. The boisterous cheers from the crowd bolstered Beau after he landed a thunderous left hook to Ike's jaw in the first round. Ike returned the favor, stunning Beau when he countered with his own left hook to Beau's jaw, followed by a hard right to his temple. In the second, Jack came out swinging like a wildcat, attacking Ike's body, while Williams countered with short hooks to Beau's face. Taking advantage of a lull in Williams' attack, Beau won the second round. Williams fought back vigorously in the third, landing blistering rights to the head and body.

As Beau tired in the fourth round, Williams jammed him momentarily against the ropes and used him as a punching bag. Ike had youth, stamina, a 3½" height advantage, and overwhelming power. On the other hand, Beau appeared sapped by dropping weight for the bout. Against the ropes, Ike landed jabs, powerful body shots, and left hooks to Jack's head. In the middle and at the end of the fifth-round, Ike again trapped Beau on the ropes, where he shook him with heavy blows.

Williams came out in the sixth round seeking to end the fight. Everyone in the crowd was on their feet screaming with excitement. Williams swiftly connected a brilliant left hook to the challenger's chin. The champion then landed a right hand, forcing Beau into the ropes midway on one side of the ring. Beau sluggishly attempted to avoid the onslaught, moving along the ropes into a neutral corner, but he couldn't get out of the way of William's attack. Ike reacted by unleashing vicious power punches on Jack, combining left hooks and rights. Under tremendous pressure, Beau, with legs shaking, "grabbed the top ropes with his arms shoulder-high and extended as far as they could go in the classic posture of Crucifixion."[6] Jack's face was swollen and bleeding badly, but he gallantly refused to go down. All that was holding Beau up was his tremendous heart and the corner ropes.

Sickened by the scene, Williams motioned with his gloves for Referee Charley Daggert to intervene. Daggert didn't respond, so Ike implored him verbally to stop the fight. "Stop it," Williams said to Daggert. "You want me to kill him."[7] Finally, Daggert stopped the fight 33 seconds into the sixth round, awarding Williams a technical knockout over the nearly unconscious Beau Jack. That night, Williams proved, "a fighter can win without being merciless—and still be a great fighter."[8] As to why he withheld punches at the end of the fight, Williams said, "I didn't want to hit him around the head anymore."[9]

Even though Beau's knee appeared to hold up during the battle, he lacked his previous speed and quickness. Perhaps dropping down to the lightweight division took too much out of him. It was only the second time Jack had been knocked out, and it took a broken kneecap to stop him the first time. This time, Beau never tasted the canvas. It was only through his amazing will and the ropes that he did not collapse to the canvas. Following the fight, Beau humbly uttered, "I didn't go down. Why the man stop it when I didn't go down?[10] I just forgot to duck that left hand," explained Jack.[11]

Remarking on Williams' strength, Beau said, "He's some fighter. He's some fighter."[12] Meanwhile, in his dressing room, Williams replied to reporters. "Yes, Beau was a good fighter, but he left himself open too much." When asked how Jack compared to Bob Montgomery, Ike stated, "Montgomery was harder to hit. He didn't leave as many openings as Jack. I don't want to say which was tougher."[13]

The Ike Williams fight would be Beau's last contest producing a gate over $40,000. The gates for his remaining bouts would only average $12,577.75. Jack, however, was unwavering that he had better days ahead in the ring. "Fighting's my life. It's the only thing I want to do."[14] After his reappearance in the lightweight division for the title fight, Beau quickly returned to the welterweight division, blaming his loss of stamina to making the lower weight.

Ike Williams, on the other hand, always known for giving back to the community, graciously donated $1,000 of his winnings to the U.S. Olympic fund and scheduled a benefit bout for the YMCA[15] before attending the Olympic Games in London.

The Olympic Summer Games were returning after a 12-year hiatus due to World War II. Although there had been years of destruction, rationing of food and clothing, the International Olympic Committee (IOC) felt the games of the XIVth Olympiad needed to continue as soon as possible. During the games between July 26, 1948, and August 14, 1948, the U.S. won 48 gold medals, the most medals by any country. In boxing, however, the U.S. only won one medal. Hank Herrington won silver in the welterweight division.

Racial Indignation

The date was February 12, 1946. The place was South Carolina. Isaac Woodard (1919–1992) had just been honorably discharged from the Army at

Camp Gordon in Augusta, Georgia. While still wearing his uniform, he boarded a Greyhound bus to travel home to North Carolina. Shortly after departing the Augusta station, Woodard asked to take a bathroom break. The bus driver responded by ridiculing the veteran. At the next stop in Batesburg, South Carolina, the chief of police, Linwood Shull, and several of his deputies met Woodard outside the bus and brutally beat him with nightsticks, leaving him completely and permanently blind. To add insult on top of injury, Woodard was charged with drunk and disorderly conduct before he was finally taken to a hospital in Columbia, South Carolina.

South Carolina refused to pursue a case against Chief Shull. An outraged President Harry S. Truman ordered a federal investigation. Although Shull was indicted and tried in a South Carolina federal court, he was acquitted within 30 minutes of deliberation by an all-white jury.

Nearby, in Monroe, Georgia, 50 miles east of Atlanta, another African American veteran who had served four and a half years on the Pacific front, George Dorsey, along with his wife and another black couple, were gunned down on July 25, 1946, by a white mob in what became known as the "Moore's Ford Lynching." Loy Harrison, a white farmer, who employed George Dorsey, had just posted bail for another of his black employees, Roger Malcom. Malcolm had been accused of stabbing a white farmer during a fight several days earlier. Harrison was driving Dorsey and his wife Dorothy, as well as Malcolm and his wife Mae, back to his farm.

After a curve in the road, Harrison's car was met by a white mob of 20 or more unmasked white men who stood, blocking the way. As Harrison stopped, the mob dragged the two black couples out of the car, while holding Harrison at gunpoint. Women were not usually lynched, but apparently one of the wives recognized someone in the mob. Therefore, both black couples were lined up next to each other, and at the count of three, their bodies were riveted with more than 60 bullets. Investigation of the incident was hampered by silence and lack of cooperation by local authorities. The case remains unsolved.

Again, President Truman responded, creating the first President's Committee on Civil Rights (PCCR) by Executive Order 9808 on December 5, 1946, to safeguard and strengthen the civil rights of all Americans. In December 1947, it issued its landmark report, "To Secure These Rights," condemning racial segregation, especially in the Services. Soon after that, on July 26, 1948, to avoid a legislative filibuster on the issue, President Truman issued Executive Order 9981, establishing equality of treatment and opportunity and demanding the end of racial segregation in the Armed Services. Even so, it would still take five years for the Armed Services to become integrated.

24

Beau Seeks
Welterweight Title

Beau took a three-month break to rest and collect himself after his devastating loss to Ike Williams. In the meantime, Beau lent his support to amateur boxing. Jack, along with Joe Louis and Ray Robinson, joined the newly formed amateur boxing club known as the Glovers Social Club as honorary members. Established by Bill Miller, Ben Wilson, Jack Corprew, and Wilbur Walcott, the club sought to acquire its own community center and initiate a fund to help injured amateur boxers. Beau also took some time to enjoy one of his favorite hobbies, fishing for tuna out of Sheepshead Bay.

During his layoff, Beau and his three children, along with 100,000 mourners, paid respect to Babe Ruth (1895–1948) at Yankee Stadium. Ruth died two days earlier on August 16. His bier was visited by more than 150,000 fans while it lay in rest at Yankee Stadium. One of the most celebrated athletes of his era, the "Great Bambino" started his professional baseball career as a left-handed pitcher for the Boston Red Sox. While there, he set the World Series record for consecutive scoreless innings. After joining the New York Yankees in 1920, Babe led the team to seven American League pennants and four World Series titles. He ended his 22-year career with 714 home runs, 2,873 hits, 506 doubles, 2,174 runs, 2,213 RBI, a .342 batting average and a .690 slugging percentage. Ruth held the home run record until 1974 when it was broken by Hank Aaron. Babe Ruth was honored as a member of the inaugural class inducted into the Baseball Hall of Fame.

Following his three-month hiatus, Jack was ready to enter the ring again. Beau decided to stay in the welterweight division in hopes of earning a shot at the welterweight title held by Sugar Ray Robinson. Losing weight to reach the 135-pound weight limit for his title fight with Ike Williams physically weakened his fighting abilities.

On October 28, 1948, Jack entered the ring at Uline Arena in Washington, D.C., to face former English welterweight and lightweight champion Eric Boon (1919–1981). Boon, at 28 years of age, had a professional record of

97–16–5, knocking out 61 opponents in 115 fights, but his talents had not been tested in the States.

Uline Arena, also referred to as the Washington Coliseum, was built in 1941 by Migiel Uline, entrepreneur and inventor of an ice cube-making machine. The arena quickly became Washington's premier entertainment and sports venue. Uline Arena hosted the first concert by the Beatles in the United States on February 11, 1964. It was also the site of President Dwight Eisenhower's first inaugural ball. The arena had seating for 6,000 when configured for hockey and 10,000 for entertainment events.

A minimal crowd of 1,994 gathered on a mild fall evening to witness the October 28 welterweight bout. Boon weighed in at 144 pounds and stood just 5'4" tall. Jack weighed in at 143½ pounds. In a close first round, Boon held his own and even staggered Beau with a right. As the second round began, Beau started applying considerable pressure. Beau "pounded his foe unmercifully, holding him at arm's length with his left and bringing up one sizzling right bolo after another."[1] He bloodied the nose of the former British champion and swarmed in like a tiger taking its quarry down. He landed almost at will. At the start of the third round, Beau threw a massive bolo punch, flooring the Englishman. As Boon stood back up, Beau staggered him across the ring and into the ropes with a stiff right. Enough was enough. Referee Eddie LaFond called the fight one minute and 31 seconds into the third-round, awarding Jack the decision by technical knockout.

After the fight, Jack Solomons, an English fight promoter, offered Beau a rematch with Boon in London. Chick Wergeles, however, rejected the offer, stating that he was not accepting any bouts until Beau fought Chuck Taylor, scheduled for November 23. Of course, Jack had his sights on Sugar Ray Robinson.

In what was promoted as the "greatest all punching card ever staged in this city," Convention Hall in Philadelphia was the venue for Beau's next battle. He faced 25-year-old Chuck Taylor (1922–1988) of Coalport, Pennsylvania. Taylor had a record of 25–11–1, a powerful left jab, and was eyeing a hopeful shot at the welterweight title himself. However, he had only won three of his last nine matches. A crowd of 4,530, mostly Taylor supporters, producing a gate of $13,671 were on hand for the 10-round welterweight bout.

After a sluggish start, Beau got his punches rolling and looked like the Beau Jack of old, zigzagging, dipping, and jitterbugging. He aggressively pushed Taylor the whole fight, which was not very long. Beau rushed in on Taylor in the second, throwing barrages of lefts and rights. In the third, Beau forced Taylor to the ropes, where he plastered him with a volley of lefts and rights to his head. Then, Beau connected a tremendous bolo punch to Taylor's jaw, sending him to the canvas. Referee Charley Daggert called an end to the fight 2:43 into the third round. Commentators praised Beau's performance, declaring that Beau appeared to be in his best form since being discharged from the Army.

Beau had two fights scheduled over the next three weeks. On December 3, he was expected to meet Vince Foster, but the bout was called off due to a hand injury Beau suffered in his contest with Chuck Taylor. Next, he was scheduled to face Johnny Greco for a fourth time at Olympia Stadium in Detroit, Michigan on December 17, but Greco hurt his foot before the fight. The following day, Leroy Willis agreed to substitute for Johnny Greco in the December 17 bout.

Opened in 1927, Olympia Stadium was often referred to as the "Old Red Barn." When it opened it featured the largest indoor skating rink in the U.S. and soon become home to the Detroit Red Wings. Initially intended for hockey, the "Old Red Barn" became a multipurpose indoor arena for all kinds of events. It had a capacity for nearly 15,000 spectators and seating was steeply sloped so that it seemed like you were on top of the action.

Willis came into the fight with forty-eight professional matches and a record of 32–11–4. He was on fire, having won seven of his last nine contests.

Olympia Stadium, 5920 Grand River Avenue, Detroit, Michigan, in the 1960s (Library of Congress).

Hailing from Detroit, Willis had the advantage of the hometown crowd, but that was his only advantage. On December 17, 1948, 5,012 fistic fans paid $11,426.60 to witness the contest.

Beau gave the Detroit youngster a boxing lesson. Jack won almost every round over the Michigan lightweight champion by shuffling around and banging away at him. Beau tagged Willis under his left eye, producing blood in the second round. Willis landed some hard rights, but the broad-shouldered Jack absorbed them well. Willis did succeed in drawing blood in the eighth when he cut Beau in the corner of his left eye. Willis, using his defensive skills, weathered Beau's onslaught and avoided a knockdown by fancy footwork and head bobbing to evade Beau's nastiest punches. By the end of the contest, both fighters tasted blood. Although bloodied, Beau received an easy victory, winning nine of the ten rounds. The only stanza Willis won was the second, in which Beau was penalized for punching Willis while holding him at the same time.

Jack wanted to meet Frankie Fernandez in his next bout, hoping to achieve a little revenge on behalf of his stablemate, Tommy Bell, whom Fernandez knocked out a little over a month earlier. On January 12, 1949, Beau's camp telegraphed an offer to Frankie Fernandez (19–1), Hawaii's welterweight champion and the number three contender in the welterweight division. Fernandez, however, rejected the offer, because he didn't feel like he could adequately train for the February 18 fight. Frankie had just married and only recently resumed training. It would be another year before Jack and Fernandez would square off.

Instead of Frankie Fernandez, Beau faced off against Jackie Weber of Pawtucket, Rhode Island. Weber had a respectable record of 38–7–0, having won six of his last eight fights. The bout was scheduled for January 17, 1949, at the Boston Garden. Like the third version of Madison Square Garden, Tex Rickard built the Boston Garden. Located above North Station, the $10 million Boston Garden opened in 1928, with seating for more than 15,000 fans. It was demolished in 1998 after the FleetCenter, now referred to as TD Garden, opened in 1995.

Fighting before a crowd of 8,776 fans, Jack pounded Weber from the opening bell. Grinning at Weber, Jack limped around the ring, stalking him. When he got Weber in range, Beau battered him with imposing body punches and stunning looping rights and uppercuts. In the sixth round, he cut Weber beneath the left eye and bloodied his nose in the seventh. In the ninth, Jack dropped the New England lightweight champion to the canvas for a nine-count with a brutal uppercut. Despite still showing the effects of his lame knee, he easily defeated Willis by unanimous decision. The paid gate was $23,262.

It was more apparent than ever, since suffering a broken kneecap in the

Janiro bout almost two years earlier, that something was dreadfully wrong with Beau's left knee. No matter how hard he tried, he was forced to limp around the ring after his opponents. Notwithstanding, a lame leg was not going to hold Beau Jack down.

Two days later, it was announced that Beau would meet Canadian welterweight titleholder Johnny Greco for a fourth time on January 31 at the Montreal Forum. Initially scheduled for December 17, it had been postponed due to a foot injury suffered by Greco. However, on January 24, promoter Raoul Goddout indefinitely postponed the fight at the request of Beau's camp, maintaining that Beau had injured his hand while training.

Because of Beau's injury, the fight was rescheduled for March 14. Not long after that, the match was postponed for a second time at the request of Jack's camp. The new date was March 21. Once again, the fight was delayed by Beau's camp and rescheduled for March 28. In response, the NBA, in conjunction with the Montreal Boxing Commission, suspended Jack until he fulfilled his contract to fight Greco. NBA Commission Abe J. Greene stated the suspension was "not a punitive measure." Instead, it was a protective measure. The Massachusetts Boxing Commission followed suit, announcing that they had also suspended Beau.

The fourth meeting between Beau Jack and the "Joltin'" Johnny Greco finally transpired on March 28. Beau had won two of their three previous meetings, while the other bout ended in a draw. A crowd of 10,394 filed into the Montreal Forum to cheer for the "Montreal Mauler," producing a gate of $38,428. Greco had the hometown crowd and nine-pound weight advantage over the former champion, scaling 147 pounds to Jack's 138 pounds. Greco had also won his last five bouts.

The furious battle began at the opening bell. Both men rushed out at each other, brawling feverishly. By the third round, it looked like Greco's weight advantage had given him control of the bout. Crouching to avoid Beau's jabs, "Jolting" Johnny cornered him against the ropes in the fourth, where he unleashed vicious blows to Jack's body. During the last minute of the fifth stanza, Greco pounded Beau repeatedly without return. Beau looked finished. However, in the sixth, Beau rumbled back and placed Greco in distress, bombarding him with body punches. Greco retaliated in the next round, scoring the fight's only knockdown when he landed a tremendous short right on Beau's jaw for a mandatory eight count.

Beau, favoring his injured knee on which he wore an elastic support, suffered a ruthless beating in the late rounds. In the ninth, Johnny bloodied Beau's mouth and then sent him reeling into the ropes with another right to the chin. Only by grabbing the ropes, did Beau avoid the canvas. Greco fervently tried to finish Beau off, but Jack refused to go down. The ninth was all Greco. He again drove Jack to the ropes again where he belted him for 90 seconds with fierce lefts and rights. Beau endured with some crafty counter-punching, but much to the crowd's liking, Greco won a unanimous decision, consistently scoring points when he had Beau corned on the ropes. Judges Johnny Gow and Rene Ouimet gave Greco six rounds, Jack three and one even. The third judge, Dr. L.O. Geoffrion, gave Greco five rounds, Jack three and two even.

Greco finally attained vengeance, winning the fourth and final meeting with Jack. Unfortunately, Johnny Greco soon met an untimely death at age thirty-one. While driving in the Westmont neighborhood of Montreal, he lost control of his car. It jumped a sidewalk and slammed into a tree. The impact broke Greco's neck. Johnny was posthumously inducted into the Canadian Boxing Hall of Fame with an overall record of 78–18–5.

Beau would not fight again until July 13th, three and a half months later. Meanwhile, Beau parted ways with his longtime trainer, Sid Bell. Bell's assistant trainer, Ted Williams, took over the reins as head trainer.

In his third fight of 1949, twenty-eight-year-old Jack met Eddie Giosa on Wednesday, July 13th, marking his fifth appearance at Griffith Stadium in Washington, D.C. He had never lost a contest at the venue. Armando Eddie Giosa (1924-2007) grew up in South Philly along with his nine siblings, the child of Italian immigrants. He was undefeated as an amateur, winning the Philadelphia Golden Gloves tournament as a featherweight and as a light-weight before turning pro. Not a powerful puncher, Eddie preferred to out-box his opponents, often dazzling them with double and triple left hooks. Ranked as the number eight welterweight by the NBA, Philadelphia's Giosa boasted a 57–18–6 record and was seeking his sixth straight victory. Both men came in at 139½ pounds. Beau was a slight favorite.

As in Beau's last two bouts at Griffith Stadium, a wet evening was forecast for fight night. Washington had already received over two inches of rain, flooding numerous streets and snarling traffic. Continuing rain and threatening storms kept the crowd down to 3,000 weather wearied fans. The gate was $6,752.23.

Beau and Eddie went to work at the opening bell, both throwing flurries of punches. The first round, however, would last longer than expected. Early in the round, Beau smashed a hard right below Giosa's belt. Giosa was in so much pain he had to be carried to his corner. Referee Marty Gallagher halted the round for five minutes so that Eddie could regain his composure. In the meantime, a fight almost broke out between the two boxers' managers in the middle of the ring arguing over the call. Chick Wergeles and Giosa's manager, Gary Barrett, almost came to blows before officials were able to calm them down.

After the contest resumed, Beau floored Giosa in the second round for a no count. The outcome was inevitable by the third round. Beau was in control and punishing Giosa. Giosa barely survived the round. Beau started the fourth by pounding Giosa with rapid lefts and right hooks. He then landed three quick lefts to Giosa's body and a smashing right to his jaw, sending Giosa to the canvas. Only the closing bell saved Giosa. The rest of the fight featured Beau swarming over Giosa. In the remaining rounds, Beau connected with a barrage of painful roundhouse punches in virtually every round.

Giosa was beaten up by the fight's end, tasting the canvas in the second, third and ninth rounds. The only rounds awarded to Giosa were due to penalties assessed Beau for low blows—the first, fifth, and seventh. The crowd roared with a thunderous ovation as Referee Marty Gallagher raised Beau's hand in victory. The unanimous decision over Giosa gave Beau his fifth victory at Griffith Stadium. Eddie finished his career with a record of 67–30–9 and was inducted into the Pennsylvania Boxing Hall of Fame.

As a result of the ruckus between the managers, Chick Wergeles was handed a thirty-day suspension by the NBA for "loud coaching and demonstrations" during the bout. Giosa's manager, Gary Barrett, was suspended for sixty days for "obscene and abusive" language.

Beau was soon making his first trip to California, where Chick had two fights lined up for him against young undefeated opponents. Upon his arrival on August 24, Beau was honored by more than 50 Oakland civic leaders and dignitaries at a dinner sponsored by promoter Jimmy Murray. Afterward, Beau was ringside at the Oakland Auditorium to watch local welterweight sensation, eighteen-year-old Maurice Harper, battle Earl Turner in his fifth professional fight. Harper had recently won the National Amateur Welterweight title in Boston, Massachusetts. Harper destroyed Turner in their ten-round battle.

Upsetting news came out in Oakland while Beau was finishing his fight preparations. Following an interview with Chick Wergeles, Allen Ward, sportswriter for the *Oakland Tribune* wrote a heartbreaking news story. Ward questioned Wergeles about Beau's financial status. Chick embarrassingly acknowledged that although Beau had made over $250,000, he was virtually penniless and was fighting for money. Chick explained that after the first Janiro fight, Beau found out that he only had $500 in the bank. "If only he had been as careful with his money before the knee accident," Chick said, "he'd be up to his chin in chips today."[2] Commenting on the situation, Wergeles stated, "He gave most of it away…. Softest touch you ever saw. At least, he used to be. Everybody was his friend or relative—but now instead of handing out $20 bills he gives autographs."[3] On a positive note, Chick said that Beau had earned more than $80,000 so far on his comeback tour and had banked half of it. Beau needed to fight. He needed the money.

The first opponent of Jack's California tour was 18-year-old Johnny Gonsalves (1930–2007) of Oakland. Managed by U.S. Olympic team coach Curley

Mendonca, Gonsalves, the former national amateur champion, entered the bout on August 31 with an undefeated professional record of 14–0 in less than a year of professional boxing.

Prior to the fight, Beau trained at Harry Fine's gym on 11th Street and Newman's in San Francisco. Jack worked out at 1:30 p.m., whereas Gonsalves worked out in the same ring a half hour earlier. When questioned about the fight between the veteran former world champion and the novice, Wergeles apprehensively responded, "We're regarding this fight as being as hard as any Beau has had. We're not underestimating your boy."[4]

The next day, Chick Wergeles and Harry Fine almost got into a fight themselves. Someone tipped Chick off that the sparring partner Fine obtained for Beau was actually a stablemate of Johnny Gonsalves. "The sparring mate, Eddie Johnson, was in full gymnasium regalia and ready to step in the ring with Jack when Wergeles was informed of the spy in his camp," wrote Alan Ward. "Wergeles held up the workout, called Fine to the center of the gym and screamed his indignation. A large crowd of spectators were vastly entertained."[5] Afterward, Fine retreated to his office and substituted two of his own fighters as sparring partners for Beau.

The venue for the bout was the Oakland Auditorium. Built in 1914, the Beaux Arts style building, was the center for entertainment in Oakland for years. It was renamed the Henry J. Kaiser Convention Center in 1984 after a $15 million renovation.

A rowdy near-capacity crowd of 6,000 fans, wanting to witness the former lightweight champion and their local boy in action, packed the auditorium, producing a $13,981 gate. Gonsalves entered the ring with a 3½ pound weight advantage and stood 4½" taller than Jack.

The noisy crowd was deafening, cheering as the fight began and continuing until the end. As expected, the younger Gonsalves started strong, winning the first two rounds. Beau, however, took over in the third round and began to dominate the contest. Beau relentlessly charged into the taller Gonsalves, throwing brutal body punches, dazing Gonsalves in the fifth round. Later in the stanza, Referee Eddie James warned Beau for punching to the kidney, which brought a loud protest from Beau's second cornerman. An argument ensued, and Chick Wergles couldn't help but interject, resulting in Referee Eddie James ejecting him from the ring. In the following rounds, Beau continued to score with sharp body punches and occasional right-hand bolo punches to Gonsalves' jaw.

At the end of ten rounds, the decision went to the scorecards. Referee Eddie James scored the bout in favor of Gonsalves, but the two judges, John Lotsey and Richard Burke, scored the fight in favor of Beau, giving Jack a split decision victory. Gonsalves suffered his first loss in fifteen professional fights, but that was not all. During the battle, Johnny suffered a cut to his eye.

It was the first cut he had received as a professional. Because of the cut and his injured optic, he had to cancel his next two matches and sit out for over six weeks.

Next up on Beau's California tour was Tote Martinez, an undefeated 23-year-old from Stockton, California with a record of 27–0. Jack changed that. A light puncher, Tote only had five knockouts and was largely untested as a boxer.

The September 6, 1949 fight was scheduled at Olympic Auditorium. The concrete slab auditorium, with capacity for a little over 7,000 spectators, was built for the 1932 Summer Olympics held in Los Angeles between July 30 and August 14. During the Olympics, U.S. boxers Edward Flynn (welterweight) and Carmen Barth (middleweight) won gold. Frederick Feary (heavyweight), Louis Salica (flyweight), and Nathan Bor (lightweight) won bronze medals.

Close to 4,300 fans showed up in the sweltering heat for the ten-round affair, producing a gate of $8,136. Beau hurt Martinez early with stiff body shots. Throwing his looping bolo punch effectively throughout the fight, Jack looked like his old self. The second was an amusing round in which Jack scarcely landed a glove on the dancing Latino, bringing cheers and laughter from the fans. The light-punching Martinez countered Beau's attack with glitzy defense, repeatedly causing Jack to miss his target. Altering his strategy, Jack overcame Martinez's defense by moving in close to him and pounding him repeatedly with both fists.

Midway through the bout, Martinez used his jab and connected with a straight right to Beau's left eye, producing an ugly lump that continued to enlarge until it was almost swollen shut by the end of the fight. The fans cheered with laughter again in the eighth round after Jack swung a punch so hard and wild that when it missed Martinez, Beau ended up on the canvas. Irrespective, Beau the aggressor throughout, earned an easy unanimous decision over the 23-year-old Martinez. Referee Frankie Van gave Beau a nine-point advantage, while Judges Tommy Herman and Frank Holborow respectively gave him a ten-point and six-point advantage.

Within a week on the west coast, Beau ruined the perfect records of two up and coming fighters, earning him a new moniker of "the spoiler." Following his California trip, Beau headed for Chicago to train for his next two bouts slated for Chicago Stadium.

Beau's next bout at Chicago Stadium was promoted by the newly formed International Boxing Club ("IBC"). Organized by the former heavyweight champion, Joe Louis, and his associates Arthur H. Wirtz and James B. Morris on March 1, 1949, it was described as "a newly formed association organized for the betterment of boxing."[6] IBC offices were opened in Chicago and New York. Years later it would be ascertained that the IBC had connections with Frank Carbo and the mafia.

Scheduled for September 30, Beau was matched against Cuban fighter Kid Gavilan in what was billed as a "not to miss" fight. Regrettably, while driving his new gold-colored car through Harlem several weeks before the fight, three men attacked Gavilan when he was stopped behind a taxi. One of the men yanked his door handle off and pulled him out of the car. Another man drew a knife, stabbing Gavilan in his neck right before gunfire from a private detective dispersed the men. The gash in Gavilan's neck required five stitches. Talking to reporters afterward, Gavilan said, "I'm all right. I'll be able to go through with the Beau Jack fight."[7] His manager Angel Lopez disagreed.

On September 16, the IBC announced that Johnny Bratton would take Gavilan's place. Bratton had knocked out his last five opponents, including a spectacular knockout of Chuck Taylor. Bratton also wanted revenge. Beau had broken his jaw on his way to victory in their first bout a year and a half ago.

A sense of hysteria broke out after the announcement. Howard Frazier, Bratton's manager, told the Illinois State Athletic Commission that the lives of Johnny Bratton and himself had by threatened by frustrated gamblers. Bratton, on the other hand, contested Frazier's claim, instead asserting that Frazier had gambled away his purse of $2,300 from an October 6, 1947, fight with Gene Burton. IBC secretary, attorney Truman Gibson, exclaimed that it was he who had received a "live or die" ultimatum from Howard Frazier. As a result, "[t]wo detectives guarded Johnny Bratton and Illinois officials opened an extensive investigation into reported death threats against boxers and managers, alleged gambling and fixed fights."[8] Subsequently, Frazier denied that he and Bratton had been threatened and admitted that he had bet on nearly all of Bratton's fights. As a result, Frazier's license was revoked by the Illinois State Athletic Commission.

Ultimately, Bratton was removed four days before the fight at the suggestion of New York Boxing Managers Guild when IBC representatives were unable to come to terms with Bratton's managers. The Guild claimed that the IBC did not have the rights to promote Bratton. Meanwhile, Bratton himself was trying to break his contract with his managers, Howard Frazier and Danny Spunt, alleging that they had embezzled his money.

Four days before the fight, the IBC announced that twenty-three-year-old Livio Minelli (1926–2012), the European welterweight champion, would be Beau's opponent. The curly black-haired Italian, boasting a record of 43-6-6, was known for his speed and left jab and had only lost one out of his last ten bouts. Coincidentally, Minelli's manager, Charley Johnston, also directed the New York Boxing Managers Guild.

Perhaps because of the continual substitutes, the crowd on fight night was disappointedly less than expected. Only 2,360 fans turned out at Chicago Stadium on September 30 to witness the IBC's first boxing show in Chicago. The gross gate was only $8,290, producing a net gate of $6,377.37.

As the opening bell sounded, Jack rushed out in his typical style and forced the fight all night, lunging forward, throwing left and rights. Minelli held his own. In the second stanza, he landed his left jab on Beau's jaw and connected left hooks to the body. In the fifth, Minelli fell a hard right to Beau's left eye socket, causing it to swell until Beau only had a slit to see through. Virtually the same thing happened a couple of weeks earlier when Tote Martinez landed a hard right to Beau's left eye. Livo also opened a cut over Beau's right eye when the two clashed heads. Minelli took the eighth round, again pounding Beau with left hooks to the body.

After ten rounds, the decision went to the scorecards. Losing two rounds on low blows made the scoring closer than it would have been for Beau. When the scorecards were tallied, Referee Tommy Gilmore scored the fight for Minelli, 52–48, while the two judges, William O'Connell and Ed Hintz, awarded the fight to Beau 52 to 48. In a close match, Beau was awarded a split decision. A reprise of boos from the disappointed crowd greeted the decision.

Jack's bout with Kid Gavilan (1926–2003), the "Cuban Hawk," was rescheduled for Friday night, October 14, 1949, at Chicago Stadium. Gavilan, whose birth name was Gerardo Gonzalez, grew up in Cuba. At the age of ten, he dropped out of school to box. His manager Yamil Chade bestowed him with the name "Kid Gavilan" after a nightclub that he owned in Cuba called the "El Gavilan," which means "the hawk." Like Beau, Gavilan was a fan favorite and featured a signature windup bolo punch that he developed while cutting sugar canes in the field.

Kid Gavilan was a tenacious fighter and entered the bout as a 4–1 favorite. Fighting out of Havana, Cuba, Gavilan sported a record of 54–7–2, including two victories over Ike Williams. Three months earlier, he lost his first

Kid Gavilan on the cover of *El Grafico* magazine, 1953 (Wikidata.org).

title bout in a close match with the welterweight champ, Sugar Ray Robinson. The 23-year-old youngster was five years younger than Beau and weighed eight pounds heavier; 148 pounds to 140 pounds. Moreover, he stood 5'10½" tall, five inches taller than Beau.

The fighters arrived in Chicago on Sunday, October 9 to complete training for the fight. Both men conducted final preparations at the Midwest Athletic Club. The stakes were high for Gavilan. He needed a win to remain a top contender for succeeding Sugar Ray Robinson's 147-pound belt, which he was expected to vacate. Pursuant to agreement, both fighters received 27½ percent of the gate and $500 from radio and television proceeds. Jack also received $300 for travel expenses.

A crowd of 5,189 fistic fans gathered on the windy night of Friday, October 14 to witness the battle. They had already seen Edward Smith put Jerry Dwain on the canvas in the first round of the opening bout and they were eager for action. The gross gate was $22,429.60, with a net gate of $17,253.54.

It was a blistering ten-round fight. Beau started the first round well, hurling a succession of lefts and hooks to Gavilan's head. Connecting with a deluge of rights when Gavilan fought at close quarters, Beau kept his momentum going in the second round. Gavilan responded by tying Beau up and retaliating with his own punches. In the third round, however, Gavilan took control of the fight, backing Beau up on the ropes and pounding him with shuddering blows to his head and body. In the fourth, Gavilan's onslaught continued. Gavilan landed a hard right into Jack's left eye socket, causing immediate swelling around his left eye, marking the third consecutive fight in which Beau's left eye socket had been pounded with punches. With his left eye virtually shut, Beau fought gallantly through the last five rounds. Every time Beau rushed in, Gavilan met him with shuddering left hooks to the head and body and sharp right crosses. Gavilan was simply bigger, heavier and sturdier than Beau.

The winner was not in doubt. After ten rounds, Gavilan was awarded a unanimous decision by the Referee Frank Sikora and Judges Harold Marovitz and J. Franklin Chiles. Given Beau's performance, he was virtually eliminated from any hope at the welterweight title. Gavilan, on the other hand, would proceed to earn the welterweight world title. With a career record of 108–30–5, Gavilan was inducted into the Boxing Hall of Fame in 1966.

Another heartbreaking story about the "Georgia Shoe Shine Boy" appeared later in the month. According to what Wendell Smith printed in his *Sports Beat* column, Beau's winnings had disappeared. "I had me $100,000 salted away," Beau told us the other day, "but when I checked up I found out it was all gone."[9] According to Smith, whomever was handling Beau's money lost it on betting on horses at the racetrack. Beau, however, spoke no malice and had no plans to take any action against the culprit. "Despite the financial loss, Beau holds no malice," wrote Smith. "The guy who bet up his money is still around. Under ordinary circumstances he would probably be one of the permanent tenants in somebody's jail…. But Beau refused to press charges. He's a deeply religious man."[10]

25

Beau's 27th Appearance Makes Madison Square Garden History

Beau Jack made his first appearance in Madison Square Garden in 1941. An iconic figure in the Garden during the forties, Beau appeared thirteen times between 1942 and 1946. He initially established the record for appearances in the Garden's main event in February 1948, when he fought his 26th featured contest. Now, almost two years later, Jack would extend his record to 27 main events. Appearing in his historical record-setting 27th main event at Madison Square Garden, Beau faced Tuzo Portugez on Friday, December 16, 1949. Beau's multitude of fights in the Garden during the Golden Era of Boxing was instrumental in branding Madison Square Garden the legendary arena that it still is today.

Sam Crawford, a Pennsylvania welterweight, began training Beau at Stillman's Gym in early November for his upcoming fight against Tuzo Portugez (1927–2013) scheduled for December 16. Portugez, a 22-year-old boxer and holder of the Central American welterweight and middleweight titles, hailed from San Jose, Costa Rico. In his November 16 U.S. debut, Tuzo defeated Bobby Mann. Coming in with a 24–5–4 record, the 5'7" tall Tuzo held a 4½ pound weight advantage over Jack, weighing in at 146½ pounds. At fight time, the oddsmakers had Tuzo a 6½ to 5 favorite.

Most of the male fans in the small crowd of 7,281, including Jack, were sporting beards. The country, especially the Midwest, southwest, and far west were suffering from a severe water shortage with water tables dropping well below the ground surface. Agriculture and industry were two main culprits. Experts in southern Arizona estimated that water was being taken from the water table for irrigation at a rate three to four times faster than it could replenish.[1]

In New York, residents were requested to cut 200,000,000 gallons from the 1,145,000,000 gallons of water used daily. Officials estimated that residential water consumption comprised 57 percent of the water usage in a given day. New York's water shortage was heightened by an eight-inch rainfall deficit and city reservoirs 37 percent below capacity. The high water consumption and waste led city officials to institute its first "Dry Friday," a bathless, shaveless day. New York's population of 8,000,000 residents were asked to not bathe or shave that day. GIs were faced with demerits if they were not smooth-faced and Army officials ordered all showers closed for 24 hours. Water for the fighters had to be imported from Saratoga Springs and was limited to five gallons.

As the bout got underway, it was apparent that the San Jose youngster had a significant edge in energy. By the second round, the strong Central American belter gained power and stamina, while Jack began to weaken. Beau's famous windmill attack seemed to be a thing of the past. In the third round, the dark-haired Tuzo smacked Beau with his jab and right hand, bloodying his mouth and nose. Beau struck back in the fifth stanza, cutting Tuzo over his left eye. In the later rounds, the former champion was visibly drained and dancing around the ring in an attempt to mask his fatigue. There were no knockdowns in the fight, but both men were bloodied at the end. Beau put up a fight, but it was becoming more and more evident that his years of competitive boxing were coming to an end.

The decision went to the scorecards. After penalizing both fighters for low blows, Judge Jack Gordon scored the contest six to three for Portugez, with one round even. Judge Art Ardala scored the fight five to four for Beau with one round even. Referee Al Berle scored Portugez the winner, seven rounds to three. The AP scorecard scored the fight five to four for Portugez, with one round even. Portugez emerged victorious with a split decision victory. The gate for Beau's 27th main event appearance was $20,382, the lowest of all of his previous main events at the Garden. Sadly for Beau, it was his last fight in Madison Square Garden.

Following the bout, Beau announced that he was nearing retirement. He had given boxing and his fans the best of what he had. "I made a promise to God at the start of my career to fight for 10 years and then quit," said Beau. "The time is drawing near. I'll continue until the middle of next year, then quit the ring forever."[2] It was a gloomy announcement for Jack. Boxing was his life. "I was always eager to give my best and please the public every time I pulled on a pair of gloves," voiced Jack. "I think I filled that part of the bill and will continue to do so until I quit."[3] Beau confided that he planned to retire to his 40-acre farm near Augusta.

To make matters worse, on January 17, 1950, Jack was admitted to St. Claire's Hospital due to the recurrence of his previous knee injury to his right knee. His medial semi-lunar cartilage was torn yet again. Following surgery, he recuperated in the hospital for a couple of weeks. Regardless of his most recent setback, Beau expected to continue in the welterweight division after his knee healed, hoping to earn his way into some lucrative fights. Regrettably, his opportunities to collect substantial purses had significantly depreciated. His bout with Tuzo Portugez would be the last of his contests with a gate of $20,000 or more.

Discharged from the hospital, Beau headed to St. Petersburg to see his mother and rest. In the middle of March, Chick Wergeles reported to the media that Beau was doing well and was jumping around again. Answering questions about Beau's boxing career and age, Chick countered, "He's only a baby."

Following a four-month layoff to allow his right knee to heal, Beau was ready for action. On April 3, 1950, two days after his 29th birthday, Beau entered the ring for his second appearance at the Hartford Auditorium. His opponent was a battle-scarred veteran from Youngstown, Ohio, Joey Carkido (1929–2004). When Carkido was sixteen years old, he used his Brother Louis' birth certificate to begin his professional career, joining fellow Youngstown boxer Tony Janiro. Carkido had a professional record of 54–19–7 but had been knocked out four times in the last year and had lost eight of his previous nine contests. He also had a longstanding issue with cutting around his eyes. At fight time Joey was a significant underdog.

Many of the 1,061 fans at the Auditorium would be unexpectedly surprised when the contest ended. As usual, Beau came out swinging, trying to overwhelm his adversary with punches. Although he may have missed more punches than he threw, Jack was the aggressor throughout the fight, continuously attacking Carkido's head and body with punishing blows. Joey, however, was unable to hurt Jack, even with his best punches. Jack simply mauled Carkido. The best Joey could offer was a little inside fighting.

The fight appeared so lopsided that many of the fans left during the eighth and ninth rounds. Astonishingly, when the victor's hand was raised by Referee John Cluney, it was Carkido's hand. Cluney scored the fight one-sidedly in Carkido's favor by a margin of forty-eight points to thirty-eight points. He gave Carkido eight rounds to Beau's two. The *Hartford Courant*'s press scorecard, on the other hand, was almost opposite, giving Beau the victory, five rounds to two, with three rounds scored even, for a score of forty-eight to forty-three. Enraged fans were so upset they rushed forward to question how Referee Cluney arrived at his verdict.

Beau's boxing career had encountered an unscrupulous bump in the road. For the first time in his career, Jack suffered three losses in a row. Beau was frustrated with his unjust loss to Carkido but determined to resume his comeback, believing better days were ahead.

Jack didn't have much time to worry about it. He was on the road to Augusta to work the 13th Masters Tournament held on April 6 through 9.

Jimmy Demaret, dressed in his Easter finest, snagged the Green Jacket with a round of 69 on the final day and an overall score of five under par. He was the first person to ever win three Masters, previously winning in 1940 and 1947.

After the tournament, Jack made his way back up the east coast to Washington, D.C., to clash with the former lightweight champion, Lew Jenkins (1916–1981). The hard-hitting Jenkins held the title from May 10, 1940, when he knocked out Lou Ambers until December 19, 1941, when he lost the title to Sammy Angott. Having battled in 118 professional scraps, the scrawny 33-year-old boxer from Sweetwater, Texas had his share of battle scars. The "Sweetwater Swatter" was also a heavy drinker and on occasion was known to fight drunk.

The ten-round welterweight bout was Beau's second at Uline Arena. In the buildup for the fight, the press underscored that both timeworn fighters were beyond their glory days.

> A pair of former lightweight champions, now in the twilight of their fistic careers, regain the national spotlight once more Friday night when they clash in Washington, D.C.… There is no hope for further championships—just the desire and necessity to keep going in the only trade they know.[4]

Only 937 die-hard fistic fans showed up for the match. Regardless, the April 14 fight was carried on ABC radio and via video by NBC-TV.

Beau came out fanatically at the opening bell, bombarding the 5'8" tall Jenkins with body punches. The fight quickly turned into a free-for-all with Jenkins taunting Jack with racial slurs. "It didn't bother me," Jack said later, "I've heard it all my life."[5] Then Lew callously spit in Beau's face four times. All of Lew's vulgar mannerisms and tactics just provoked Jack even more.

Each pugilist appeared to be loading up their punches, eyeing a knockout, but Beau was rapidly winning the skirmish with barrages of body shots. Jenkins' form rapidly vanished in the third round. After throwing a straight right past Beau's jaw, Beau countered, landing a hard blow to Jenkins' left kidney. Jenkins went down hard for a nine count. After Jenkins raised himself off the canvas, an incensed Beau immediately landed a hard right to Lew's forehead, opening an old cut above Lew's scarred right eye, producing a stream of blood.

Beau pummeled Lew again in the fourth round. The fifth was all Beau as well. With twenty-eight seconds left in the round, Beau landed a sharp punch to Jenkin's midsection that sent him to the canvas, clutching his groin. In agony, Jenkins immediately grabbed his crotch, as the disapproving crowd roared in protest, reacting to a palpable low blow. In pain, Jenkins' handlers had to carry him to his corner. Referee Ray Bowen quickly ruled Beau's punch low and gave Jenkins five minutes to recover. It was Beau's third penalty for low blows.

Beau Jack dodges a punch by Lew Jenkins at Uline Arena, April 14, 1950 (ACME Telephoto).

Taking his time to recover, Jenkins slumped on his stool, his face cut up and swollen. As the recovery time expired, Jenkins was ready to return to battle, but his manager Blinky Palermo and trainers restrained him from going back out. Referee Bowen immediately called Dr. Leon Gordon of the District of Columbia Boxing Commission inside the ring to determine whether Jenkins could continue. Gordon quickly concluded that Lew was perfectly able to carry on with the bout. Jenkins, however, stayed on his stool.

After the fight, Dr. Gordon commented on Jenkins' condition. "In my opinion Jenkins was perfectly able to continue and was willing to," stated Dr. Gordon. "His handlers refused to permit him to fight. He was hit by a glancing blow on the groin, but the five-minute rest had enabled him to recover and he should have continued."[6] Since Jenkins failed to come out in the sixth, Referee Bowen had no choice but to award Beau victory by TKO.

There was mass confusion regarding which round the knockout occurred. Thousands of people who were watching the fight on television began calling newspapers across the country for clarification. Since the "knockout" happened at the end of the fifth round, boxing aficionados thought it must have been scored a fifth-round knockout. However, Bowen scored it as a sixth-round knockout, due to Jenkins' failure to come out in the sixth round. Amidst the agitation of the crowd, Jack won an unpopular technical knockout against the Texas mauler and former lightweight champion, Lew Jenkins. Jenkins retired after his loss to Jack with an overall record was 73–41–5. Subsequently, he enlisted in the Army, where he earned a Silver Star in the Korean War for bravery. In 1999, eighteen years after his death, he was inducted into the International Boxing Hall of Fame.

Beau had a little over three weeks off before he appeared in the ring again, this time in Providence, Rhode Island. Jack met Jackie Weber for the second time on May 8, 1950. In their previous match 16 months earlier, Beau earned a unanimous decision. Weber was 7–6–2 since then and had lost four of his last six fights.

Weber, the local boy from Pawtucket, didn't stand a chance against the two-time former lightweight king. Beau, at 29 years of age, displayed speed and power, battering Weber around the ring. Perhaps Beau's best attack of the night was his savage attack on Weber's body. Following a barrage of hooks and rights to the body, Weber painfully uttered to his corner at the end of the sixth round that he was nauseated and incapable of continuing. Failing to answer the bell in the seventh round, the local boy suffered defeat at the hands of Jack, who recorded a seventh-round technical knockout. For the second consecutive time, Beau scored TKOs over his foe due to their inability to finish.

Two weeks later, on May 22, 1950, Beau entered the ring against the dark-haired, Italian-American Johnny Potenti (1923–1981) of Worcester, Massachusetts. The ten-round preliminary fight took place in Boston Garden before a mediocre crowd of 3,645. No longer was Beau fighting in the main event. Middleweights Joe Rindone and Joe Blackwood earned that honor. The twenty-seven-year-old Potenti was 42–1 in his professional career and had knocked out nineteen of his opponents. Known as a tommy-gun fighter, Johnny had a stiff left jab, a hard right, as well as respectable ring skills and was undefeated in his last 20 bouts. Potenti also had seven and a half pounds on the veteran and was two years younger. Potenti weighed in at 148¾ pounds to Jack's 141¼ pounds.

At the opening bell, both men came out ready for battle, but Beau rapidly gained control of the fight, belaboring Potenti with heavy rights to his body in every round. Throwing wild punches along with straight punches, Beau puzzled the Worcester fighter. Beau put his adversary on the canvas twice in the third round with wide left hooks to the body. The first time Potenti went down to a knee and came back up immediately. The second time, he fell to both knees and took a mandatory eight count. When Johnny came inside, Beau clinched and dished out an inside battering. Potenti attempted to rally in the tenth round, jolting Beau with a hard right to his chin, but his rally was short-lived. Beau went on to win a unanimous victory. It was only Potenti's second loss in 44 professional fights. Like Lew Jenkins, Potenti retired after the match with a record of 32–2–0. The fight card produced a gross gate of $8,881 and a net of $6,501.

The next day, Beau, along with members of the Brooklyn Dodgers, made a guest appearance at the 10th annual Fathers' Children's and Orphans' Dinner. Held at the Men's Club of Union Temple in Brooklyn, the honored guests were the 150 orphans and underprivileged children. It was an honor for Beau, an "orphan" himself, to spend time with the children.

Within a couple of weeks, Jerry Sacks, promoter for the Hoosier Boxing Club, announced that the club would be hosting a charity bout between Beau Jack and 22-year-old Ronnie Harper at the Indianapolis State Fairgrounds to benefit the Marion County Cancer Society. Harper hailed from Logan, West Virginia, but fought out of Detroit, Michigan. His young journeyman record was 26–21–4, but he had won his last five fights.

The ten-round main event was scheduled for Wednesday, June 28. Beau arrived in Indy a couple of days before the fight to finish up his training. On Monday night, Beau made a guest appearance at the Golden Gloves tournament taking place at Hagerstown High School to watch the action and meet with the young amateurs.

It was a mild Indiana evening with temperatures in the upper sixties on fight night. With the boxing ring placed inside the fairground's race track, over 4,000 spectators assembled in the grandstands.

Ronnie was a gritty young man, but experience got the best of youth. Beau dominated the fight from the opening bell. Throwing right crosses and left hooks, he repeatedly rocked Harper. His vicious body attack wore the young lad out in the early rounds. Late in the fourth, Beau landed four pounding lefts to Harper's midsection followed by two stunning rights to the jaw. Referee Frank Arford had seen enough. He refused to let Harper come out in the fifth round. Although Harper's corner contested the decision, Arford maintained that Harper was listless and wasn't even aware of what round of the fight it was. Alleviating any doubt, the two judges concurred with the stoppage. Beau netted victory by technical knockout 2:13 minutes into the fifth round.

In his tenth year of professional boxing, Beau fought his first bout in his home state of Georgia. Scheduled for Thursday, July 17, Beau's next contest was in Atlanta. Jack arrived at Hartsfield Airport on July 13 to prepare for his upcoming combat with Bobby Timpson. Timpson, hailing from Youngstown,

Ohio, excelled as an amateur, winning the Golden Gloves Championship of Eastern Ohio. Debuting on July 19, 1945, his record was 32–27–3. Since defeating Joey Freda on October 14, 1947, however, Bobby began to fade, losing 13 of his last 16 bouts.

Following Beau's arrival in Atlanta, he held a news conference announcing once again that he would retire from boxing at the end of the year to live with his family in Augusta. "This will be my last year in pro boxing," said the one-time shoe shine boy. "New York is a great place to fight and make money, but I am anxious to live with my family and friends back in Augusta."[7]

Three thousand fans showed up at the Municipal Auditorium to watch Beau's first fight in Georgia. Opened in 1909, the auditorium was home to concerts, theatre, the Atlanta Symphony Orchestra, and frequent boxing and wrestling matches. Although Beau had a four-pound weight advantage, Timpson had the benefit of youth. Timpson, at 23 years of age, was six years younger than 29-year-old Jack.

At the opening bell, both men came out with poised fortitude in their eyes, battling on even terms during the first three rounds. In the fourth, the former world champion seized control. Beau assaulted Timpson with his "famous bolo right to the body," dumping him onto the canvas for a two count. Timpson went down for a second time in the fifth after Beau smashed him with a right uppercut. Looking for a knockout as the sixth round began, Beau rushed Timpson with malicious intent, landing a smashing left hook to Timpson's eye, followed by an authoritative right bolo punch to the body. Within 40 seconds of the sixth round, Referee Sgt. Bryant Bass, Beau's previous sparring partner, stopped the bout, declaring Jack the winner by TKO. Following the contest, Beau called his wife and kids who were now living in Philadelphia. He proudly boasted that his kids would not go to sleep until he called them after a fight.

Within the next week, Beau's financial turmoil made headlines again. At the end of July, it was learned that the Internal Revenue Service was garnishing Beau's bank account in Augusta for back taxes. The previous fall, sportswriter Wendell Smith had announced in his *Sports Beat* column that Beau's earnings had disappeared. Management was blamed. Smith's conclusion appeared particularly valid given this latest news that whatever money Beau had in his bank account was being garnished for back taxes. Taxes should have been paid on Beau's behalf by his management. Given his financial turmoil, Jack was compelled to continue boxing.

Hawaii was next on Beau's travel itinerary. Promoter Al Karasick was intent on bringing Beau to Hawaii for a couple of fights. Beau had never been to Hawaii, but he was excited about spending time on the Islands. He figured he could relax by fishing while making needed money boxing.

On August 29, Karasick announced that he had signed Jack to fight local welterweight Frankie Fernandez in Honolulu on October 3. As an enticement, Karasick provided Beau a $5,000 guarantee, plus two round-trip airplane tickets from New York. Jack had eagerly waited for a chance at Fernandez so he could avenge his stablemate Tommy Bell's loss to Frankie two years earlier. The next week, however, Fernandez backed out of the bout, declaring that he had been battling a severe case of the flu and had been bedridden for over a month.

Not wanting to lose his promotion, Karasick suggested another Hawaiian fighter, "Wildcat" Philip Kim (1926–1958), as a substitute. Karasick, however, needed to strike a new deal with Chick Wergeles, as Kim was not as powerful of a draw as Fernandez. A compromise was reached, and on September 19, Karasick announced that Beau would face Philip Kim at Honolulu Stadium on October 3.

Beau and Chick arrived in Honolulu on Monday night, September 25. Fishing was Jack's first concern upon arrival. "One of the reasons I signed for a bout in Hawaii is because of the fine fishing grounds here," Jack said. "That's my chief hobby."[8] Beau proudly boasted that his biggest catch to date was a 580-pound tuna off the coast of New Jersey.

Zealous Hawaiian pugilists clamored at the opportunity to see Jack in action. As Beau completed his prefight training at Sad Sam's Gym, locals turned out in hordes to witness the former lightweight champion in person. Beau didn't disappoint. He showed off his form as he worked the speed bag, heavy bag, and performed some shadow boxing. Beau lived for training and pleasing the fans. Chick actually had to sternly order Beau to quit working out before Beau would leave the gym. After Beau's workout, Kim arrived at Sad Sam's for his training.

Kim was a powerful puncher and boasted a 25–2–2 record with 17 of his victories coming by way of knockout. This was by far the biggest opportunity of his young career. "Wildcat" Kim's manager, Eishie Toyama, confidently declared that Kim was prepared for Jack. "The Wildcat has only one thing in mind," his manager, Eishie Toyama, said, "He wants to beat Beau Jack. And he is more confident and determined than I have ever seen him. He's right physically and mentally."[9]

Unfazed, Chick Wergeles acknowledged that Beau was not as good as he once was, but promised local sportswriter Red McQueen, "If Jack doesn't give your fans one of the greatest performances they have ever seen here, I'll buy you the best hat in town."[10] In another interview, Wergeles continued to brag about his boxer. "Beau has fought the best fighters in the world in his division and as a result is long on experience," Wergeles bragged, "and we didn't come all the way from New York to lose. Beau likes it here, and he wants to spend several extra weeks in Honolulu. And he wants to fight Frankie Fernandez."[11] Holding the edge over Kim in experience, Jack was anxious to get past Kim so he could face Fernandez. He had been gunning for a bout with Fernandez for almost two years.

Honolulu Stadium was the venue for the fight. Honolulu Stadium, as described in Arthur Suehiro's book *Honolulu Stadium: Where Hawaii Played*,[12] was a part of Honolulu's golden era. Built in 1926, the landmark venue hosted the Hula Bowl, University of Hawaii football team, stock car racing, boxing, baseball, etc. Babe Ruth, Joe DiMaggio, and Jessie Owens played within the walls of the stadium, as did Elvis Presley. The stadium had seating for 24,000 but was subsequently outdated and replaced by Aloha Stadium in 1976.

A mediocre crowd of 5,176, paying a gate of $12,204, impatiently assembled to see Beau Jack in action against their local fighter. Both men had a reputation for aggressiveness and throwing heaps of punches, and the pugilistic fans were counting on a brawl. They would not be disappointed.

A scrap broke out in the first round. Right after the bell rang, Beau belted Kim with a roundhouse uppercut. Beau buffaloed the young boxer with his constant movement and bolo punches. Astonished, Kim retreated as in awe of Beau, while Beau just kept landing blows to his body, coupled with sharp left hooks, wearing the younger fighter down. Nevertheless, Beau didn't start out well in the scoring. Referee Willie Whittle deducted a point from Beau for throwing two low blows in the first round. Chick Wergeles protested so adamantly that after the fight Whittle demanded the Territorial Boxing Commission punish Wergeles for pushing him and acting belligerent while opposing the point deduction.

The only highlight for Kim in the first six rounds occurred in the second stanza when Kim managed to inflict a nasty cut on Beau's lip that would require nine stitches. Unfortunately for Kim, it didn't slow down Beau's attack. Bleeding freely from his mouth and swallowing a lot of blood, Beau battled through the next couple of rounds. Kim finally showed up in the seventh round, landing a stiff left and a jolting right just before the closing bell rang. Beau was still groggy and confounded when the eighth round began. Forcefully, Kim thundered a right to Beau's jaw and hit him with a flurry of shots, backing Jack into the ropes. Hurt against the ropes, Jack couldn't defend himself, but Kim failed to inflict more damage on the defenseless former champion when he had him wounded. In a moment of bad judgment, Kim backed off, instead choosing to box with Beau. That is just what Beau needed, a chance to recover. At the end of ten rounds, Judge Bill Pacheco scored the contest even. Judge Kenneth Olds and Referee Willie Whittle, however, gave the edge to Beau 14–13 and 18–2 respectively. Beau emerged from the blood-spattered bout a victor on points.

In his post-fight comments, Kim responded to criticism that he hadn't taken advantage of Beau when he wounded him in the eighth round. Kim explained that he hurt his hands earlier in the stanza and feared damage to his knuckles if he continued to barrage Beau on the ropes. In their dressing rooms, both fighters expressed admiration for each other. Kim stated, "He's still a champion in my book." Reflecting on Kim, Beau declared, "He's tough. I like to fight a guy like Kim who throws a lot of punches."[13]

Unfortunately, eight years later, Kim was found shot to death lying in the front seat of his car in a Los Angeles parking lot, just three blocks from the central police station. Kim, known for brushing with the law and gambling, was 32 years old. He had retired a couple of years earlier with a record of 43–15–3.

Beau returned to New York to prepare for his next bout. However, he had to cancel his upcoming contest with John L. Davis because his lip was so chopped up from the Kim fight. A couple of days later, Beau's aspiration to meet Frankie Fernandez (1919–2004) was granted. He entered into a contract to fight Fernandez in Honolulu on November 7. For his efforts, Jack was provided a $4,000 guarantee, plus two round-trip airline tickets and expenses for himself and Chick. Due to unforeseen circumstances, the bout was postponed until the 14th. Beau would have to wait one more week.

Before long, Beau and Chick boarded their flight for a return trip to Hawaii. Thirty-one-year-old Frankie Fernandez, two years older than Beau, was the greatest Island fistic attraction of the day. He was the TBC welterweight champ and had a stellar record of 24–2–0. Although Frankie had won his last four bouts, there were some questions about his readiness, as he was coming off an eight-month layoff, last fighting on February 28, when he outpointed Milo Savage of Seattle, Washington.

Hawaiian Sportswriter Red McQueen, having previously witnessed Fernandez fight, predicted Fernandez would take Beau out before the sixth round. One thing for sure, the bout, like Beau's first bout in Hawaii, was anticipated to be a brawl. Commenting on the upcoming match, Beau said, "I know it will be a tough fight and I am going to do my best. You asked if I knew anything about Fernandez. Well, Tommy Bell was telling us something about him. But I didn't pay much attention. You see, I don't like to be told about my opponents. I prefer to find out about them in the ring and fight them accordingly."[14] Beau was about to find out more than he desired to know about Fernandez.

The November 14 welterweight bout at Honolulu Stadium was a mêlée with punches soaring. Fernandez came out early in the first round, catching Beau off guard with his aggressiveness and boxing skills. He kept beating Beau to the punch, staggering him with straight rights and lefts to Beau's jaw and temple. When Beau attempted to throw his looping bolo punch, Fernandez just stepped inside and cracked Beau's jaw with rights and lefts. The second round was much the same, except Beau was penalized for a low blow. During the third, Frankie ripped a hard right over Beau's left eye, opening his previous wound, which began to bleed. With 30 seconds left in the fifth round, Fernandez pinned Beau against the ropes, leaving him stunned from rights and lefts. At the sound of the bell, Beau sarcastically straightened up and threw a salute to Fernandez.

Jack came back vigorously in the sixth round, belting Frankie in the midsection with his famous right-hand bolo punch. However, there was little Beau could do. He was merely outclassed and out boxed by Fernandez. To make matters worse, Beau had another point taken away in the ninth round for a kidney punch.

Although both men were brawling, they valiantly displayed honorable sportsmanship. In the third round, Fernandez fell into the ropes after losing his balance. Beau graciously permitted Frankie to come back up and regain his composure before continuing. In the eighth round, Frankie reciprocated when Jack's head went outside the ropes, allowing Beau to re-gather himself.

In the end, Beau lost a unanimous decision to Fernandez. Referee Willie Whitle scored the contest 18–8, Judge Richard Bearse 20–9, and Judge James Carreira 22–8, all in favor of Fernandez. "Fernandez ripped the Georgia windmill to earn a convincing decision last night at the Stadium," wrote Andrew Mitsukado of the *Honolulu Advertiser*.[15] After the fight, Gene Wilhelm, sportswriter for the *Honolulu Star-Bulletin*, spoke with both men. Questioned about Frankie's punching power, Beau responded, "Well, I took everything he threw. But he's sure a strong boy, very strong."[16] Fernandez praised Beau. "He sure can hit.... When he starts winding up like a windmill, you just gotta do something and quick."[17]

Beau lost the decision, but the promoters suffered a knockout when the weather forecast for fight night included thunderstorms and rain. Contrary to predictions, the night was nice and dry. Irrespective of the improved weather, at least half of the expected fans did not turn out. The purse of $11,322.40 provided by the relatively small crowd of 4,649 fans did not even cover the main event after taxes.

On November 16, promoter Lou Thomas announced that he had once again signed Beau Jack and John L. Davis for a ten-round welterweight bout at the San Francisco Civic Auditorium for Friday night, November 24, 1950. Beau had canceled their previously scheduled contest because of injuries suffered to his mouth during his clash with Kim. Jack and Chick flew into San Francisco from Hawaii on Friday night, November 17. Four days later, Wergeles called the bout off again, this time asserting that Beau's left eye had not healed from the Fernandez bout. Moreover, Chick pleaded that unexpectedly the cut above Beau's eye was re-opened during training for the upcoming combat. In a terse reply, California State Athletic Commissioner Joe Phillips proclaimed that if Beau did not appear for the fight, he faced suspension in California and possibly the rest of the states affiliated with the NBA.

Beau complied and appeared before the Commission for a physical. Following their examination, the Commission's physicians concluded that Beau's eye did not seem problematic and should be fully healed in time for the fight. Adamantly rejecting their opinion, Wergeles commented, "The state athletic commission told me today they would have me suspended all over the country if we didn't go through with the fight, but I'm not going to endanger the health of my fighter."[18] Even after promoter Jimmie Murray said he would be willing to postpone the fight a week, Wergeles refused.

Alan Ward, the sports editor for the *Oakland Tribune*, provided another motive as to why the bout was called off. "The grapevine has it that Wergeles was touted off the fight by interests unfriendly to Thomas, and Thomas' associate, Jimmy Murray of Oakland."[19] Commissioner Joe Phillips concurred, stating he was confident that pressure had been put on Wergeles not to fight. With the Commission's understanding, Beau and Chick flew back to New York on Monday night, November 20, four days before the scheduled bout.

Beau next entered the ring at the Milwaukee Auditorium in Milwaukee, Wisconsin. He faced 24-year-old Fitzie Pruden (1927–1990), a 144-pound, 5'8" tall fighter from Toronto, Canada. The double headliner took place on New Year's Day, January 1, 1951. Since his debut in 1947, Pruden had racked up a notable record of 45–10–0 and earned the right to face Beau by impressively outpointing John LaBroi on Thanksgiving Day. Six years younger than Beau, Pruden had a three-pound weight advantage.

As usual, Beau came out strong. His very first punch was a stunning right to the Canadian's chin. Barely standing upright on his unsteady legs, Pruden almost toppled over. The contest appeared like it might be over, but Pruden weathered the round. Resiliently, Fritzie came back fiercely in the second round, driving Beau back. From there on it was a bloody slugfest. At the end of ten vicious rounds, the decision went to the scorecards. Referee Dauber Kaeger scored Beau the winner but the two judges favored Pruden. Pruden was declared the winner by split decision. The crowd of 4,156 fans produced a gate of $12,697.

Seventeen days later, Jack met Irishman Del Flanagan (1928–2003) from St. Paul, Minnesota. Flanagan came into the fight riding a 47-bout win streak and was determined to increase his streak to 48 victories. Beau entered the ring with two consecutive losses.

The venue for the contest was the Auditorium in Minneapolis, Minnesota. Built in 1927, the Minneapolis Auditorium had seating for 10,545. It was also the initial home of the Minneapolis Lakers of the NBL, which subsequently joined the NBA and moved to Los Angeles, where they changed their name to the Los Angeles Lakers.

Beau arrived in St. Paul two days before the bout to finish up preparations. Both men trained at the Ringside Gym. Arrogantly, 22-year-old Flanagan told the press that he was going to knock Beau Jack out. "I've scored 23 knockouts in 47 professional fights, and after I put Jack away it'll be 24 knockouts in 48 fights."[20] Flanagan was a slick and elusive boxer. It was difficult for most of his opponents to land a glove on him, even if he was standing in front of them. Del possessed a hard-straight left that he fired off like a machine gun. On fight night, January 18, the crowd numbered 4,784, producing a gate of $15,678.60. Beau weighed in at 138 pounds, while Del weighed in at 139¼ pounds.

Flanagan stormed out at the opening bell, taking command of the battle. Within two minutes, he had blood flowing from Beau's nose. Using his speed and left jabs, the 5'8" tall Flanagan kept the former champion at distance. Del pounded Beau with his left jab. When there was no opening for his jab, he tagged Beau with his left hook. Jack finally showed a little life in the fifth, throwing left hooks to the body and catching Del with a hard bolo punch. A crafty boxer, Flanagan learned fast and was prepared the next time Beau wound up his bolo punch, detonating a left hook to Beau's chin. Del was also ready when Beau came rushing out in the sixth round. As Beau rushed forward, Flanagan landed two rights directly on Beau's button. Beau came on yet again in the eighth round with lefts to the body. Flanagan, however, was not an easy target to hit, retreating at times behind his left jab. Jack managed to win the ninth round, working Flanagan's body with lefts and bolo punches. In the final round, both fighters gave their all, standing toe to toe as they eyed a knockout. Flanagan, however, was too much for Beau, winning a unanimous decision and his 48th consecutive victory. It was only the second time in Beau's career that he had lost three fights in a row. In his last twelve matches, Beau was six and six.

In his post-fight comments, Flanagan said Beau never hurt him, but admitted "he is the trickiest fighter I have ever fought."[21] Beau sang Flanagan's praises. "That boy is going to be the next lightweight champion. He isn't a hard puncher but how he can box. You just can't hit the boy solid.[22] What a boxer," exclaimed Jack. "You don't know until you are in there with him how hard he is to hit cleanly. Even my good shots, where I thought I had him where he could be hurt, seemed to go soft the way he moved with them or tipped me off balance. Yes, he can be a champion."[23] Agreeing, Chick Wergeles declared, "There is the next world lightweight champion. He is a master boxer."[24] Del would never get a title shot, but he would end his professional career with a record of 105–22–2. Both he and his Brother Glen were inducted into the World Boxing Hall of Fame in 2003.

In less than two weeks, Beau was back on the West Coast for his upcoming fight against Emil Barao (1926–2008) of Hayward, California. The bout was scheduled for January 31, 1951, at the Oakland Civic Auditorium in Oakland, California. Built in 1914, the arena had a beautiful glass covered roof and seating for 4,000 spectators.

Oakland Civic Auditorium, c. 1917 (Wikimedia Commons).

For the first time in two years, Beau was entering the ring for the third time in less than a month. A significant step down in opponents, Emil had lost his last three fights and had a journeyman record of 33–33–9.

Barao and Jack circled each other at the opening bell. Barao seemed in awe of Beau's windmill attack, backtracking while Beau pursued him, scoring with bolo punches and lefts to the body. Beau focused most of his attack on Barao's head and body, scoring as he landed punches. In the eighth round, Jack bombarded Barao with body punches and then went to his head. At the end of the round, however, Barao stood his ground and landed a right hand on Beau's jaw, knocking him to the canvas for a no count. Barao also came out strong in the tenth round, rattling the former champion with flurries of rights and lefts. Beau looked as if he had been in a barroom brawl after Barao opened a cut on his mouth and bloodied his nose with brutal left hooks. Nonetheless, he couldn't overcome Beau's domination in the earlier rounds. At the end of ten rounds, a battered Beau was declared the victor by unanimous decision, winning eight rounds to Barao's two rounds.

On February 8, promoter Manny Almeida announced that he had signed lightweight champion Ike Williams and former champion Beau Jack for a ten-round overweight bout scheduled for March 5. The contest would take place at the Rhode Island Auditorium in Providence. Beau had lost to Ike by TKO in a lightweight title fight a couple of years earlier. Even though Ike lost his last bout, dropping a unanimous decision to Joe Miceli in a non-title match on February 19, he was heavily favored over Jack, 10–1. The only advantage Beau had was that he came in four pounds heavier than Williams, weighing 146 pounds to 142 pounds for Williams.

Astonishingly, Beau surprised the oddsmakers and pugilistic fans. Fighting with a distinct advantage in the early rounds, Beau pelted the taller Williams with left hooks and uppercuts. Jack landed two hard right uppercuts in the third, bewildering Williams. Beau was in a groove as he fought from his crouched stance. In the fifth round, he bombarded Williams and landed, perhaps his best punch of the night, a left hook to Ike's body dazing the champion. In the sixth, Beau knocked Ike to the canvas with an overhand right. Unfortunately, Referee Sharkey Buonanno inadvertently called it a slip, instead of a knockdown. Both fighters ended up falling out of the ring twice as Williams tried to push Beau out of his crouching stance. Ike fought back hard, outpunching Jack ten to one in the later rounds.

At the final bell, the underdog Beau Jack was cheered rowdily by the 3,695 appreciative fans. Ike Williams, however, was awarded an immensely unpopular split decision, with the two judges giving the victory to Williams and Referee Sharkey Buonanno giving Beau Jack the victory. When the decision was announced, the disgruntled crowd condemned the decision with choruses of boos. The gate was only $7,095.

To meet his next adversary, Beau traveled to Coliseum Arena in New Orleans. He faced Leroy Willis for the second time on March 30, 1951. Beau had defeated Willis by unanimous decision in their previous bout on December 17, 1948.

Like their first contest, the bout wasn't much of a fight. Beau consistently landed bolo punches, a sweeping arched uppercut, on Willis' head, as well as some heavy blows to his chin. Enduring the storm, Willis connected with some good punches, but couldn't score often enough. Using his "neck-stretching bolo punch," Beau again won an easy unanimous decision over the Detroit fighter.

Gil Turner Puts the Nail in the Coffin

Beau at thirty years of age wasn't as good as he once was, but he kept going. After the Willis bout, Jack signed to fight a young unbeaten boxer, twenty-year-old Philadelphian Gil Turner (1930–1996). As an amateur, Turner had won the National AAU Welterweight Championship. Since recently turning professional, Turner had a record of 17–0, with 16 knockouts.

Before the fight, Beau worked out at Olympia Gym in Philadelphia where he impressed onlookers. One of those present was "Jersey" Joe Walcott, who said: "That Beau looks real good. In fact, he looks like a winner to me!"[25] At the weigh-in, Beau was 142 pounds, while Turner was 142½ pounds. Gil had a four-inch height advantage but came in as a 6–5 underdog mainly because of his lack of professional experience. It was also his first ten-round bout.

John DaGrosa, a member of the Pennsylvania Athletic Commission, cautioned the fighters before the bout, but he spoke most directly to Beau. Talking to Jack, he said, "I know that you have been a tremendous credit to the game. You know all the tricks," said DaGrosa as he looked at Beau. "Turner is a promising fighter. He has been winning his fights cleanly and fairly. He has never resorted to questionable tactics in the ring. To your credit, you do not do anything that is illegal. But I also know that, if the occasion arises, you can use trickery."[26] Clearly, DaGrosa wanted a clean fight from Beau.

The fight took place before 6,094 spectators, mostly Turner fans, at the Arena in Philadelphia on April 16, 1951, producing a gate of $18,884.35. The raucous crowd was in an uproar from the opening bell until the final bell. It was a big test for the young unbeaten Philadelphia fighter. What Turner lacked in professional experience, he made up in quickness, stamina, and power. He dished out every punch he had, but Beau's resilience carried him through the fight.

Turner took command of the fight early and never lost it. As Jack rushed in at the opening bell, Turner pounded him with a two-fisted attack to his head. Both men traded bolo punches, but Gil shook Beau up, beating him with left hooks and rights to the head. He continually rocked Beau twice with hard rights and lefts to his jaw. As instructed by his corner, in the seventh round, Turner took a breather. It was the only round that Beau won. In the final stanzas, Turner coasted, throwing flurries of punches to discourage Beau and win the rounds. Astonishingly, Beau was able to withstand Turner's punishment and keep standing. At the final bell, Beau waived an "airy greeting to his young adversary," but the outcome was a foregone conclusion.[27] Turner cruised to a unanimous decision victory over the former champ, winning all ten rounds on Judge Frank Knaresborough's scorecard and eight rounds on both Referee Charley Daggert and Judge Zach Clayton's card.

Sitting in his dressing room after the fight, Beau praised Gil. "Turner seems to have everything," Beau said appreciatively. "He's got the making of a ring champion. If he's not rushed too fast, he ought to get there."[28] Beau iterated that his heart wasn't in the fight. "I fought the best I could, but it wasn't good enough," said Jack. "I was in good shape … but I was worried. My heart wasn't in the fight."[29] Apparently, Jack was in the middle of a dismal domestic quarrel that had kept him from focusing on his training. It was so bad, he purportedly almost called off the fight.

Several days later, contemplating a rematch, promoter Herman Taylor asked Chick how Beau was doing. Chick stated that Beau had patched up his domestic issues and was in harmony again. On May 13, Taylor announced that he had signed Beau Jack and Gil Turner for a rematch scheduled for May 21. One month after their first bout, the two warriors entered the ring again at the Arena in Philadelphia. A crowd of 4,649 fans gathered for the contest. Beau weighed 145 pounds. Turner weighed 143 pounds.

As in their first bout, Turner jumped on Beau early, consistently pounding rights against his jaw. Jack's best round was the third when he traded evenly with Turner. No matter how hard Beau tried, however, he couldn't endure the punching power of Turner. By the eighth stanza, Gil had hammered Beau helpless. Turner stormed Beau with a flurry of rights and lefts. Then Turner landed a massive right uppercut that sent Beau reeling into Turner's corner. Stepping between the fighters, Referee Charley Daggert had seen enough punishment. He stopped the fight 1:26 minutes into the eighth round.

It was a devastating loss for Beau Jack. A dejected Beau cried as he was led to his corner. "I love to fight," he sobbed, "why did he stop it?"[30] It was only the third time in his 12-year career that Beau had been stopped. Following the fight, the Pennsylvania Athletic Commission, impressed by Turner, announced that it would not recognize any welterweight champion who had not fought Gil Turner. Beau had now lost six of his last eight contests.

26

Tissue Paper Legs

After Beau's thrashing by Gil Turner, his trainer, Sid Bell, who had rejoined Beau's camp, finally convinced Beau to retire from boxing. He spoke earnestly to Beau. "Beau, you got the heart of a lion, the strength of an elephant the punch of a lightning bolt—but your legs are tissue paper. Promise me you won't fight anymore."[1] Bell stressed to Beau that his legs were just too weak. Jack had suffered through multiple operations on both knees. He just wasn't as competitive as he used to be and at his age and condition was prone to serious injury. With his trainer's advice and back to back losses to Gil Turner, Jack, at thirty years of age, retired in 1951. Jack's career appeared over. His record was 80–23–4. Beau and his trainers, as well as his longtime manager and friend Chick Wergeles, parted ways.

Beau stuck around New York for a couple of months. In addition to the shooting galleries and dime movies, Beau found relaxation attending shows and movies at the Apollo Theater. Opened in 1914, the neo-classical theater became a landmark in the Harlem section of New York City. Although African Americans were not originally allowed to attend or perform at the Apollo, that changed after Sidney Cohen and Morris Sussman purchased the theater in 1934 and marketed entertainment toward the predominantly African American citizens living in Harlem. The Apollo Theater was instrumental in the development of numerous musical genres, such as the blues, gospel, jazz, R&B, swing, and soul. Outstanding performers were commonplace, featuring such artists as Ella Fitzgerald, Sarah Vaughan, Billie Holiday, Sammy Davis, Jr., the Johnny Otis Rhythm & Blues Caravan, Josephine Baker, and James Brown.

Over the next couple of months, Beau was frequently spotted at the Apollo holding hands with his lady friend Ruby Valdez. It could have been a reason for his recent domestic troubles, but Beau was captivated by Ruby. In addition to attending the movies and Saturday night shows, the couple were regulars at Amateur Hour on Wednesday nights. Some of the best up and coming artists vied for prizes at Wednesday night's Amateur Hour. Begun in 1934, the Amateur Hour was one of the Apollo's most popular ongoing shows during the 40s and 50s. One of the first winners was 15-year-old Ella Fitzgerald. Over the years, Amateur Hour contestants included numerous artists and musicians, such as the Esquires, James Brown, Sarah Vaugh, Dinah Washington, and Ruth Brown.

Within weeks of Beau's retirement, the press aired his financial difficulties again, broadcasting that he was broke. Future Pulitzer Prize winner (1956) and distinguished sports journalist for *The New York Times* Arthur Daley (1904–1974) reported that Beau Jack, at thirty years of age, was broke because his associates swindled his money. "He's broke," Daley wrote, "because he was robbed of his heritage, his earnings squandered away.[2] This is one of the most contemptible episodes in a sport that has had far more than its share of disgraceful actions by the thieves and hoodlums who infest its outer edges," penned Daley. "The Beau can read now and his favorite book is the Bible. Perhaps he can take some comfort from the passage relating to the man who fell among thieves. It's the only comfort he has left."[3]

Adding credence to Daley's story, three months after his final fight with Gil Turner, Beau was reportedly receiving $55 a week from the National Sports Alliance Boxers' Pension Fund. Formed in New York City on December 11, 1921, largely through the work of New York Senator Jimmy Walker, the National Sports Alliance's offered assistance to indigent boxers. Jack Dempsey and his manager Jack Kearns were among the initial members. Members paid dues, and surcharges were added to ticket prices to aid the Alliance and its efforts.

Back Home in Augusta

Beau left New York and was back in Augusta by 1952, where he reconciled with his first wife, Josephine. Much of his time was spent tending his small farm off of New Savannah Road. Yet, boxing was in his blood. Beau may have retired from his career, but he was still in demand. As a former world champion, Beau was often called upon to referee bouts around the area. For instance, in March he traveled to Spartanburg, South Carolina, where he refereed a preliminary match before the main event between Rib Bill Wilson and Guard Wyatt. The appreciation and applause he received from his fans were priceless to Beau Jack.

As was customary, in early April, Jack was back at the Augusta National, shining golfers' shoes during the Masters Tournament. Beau was once again a bootblack. Apparently, Beau not only shined shoes and waited on golfers, but he was also an excellent masseur. While attending the 1952 Masters Tournament, sportswriter John Wheeler had the pleasure to experience one of Beau's massages. Wheeler asked Bowman Milligan if there was anyone at the clubhouse that could give him a rub down. Wheeler recalls the incident in his own words.

> "Beau will take care of you," replied Bowman. I looked a little puzzled. "I mean Beau Jack, the old lightweight champion," he explained. "He gave Gene Tunney one every day he was here, and he claimed they were the best he'd ever had."
>
> What was good enough for Tunney wasn't too good for Wheeler, so I stretched out on the table. He had come the full circle, and then was back where he started from in the locker room of the golf club. He is a polite, genial, modest man with a ready smile, and an excellent masseur.[4]

Beau Jack, the pleaser, knew how to nurture the guests at the Augusta National.

Wheeler questioned Beau how he made out financially from his boxing career. Beau replied, "Oh, I did all right. Managed to save some money and didn't wind up punchy."[5] After asking around, Wheeler was told that Beau "finished up with about $75,000 and received an income of $150 to $200 a month."[6] Of course, this information conflicted with earlier press reports that Beau was broke.

As the days went by, Jack continued to yearn for boxing. On a gloomy, warm, humid day in April, following the conclusion of the 1952 Masters Tournament, Beau began contemplating a return to boxing. Stan Hochman, a reporter for the *Augusta Chronicle*, related it to "a salmon returning to its spawning grounds for it was here that Beau Jack got his start."[7] Beau was still in good shape, but his years in the ring had taken their toll on him. He was ten pounds over his fighting weight. He was scared above his eyebrows from all the cuts suffered in the ring, and his vision was waning. Scar tissue covered his left knee, which had been broken twice. Was a comeback feasible? Ironically, it was Beau's former manager Bowman Milligan that assisted Beau in mapping out a return route.

In late May, Beau Jack announced that he was resuming his boxing career. In an interview with Bill Ferguson of *The Times*, Beau was optimistic. "I'm just 31 and that's not too old, is it?" questioned Beau. "I've just gotta' make a comeback.... I'm still in good shape and I been workin' out regular. I know I can come around.... I'll be back, it's in my blood."[8] Beau was ready to mount a comeback, but was the boxing world ready for him?

Determined, Beau traveled to New York to obtain his boxing license from the New York State Athletic Commission. Before permission could be granted, Beau was required to undergo a physical examination by the Commission's physician, Dr. Ira McCown. After completing the physical, Dr. McCown gave his report to the Commission. The Commission consulted with Dr. McCown and carefully reviewed Beau's physical record before reaching a decision. Citing his previous knee injuries and the probability for further harm, on

November 21, 1952, the NYSAC denied Beau's request for a boxing license. Beau was heartbroken but as the man he was, took the rejection in stride.

Being denied a boxing license, Jack returned to Augusta and opened up a barbecue restaurant, Beau Jack's Drive-In, located at the intersection of New Savannah Road and Molly Pond Road. Nevertheless, even though Jack had his family and restaurant in Augusta, he just couldn't seem to settle down. During the early summer of 1953, Beau headed to Florida, where he found employment at the glamorous Fontainebleau Hotel on Miami Beach, shining shoes.

After the summer season, Beau returned to Augusta, where he again turned his attention to boxing, this time as a trainer. Not only was Jack able to spend time in the gym, but he was also able to give back to his sport by instructing young boxers. He worked with fighters such as Aman Peck of Hartford, Connecticut, and Eddie Green of Kannapolis, North Carolina, as well as several Augusta boxers, including Claude Chapman, James Bussey, the Tornado Kid, and Raymond Jones.

Beau was once again back at the Augusta National for the 18th Masters Tournament held on April 8–12, 1954. It was a memorable tournament with Sam Snead defeating Ben Hogan in a Monday playoff. On the eve of the play-off between Snead and Hogan, Beau traveled to the Asheville Auditorium, as two of his pupils, Eddie Green (29–13–1) and Raymond Jones (5–6–2), were on the Monday night boxing card. Eddie Green met Jackie O'Brien (58–12–7) in the featured welterweight bout, and Raymond Jones faced Joe Green (33–14–2). With Beau working the corner and shouting directives, both of his fighters scored victories that night. Two weeks later, Beau was at the Armory in Charlotte with Eddie Green. Eddie faced Gene Burton (54–20–10), a former number one welterweight contender. Green earned a unanimous decision over the formidable Burton.

Later that summer, Beau made local headlines, but not of the kind he was used to when he was boxing. At 2:00 a.m. on Sunday, August 29, 1954, his restaurant, Beau Jack's Drive-In, was raided by a county racket squad. Upon entering, the squad found nine men, including Jack, playing a game of "skin." The men were arrested and charged with gambling. One of the men was also charged with carrying a concealed weapon. Authorities confiscated $9 in cash and three decks of cards. Beau was fined $18 for gambling and $28 for running a gaming house.

Racial Segregation in Schools Declared Unconstitutional

For years, Americans lived in a racially segregated life under the "separate but equal" doctrine set forth in 1896 by the U.S. Supreme Court in *Plessy v. Ferguson.* According to seven of the Supreme Court Justices, as long as public facilities were equal for blacks and whites, racially segregated facilities were permissible. There was one lone dissent, that of Justice John Marshall Harlan.

> [I]n view of the constitution, in the eye of the law, there is in this country no superior, dominant, ruling class of citizens. There is no caste here. Our constitution is color-blind, and neither knows nor tolerates classes among citizens. In respect of civil rights, all citizens are equal before the law. The humblest is the peer of the most powerful. The law regards man as man and takes no account of his surroundings or of his color when his civil rights as guaranteed by the supreme law of the land are involved.

His dissent on the grounds that all citizens, black or white, are equal before the law would set the stage for the civil rights movement, but it would take five decades.

Times were challenging for black Americans as the civil rights movement began in the late 1940s, seeking to end racial discrimination and gain equal rights under the law. At the time, South Carolina required segregation in public schools. The state's constitution required separate schools for white and "colored" children and prohibited integration of schools. Of course, education facilities for black students were significantly inferior to those of white students.

In Clarendon County, South Carolina, busing was provided for the white schools but not black schools. In addition to having separate and significantly inferior facilities, black children had to walk to school, sometimes many miles. Harry Briggs, a service station attendant, and his wife Elizabeth Briggs, a maid, rallied 21 other families to find a bus for their children. When they asked school superintendent R. M. Elliot for the use of one of the 33 buses owned by Clarendon County, he refused.

In 1949, the National Association for the Advancement of Colored People (NAACP) agreed to assist the Briggses and other black families in Clarendon County to not only obtain school transportation but to seek equal facilities and educational opportunities. A three-judge panel of the U.S. District Court found segregation lawful by a vote of 2–1. On appeal to the Supreme Court in 1952 as *Briggs v. Elliott*, evidence was provided by Clarendon County that progress had been made on equalizing facilities. Therefore, the case was remanded back to the district court. In the subsequent district court hearing, Thurgood Marshall argued that as long as segregation existed, schools would be unequal. Inevitably, the case was appealed back to the Supreme Court, where it would become the first of five cases combined into *Brown v. Board of Education* (1954).

In one of the other cases, Oliver L. Brown, a welder and assistant pastor, filed a class-action suit against the Board of Education of Topeka, Kansas after his daughter was denied entrance to Topeka's all-white elementary schools. His daughter Linda Brown, a third-grade student, had to walk six blocks to her school bus stop to ride to Monroe Elementary, a mile away. A white elementary school was only seven blocks from her house. The NAACP directed Brown to attempt to enroll her in the closest school, i.e., the white school. Needless to say, enrollment was refused.

Brown subsequently filed suit against the Board of Education. Arguing that schools for black children were not equal to those for white children, Brown asserted that segregation violated the "equal protection clause" of the 14th Amendment, prohibiting any state to "deny to any person within its jurisdiction the equal protection of the laws."

In all, five cases were consolidated into *Brown v. Board of Education* as heard before the Supreme Court—*Brown v. Board of Education of Topeka* (Kansas), *Briggs v. Elliott* (South Carolina), *Davis v. County School Board of Prince Edward County* (Virginia), *Gebhart v. Belton* (Delaware), and *Bolling v. Sharpe* (Washington, D.C.). In a landmark opinion, the Supreme Court unanimously ruled that racial segregation in public schools was unconstitutional. Although the decision would become a cornerstone of the civil rights movement, many schools remained segregated.

Rosa Parks

Another critical moment in the civil rights movement occurred on December 1, 1955. A black seamstress named Rosa Parks (1913–2005) was coming home from work on a city bus in Montgomery, Alabama. Blacks were expected to sit in the back of the bus, with the front reserved for whites. When a white man got on the bus at one of its stops, there were no seats left in the "white" section. Therefore, the driver demanded riders in the first row of the "colored" section to stand. Three of the riders stood, but Rosa Parks refused. She was arrested and found guilty of violating segregation laws. Rosa Parks' defiance led to a year-long Montgomery bus boycott led by the young Rev. Dr. Martin Luther King, Jr. Rosa Parks suddenly became a national symbol of dignity and strength in the struggle to end racial segregation.

27

Reentering the Ring

As Jack managed and trained fighters, he once again began to contemplate his own return. Beau hadn't retired on a good note. He had lost his last two fights in 1951 to Gil Turner. Even worse, in their previous bout, Turner knocked him out. Beau was 33 years old and had been out of the ring for almost four years. He also had two bad knees that had been operated on several times. According to Beau, however, his body and mind were prepared to return to boxing.

Boxers rarely succeed in revisiting the ring after retirement. One of boxing's greatest heavyweight champions, Joe Louis (1914–1981), failed in his comeback attempt several years earlier. The "Brown Bomber" retired as the heavyweight world champion after he knocked out "Jersey" Joe Walcott on June 25, 1948. It's a title Louis held over twelve years while amassing an incredible professional record of 49–1. After retiring, Louis was informed by the IRS that he owed over $500,000 in back taxes and penalties for incomplete tax returns filed by his manager's accountant.

Although Louis grossed near $4.6 million during his career, he received less than $800,000. With his numerous businesses that he invested in failing and his back taxes continuing to accumulate interest, the former champ was in dire financial straits. Louis had no choice but to return to the ring. A year after returning to the ring, the 37-year-old "Brown Bomber" ran into 27-year-old and future boxing legend Rocky Marciano in Madison Square Garden. In a nationally televised fight on October 26, 1951, Marciano destroyed Louis, knocking him out and giving him the third loss of his career. "At 2:36 of the eighth round in Madison Square Garden last night, the old Brown Bomber was stretched on his back on the apron of the ring in a pathetic finish to one of the most fabulous stories in all sports."[1] It was sickening to see one of America's first popularly idolized black champions on the canvas.

The great Joe Louis was finished. Tears filled his dressing room after the fight. His Army buddy and middleweight champion Sugar Ray Robinson cried, reporters were choked up, and even Rocky Marciano stopped by Joe's dressing room to say he was sorry.

Another legendary boxer, former welterweight and middleweight champion Sugar Ray Robinson (1921–1989), was also attempting a comeback. Robinson retired in 1952 with a record of 133–3–2 after fighting for almost twelve years. Although he won his first comeback fight on January 5, 1955, knocking out Joe Rindone, he was embarrassed on national television in his second contest against unranked Ralph Jones. Jones knocked Robinson around the ring, leaving the former two-time champion bleeding from his nose and with a cut over his right eye on his way to winning a stunning decision. It was only the fourth time Robinson had tasted defeat in 140 bouts.

Unbeknownst at the time, Robinson, unlike Joe Louis, survived his initial disappointments to carry on for over 10 more years, finally retiring at 44 years old. Surprisingly, he even won the middleweight title two more times, holding the title for a record five times. But, Beau was not Robinson.

In the midst of Louis' failed comeback attempt and Robinson's beating on national television, Beau was determined to fight again, and boxing would furnish needed money. Moreover, in his mind, he still believed he could contend for a title. Several months later, on December 28, 1954, promoter Dick Wilson announced he had signed Jack for the first fight of his 1955 comeback attempt. His opponent was none other than his former pupil, Eddie Green (1926–2013). The ten-round middleweight bout was scheduled for January 20, 1955 at the Township Auditorium in Columbia, South Carolina.

Constructed in 1930, the Township Auditorium is a three-story brick building, featuring Georgian Revival architecture and a columned entrance. It has a seating capacity of 2,500 to 3,500. At the time, it was strictly segregated. White and black patrons sat in separate areas, had separate entrances, and separate restrooms. Subsequently, in 2005, the Township Auditorium was listed in the National Register of Historic Places.

Beau's comeback efforts at 33 years of age with a twice-broken kneecap were condemned by many. Syndicated International News Service (INS) sportswriter Pat Robinson was aghast that a boxing commission anywhere could even contemplate issuing a boxing license to Beau. "We read with jaundiced eye a story advising us that somebody down in South Carolina is going to promote a comeback fight for Beau Jack," wrote Robinson. "If the cops don't step in and stop such an atrocity, the SPCA should."[2] The risk of injury was just too high. Although Jack was reportedly broke, "it is better for a man to be broke than to take a chance on permanent injury for a few bucks."[3] He was jeopardizing too much just to make a little pocket change. He was simply too old and battle-scarred to box again.

Jack's former manager Chick Wergeles was incensed when he heard the news of Beau's plan to return to the ring. "I read a report that Jack is going to make a comeback in Columbia, S.C., next month," said Wergeles. "He won't fight if I can help it. I signed him to a five-year contract back in 1952, so he couldn't fight again. He'd get hurt."[4] Concerned for his former fighter, Chick emphasized that his knees were still bad. Wergeles saw firsthand what happened in Beau's last fight with Gil Turner and predicted with apprehension that Beau would get hurt because of his bad left knee."

Promoter Dick Wilson wanted none of the criticism. He retorted publicly that the fight would go on unless legal action was taken to prevent it. "We will endeavor to go through with the fight for I feel after personally observing Jack that he is in good physical condition."[5] Furthermore, as far as he knew, Chick was no longer Beau's manager. Alarmed, Wergeles tried to prevent the contest, insisting that he had a private contract with Jack through 1957 and would not permit him to fight again.

Jack kept training during all the confusion and proudly proclaimed that he was ready for action and that his bum knee was resilient again. Meanwhile, on January 5, 1955, the Richland County Boxing Commission governing the bout declared that Beau had passed physical examinations by two Columbia physicians and was adequately ready for his fight against Eddie Green.

Having entertained Wergeles' plea, the New York State Athletic Commission investigated the managerial contract and several days later concluded that the contract Wergeles had with Beau expired in 1951. Wergeles countered the Commission, admitting that his contract on file expired in 1951 but insisted that he had a private agreement with Beau to prevent him from boxing and suffering permanent injury. Wergeles' contract allegation was quickly dismissed. However, the NYSAC continued to refuse to issue a license to Beau Jack.

Fran Walosin of the *Elmira Advertiser* took the Richland County Boxing Commission to task, proclaiming that the Commission exhibited boxing's cruelest characteristic by issuing Jack a license. "For anyone interested, this is the boxing game displaying its cruelest side—the squeezing of a last few bucks out of a once great at the risk of permanent injury to the fighter," denounced Walosin. "The fact that the Richland County, S.C. Carolina Boxing Commission has reinstated Jack after his license has been revoked for 44 months despite warnings from the fighter's ex-manager that Jack is risking severe injury, is another example of the glaring need for a national body to govern boxing."[6] Irrespective of the warnings, the bout was set to occur on January 20.

Beau was frustrated about all the condemnation regarding his comeback but was not thwarted in his efforts. He affirmed that he was ready and able to fight again. "I'm beginning to get that killer feeling again…. I won't disgrace myself…. If the fight lasts only one round, it'll still be a good fight, because I'll be giving everything I've got for every second."[7]

Beau trained laboriously at his old stomping grounds, Stillman's Gym in New York. First things first. Jack cut his weight from 169 pounds to 147 pounds. His trick to trimming his weight was purportedly "having 'those little fellers,' boys of 95–100 pounds, run on his stomach while he was lying flat on his back."[8] His training also included arduous road work, and he began sparring regularly. When in Augusta, he worked out at the YMCA and Camp Gordon. Beau was eager to thrill his fans and hear their thunderous ovations once again. It had been four years, one month, and three days since he had last stepped in the ring.

His opponent and former apprentice, middleweight Eddie Green, had credentials that would worry any fighter contemplating a comeback. Green was 27 years old, almost seven years younger than Beau. He was taller and outweighed Beau 159 pounds to 147 pounds. Moreover, Green had never suffered a knockout and had won 48 of his 60 professional fights.

On fight night, the scene was tense. Everyone was anxious to see how Beau would perform. As usual, Jack came out the aggressor at the opening bell. Unlike his previous fights, however, Beau was flat-footed and showed little of his previous whirlwind style. Green, for his part, kept Beau at bay using long left jabs, driving Beau off balance, while he scored hard body punches. Disconcerting, it was evident that Beau's left knee was bothering him during the fight, the same one that had led to his retirement. He dragged his left leg at times, and his bounce was merely a memory of the past. Beau still put up a decent showing, managing to land stinging left hooks before Green could tie him up to avoid further damage. He was most effective when he worked his way inside Green's long arms.

Neither fighter was in trouble during the fight, though Beau did open up a slight cut under Green's right eye. After ten rounds of action, the outcome went to the scorecards. Referee Ray Moore called it 97–95 for Jack. Judge Bee Harper called it 99–95 and Judge Don Busci scored it 98–93, both in Jack's favor. Beau's arm was lifted in victory as he emerged from his first fight in three and a half years with a unanimous decision.

Beau was euphoric. In the post-fight press conference, Beau called out his old adversary, Ike Williams, the former lightweight champion who had defeated him in both of their previous meetings. Beau wanted revenge, and Ike seemed like a reasonable opponent. Ike too was seeking to make a triumphant return to boxing. Like many that had tried before, Ike was having a difficult time of it. He had lost his last two fights and had only fought once since November 9, 1953. In his dressing room after his victory over Green, a delighted Jack announced, "I think I'm set to fight Ike Williams next here."[9]

Encouraged by his performance, Beau was eager to enter the ring again. On the other hand, Eddie Green retired after one more fight. Promoter Dick

Wilson was also enthusiastic and ardent for Beau to continue fighting. Look-ing for a big payday, he announced that Beau would not fight anyone but named fighters from there on out on his comeback trail. Thus, Wilson as-sertively announced he was seeking to match Beau with Ike Williams in Co-lumbia sometime in April. Beau quickly left for New York to begin training at Stillman's Gym, in hopes of avenging his two losses to Ike. However, before Wilson could schedule the bout, Beau and Wilson parted ways.

What Jack really desired was to fight once again in Madison Square Gar-den and for a chance at the title. Once again, he applied for a license with the NYSAC. It was denied. Chairman Julius Helfand, speaking on behalf of the Commission, explained that Beau's request was rejected because of "Jack's record, his physical condition, his age, his long years of inactivity and because of a letter from Chick Wergeles, Jack's manager."[10] A return to the Garden did not appear to be in the cards for Jack.

With Dick Wilson out of the picture, three Augusta promoters began vying to promote the potential bout between Beau Jack and Ike Williams in Augusta, Georgia. In late February, Tony Mahoney, a wrestling promoter, proclaimed that he should have first dibs at promoting the contest as he was first in line. Teddy Norris, a small-time boxing promoter, stated that he had been in touch with the camps of both Beau Jack and Ike Williams and was hopeful something could be worked out. Lastly, George E. "Slim" Griffin, also a small-time boxing promoter, aggressively declared he had already reserved the Bell Auditorium as the venue for a March 31 rematch between Beau Jack and Ike Williams. None of the three would get the fight.

On Wednesday night, March 2, a new, inexperienced promoter named Nathan Williams emerged, announcing that he had matched Beau Jack and Ike Williams for a bout in Augusta to occur on the eve of the Masters Tourna-ment in April. Nathan, however, had not even applied to the Augusta Boxing Commission[11] for a license to promote the fight; nor did he know that the Commission existed until he read about it in the afternoon paper on March 3. Likewise, the Commission did not know about a potential match between Beau Jack and Ike Williams until they saw the March 3 announcement from Nathan Williams in the morning paper.[12] The following day, a spokesperson for the Commission vehemently stated that until someone applies for a li-cense and the application is approved by the Commission, there will be no fight. The Commission also expressed concern, stating that Jack had previ-ously been denied the right to fight in Augusta because he refused to undergo the required physical examination.

Before issuing Jack or Ike a license, the Augusta Boxing Commission required both fighters to obtain approval from the Commission's physician, Dr. J. E. Hummel. Somewhat startling, both fighters were able to pass their examinations. On March 16, Ike Williams signed the contract to fight Beau on April 9, 1955, at Augusta's Bell Auditorium. The pre-fight hype began to build as two former lightweight champions were set to battle it out in Beau's hometown.

For the first time, Beau was scheduled to fight in Augusta. The venue was Augusta's Bell Auditorium. Constructed in 1939 and early 1940 at a cost of $500,000, the 2,690-seat auditorium was named in memory of Augusta's Mayor William B. Bell. At the time, Augusta was still plagued by racism and segregation. As late as 1961, legendary singer/songwriter Ray Charles canceled his show at the Bell Auditorium upon learning from some Paine College students that the dance floor would be reserved for "whites," with blacks being relegated to the upper balcony. The firm stand by Ray Charles would be instrumental in dismantling segregation in Augusta.

Beau was excited to be fighting in front of the hometown fans. It was on the eve of the final round of the 1955 Masters Tournament. Cary Middlecoff, a dentist turned golfer from Halls, Tennessee, had a four-stroke lead over Ben Hogan after making four straight birdies and an eagle putt over 80 feet long on the 13th hole in the second round. He went on to win the tournament by seven strokes.

Beau's opponent, Ike Williams, had defeated Beau twice, once by TKO and the other by split decision. After winning the lightweight title in April 1945, Ike reigned as champion for six years until he lost to Jimmy Carter of Aiken, South Carolina on May 25, 1951. Ike retired in 1953 following a beating from Jed Black. The last time he was in the ring on July 2, 1954, he lost a unanimous decision to Rafael Lastre.

The Bell Auditorium was filled with 2,500 enthusiastic hometown fans seeking to see their local champion, Beau Jack, battle with Ike Williams. Williams came into the fight with a 10-pound weight advantage at 155 pounds and a 4" height advantage. Ike also held a three-year age advantage. Williams was 31 years old, whereas Jack was 34 years old.

The air was tense with excitement as the bout began. Contrary to the crowd, the two former champions appeared sluggish. The two fighters appeared to be lightly sparring in the first two rounds. In the third stanza, Williams warmed up and started to assert his inside game over Beau. However, in the fifth round, Beau caught Williams coming in with a hard left that staggered Ike and opened a cut over his eye. It obviously angered Williams. He stormed out in the sixth, quickly cornering Beau and landing a looping right that dropped Beau to his knees. Beau jumped back up in defiance but was met with an onslaught of rights and lefts, leaving him groggy on his feet. Beau regained his composure and retaliated strong in the ninth and tenth rounds, hurting Williams with a whirlwind of rights and lefts. The crowd went wild and rose to their feet when Beau knocked Ike through the ropes in the ninth round, but it was not scored a knockdown.

After ten rounds, the decision went to the scorecards. Referee Pete Tarpley scored the bout even, giving both fighters four rounds and scoring two rounds even. Judge Denny Leonard scored the fight in favor of Beau Jack. He scored five rounds for Beau, three for Williams and one even. Judge Joe Armstrong scored the bout in favor of Ike Williams, giving Ike five rounds, Beau three rounds, and scoring two rounds even. The contest was ruled a draw.

Having lost his first two fights with Williams, Beau was content with a draw. In his post-fight comments, he boasted that he wanted a crack at welterweight Chico Vejar, a popular fighter among boxing fans with a 59–4–1 professional record. Ike Williams, on the other hand, said he just wanted one more fight in hopes to make enough money to buy a pool hall in Trenton, New Jersey.

In late spring, Beau returned to Miami, looking for opportunities to fight while shining shoes at the Fontainebleau Hotel. Somehow, Beau secured another fight. His opponent was Willie "Kid" Johnson. They were initially scheduled to fight on February 21, but logistics did not work out. Jack and Johnson eventually met on July 4 in a ten-round bout at Beach Arena in Daytona, Florida. Hailing from Jacksonville, Florida, Johnson was the Bahamas welterweight champion and had recently knocked out Ike Williams. It was a tough fight, but Beau eked out a split decision.

Resolved to continue boxing, Beau knew he had some convincing to do. He made several appeals to various promoters, seeking assistance in lining up additional fights. One promoter he talked to was David Coapman, boxing enthusiast and staff writer for the *Capital Post* in Tallahassee, Florida. Coapman, a native of Rochester, New York, sought to match Beau Jack for a bout in Rochester, but it never happened. In a significant turn of events, several years later, Coapman became referred to as "Rochester's watchdog of pugilism." He wrote state governors pleading to have old fighters retired for their own good. For example, he was successful in getting Manuel Batista's California license removed because he had been kayoed at 21 times.

Babe Lancaster, another Florida promoter, was also interested in staging a fight for Beau in Miami or Tampa. Beau spent a week at Lancaster's training beach on Washington Shores in Orlando, Florida, where he trained and sparred. Like Coapman, Lancaster was unsuccessful in booking Beau a contest. Therefore, Beau went back to Miami and tried to get boxing promoter Chris Dundee to let him fight at the Miami Beach Auditorium. Dundee refused to entertain the idea without Chick Wergeles' blessings, which was not going to happen.

Beau still had a strong resolve. When asked by Art Grace of the *Miami News* whether he thought he was still a respectable fighter, Beau replied, "YES SUH."[13] Naively, he continued, "I know I slowed down a little bit but I gained punching power. I hit harder. Still fight the same way though…. Whirlwind style, keep coming all the time. I had three fights this year trying to get back, and honest, I ain't seen no difference in me."[14] Beau wanted to fight. That was his life.

Whether Beau desired to admit it or not, his boxing days were coming to a rapid close. Beau Jack's last fight would take place in his hometown. On August 2, 1955, promoter Nathan Williams announced that Beau would face Ike Williams in an August 12 rematch at the Bell Auditorium. This time, Williams came in with an eight-pound weight advantage, weighing 154 pounds to Jack's 146 pounds.

The first three rounds were close. Vigorously, both men mixed it up as they stood toe to toe. In the second round, Beau connected with a right-hand uppercut to Ike's head, staggering the former champion into the ropes. He later landed a left on Ike's head. Williams, however, gained momentum in the third and unequivocally took charge in the fourth round after knocking out Beau's mouthpiece. In the fifth, Williams staggered Beau with two rights and a left. Then, he landed a right cross, knocking Beau senseless. When the bell rang, Beau was dazed and disoriented and stumbled over to Ike's corner to take a seat, only to be led back to his corner. Beau was bleeding profusely out of his mouth. Similar to their first fight on July 12, 1948, Williams knew Beau was severely hurt and didn't want to continue dishing out punishment.

Ike was pleading that the fight be stopped, but it continued. At the end of the seventh, Williams backed Beau up and left him hanging on the ropes. As the bell rang to start the eighth round, Williams hit Jack with a hard right, backing him up into a neutral corner. Then Ike bombarded Beau with both fists to the head and body for at least 15 seconds. Again, Williams backed off, pleading through his actions that the fight be stopped, again to no avail. So, Williams backed Beau into the ropes again and began using him as target practice. *Augusta Chronicle* sports editor, Johnny Hendrix, sitting ringside, uttered, "Williams, with concern in his eyes and mercy in his heart, pulled his punches in the sixth and seventh rounds, but when the bout wasn't stopped he went back to work in the eighth."[15]

With blood pouring out of Jack's mouth, the crowd started yelling for the fight to stop. For the fourth time, Williams backed off, pleading with the referee to stop the fight. "It sickened Williams, who is not a sensitive man," wrote Jimmy Cannon. "He profanely demanded the referee stop the fight and relieve him of this awful duty."[16] Finally, Referee J. T. Gilliam took control of the fight and prevented the infliction of further damage to Jack, refusing to let Beau answer the bell for the ninth round. Jack's eyes were glassy, and blood was gushing out of his mouth. Even at the end, Beau insisted that the fight continue. Williams, however, completely dominated the match, earning a devastating technical knockout over Jack.

A distraught Beau wept after the fight. He was disheartened that he had essentially been knocked out on his feet. But with his pride intact and his chirpy sense of optimism, Jack stated, "I went out on my feet. They can't ever take that from me."[17] When questioned whether he was hurt during the fight, Beau, with zealous pride, disavowed that he had been injured. Jack merely pointed to his left elbow and said, "No suh, I hurt my arm in the third round. He never knocked me down. I never been down my whole life, you know that."[18]

Beau's stellar boxing career ended after the horrific thrashing he took from Ike Williams. After one hundred twenty-two professional bouts and a record of 92 wins (44 knockouts), 25 losses and 5 draws, Jack's incredible ring journey finally concluded.[19] Beau had been to the top of the mountain. Before suffering a broken knee, he only had ten losses. He fought in five title bouts and held the world lightweight title twice, earning his first championship at the young age of 21. He is the only boxer to fight in three main events at the Garden in one month. Jack, along with Bob Montgomery, set the record for the highest priced sports ticket—$100,000 for a ringside seat. Along with Montgomery, Beau raised $35,864,900 in war bonds to help the U.S. war effort in World War II. Jack was named "Fighter of the Year" by *The Ring* magazine in 1944. During his 15-year professional career, Beau fought in a record 27 main events at the Garden and produced gates over $2 million.

It wasn't easy for Beau to retire from boxing. Three weeks after he lost to Ike Williams, Art Grace caught up with Beau at the Miami Beach Auditorium. He asked Beau whether he still wanted to fight. Beau emphatically stated, "I got to. It's my heart."[20] Trainer Angelo Dundee, a friend of Beau's, was listening to the conversation. "Beau," he said. "I wish you'd get that idea out of your head. Comes a time you got to realize you just ain't as good as you used to be. You were great but you can't fight no more. I'm scared to death you're going to get hurt one of these nights."[21] Whether he liked it or not, Jack's boxing days were over.

Beau Jack returned to his seasonal job as a bootblack at the Fontainebleau Hotel. Although Beau spent time over the next year or so in Augusta, most of his time was spent in Miami. Jack gave up on his restaurant and sold it to his uncle, John Henry "Punch" Harris. Beau may have wanted to fight again, but he found solace in shining shoes. "I'm sending money home to the wife and kids every week. I can shine shoes—I'm the champ. You got to come over and let me shine you up."[22]

Ike Williams also retired with an overall record of 126–24–4, with sixty-one victories coming by way of knockout. He was *The Ring's* Fighter of the Year in 1947. In 1948, Ike was awarded the Edward J. Neil memorial plaque as the fighter who had done the most for the sport of boxing that year. In 1990, he was inducted into the International Boxing Hall of Fame.

In 1960, boxing came under scrutiny for its connections with organized crime. Ike Williams was one of the boxers questioned about his ties to the mafia. He was called to testify before the U.S. Senate Special Committee to Investigate Organized Crime in Interstate Commerce (Estes Kefauver's committee), based on his connections with his manager, Frank "Blinky" Palermo, an organized crime figure. Blinky and his partner, Frankie Carbo, were notorious mobsters. They controlled numerous boxers and fixed fights. One of the most well-known of the fixed fights was the Jake LaMotta/Billy Fox fight in 1947, which served as the story behind Martin Scorsese's film *Raging Bull*. LaMotta purportedly paid the mob $20,000 and threw the fight for a chance to fight for the middleweight title.

There was a rumor before Ike Williams lost to Jimmy Carter in 1951 that Palermo had loaned money to Carter's manager, Willie Ketchum. Of course, when questioned by the New York State Athletic Commission, the allegation was denied. In his testimony before the Kefauver Committee, Ike testified that Blinky had brought him offers as large as $100,000 to throw fights. Williams, himself, admitted to carrying fights to specific rounds but was adamant that he never willingly lost a fight.

Although Ike made over $1,000,000 during his 15-year career, he didn't have much to show for it. Unfortunately, he even had to pay income taxes on money he never received. By 1960, Williams was broke, having gone through all the money he had and losing his rental properties.

Fortunately, numerous boxers came to Ike's support. Muhammad Ali admired Ike's style and rebellious attitude toward the boxing establishment. He went to see Williams in Trenton, New Jersey, where Ike was working at a warehouse and living at the local YMCA. Ali offered Ike a job at his training camp in Pennsylvania. Williams, however, was a bit too rebellious, even for Muhammad Ali. Mike Tyson and boxing promoter Don King also came to Ike's aid. They were foremost among a group who took an interest in Williams's welfare during the 1980s, helping to arrange an apartment for him to live in Los Angeles, California.

As with several boxers Beau faced during his career, he and Ike became friends. At Beau's 1991 induction to the International Boxing Hall of Fame, he and Ike had a chance to catch up with each other. As they stood talking, Williams recalled battles against each other.

"I fought Beau Jack three [four] times," Williams said, glancing over at his ex-foe. "The last two times, he was past his prime, but he was still a helluva man."

"The last time we fought, I was giving it to him pretty good. All of a sudden, he comes up with a bolo punch." Williams brings up his right hand in uppercut fashion. "And catches me right here."

He opens his mouth, displaying a single gold bottom tooth sprouting up among a row of white ones.

"I was sick," Williams said, glancing over at Jack again. "Sick. I had a perfect set of teeth. One-hundred and fifty-three fights and he had to knock that tooth out in my last one."[23] Jack may have lost the battles, but Ike lost his perfect set of teeth thanks to Beau.

During his acceptance speech, at the next day's induction ceremonies, Jack stood before the microphone and looked at his friends Ike Williams and Kid Gavilan, sitting among the honored guests. "I wished I was fighting now, but it ain't possible," Jack said. "The two guys up here who beat me (Gavilan and Williams), I want to fight again. But they keep moving away."[24]

PART VII

Retirement from the Ring

Not everybody can make a pair of shoes shine, you know. I'm doing what I want to do—satisfying people with my work. And that's all I've tried to do all my life.

—Beau Jack

28

Financial Woes

Even before Beau Jack hung up the gloves, stories came out about his financial woes asserting how he had been robbed by his management team and/or the Syndicate that promised to stow his earnings into a trust account. Numerous reports indicated that Beau grossed over $2,000,000 during his boxing career but was left penniless. Beau, himself, declared that he was broke. Were his earnings gone? If so, was there someone to blame? Some commentators suggested that an unethical split of his purses in favor of Bowman Milligan was to blame, while others asserted it was due to Beau spending his earnings on a lavish lifestyle. Yet others faulted the Syndicate for failing to properly invest his money. How much did Beau really make in the ring? Was he broke?

Accounts suggest that Beau personally earned between $300,000 and $500,000 during his career. By the end of his career, however, Beau appeared broke. Beau said it was after his fight with Tony Janiro on February 21, 1947, that he learned that his ring earnings had disappeared. He wasn't quite sure what he made, but stated, "I hardly saw a cent of it."[1] Jack was infuriated. "I wanted to take a gun and do something about it," rasped Beau. "People have killed for less than that. But then I thought about my family and how they would feel if I was on my way to the electric chair."[2] Beau was angry and distraught when he learned that he had been the victim of deception.

More stories came out in the following years. In January 1949, a visibly shaken Chick Wergeles told Dan Burley (1907–1962),[3] sportswriter and future editor of the *New York Age*, that Beau's earnings had evaporated into thin air.[4] In March, a headline in the *Winnipeg Tribune* read, "Beau Jack Is 'Broke.'"[5] In October, Beau corroborated his financial woes in an interview with Wendell Smith of the *Pittsburgh Courier*. "I had me $100,000 salted away," grumbled Beau, "but when I checked up I found out it was all gone."[6] That same year, his manager Chick Wergeles, in an interview with Allen Ward, sportswriter for the *Oakland Tribune,* again confirmed that Beau was virtually broke. *New York Times* sports columnist Arthur Daley also corroborated it in 1951.[7] Moreover, in August 1951, Beau, apparently penniless, was reportedly receiving $55 a week from the National Sports Alliance Boxers' Pension Fund, which offered assistance to indigent boxers.[8]

Beau's financial difficulties were well known, and he didn't mind acknowledging it publicly. Jack appeared on the CBS game show "Strike It Rich" in New York during the week of July 12, 1957. "Strike It Rich" aired on radio and television from 1947 through 1957. People in need of money due to unfortunate circumstances were selected as contestants. Contestants told their unfortunate tales of despair and then tried to win money by answering four reasonably easy questions. Each player would receive $30 to bet with, answering each question after being given a category. If a contestant didn't win any money, the host Warren Hull opened the "Heart Line," a phone line that allowed viewers to donate money or merchandise to the contestant and his or her family.

Jack sat backstage before his appearance on "Strike It Rich," waiting for his cue with his wife and seven of his ten children. When Warren Hull called on Beau Jack to tell his story, Beau described his financial woes. "I'm broke," he explained. "Not dead broke, just broke."[9] Beau did well on the show. He collected $444 and with "Heartline" calls his total was $600. Beau won three fishing poles as well. With the money he won, Beau announced he was planning to add on another room to his four-room house in Augusta, where his family lived. If Beau was broke, where did his earnings go?

Unethical Split

In 1950, Red McQueen of the *Honolulu Star-Advertiser* blamed the disappearance of Beau's ring earnings on the unethical percentage retained by Bowman Milligan.[10] In other words, Beau didn't receive a boxer's legal share of his purses. McQueen pointed the finger at the management deal established by the Syndicate between Beau Jack and Bowman Milligan. Milligan landed an exceptionally unethical and unfair deal for helping Jack. At the time in New York, a manager was legally not entitled to collect more than 1/3 of a boxer's earnings. Milligan, however, received fifty percent of Beau's earnings. Then when Chick Wergeles was hired in the summer of 1941, he received twenty-five percent, leaving only twenty-five percent for Beau.

Sportswriters were generally in consensus that Beau's financial difficulties were primarily due to the unethical, if not unlawful, agreement granted Bowman Milligan. Stanley Woodward of *The Miami News* and Dan Parker of the *Courier-Post* agreed with McQueen, blaming Beau's financial woes on the Milligan contract.[11] The split was great for Milligan but left Beau with the short end. Thanks to Beau's success, Bowman's pockets were virtually lined with gold. Milligan also received the purses on behalf of the team. It was his responsibility to ensure the money was appropriately divided.

Only after his best paydays were behind him and Bowman had departed, did Beau finally began to receive his fair share of the earnings. Chick Wergeles saw to it. Under the sole handling of Wergeles, Chick made sure that his fighter received two thirds of his earnings as required by the New York State Athletic Commission. Unfortunately, after breaking his knee in the Janiro fight, Beau's earning would never be as high as they once were. In fact, he only appeared in four more matches with gross gates of $50,000 or more. Chick, however, stuck it out with Beau, knowing that Jack had to keep fighting to stay afloat.

Lavish Lifestyle and Women

Did Beau squander his earnings by living a lavish lifestyle? Bill Plaschke (1958–), a writer for the *Fort Lauderdale News*, attributed Beau's financial woes to his lifestyle. "The homeless boy who was so used to poverty discovered the fun of buying fancy clothes, nightclubs and entertaining a gang of friends," wrote Plaschke. "Beau Jack's chief interest in life out of boxing … became the sleek beauties of Harlem who were only too pleased to entertain the champion."[12] Even after Beau broke his knee and was no longer earning big purses, Plaschke, a five-time winner of the Associated Press's National Sports Columnist of the Year, asserted that he was spending money at the same old fast clip.

Chick Wergeles also attributed part of Beau's misfortune on the women in his life. "There were three wives," Wergeles said. "He was serious, but they were just out to take his money and one by one they left him when they thought he was broke. The first wife left him with three children. Beau has to pay $200 a month for their support and $2,000 a year alimony."[13] Expensive paternity suits may have also been a contributor.

It is unclear how many wives Beau had, but by most accounts it was two. Nonetheless, he was undeniably a ladies' man. He married his first wife, Josephine Jones, before leaving for Springfield in 1940. In April of 1948, a photo and story came out detailing Beau and his "wife" Margaret Shepherd Walker's trip to Vero Beach, Florida. Margaret was photographed picking an orange after the couple watched Jackie Robinson hit a home run in spring training. Later that year, there were rumors that the couple was divorcing, and that Beau was dating Mary Swiggert. Three years later, he and his first wife Josephine were reportedly living together at their place on New Savannah Road in Augusta. In between, Beau made news in New York when he was dating Ruby Valdez during the summer of 1951. His former wives or girlfriends were undeniably a toll on Beau financially.

Sportswriter Pat Robinson of the *Arizona Republic* concurred in attributing

Beau's financial demise to himself. Beau, apparently, gave in to the temptations of the nightlife, as well as gambling. Pat Robinson explained. Early in Beau's career, wrote Robinson, he was a "sweet, lovable kid." He didn't have a sweetheart and "he was not the kind of a boy who would ever be lured by the bright lights of Broadway." Later, it was discovered that Beau had left a wife and children in Georgia. As for never being "lured by the lights of Broadway" it didn't take him long to not only discover the lights of Broadway but also those up in Harlem. Robinson also blamed Beau's fancy with horse racing. "He also quickly discovered that horses were running at Belmont, Aqueduct and Jamaica, and that those places were easily accessible and that bets could be made there."[14] Sportswriter Red McQueen and Fred Young (1892–1980), sports editor for *The Pantagraph* in Bloomington, Illinois, agreed in part, imputing Beau's finances partially on his lavish lifestyle.

Other people faulted Beau's big heart as the conundrum. Beau undeniably was willing to spend money on others, especially if he thought he could help them. Les Matthews with the *New York Age* reported, "Beau Jack picks up every fighter he sees roaming the street at night and takes him fishing."[15] Beau enjoyed helping others, but it does not seem to be an adequate explanation as his earnings were sent to Augusta to be placed in a trust account.

Of course, many disagreed that Beau Jack lived lavishly. Sportswriter and scout for the Pittsburgh Steelers Bill Nunn (1924–2014) was one of those who disagreed. "Funny part about Jack was he didn't squander his money," commented Nunn in 1955. "During the height of his career he lived in a far from glamorous single room in Harlem and received all of $15 a week to live on."[16] Living in a single room in Harlem does not sound very lavish.

Were a lavish lifestyle and the numerous women a reason for Beau to be broke? It can only explain a small portion of his financial situation. Chick Wergeles stated that when purses were collected for Beau's fights, Beau's twenty-five percent was sent to Augusta to be placed in trust for him at the Georgia Railroad Bank. Fred Young was in accord. Even if "Beau was throwing his money around like a Texas oil baron doing the town," stated Young, "the competence was being salted away against the time when Beau had fought himself out."[17]

How Much Did Beau Make?

How much did Beau make in the ring? It is not an easy question to answer, but accounting for different variables, one can obtain a fair idea. First, one must distinguish between gross receipts and actual money received by Beau's management team ("BJ's Team"). A fighter receives a guarantee and/or a percentage of the gate after the promoter takes their share and expenses are paid. The amount paid the boxer is then split with a portion being taken out for his manager and costs for a trainer, etc.

What were the gross gates for Beau's matches? Red McQueen calculated Beau's total revenues during his best five years at almost $2 million.[18] Bill Nunn, Jr., and numerous other sportswriters agreed, asserting that Beau drew gates totaling more than $2 million.[19] Stanley Woodward (1895–1965), outstanding sports writer and future member of the National Sportscasters and Sportswriters Hall of Fame, presented a more detailed calculation of revenue produced by Beau, but only examined 19 fights during Beau's best five years. He calculated that net gates amounted to $1,491,756.[20]

The above interpretations are rudimentary at best. Table 1 presents the gross gates for 51 contests in which Beau was featured in main events between 1941 and 1951. Gross gates equal $2,223,770. See Table 1. Of course, that does not account for 69 other small "money" contests.

Table 1
Beau Jack's Gates & Earnings

Date	Opponent	Gate	BJ's Team Share	Date	Opponent	Gate	BJ's Team Share
10/31/41	Guillermo Puentes	*$850	$850	03/03/44	Bob Montgomery	$111,954	$30,000
8/18/42	Carmine Fatta	*$1,000	$1,000	03/17/44	Al Davis	$132,823	$30,402
8/28/42	Billy Murray	$18,752		03/31/44	Juan Zurita	$87,802	$25,000
11/13/42	Allie Stolz	$34,786	$6,000	08/04/44	Bob Montgomery	War Bonds Fight	$0.00
12/18/42	Tippy Larkin	$58,468	$17,000	12/14/45	Willie Joyce	$70,071	
02/05/43	Fritzie Zivic	$70,291	$15,000	01/04/46	Morris Reif	$73,280	
04/02/43	Henry Armstrong	$104,976	$24,158.17	02/08/46	Johnny Greco	$148,152	
05/21/43	Bob Montgomery	$94,500	$32,076	05/31/46	Johnny Greco	$66,922	
07/19/43	Johnny Hutchinson	$50,057	$18,000	07/08/46	Sammy Angott	$41,028	$10,869.28
10/4/43	Bobby Ruffin	$43,429	$13,028.70	08/19/46	Danny Kapilow	$32,000	$15,000
11/19/43	Bob Montgomery	$96,573		10/22/46	Buster Tyler	$7,600	
01/07/44	Lulu Costantino	$43,161		02/21/47	Tony Janiro	$98,053	
01/28/44	Sammy Angott	$84,870		11/03/47	Humberto Zavala	$9,518	
02/15/44	Maxie Berger	$30,040		12/16/47	Frankie Vigeant	$427.70	

Date	Opponent	Gate	BJ's Team Share	Date	Opponent	Gate	BJ's Team Share
12/29/47	Billy Kearns	$4,429		09/30/49	Livio Minelli	$8,290	
01/23/48	Johnny Bratton	$57,499		10/14/49	Kid Gavilan	$22,429	$6,467.98
02/20/48	Terry Young	$66,317		12/16/49	Tuzo Portuguez	$20,382	
04/09/48	Johnny Greco	$51,832		04/03/50	Joey Carkido	$1,688	
05/24/48	Tony Janiro	$27,473		05/22/50	Johnny Potenti	$8,881	
07/12/48	Ike Williams	$83,787	$13,671.45	10/03/50	Philip Kim	$12,204	
11/23/48	Chuck Taylor	$13,671		11/14/50	Frankie Fernandez	$11,322.40	$4,000
12/17/48	Leroy Willis	$11,426		01/01/51	Fitzie Pruden	$12,697	
01/17/49	Jackie Weber	$23,262		01/18/51	Del Flanagan	$15,678.60	
03/28/49	Johnny Greco	$38,428		01/31/51	Emil Barao	$3,278	
07/13/49	Eddie Giosa	$6,752.25		03/05/51	Ike Williams	$7,095	
08/31/49	Johnny Gonsalves	$13,981		04/16/51	Gil Turner	$18,884.35	
09/06/49	Tote Martinez	$8,136		05/21/51	Gil Turner	$13,451	
					TOTAL	$2,225,620	$277,523.58

*Although the gross gate is unknown, Beau received $850 for his October 31, 1941, contest with Guillermo Puentes and $1,000 for his August 18, 1942, bout with Carmine Fatta.

How much did BJ's team receive from the gross gates? McQueen and Nunn estimated that during Beau's best five years, his team collected purses totaling over a half million or one fourth of the gross gates.[21] When known, BJ Team's share of the purses is presented in Table 1, but it only accounts for seventeen matches. In the 15 contests in which both the gross gate and the amount received by BJ's Team are known, the gross gate was $1,050,997. Out of that amount, BJ's Team received $275,674 (or 26.229 percent of the gross gate). Although not perfect, if 26.229 percent is applied to the thirty-six bouts in which only the gross gate is known ($1,172,773), BJ's Team would have received $307,614.94. Adding the estimated receipts to the known proceeds, BJ's Team received $583,289 for the 51 contests listed in Table 1.

How much did Beau personally receive? Several sportswriters have attempted to estimate the amount. In 1951, Jack Cuddy calculated that Beau should have personally earned over $300,000.[22] In 1956, Dan Parker's computations resulted in a much lower amount. He estimated that Beau earned $123,778. Parker went further to explain that out of the $123,778 received by

Beau, he "paid $44,873 in taxes and was allowed to keep 25 percent of the balance of $78,905, or $19,726.25."[23]

Sportswriter J. Suter Kegg (1917–2002) of the *Cumberland Evening Times* emphasized the impact of taxes and explained that Beau never made much money. "The fact is that Beau Jack never earned more than $25,000 a year (net after taxes) in his best days, and the fact is that Beau Jack squandered most of his money despite the charitable and philanthropic attitude of his original sponsors in Augusta. It also should be remembered that the Beau's big years were also big tax years because of the war."[24] No doubt taxes were extremely high. The Revenue Act of 1942 increased taxes to help support the U.S. war effort in World War II. For example, the tax bracket used for income received in 1943 imposed a 78 percent federal income tax on income of $50,000 and 90 percent on income of $90,000.

Table 1 presents the most detailed analysis of Beau's earnings. If BJ's Team received $583,289, Beau would have been entitled to one fourth or $145,822.25. As pointed out by Dan Parker, taxes would have reduced that amount. If we use the same rate as Parker, Beau would have paid $52,933.48 (36.3 percent) in taxes, leaving him with $92,888.78. The tax rate utilized by Parker, however, appears to be on the low side.

Did the Syndicate Squander Beau's Money?

Chick averred that Beau was fleeced by people he thought were his friends and spoke harshly of the "so-called southern millionaires who originally backed Beau Jack."[25] In 1951, Arthur Daley of the *New York Times* reported that Beau was broke because his associates swindled his money. "He's broke," Daley wrote, "because he was robbed of his heritage, his earnings squandered away."[26] In 1955, Bill Nunn, Jr., also blamed the Syndicate for not correctly investing his earnings.

On the contrary, Beau's hometown newspaper, the *Augusta Herald*, disagreed that Beau was "down and out" or that his earnings had been poorly invested. Randy Russell, an editorial writer for the *Augusta Herald* and former sports editor, writing in 1955 for *Sport* magazine, disputed that Beau's earnings were stolen or misspent. In fact, he praised those that invested Beau's earnings. According to Russell, in 1955, Beau's assets included a $10,000 life insurance annuity, a $15,000 trust account, and an $18,000 farm.

The initial investment in the trust fund was $12,000, but since then the trust fund had produced a return of $35,000. Russell touted the savvy investment of Beau's money. "Even the bank officials were surprised," said Russel, "that they had taken a $12,000 investment from Beau and provided a $35,000 return."[27] From that amount, Jack had withdrawn $20,000 of the profit.

Utilizing Russell's accounting, it appears that between $22,000 and $40,000 was invested on Beau's behalf. If the farm was bought from Beau's $20,000 withdrawal, the total amount deposited in the Georgia Bank and Trust on Beau's behalf would have been $22,000 ($12,000 trust + $10,000 annuity). The trust amount grew to $35,000 through the bank's investments. Deducting $20,000 withdrawn by Beau, the amount would correspond with what Russell stated was in the trust, $15,000. On the other hand, if Beau's farm was purchased with undisclosed bank funds, the amount originally invested would have been $40,000 ($18,000 farm + $12,000 trust + $10,000 annuity).

Although the return on the trust was remarkable, if the $92,888.78 roughly calculated above is accurate, there is a discrepancy of $52,888.78 to $70,888.78 that is not explained. Therefore, there appears to be some validity in the assertions that Beau did not receive a substantial portion of his earnings. Perhaps the tax rate applied to Beau's earnings was higher than that utilized by Dan Parker.

Beau, however, did not blame the original group of people or the Syndicate that raised the money to start his boxing career. In 1955, Art Grace of the *Miami News* questioned Beau whether the Syndicate gave him the short end of his earnings. Beau said emphatically, "NO, SUH." "That's not so. I got a good annuity back home. But that's for the kids when they go to college and all. I don't want to touch that money. Those men in the syndicate were all fine men."[28] He appeared to hold no ill will against the Syndicate that gave him his start in boxing.

Beau Not Angry

Although Beau could never explain where all his money went, he persistently made light of his situation. He put it like this: "[A]ny time you have a bottle of milk and it breaks, it's gone. You can't bring it back."[29] Beau was distraught when he learned that he had been swindled. As was typical for Beau Jack, however, his anger and frustration were short lived. "I don't worry about money," Jack replied, "I got a good job. I got my health and strength. I have nothing to worry about except to stay healthy."[30] Beau continued to forgive and not worry about his finances. In an interview with Dave Condon of the *Chicago Tribune* in 1969, Beau was troubled that he didn't receive the money he thought he deserved but did not express anger. "My biggest purse was about $48,000," stated Beau. "So many years ago I don't care. Don't even want to think about what I used to make, because I never got all of it, anyhow. Way I see this life," explained Beau, "every day a man has to do a day's work. One day he gets paid $48,000. Another day, maybe $5."[31] Irrespective of his finances, Beau relished the opportunity he was provided. All he wanted to do was fight, even if he never made any money. Fighting was the highlight of his life, and he climbed to the pinnacle, winning two lightweight world titles.

Beau was encouraged numerous times to prosecute Bowman Milligan and his former handlers. In early 1951, Chick Wergeles asked Beau to prosecute those who had "milked" him of his money, but Beau refused. "Naw, ah can't do that," said the deeply religious Beau. "Ah cain't be a revenger. God'll punish 'em."[32] Sportswriter Jimmy Cannon suggested, as Wergeles did years earlier, that Beau go to the District Attorney to seek help for his losses. Beau, however, would have none of it. "God take care of that," said Beau Jack. "He want you poor, you be poor. He know what they do to me. He know all about it. You can't tell God nothing He don't know."[33] Again, Beau responded that God will take care of those who mistreated him. He was not looking for a conflict outside of the ring and relentlessly maintained his optimistic attitude.

Beau Not Broke

There is an alternative explanation of Beau's finances. Perhaps, he just acted broke. In a 1988 interview with Gary Smith of *Sports Illustrated* magazine, Smith asked Beau how he got by. Beau responded, "Don't you worry. There's a famous man sends me a check every month, enough to live on."[34]

Subsequently, Gary Smith spoke with Beau's son Jonathan. Jonathan also disputed the notion that his father was broke and had to shine shoes for a living. "My dad didn't need to shine shoes," said Jonathan. "He just went back to what he knew before boxing."[35] Jonathan explained that Beau had five of his children in private school while he was shining shoes and that he had a closet full of suits at his mother's house.

Jonathan went on to praise Beau's big heart and giving attitude. "We could get anything from my dad—all we had to do was ask," said Jonathan. "I tested him once. I asked him to buy me a DeLorean. He looked at me for two minutes. 'Are you a good son?' he asked. I said, 'I guess so.' He said, 'Listen to your mom, and I'll get it for you.' I started feeling guilty. I said, 'No, that's O.K., Dad.' So, he bought me a Mustang instead."[36]

Although Jonathan believes his dad's manager swindled him, Beau still had assets. "His manager ripped him off, but not everything," Jonathan said. "He's got land in Georgia, some investments. And he doesn't spend money, lives real simple." Jonathan begged him to move out of his one-room apartment he lived in because it was in a bad area. Beau responded, "Son, always play broke. Don't let people know you have a cent."[37]

Beau had 15 children (ten boys and five girls). According to Jack, even while he was shining shoes, he managed to send them all to college. Furthermore, he also paid for his second wife to go through Miami-Dade Junior College. Shining shoes would not be adequate to pay for their educations.

29

On His Knees Again

After hanging up the gloves in 1955, Beau tried living in Augusta, but it just wasn't close enough to the world of boxing. Ultimately, he headed back to Miami Beach, a boxing haven, where he would shine shoes at the Fontainebleau Hotel. In what little spare time he had, Beau enjoyed working with young boxers and hanging around the numerous local boxing gyms.

Fronting the Atlantic Ocean, Miami Beach is located on the barrier islands across Biscayne Bay from Miami. With its pristine white sand and beautiful waterfront vistas, the stretch of oceanfront luxury became the playground for the rich and famous during the mid 1900s. Miami Beach was a bustling center of entertainment with glamorous nightlife, swanky hotels, jazz clubs, restaurants, and celebrities. Tourism was booming. The stretch of Collins Avenue between 41st Street and 62nd Street was named Millionaires Row in acknowledgment of the opulent homes of the rich and famous and grand hotels, such as the Hotel Deauville, Eden Roc Miami, Carillon Hotel and Beach Resort, Algiers Hotel, Nautilus Hotel, and of course, the Fontainebleau Hotel.

The nightlife and entertainment were incredible. There was something to do every evening. There were spectacular cabaret shows and lavish nightclubs ranging from Copa City to the Latin Quarter, and the Birdland Jazz Club. Beautiful ladies in chorus lines served as the backdrop for the nightly dinner shows. The Beatles' first American performance was on the *Ed Sullivan Show*, broadcast live from the Deauville Hotel on February 16, 1964. Jackie Gleason brought his *Jackie Gleason Show* and *American Scene Magazine* television show to Miami Beach in 1964. A variety talk show, it was broadcast from the Miami Beach Municipal Auditorium at 17th and Washington Avenue.[1] In the 1960s, the Municipal Auditorium also hosted *The Dick Clark Show*, *The Ed Sullivan Show*, the Miss USA and Miss Universe pageants. Celebrities such as Frank Sinatra, Jack Benny, and Bob Hope not only performed at the auditorium, but they also frequented many events held at the venue.

There was no telling which celebrities and entertainers you might see on any given day. Frank Sinatra and his Rat Pack—Dean Martin, Jerry Lewis,

Peter Lawford, Joey Bishop, and Sammy Davis, Jr.—were often seen strolling the streets and enjoying the nightlife in Miami Beach, especially at the La-Ronde Super Club where Sinatra was a frequent performer. Marilyn Monroe (1926–1962) had a condo at The Flamingo, and in 1954 was often seen on the beach with her husband Joe DiMaggio, "The Yankee Clipper" (1914–1999). Milton Berle (1908–2002) was a regular performer at the Redbury Hotel. Judy Garland (1922–1969), Louis Armstrong (1901–1971), and Tony Bennett entertained guests at the Napoleon Ballroom. Lena Horne (1917–2010) and Lucille Ball (1911–1989) frequented the Eden Roc. Dolores Hawkins (1929–1987) performed in the *Cavalcade of Broadway*. Singers such as Johnny Desmond (1919–1985), Elvis Presley (1935–1977), and Johnny Mathis performed in various venues. Danny Thomas (1914–1991) often performed his comedy act at local nightclubs. The list of celebrities frequenting Miami Beach at the time was simply astonishing.

During the time, Miami Beach was also a gambling haven. Betting on horse races in Miami during 1949 totaled over $50 million. As early as the late 1920s, Al Capone, aka Scarface, began to winter in Miami and had a mansion on Palm Island. Meyer Lansky, the "Mob's Accountant," ran casinos. There was also the gambling industry controlled by Frank Costello, an Italian American mafia gangster known as the "prime minister of the underworld."

In 1950, with the arrival of boxing promoter and manager Chris Dundee and his brother, legendary trainer Angelo Dundee, Miami's recognition as a boxing center took off. Miami Beach became a boxing mecca, hosting a steady stream of boxing matches. Chris Dundee promoted major bouts in the Miami area, such as the welterweight match between Kid Gavilan and Bobby Dykes, and world title fight between light heavyweights Harold Johnson and Jesse Bowdry. Miami Beach also became a training center for fighters, anchored by the world-renowned Fifth Street Gym, managed by the Dundee brothers.

The Miami Beach Auditorium, Bay Front Auditorium, and the Orange Bowl were all scenes of major boxing matches. Such venues attracted some of the best boxers, such as Ezzard Charles, Chico Vejar, Archie Moore, Sugar Ray Robinson, Jake LaMotta, Johnny Gonsalves, Gil Turner, and Jimmy Carter. They all clashed in Miami. Amateur boxing was flourishing, and Golden Gloves tournaments were highly anticipated events in Miami. In 1955, boxing was so prevalent, the sport was added to the City of Miami's official recreation program.

Regrettably, Miami Beach was also strictly segregated during the 50s. Seasonal workers, mostly black, were required to register with the police department, where they were photographed, fingerprinted, and forced to carry a registration card. Black people were not allowed in many of the hotels and nightclubs unless it was for work there. In March 1955, Lena Horne defiantly took a stand against segregation when she refused to perform an $8,000 a week engagement at Copa City because her reservation was not honored at a Miami Beach hotel.

Shining Shoes at the Fontainebleau Hotel

Going back to Miami Beach was a natural move for Beau. Jack had shined shoes on a seasonal basis at the Fontainebleau Hotel in the heart of Millionaire's Row for the last several years, so it made sense for him to obtain a permanent job at the fabled hotel. The Miami icon ushered in an era of glitzy and luxurious hotels on Miami Beach. Opening on December 1954, the Fontainebleau featured 565 rooms, 265 cabanas, a marina for 50 yachts, and a staff of 847. Located on the 14-acre estate of the former Firestone Mansion owned by Harvey Firestone at Collins Avenue and 44th Street, its grounds were adorned with gardens fashioned after Fontainebleau and Versailles, France.

A 17,000 square foot lobby highlighting a glamorous spiraling marble staircase, known as the "staircase to nowhere," greeted guests upon their arrival. At the top of the staircase was a small coat closet. The hotel, built at the cost of $14,000,000, was branded as a "decadent paradise of 'flashy diamonds, illicit sex, and overflowing ice cream sodas.'"[2] It was not uncommon to see half-naked women walking through the halls or to spot celebrities in the posh lobby. Levi Forte, a bellman at the Fontainebleau, said, "The floor was like a mirror, so shiny you could see yourself."[3]

The glitzy hotel hosted marvelous entertainment and nightlife in the Bleau Bar and LaRonde Supper Club. Lucille Ball, Judy Garland, Jackie Gleason, Sammy Davis, Jr., Bob Hope, and Frank Sinatra were regular performers. Frank Sinatra's s last Timex-sponsored variety television show was broadcast from the Fontainebleau on March 26, 1960. Titled *Welcome Home Elvis*, it was Elvis' first television appearance since his discharge from the military. The show co-featured Sammy Davis, Jr., Joey Bishop, Peter Lawford, and Nancy Sinatra. The opulent hotel and its grounds have also been the backdrop for numerous movies, such as *Goldfinger*, *Scarface*, *The Bellboy*, and *The Bodyguard*. A magnet for boxers, the Fontainebleau hosted Roberto Duran's defense of his lightweight title on Jan 29, 1977, when he defeated Vilomar Fernandez.

Beau's shoeshine stand was in the hotel barbershop on the lower level of the Fontainebleau. During the day, Beau shined shoes, starting as early as 7 o'clock in the morning. Instead of going home after closing down his shoe shine stand at 5:30 p.m., Beau would walk over to the men's bathroom where he worked as a restroom attendant, handing out towels, often working until midnight. On a good week, he would make $55.

At one point there was a sign outside the hotel barber shop that read,

Fontainebleau Hotel, c. 1955 (Library of Congress).

"Come and have your shoes shined by the former lightweight champion of the world." Beau, however, maintained an unpretentious presence. He wore a simple white jacket to work. Unlike others, he did not inscribe his name over his jacket pocket. "I would not put my name there," said Jack, "because that would be too much like begging."[4] Beau didn't mind shining shoes again. In fact, he embraced it. "I like this job because I know what a shoe needs," he said. "I know what the people want with a shoe. I do a good job."[5]

"I accept fate. I began as a shoeshine boy and I'm resigned to end as one," Beau unpretentiously articulated. "All the good things that happened to me in between have been a blessing."[6] Jack was content with shining shoes and serving guests. He was a simple, homely man that didn't appear to care about the money, only his friends. "Good week I make $50. Bad week $35.... The smallest tip? Fellow give me just seven cents once. Didn't bother me. The way I looked at it, if I already had 93 cents, that extra seven cents would make me one big dollar."[7]

Esteemed Visitors Show Respect

Beau was one of the best-known athletes during the forties. Throughout his time boxing in New York, Beau met various celebrities, many of whom became lifelong friends. For instance, Frank Sinatra and Humphrey Bogart often visited Beau in his dressing room after his battles in Madison Square Garden. Other celebrities dropped in at soirees hosted by the Syndicate before Beau's fights. Jack was also well revered by the boxing community, from the boxers he fought to managers and trainers. What is remarkable is the everlasting respect they had for Beau. When in Miami, they made a point to drop in on Beau for a visit.

During his twenty-five years of shining shoes at the Fontainebleau, renowned visitors such as Rocky Marciano, Irving J. Bottner, Cus D'Amato, Irving Rudd, Jackie Gleason, Frank Sinatra, and Jimmy Cannon, came by to express their love and respect for Beau. Recalling the bygone days, Beau said, "Lots of movie stars used to see me fight. They were my friends and helped me out a lot. It was so beautiful to know that people cared for you."[8] As Jack elucidated, "Boxing's been good to me. It was real good to me. It made me a lot of friends, that's the thing."[9]

The heavyweight champion Rocky Marciano (1923–1969) took a brief vacation at the Fontainebleau in late 1955. He had just fought the last fight of his stellar career on September 21 and would vacate the title and announce his retirement on April 27, 1956. Astonishingly, Marciano never lost a fight in his forty-nine-bout career and reigned as heavyweight champion from 1952–1956. While the champ was upstairs in his luxurious oceanfront suite, the former lightweight champ was downstairs shining shoes.

Having sincere admiration for Jack, Rocky undertook to seek him out during his stay. Beau jumped at the opportunity when Marciano invited him to be his dinner guest and appreciated the fellowship and conversation. "We had a big time," said Beau animatedly, "talking about fights and fighters. He told me how Moore had blacked him out, and how he could have lost that fight and his title. What a big strong man that Rocky is, and what a wonderful man he is with it, too."[10] Tragically, Rocky died on the eve of his 46th birthday, when the private plane in which he was flying crashed after encountering bad weather on the way to Des Moines, Iowa.

During the summer of 1959, Irving J. Bottner (1916–2006) paid Beau a visit to surprise him with a special present. The president and owner of Esquire Shoe Polish, a subsidiary of Revlon, Bottner was a progressive businessman who once was a bootblack himself. His Esquire brand was one of the most popular shoe polishes of the day. Bottner, an enormous fan of Beau Jack, knew of Beau's shoe-shining notoriety. While in Miami, Bottner presented Beau with a specially designed shoeshine box and a lifetime supply of shoeshine products. He also offered Jack a contract to conduct public relations for the Esquire Shoe Polish and exhibit the sweet art of shoe shining at sales meetings.

Hall of Fame boxing manager and trainer "Cus" D'Amato was another distinctive visitor that dropped in on Beau at the Fontainebleau. Constantine "Cus" D'Amato (1908–1985) excelled in psychologically motivating his fighters. One of his well-known quotes was, "A professional fighter has got to learn to hit and not get hit, and at the same time be exciting. That's what professional boxing is about."[11] D'Amato handled the careers of three Hall of Fame boxers, heavyweight champions Mike Tyson and Floyd Patterson, and light heavyweight champion Jose Torres. As "Cus" stood in front of him, Beau knelt down to shine his shoes, but D'Amato would have none of that. Instead, "Cus" insisted on shining Beau's shoes, which he did.

Another of Beau's renowned visitors was press agent Irving Rudd (1917–2000). The quick-witted press agent and Boxing Hall of Famer enjoyed calling on Beau in the Fontainebleau barber shop. During Rudd's life, he served as press agent for legendary promoters such as Mike Jacobs, Don King, and Bob Arum. He also worked with Muhammad Ali, Sugar Ray Leonard, Ray Mancini, and Thomas Hearns, as well as the Brooklyn Dodgers. When Beau caught a glimpse of Rudd, he asked if he could shine his shoes. Jim Murray of the *Los Angeles Times* described the interaction. "Why, Mr. Rudd! Can I shine your shoes-for-nothing?" Rudd looks at him. "No, Sidney, you can't shine my shoes," Irving says. "Why not?" Beau Jack says. "Because," says Irving Rudd, "you were the lightweight champion of the world."[12] Out of admiration, Irving would not let the former champion shine his shoes.

Famous comedian and actor Jackie Gleason (1916–1987), known for his role in *The Honeymooners*, lived in Miami and frequently visited with Jack. They enjoyed reminiscing about his fights and boxing. Beau proudly sported a button Gleason gave him that said, "How Sweet It Is."

Beau Jack had an extraordinary relationship with Frank Sinatra (1915–1998). The legendary Sinatra rose to fame during the early '40s, becoming one of the most famous singers of the 20th century. He sold over 150 million records and was an eleven-time Grammy winner. Sinatra had hit songs that are still popular today, such as "My Way," "Fly Me to the Moon," and "New York, New York." Appearing in numerous films, he was also an award-winning actor. He received an Academy Award for his role in *From Here to Eternity* (1953) and critical acclaim for his performance in *The Manchurian Candidate* (1962). Sinatra even gave Beau a cameo appearance in his film *Tony Rome* (1967).

Introduced to boxing by his father, Sinatra was a rabid fight fan and supporter of charities. He knew boxing and enjoyed mingling with boxers such as Rocky Graziano, Joe Louis, Sugar Ray Robinson, and Jake LaMotta. Sinatra was generous and compassionate in his giving. During his life, he raised over a billion dollars for charities, including $1.2 million for orphaned and handicapped children. He also silently paid Joe Louis' bill when he was in the hospital. Likewise, when Sugar Ray Robinson fell on hard times, Sinatra

Beau shining shoes at the Fontainebleau Hotel, c. 1968 (United Press International).

had a monthly check sent from his Anheuser-Busch interests to Robinson.

Sinatra not only witnessed many of Jack's fights in New York, he often paid him a visit in his dressing room after his bouts. Sinatra and Beau developed an eternal bond of friendship and mutual respect. When Sinatra was in Miami, he regularly dropped by the Fontainebleau to give Beau a hug and procure a shoe shine. Admiringly, he would say, "This is my Beau Jack."

When Beau started out shining shoes at the Fontainebleau, his shoe stand was right outside the hotel. While Frank Sinatra and Tony Consiglio, a lifelong friend of Sinatra, were staying at the Fontainebleau, Consiglio saw Jack shining shoes. Consiglio went upstairs and told Frank that Beau was shining shoes outside. When Sinatra found out Beau's stand was outside, he immediately called Ben Novack, the hotel's manager, and instructed him to find a respectable job for Jack in the hotel. Beau was offered a position inside the hotel that very day.[13]

Beau treasured Sinatra and would do anything for him. In a 1988 interview with Gary Smith of *Sports Illustrated* magazine, Beau spoke of his relationship with Sinatra. "If that man needed me any hour, any day, I'd go to him," proclaimed Beau. "Not walkin'. **Runnin'.** After I'm gone, I'm gonna remember him. When he came to Miami he would try to give me his shoes when I shined 'em, but they were so small I couldn't get two toes in. He was always worried that I didn't have money."[14] Frank Sinatra was an essential link to Jack's boxing days and a genuine friend that respected and cared for Beau, as Beau did for him.

When asked if Sinatra was a good tipper, Beau replied "Oh, I can't tell you that. Mr. Sinatra always made me promise not to tell anyone what he gives."[15] Like many others, Sinatra resisted Beau's efforts to shine his shoes. Frank told Beau that he should be polishing his shoes for all of the exciting thrills Beau had provided him during his spectacular boxing career. It is said that Frank would give Beau several hundred dollars and even $1,000 when he visited with him. Who knows, but when Beau referred to a famous benefactor, Frank Sinatra comes to mind.

Sports columnist and future Boxing Hall of Famer Jimmy Cannon (1909–1973) was a friend of both Frank Sinatra and Beau Jack. Cannon was a widely popular sportswriter and columnist for the *New York Post*, *New York Journal-American*, and King Features Syndicate. His boxing coverage was renowned, and he knew the impact of the black boxer. Speaking about the legendary Joe Louis, Cannon wrote, "He's a credit to his race—the human race."[16] Cannon was famous for starting his sports column with, "Nobody asked me, but..." Ernest Hemingway praised Cannon. "He's an excellent sportswriter and he's also a very good writer aside from sports," Hemingway said. "I don't know anybody who takes his job more seriously or with more confidence. He's able to convey the quality of the athlete and the feeling, the excitement, of the event."[17]

Cannon followed Jack's boxing career and called on Beau when he was in Miami. In an article Cannon wrote in the *New York Journal-American* following a visit with Beau, Cannon stated, "Some of his customers still call him the Champ, but many address him as boy. They couldn't have seen him fight because there was never more of a man."[18] It took a courageous man to continue fighting against Tony Janiro with a broken kneecap.

In 1979, Beau ended his time at the Fontainebleau Hotel and moved down the street to start working at another famed luxury hotel, the Doral Beach Hotel. Opened in 1963, the luxurious swanky seventeen-story hotel was located on the corner of 48th Street and Collins Avenue. It had 430 rooms, plenty of convention space, a marina, and a double deck cabana area. Its exterior was pre-cast white quartz stone. Its floors were marble. A spectacular view of Miami Beach and Miami greeted guests to the Starlight Roof Garden, where they could enjoy entertainment such as Freddie Martin and his orchestra and Count Basie. "The theme is unadulterated pleasure," wrote Bill Plaschke of the Fort Lauderdale News, "lavish leisure, the best of the good life."[19]

Today, the Hotel is the Miami Beach Resort and Spa. Paired with the Doral Country Club, the Hotel was built for $10,000,000. The Country Club began hosting the now-defunct Doral Open Invitational, a major PGA golf tournament in 1962. In 2012, Donald Trump bought the country club and renamed it the Trump National Doral Country Club.

Beau's shoe shine stand was located in the barber shop, past the boutique stores, on the basement floor of the Doral. He worked fourteen hours a day, five days a week. After shining shoes for eight hours, Jack would go upstairs and work the evening washing dishes in the kitchen until midnight. Although Beau missed boxing, he was content.

> I've heard a lot of people say, "A boxing champ shinin' shoes?" They can't seem to take it. I just say I'm here and if you got any shoes, I'll shine 'em. The days of being a star are over. The money's gone. I'm just glad I'm healthy and able to work. I'm proud that I'm not afraid to work.[20]

Beau was delighted, encountering people from all over the world and making new friends every day. "I'm happy about everything," stated Jack. "I have my friends and you can't beat that. When you have friends, you have everything."[21] Beau was content. "I ain't complaining," Jack said smiling. "I've shined the shoes of President Kennedy, Frank Sinatra and Sammy Davis, Jr."

Moments from the Civil Rights Movement

The Civil Rights movement was in full swing working to gain equal rights. Some people, however, just couldn't accept change and tried their best to thwart it. On January 14, 1963, following his election as Governor of Alabama, George Wallace declared in his inauguration, "segregation now, segregation tomorrow, segregation forever." On June 11, 1963, when two black students attempted to enroll at the University of Alabama, Governor Wallace stood in a doorway to prevent their entry in what is often referred to as the "Stand in the Schoolhouse Door." President John F. Kennedy had to call for one hundred troops from the Alabama National Guard to assist federal officials before Wallace would step down, permitting desegregation of the University.

A little over two months later, on August 28, 1963, Martin Luther King, Jr., gave his famous "I have a dream" speech in front of the Lincoln Memorial after 250,000 people took part in "The March on Washington for Jobs and Freedom." In a visionary proclamation he spoke, "I have a dream that one day this nation will rise up and live out the true meaning of its creed: 'We hold these truths to be self-evident: that all men are created equal.'"

Progress, albeit slow at best, was taking place. The following year, on July 2, 1964, President Lyndon B. Johnson signed the Civil Rights Act of 1964 into law, preventing employment discrimination due to race, color, sex, religion or national origin. It also established the U.S. Equal Employment Opportunity Commission (EEOC) to assist in preventing workplace discrimination. A year later, on August 6, 1965, President Johnson signed the Voting Rights Act of 1965, prohibiting the use of literacy tests as a voting requirement.

Then there was the tragedy of April 4, 1968. Dr. King was on a return trip to Memphis, Tennessee, to protest the inferior treatment of black sanitation workers. In his last sermon on April 3, Dr. King remarked:

> We've got some difficult days ahead. But it doesn't matter with me now. Because I've been to the mountaintop…. And He's allowed me to go up to the mountain. And I've looked over. And I've seen the promised land. I may not get there with you. But I want you to know tonight, that we, as a people, will get to the promised land.

The following day, 40-year-old James Earl Ray assassinated Martin Luther King, Jr., on the balcony of his second-floor motel room.

Race riots broke out across the United States. National Guard units were deployed in Memphis and Washington, D.C., to restore peace. A week later, President Johnson signed the Civil Rights Act of 1968, also known as the Fair Housing Act, providing equal housing opportunity regardless of race, religion or national origin.

30

Beau Jack the Trainer

Even when Beau was not engaged in ring combat himself, he cherished being in the gym working with amateurs and young professionals. After Beau initially retired in 1951, he began utilizing his experience training boxers.[1] Simply put, Jack believed that every man has the same things inside him that he did, but that the trainer has got to get it out of him. His young stable of fighters included Aman Peck of Hartford, Connecticut; Eddie Green of Kannapolis, North Carolina; Claude Chapman of Boston, Massachusetts; and Augusta product James Bussey. He continued to stay connected to boxing, working in the gym and giving back to the sport that gave so much to him, until the day he died.

Aman Peck was a middleweight boxer initially from Tampa, Florida. The winner of only four of his first 13 professional fights (4–8–1), the Tampa club fighter was quick and aggressive, but his punches didn't pack much power. His best performance came on January 13, 1953, when he went ten rounds in a tune-up bout for the welterweight champion, Kid Gavilan. Following his bout with Gavilan, Peck arrived in Augusta to train under Beau Jack. Under Beau's guidance, Peck won his next three fights over mediocre opponents. Sensing the opportunity, in late May, the Augusta Athletic Club issued an offer to Kid Gavilan to fight Peck in a rematch at Jennings Stadium on June 27. To sweeten the pot, the proposal included a $2,500 guarantee for Gavilan, but Gavilan rejected the offer. Aman Peck would end his fourteen-year career with a record of 25–60–6.

Eddie Green (1926–2013) was another pupil of Jack's. Hailing from Kannapolis, North Carolina, Eddie fought mostly in the middleweight division. Beau traveled around the southeast with Eddie, working his corner at the Asheville Auditorium, as he battled out a unanimous decision over Jackie O'Brien (58–12–7) in the feature welterweight bout on April 12, 1954. He was also in his corner on April 29 when Eddie battled to a victory over Gene Burton (54–20–10), a former number one welterweight contender, at the Armory in Charlotte, North Carolina. Eddie Green, of course, was the first opponent Beau met in his final 1955 comeback attempt. Green retired in 1955 with a record of 33–14–1.

Augusta middleweight James Bussey, aka "Young Joe Louis," or the "Georgia Kid," trained under Jack throughout his seven-year career. The 164-pound Bussey won seven of his first eight bouts, including his TKO victory over Richie Rhodes (16–6–7) of Miami on May 21, 1954. Jack was also in the Bussey's corner when he fought Billy Kilgore at the Lake Worth, Florida arena on February 2, 1956. Bussey retired in 1961 with a record of 15–19–4.

Light heavyweight Claude Chapman (1928–2009) also received instructional training from Beau. On May 22, 1954, Beau and 20-year-old Chapman were at the Armory in Charlotte for a bout against Leo Johnson in the light-heavyweight division. Chapman, weighing 186 pounds, defeated Johnson on points. Winning 23 of his first 25 bouts, Chapman went on to earn a 29–8–0 record and the New England heavyweight title over his 12-year career.

Golden Gloves—Moore Park—Kid Gavilan

Beau had a "sweet spot" for young amateur boxers. "I tell a kid," Jack said, "If you want to box, it's got to be your whole life. You can't smoke, you can't drink, you can't do narcotics, and you got to beat your brains out to be any good."[2] Jack savored working with amateur boxers through the Golden Gloves program. Sanctioned by USA Boxing, the Golden Gloves program provides young amateur boxers a chance to qualify for local, regional and national tournaments, while developing conditioning, sportsmanship, self-confidence, and character. In 1980, Beau worked alongside former welterweight champion Luis Manuel Rodriguez as a cornerman and instructor at the Sunshine State Golden Gloves Tournament at Dinner Key near Coral Gables, Florida. At least three of the competitors developed into professional fighters.

The following year, in 1981, Beau began volunteering as a boxing instructor at Moore Park in Miami. Located at 795 N.W. 36th Street, Moore Park had a strong renowned amateur boxing program for youngsters twelve years and older. Its boxing program was operated by Jimmy Mackey, a former welterweight fighter. An outstanding amateur boxer, Mackey racked up a record of 25–16–4 between 1957 and 1966. A significant figure in Florida's Golden Gloves program, he excelled at working with amateurs. He was also instrumental in the development of amateur boxing in the Bahamas.

Volunteering alongside Beau was former welterweight champion Kid Gavilan (1926–2003). In May 1951, at age twenty-five, Gavilan won the welterweight title when he defeated Johnny Bratton. He fought for 15 years between

1943 and 1958, amassing a record of 108–30–5, and breaking the jaws of seven men in the ring. Like Beau, Gavilan featured a signature windup bolo punch and was a furious fighter. He reigned as champion for three years, was never knocked out, and only tasted the canvas three times in his career.

After Gavilan retired from boxing, he went back to Cuba before returning to the United States in 1968 on a Freedom Flight. He worked in Tampa as a caregiver for twelve years and then moved to Pennsylvania, where he was employed as a boxing instructor. When that position ran out of funding, he ended up in Miami in March of 1980, where he began selling sausages on the streets.

Boxing was a staple of life for both Jack and Gavilan. They had met once in the ring during their careers when Gavilan battered out a unanimous decision over Jack in 1949. As the two former champions worked with the amateurs, they developed a long-lasting friendship. Similar to Jack, Gavilan won a lot of money in the ring, estimated at $3.5 million, but was virtually penniless. Gavilan apparently spent his money on fast cars and jewelry. He enjoyed buying expensive suits and even had a chauffeur to drive him around. Although he had lost his earnings and suffered three strokes, he was still full of life. "Life is beautiful," stated Gavilan in 1980. "I feel terrific, like a little boy."[3]

Taking a personal interest in the youngsters, Jack expressed the importance of living right. "I tell the boys if you want to get in the limelight and have people love you and come and see you and talk about you, you've got to give them everything you got and that means staying away from drugs," declared Jack. "I want to keep the boys out of trouble and let them enjoy boxing like I did. I don't let 'em have an easy tick around me."[4] A taskmaster, Beau conveyed parental life messages through his training. He practiced what he preached, jogging every morning from 51st Street to 36th Street. "I think that helps me stay in good shape," said Jack. "I come by the gym and do a lot of things with these kids."[5]

Beau Jack's All-Star Boxing Gym

The year was 1985 and Beau was 64 years old. He had been shining shoes for the past 20 years while training boxers during his free time. Beau's full-time shoe shining job was about to end. In 1985, Stu Kaufman, an attorney by trade, was building and developing a new boxing gym located at 616 N.E. 8th Street in Hallandale, Florida, near Hollywood Beach. Originally from New York, Kaufman remembered Beau fondly from his fights at Madison Square Garden and sought him out to be his head trainer. Respecting Jack's work ethic and love for the sport, Stu hired Beau as his head trainer in May 1985. In his honor, Kaufman named the gym "Beau Jack's All-Star Boxing Gym."

Exhilarated, Jack was back doing what he cherished. He had been separated too long from his sport and was thrilled to be back in the ring. "This is beautiful. I can't think of anything that could make me happier," Beau exclaimed. "You could give me $50,000 to be with boxers again and I'd give you back the $50,000 if you let me stay with the boxers. I've got what I want."[6] Beau would have worked for free, but Kaufman paid him a nominal salary. He also gave Beau use of a small room adjacent to the gym and free meals at the Ocean's 11 Sports Lounge and Grill, Kaufman's restaurant across the street.

Jack praised Kaufman for the opportunity. "Nobody else gave me a chance but Mr. Kaufman," he said. "The man has given me an opportunity to prove to the world it could be done, that I could train good. This is my whole life, and I'm back in it. I'd rather be in this than be rich."[7] Beau was stepping up from a part-time volunteer to become a full-time head trainer of a boxing gym.

Jack was a harsh but fair trainer. He trained fighters like he trained—mercilessly. When Beau was boxing, he woke up at 3:30 a.m. every morning to run ten miles at the crack of dawn. Conditioning was imperative. "The only thing that made me win," Beau declared, "was my conditioning. You have to be in shape with your mind, with your strength and will all your energy."[8] After observing Beau in the gym, Bob Hill of the *Fort Lauderdale News* described Beau's training style. "Jack works his boxers the same way General Motors builds cars," wrote Hill. "He lines them up and has each work on one thing at a time, one right after the other."[9]

Boxers trained by Jack attest to his mercilessness and fairness as a trainer. Mark Sanford, an ex–Marine, was one of those boxers. Even after fighting in over thirty amateur bouts, Sanford said, "He's tougher than anything you'll find in the ring. If you can take what Beau Jack gives you, you can handle anything."[10] Jack made it a point to teach his pupils to deal with fear in the ring. "You get a little jittery about a fight," he said. "Don't let anyone ever tell you they're not afraid. If they say that, they're nuts. You can't help feeling fear. It comes over you."[11]

Equality in the gym was imperative. Jack treated everybody equal no matter their status. Jon Ruiz, another one of Beau's trainees, was adamant that Beau treated everyone, whether they were a talented fighter or just a beginner, with equal dignity and respect. It didn't matter if you were a professional boxer or a young boy trying to learn the ropes. You did not receive special treatment. Future heavyweight champion Trevor Berbick found out the hard way. At the time, Berbick was the WBA's seventh-ranked heavyweight contender. When he refused to get in line with the other boxers at the gym, Beau declined to let him work out. Less than a year later, Trevor Berbick became the WBC Heavyweight Champion, defeating Pinklon Thomas on March 22, 1986. Although Jack was tough, he was well-liked by his students.

His students treasured his insightful guidance. Junior middleweight Rick Fisler summed up his purpose for training with Beau. "I've trained with a lot of trainers, but he's the best. No question."[12] Another one of Beau Jack's pupils, Bob Tumminia, concurred. "He's the main reason I came here. I figure the only way to be a champ is to be trained by a champ."[13]

Beau's position at Kaufman's gym did not last long, but Beau was able to bounce over to Fifth Street Gym in Miami Beach. Fittingly, the world-renowned Fifth Street Gym would be Beau's last hurrah.

The 5th Street Gym

Above its entrance hung a sign stating, "Miami Beach 5th Street Gym, Nationally Known Boxers." The 5th Street Gym was the brainchild of brothers and Boxing Hall of Famers Angelo and Chris Dundee.[14] Angelo and his wife, Helen, along with his older brother Chris, started the gym in 1951, putting Miami in the center of the boxing map.

Chris Dundee (1907–1998) was a fight promoter, promoting hundreds of bouts, including eight world championships. He staged matches for Kid Gavilan, Sugar Ray Robinson, Archie Moore, Jake LaMotta, George Foreman, and Sugar Ray Leonard, to name a few. He also organized the Miami Beach fight in which Muhammad Ali stole the heavyweight title from Sonny Liston in 1964.

Angelo Dundee (1921–2012), on the other hand, was a legendary trainer. Learning his trade at Stillman's Gym during the late '40s, Angelo trained fifteen world champions. His first champion was Carmen Basilio, who won the welterweight and middleweight titles during the 50s. Angelo also trained light-heavyweight champ Willie Pastrano; heavyweight champion Jimmy Ellis; welterweight champion Luis Rodriguez; welterweight champion Jose Napoles; and champion of five weight divisions, including the welterweight division, Sugar Ray Leonard. When George Foreman defeated Michael Moorer to become the oldest heavyweight champion at age 45, Angelo was working his corner. Angelo, however, is best known for training a skinny teenager named Cassius Clay, aka Muhammad Ali.

Angelo Dundee's integrity made him one of boxing's finest ambassadors. The late sportscaster Howard Cosell once said of Dundee, "He is the only man in boxing to whom I would entrust my own son."[15] One reason Angelo was so effective as a trainer was his ability to motivate his fighters. Angelo was one of the best motivators the game has ever seen. Promoter Bob Arum remarked on Angelo's skills. "He was wonderful. He was the whole package," Arum said. "Angelo was the greatest motivator of all time. No matter how bad things were, Angelo always put a positive spin on them. That's what Ali loved so much about him."[16] In a 1981 interview with the *New York Times*, Muhammad Ali esteemed Angelo, "You come back to the corner and he'll say, 'The guy's open for a hook, or this or that.' If he tells you something during a fight, you can believe it. As a cornerman, Angelo is the best in the world."[17]

Following their arrival in Miami Beach, the Dundee brothers opened the 5th Street Gym in 1951 on the corner of Fifth Street and Washington Avenue above the Miami Beach Drug Store and Howie's Bar & Liquor Store. Three blocks from South Beach, it looked dilapidated and had the feel of the slums. There was no air conditioning and it smelled like sweat. Termites had eaten on the wood floors so much that when heavyweight Sonny Liston jumped rope, "termite dust fell in the liquor store on the ground level."[18] Sounds of boxing permeated the air. You would hear the endless pounding of gloves battering speed bags and every three minutes the sound of the bell signaling the end of a sparring round.

Boxing historian Hank Kaplan (1920–2007) revered the Dundee brothers and their celebrated gym. "The Dundees may have been the best twosome in boxing history," said Kaplan. "Angelo developed 12 world champions, and during the days Chris was promoting, the Fifth Street Gym was the best, most active gym in the country. Every great fighter of the '50s, '60s, '70s and even '80s came here to train."[19] More than 30 world champions trained at the landmark during its 43-year history. Some of the clientele included names such as Jake LaMotta, Sugar Ray Robinson, Sugar Ray Leonard, Sonny Liston, Willie Pep, Ike Williams, Kid Gavilan, Joe Louis, Roberto Duran, Floyd Patterson, Emile Griffith, Alexis Arguello, Jimmy Ellis, Muhammad Ali, and Aaron Pryor. When Ali was training for his first fight with Joe Frazier in 1971, celebrities would stop by to see him train and spar. Like the legendary boxer training at the gym, the list of visitors was astonishing. The Beatles, Burt Lancaster, Jackie Gleason, Jim Brown, Robert Duvall, and Frank Sinatra all observed training sessions on the second-floor gym. Actor Mickey Rourke also trained at the 5th Street Gym when he was working with trainer Freddie Roach to prepare for his second bout in 1992. Rourke managed to compile a 6–0–2 record in the light heavyweight division.

It was commonly said that the 5th Street Gym "contains more good fighters per square inch than can be found anywhere in the land."[20] According to boxing analyst Ferdie Pacheco, the gym was like "the Note Dame and Yankee Stadium of boxing rolled into one."[21] The champs came to train alongside the upstarts. "It had a kind of grimy romance," wrote Matt Schudel of the *Sun Sentinel,* "built of spilled sweat and blood and the dreams of a thousand hungry kids."[22] Next to Stillman's Gym in New York, it was probably the most well-known boxing gym in the world.

In the late 1970s, Angelo Dundee left Miami Beach and moved up north to train his stable of boxers. Roosevelt Ivory, a Miami promoter, took over the business and hired Dr. Cool to manage the gym. Along with Beau Jack, Dr. Cool was the best-known bootblack in the country, having shined shoes for more than 40 years. He could make the brush sing and the rags pop, making calypso music with his shines. Dr. Cool, however, preferred show business over managing the gym. When the management position became available at the gym in 1987, Beau was a natural fit. Ivory quickly hired Jack to operate the renowned Fifth Street Gym.

Immediately, Beau became the soul of the place. Jack praised the rugged atmosphere. "Everybody gets sick when they first come here. You're nothin' if you can't stand this. If you wanna fight, you gotta get in shape."[23] Needless to say, Beau invited his good friend, former welterweight world champion Kid Gavilan, to join him at the gym as an assistant trainer.

Alex Daoud, the mayor of Miami Beach from 1985 to 1991, came to the Fifth Street Gym when he was a kid afflicted with polio. "What the 5th Street Gym did when I first started training was it gave me an introduction to fighters who were predominantly black, predominantly poor and overwhelmingly nice," professed Daoud. "Not once did the fighters ever pick on me or cause me any problems."[24] Daoud recalled that he used to meet other boxers at midnight to run several miles around a nearby golf course. One night, three police cars surrounded the boxers and demanded Daoud explain why they were there. "I said, 'I'm a fighter. I'm training with my friends,'" Daoud says. "And the guy said to me, 'But you're white.' And Muhammad Ali, with a straight face, looked at the police officer and said, 'It's not his fault. He's been sick lately.'"[25]

Years later, when Daoud was serving as the mayor of Miami Beach, he returned to the gym and met Beau Jack, who had taken over operations from Dr. Cool. He and Beau got to know each other quite well and became close friends. One evening after questioning Beau about his apartment, Alex was invited to visit his flat. It was quite an eye-opener. "He lives in one room, without air conditioning, without a kitchen, without loved ones around him," sadly stated Daoud afterward. "He doesn't have much money. I know that for a fact."[26] Beau essentially lived in a one-room shantytown apartment. The roof leaked. There were rats and cockroaches. Beau had to walk down the hall to use a community bathroom. Alex cried when he saw where the former champ was living. Fortunately for Beau, Daoud helped him relocate to an apartment at Murray Gillum Senior Citizen Housing. Jack was humbled and thankful. He embraced Alex and warmly said, "Thank you Alex. I love you."[27] Daoud later tried to have the Fifth Street Gym designated as a historical site but was unsuccessful.

As time went by, the gym began to die a slow death as more and more kids became involved in drugs. Drugs were an easy way to make money. Beau explained, "Boxing used to be the only way some young men could rise up from life in the streets. Today they have less demanding alternatives. They don't have to work, they don't have to sweat, they can just sell dope on the corner."[28]

Unfortunately, the landmark was demolished in May 1993. During the gym's final weeks, all the punching bags and other equipment were removed. One man, with the aid of his cane, however, continued to climb the stairs and sit looking out the corner window. His teeth were gone. Skin dropped over his left eye. That man was Beau Jack. He was losing his source of solace.

31

Final Days

The Fifth Street gym was gone, and Beau's health was deteriorating. In the early nineties, Jack was hospitalized due to an inoperable malignant stomach tumor. With the heart of a champion and courage of a lion, Jack kept plodding along, spending his last days receiving well-deserved awards and honors, appearing for autographs, attending boxing matches, and still managing to train fighters.

"Hall of Fame boxers will sign autographs at mall in Miami" was the announcement in the *South Florida Sun Sentinel*. On Sunday, March 27, 1994, Beau, along with two-time featherweight champion Willie Pep and six-time world champion welterweight Emile Griffith, appeared at Miami's West-chester Mall for an autograph session. The prizefighter who couldn't sign his name when he began his career was more than happy to autograph photos and cards.

As one can imagine, attending boxing matches were one of Beau's favorite pastimes. It was different as a fan versus a boxer, but it still brought him close to his sport and always revived memories of his ring days. Jack was on the east coast of Florida, just north of Fort Myers, to attend the middleweight title bout between Andres Arellano and Freeman Barr at the Charlotte County Memorial Auditorium on Tuesday night, February 25, 1997. Barr won the International Boxing Council Americas middleweight title that night by TKO in the tenth round. During the fight card, Beau Jack and Christy Martin,[1] the World Women's Boxing Association's lightweight champion, were recognized before the 1,200 fans.

Beau and Kid Gavilan frequently traveled together. They both boarded a plane from Miami to New York on Friday night, December 19, 1997, to witness Prince Naseem Hamed of Sheffield, England defend his WBO featherweight title against Kevin Kelley of New York at Madison Square Garden. It was a heck of a fight with abundant action. Prince (28–0, 26 KOs) was knocked down three times by Kelley (47–2, 32 KOs), before stopping Kelley in the fourth round to earn a TKO victory.

Beau was also fortunate enough to travel, expenses paid, to numerous events honoring him and his outstanding career. Jack was the featured honoree at the 1996 annual dinner of the Ring 8 Veteran Boxers Association at Tony Mazarella's Waterfront Crab House in Long Island, New York. Started in the 1930s as a social club, Ring 8, a nonprofit organization, changed its emphasis to assisting retired boxers in 1953. Funds raised by Ring 8 are used to aid retired fighters with varied needs such as financial assistance, housing, dentures, eyeglasses, and funerals.

In early March 1997, Beau and Gavilan headed to sold-out Bally's Park Place in Atlantic City, New Jersey, to join former boxing champions and celebrities for a three-day celebration of the 75th anniversary of *The Ring* magazine. Other titleholders in attendance included such boxing greats as Smokin' Joe Frazier, brothers Leon and Michael Spinks, Archie Moore, Ingemar Johannson, Sandy Saddler, Carmen Basilio, Joey Giardello, Jake LaMotta, Joey Maxim, Floyd Patterson, Sugar Ray Robinson, Eder Jofre, Ruben Olivares, Thomas Hearns, Larry Holmes, Ken Norton, Chuck Wepner, Emile Griffith, Aaron Pryor, Iran Barkley, Christy Martin, Carlos Palamino, Sean O'Grady, Arthur Mercante, Carlos Ortiz, and Gene Fullmer. Beau was right at home with his colleagues and among the most revered in the crowd.

Seventy-five-year-old Beau swapped some stories and shared his congenial sense of humor as he spoke at the 75th-anniversary dinner. During his speech, Beau spoke about his October 14, 1949, loss to Kid Gavilan. He jokingly announced that Gavilan gave him $50 to lose the fight. Sitting among the honored guests, Gavilan just grinned back at Jack. Beau also comically expressed his frustration over his three losses to Ike Williams. "When I die and go to heaven, I want to fight Ike Williams again."[2]

On April 3, 1998, two days after his 77th birthday, Jack was in Montreal, Canada. He was an honored guest of InterBox, an innovative company providing boxers training, lodging, a salary, and educational funds.[3] InterBox recognized numerous boxing legends before the Stephane Ouellet and Alex Hilton middleweight title fight at the Molson Centre in Montreal. In addition to Beau Jack, InterBox paid tribute to Jake LaMotta, George Chuvalo, Archie Moore, and Yvon Durelle.

Before the bout, the legends gathered at a local restaurant to reminisce. Following dinner, someone offered to help Beau up from his table. "Leave me alone," retorted Beau. Then another person offered to get his cane. Jack shouted, "Leave it there and leave me alone."[4] Refusing any aid, Jack stood up and began walking between the tables, but stumbled, knocking chairs and a table down on his way to the floor. Archie Moore, the former light-heavyweight world champion from 1952–61, jumped to his feet and immediately went to help Jack up on his feet. Even at 77 years old, Beau Jack shunned assistance.

Beau was in Rochester, New York, in May 1998 to receive yet another

(Left to right) Philadelphia Mayor Rendell, boxing memorabilia dealer Harry Zambelli, and Beau Jack. Former light heavyweight champion Harold Johnson is in the foreground, c. 1998 (courtesy Bruce Kielty).

award. At the Rochester Boxing Hall of Fame dinner, Jack received the John Mastrella Integrity Award. John Mastrella, always known for his honesty and integrity, was an Army captain who served in the Battle of the Bulge. After serving his country, Mastrella worked as the Rochester police commissioner and later served as a New York Supreme Court Justice. A former boxer himself, Mastrella was a welterweight boxing champion.

Several months later, Jack headed out from his South Beach apartment to catch a flight to Philadelphia to be commemorated once again. His destination was the Boxers' Ball at the Apollo of Temple. The black-tie affair, held on November 18, 1998, raised money for the Fight for Education Foundation. Among the 600 people on hand were boxing stars Sugar Ray Leonard, Bernard Hopkins, David Reid, Nate Miller, Joey Giardello, Michael Grant, Charles Brewer, Matthew Saad Muhammad, Zahir Raheem, Wesley Mouzon, Curtis Parker, Greg Sirb, Marvin Garris, Randall "Tex" Cobb, and Fred Jenkins.

"Bouts-and-Boogie" was the event's theme, featuring a remembrance of boxing in the 1940s and a special tribute to the late Bob Montgomery and to Beau Jack. The two warriors fought four times, each winning two of the bouts. Their bouts filled Madison Square Garden and raised a record total of

$35 million for war bonds in the renowned "War Bonds Fight" in 1944. Both men nobly and enthusiastically contributed to the U.S. efforts in World War II.

Speaking of the "War Bonds Fight," Beau proudly proclaimed, "The thing that means the most to me is that I felt like I was doing something to help win the war. As old as I am now, I would do it again."[5] He also fondly reminisced about his late rival, Bob Montgomery. "Bob Montgomery was a rough, tough man, a real man. That's what I was told before I fought him the first time, and it was the truth. I can't say nothing but good things about Bob Montgomery." He sadly added, "Nobody even called to let me know he was sick," Jack said, the sadness in his voice evident. "I wish I could have talked to him before he passed."[6] During the gala affair, Philadelphia's Mayor Ed Rendell presented Jack with the Liberty Bell Award commemorating his four bouts with Bob Montgomery and the great "War Bonds Fight."

Along with his journeys, Beau found a new boxing gym to train young boxers, the South Beach Boxing Gym. Founded in 1998 by Jolie Glassman and her ex-husband, the gym was created with the intent to continue Miami Beach's boxing legacy. Offering extreme workouts, several former boxers such as Beau Jack, Roberto Duran, Vinny Pazienza, Roy Jones, and Bernard Hopkins, used the gym to train their eager pupils. Although most trainers had to pay for gym space and use of the facilities, Jack was given free space and use of the gym.

32

An American Hero Passes

You have to love people to do this, to fight harder and harder
and harder. I love every human being God put on this earth.
I fight this way, and prepare this way, for love.

—Beau Jack

It was a mild winter day with scattered showers. The ocean was choppy
with swells ranging from three to five feet. Miami was celebrating Black History Month and the centennial anniversary of the black anthem *Lift Ev'ry
Voice and Sing*, with a four-part historical and musical revue telling the story
of black history in the United States. The day was February 9, 2000. It was the
same day that Beau Jack quietly passed away in a Miami nursing home.

Sidney "Beau Jack" Walker departed for the heavenly stars on February
9, 2000. His health had been declining for several years. In the end, however,
it was the damage he suffered while following his dream that led to his death.
During his 121-professional bout career, Beau suffered countless punches and
trauma to his head. Regrettably, the constant blows absorbed by his head resulted in the development of "Pugilistic Parkinson's Syndrome," also known
as "Boxer's Dementia."

The condition is directly related to recurring cerebral concussions sustained while boxing. Symptoms include memory loss, reduced thought processes, and movement disorders, such as weakness in the legs and wobbliness
of movement. The nature of boxing unfortunately leaves fighters at increased
risk of Parkinson's disease. Other notable people in the boxing world have
suffered from Parkinson's disease such as Joe Louis, Muhammad Ali, and
trainer Freddie Roach.

Jack died happily without remorse. Boxing had been his life. The money
he made was not that imperative to him. He fought to hear the applause
from the fans. "I was a whirlwind in every way," he admits. "I never looked at
the money. I lived for the cheers and the clapping of the fans."[1] Throughout
his career, he constantly encountered new people and made friends. Beau
was content and would have done it all over again if he had the chance. "I

would do it again—everything," Beau proclaimed. "I never thought about the money. I never cared for it. The crowd. That's what I cared for, the crowd. I wanted to give them excitement. I wanted them to come back and see me… The screaming and the yelling … the crowd. That's what I did it for."[2] Beau was champion of the world. "Fighting was a vacation for him from all that was bad in the world."[3]

Acclaimed as "one of the most exciting and popular figures Madison Square Garden has ever known,"[4] Beau Jack was one of the Garden's most admired and prolific fighters. During his 15-year professional career, Beau Jack fought in a record 27 main events at the Garden with gates grossing nearly $2 million. He won his first of two lightweight championship titles at the young age of 21. In 1943, he was the only boxer to yield a $100,000 gate at boxing's mecca, Madison Square Garden. In March 1944, he became the only boxer to fight in three main events at the Garden in one month, producing a combined gate of $332,579. Five months later, he set the record for the highest priced sports ticket—$100,000 for a ringside seat when he fought Bob Montgomery in the famous "War Bonds Fight" of 1944. Beau was a box office sensation. Even though Beau "fought long before the age of millionaire athletes and multimillion-dollar TV revenues, no fight anywhere has ever matched his best in ticket-sale revenue."[5] Later that year, he was named "Fighter of the Year" by *The Ring* magazine.

Beau Jack is not only a boxing legend, he is an American hero. Along with Bob Montgomery, they raised an incredible $35,864,900 in war bonds for U.S. efforts in World War II. He even bought $1,000 worth of war bonds himself and gave the respective tickets away to wounded veterans. Taking great dignity in fighting for his country, Beau donated his services for the bout. He always helped those less fortunate than himself and gave back to his fans and sport. Jack had exceptional charisma. "What they call charisma today is 1/100th of what he had," recalls Larry Kent, Beau's assistant trainer. "This guy, no matter where he went, he was loved and admired. He would stop anywhere to sign autographs."[6]

He valiantly earned the numerous honors bestowed upon him. In addition to the awards previously mentioned, Beau was inducted into *The Ring* magazine's Boxing Hall of Fame (1972), Georgia Sports Hall of Fame (1979), Madison Square Garden's Hall of Fame (1982), and International Boxing Hall of Fame (1991).

Beau began life with all odds against him. He was a poor black boy in a dark racial South. Beau lived with his grandmother because his parents abandoned him. He joyfully did everything he could to help his grandmother with chores around the farm. She instilled values in Beau Jack that he would carry for life—honesty, integrity, gritty determination, and a heart that received joy from helping those less fortunate.

It was only when he became a teenager that Sidney found a route out of poverty. With the help of golf legend Bobby Jones and other founders of the Augusta National Golf Club, the Georgia bootblack embarked on a tremendous record-setting boxing career. Cast from the grounds of the world's most prestigious golf club and racism into the prime time of New York, he boxed his way to two world titles. His success came through sheer heart and gritty determination.

Ever respectful and polite, Jack was a heartwarming ray of light and innocence in a sport infiltrated by the mob. His honor and soul could not be sold. Earl Ruby, Sports Editor for the *Courier Journal* in Louisville, Kentucky, penned, "In the fight racket there was never a classier guy than Beau Jack, who was never great at his mean game. His was a blending of innocence and ignorance and yet it was the purest of all."[7]

Even when Beau lost a controversial bout, he accepted it with class and genuine character. He may have been upset and frustrated in his dressing room after the fight, but that didn't last long. Resting on his strong religious beliefs, Beau would say, "The man say I win, … I win. He say I lose, I lose."[8]

A black American hero, Beau Jack was esteemed by millions, both black and white. His fights were broadcast throughout the States and overseas, as families and soldiers gathered around the radio. He inspired others through his actions. Even with a broken knee, he refused to quit. Whether he won or lost, the bull-shouldered battler was never accused of not always giving his best. He knew how to please the crowds, fighting in an unorthodox swarming "all out" style. "He was a great fighter," proclaimed boxing historian Hank Kaplan. "He had fantastic stamina. You couldn't find anybody more courageous than Beau Jack. He threw punches in bunches. He had a chin made of iron."[9] Richard Goldstein, a journalist for the *New York Times*, appreciated Beau's appeal. "In the years when the old Garden at Eighth Avenue and 50th Street was boxing's mecca, crowds of 18,000 and more roared for a young man from Augusta, Ga., who wasn't especially powerful or superbly skillful," wrote Goldstein. "What enthralled the fight fans was his sheer energy, the flurries of punches he threw from the opening bell to the final round."[10]

Beau rose from poverty to a boxing champion and hero in a white man's world. Following his improbable career, he went back to shining shoes on his knees once again. Jack's journey took him from rags to riches and ultimately back to rags. Through it all, he remained humble and proud. He did not want pity. "Don't be having no pity for me. I've been to the top of the mountain. I was champion of the world. I've worked hard all my life, and I'm happy doing what I'm doing. It's an honest job and a good living—and I met a lot of nice people."[11] Beau "considered it a privilege to be allowed to entertain people by suffering in public. It touched him, and the money didn't matter."[12] Pleasing the people was Beau Jack's greatest joy.

Appendix: Boxing Record

Beau Jack's weight given on left; opponent's on right. Wt.
= Weight; Rds. = Rounds scheduled; W = Win; L = Loss;
D = Draw; KO = Knockout; TKO = Technical knockout;
pts = Win/loss on points; UD = unanimous decision; SD
= split decision

Date	Venue	Wt.	Opponent	Wt.	Rd.	Outcome
Apr. 7, 1939	Richmond Arena, Augusta, GA		Unknown			W (TKO)
Apr. 12, 1939	Reynolds Street Arena, Augusta, GA		Battling Henry		6	W (TKO rd. 5)
Jan. 18, 1940	Municipal Auditorium, Aiken, SC		Unknown			W
Feb. 1, 1940	Municipal Auditorium, Aiken, SC		Jake Moseley (Bosley)		4	W (pts)
Feb. 8, 1940	Municipal Auditorium, Aiken, SC		Battling Burns		4	W (pts)
Feb. 15, 1940	Municipal Auditorium, Aiken, SC		Alvin Stevens		6	W (KO rd. 3)
Feb. 29, 1940	Municipal Auditorium, Aiken, SC		Vincent Corbett			W
Mar. 7, 1940	Municipal Auditorium, Aiken, SC		Son Jenkins			W
Mar. 21, 1940	Municipal Auditorium, Aiken, SC		Silent Stafford		6	W (pts)
Mar. 27, 1940	Municipal Auditorium, Aiken, SC		Joe James		6	W (KO rd. 2)
Apr. 4, 1940	Municipal Auditorium, Aiken, SC		Tommy Lee		4	W
May 20, 1940	Valley Arena, Holyoke, MA	131	Frankie Allen	127¾	4	D
May 27, 1940	Valley Arena, Holyoke, MA	132¾	Billy Bannick	134½	4	W (TKO rd. 3)
Jun. 17, 1940	Valley Arena, Holyoke, MA	134	Jackie Parker	137½	4	L (pts)

Date	Venue	Wt.	Opponent	Wt.	Rd.	Outcome
Aug. 2, 1940	White City Stadium, West Haven, CT	132½	Joe Polowitzer	134½	6	L (pts)
Aug. 12, 1940	White City Stadium, West Haven, CT	132	Joe Polowitzer	135	6	W (pts)
Aug 19, 1940	Valley Arena, Holyoke, MA	134	Jackie Parker	137½	4	L (UD)
Aug. 26, 1940	Valley Arena, Holyoke, MA	132	Carlo Daponde	134¾	4	W (UD)
Sep. 2, 1940	Valley Arena, Holyoke, MA	132	Jackie Small	132	4	W (TKO rd. 2)
Sep. 16, 1940	Valley Arena, Holyoke, MA	132	Oliver Barbour	131	6	W (TKO rd. 3)
Sep. 30, 1940	Valley Arena, Holyoke, MA	126	Tony DuPre	129	6	W (TKO rd. 2)
Oct. 14, 1940	Valley Arena, Holyoke, MA	129¾	Abe Cohen	130	6	W (KO rd. 3)
Oct. 21, 1940	Valley Arena, Holyoke, MA	128	Ritchie Jones	132	6	W (KO rd. 3)
Nov. 4, 1940	Valley Arena, Holyoke, MA	128	Joey Stack	125	6	W (UD)
Dec. 2, 1940	Valley Arena, Holyoke, MA	128½	Jimmy Fox	127	6	W (UD)
Dec. 16, 1940	Valley Arena, Holyoke, MA	129½	Young Johnny Buff	128½	6	W (KO rd. 1)
Dec. 30, 1940	Valley Arena, Holyoke, MA	130½	Mel Neary	129	6	W (TKO rd. 5)
Jan. 27, 1941	Valley Arena, Holyoke, MA	130½	Joey Silva	131	6	L (SD)
Feb. 10, 1941	Valley Arena, Holyoke, MA	130½	Mexican Joe Rivers	132½	6	W (TKO rd. 4)
Feb. 24, 1941	Valley Arena, Holyoke, MA	130½	Lenny Isrow	131	6	W (TKO rd. 3)
Mar. 10, 1941	Valley Arena, Holyoke, MA	133½	Nicky Jerome	135	6	W (TKO rd. 3)
Mar. 24, 1941	Valley Arena, Holyoke, MA	135	Joey Silva	133½	6	W (UD)
Apr. 7, 1941	Valley Arena, Holyoke, MA	135	Tony Iacovaci	132	6	W (KO rd. 6)
Apr. 22, 1941	Foot Guard Hall, Harford, CT	136	Bob Reilly	136	8	W (TKO rd. 7)
Apr. 28, 1941	Valley Arena, Holyoke, MA	134½	Harry Gentile	135	6	W (TKO rd. 1)
May 5, 1941	Valley Arena, Holyoke, MA	136	Chester Rico	136	8	D
May 19, 1941	Valley Arena, Holyoke, MA	135	George Salamone	134½	8	W (KO rd. 8)

Date	Venue	Wt.	Opponent	Wt.	Rd.	Outcome
Jun. 2, 1941	Valley Arena, Holyoke, MA	136½	Tommy Speigal	136½	8	W (UD)
Jun. 16, 1941	Valley Arena, Holyoke, MA	135	George Zengaras	135	8	W (UD)
Aug. 5, 1941	Ebbet's Field, Brooklyn, New York	134½	Minnie DeMore	131¾	6	W (TKO rd. 3)
Aug. 14, 1941	Ebbet's Field, Brooklyn, New York	135½	Al Roth	141	8	W (TKO rd. 5)
Aug. 26, 1941	Madison Square Garden, New York, NY	136	Guillermo Puentes	131	6	W (pts)
Sep. 19, 1941	Madison Square Garden, New York, NY	134¼	Al Reid	130¼	8	W (KO rd. 8)
Oct. 14, 1941	Broadway Arena, Brooklyn, NY	135½	Tommy Speigal	131	8	W (pts)
Oct. 31, 1941	Madison Square Garden, New York, NY	135	Guillermo Puentes	130¼	8	W (pts)
Dec. 1, 1941	Ridgewood Grove Arena, Brooklyn, NY	136½	Sammy Rivers	135	8	W (TKO rd. 3)
Dec. 8, 1941	St. Nicholas Arena, New York, NY	136¼	Freddie Archer	137½	8	L (UD)
Dec. 29, 1941	St. Nicholas Arena, New York, NY	136½	Freddie Archer	139	8	L (pts)
Jan. 5, 1942	Valley Arena, Holyoke, MA	134¾	Carmelo Fenoy	137	10	W (UD)
May 22, 1942	Madison Square Garden, New York, NY	137½	Bobby Ivy	133¾	8	W (pts)
Jun. 23, 1942	MacArthur Stadium, Brooklyn, NY	138	Guillermo Puentes	134	8	W (KO rd. 1)
Jul. 3, 1942	Fort Hamilton Arena, Brooklyn, NY	138	Bobby McIntire	140	8	W (TKO rd. 6)
Jul. 7, 1942	Queensboro Arena, Queens, NY	137	Cosby Linson	141	8	W (TKO rd. 8)
Aug. 1, 1942	Twin City Arena, Elizabeth, NJ	138	Ruby Garcia	140	8	W (TKO rd. 6)
Aug. 18, 1942	MacArthur Stadium, Brooklyn, NY		Carmine Fatta		8	W (KO rd. 1)
Aug. 28, 1942	Madison Square Garden, New York, NY	135½	Billy Murray	140¼	10	W (pts)
Oct. 2, 1942	Madison Square Garden, New York, NY	138	Chester Rico	135¾	8	W (pts)
Oct. 12, 1942	St. Nicholas Arena, New York, NY	136½	Terry Young	137¾	10	W (UD)
Nov. 13, 1942	Madison Square Garden, New York, NY	132¾	Allie Stolz	133¼	10	W (TKO rd. 7)
Dec. 18, 1942	Madison Square Garden, New York, NY	132¾	Tippy Larkin	134¼	15	W (TKO rd. 3)

Date	Venue	Wt.	Opponent	Wt.	Rd.	Outcome
Lightweight Championship						
Feb. 5, 1943	Madison Square Garden, New York, NY	137¼	Fritzie Zivic	145¼	10	W (UD)
Mar. 5, 1943	Madison Square Garden, New York, NY	135½	Fritzie Zivic	146	12	W (UD)
Apr. 2, 1943	Madison Square Garden, New York, NY	135¾	Henry Armstrong	138	10	W (UD)
May 21, 1943	Madison Square Garden, New York, NY	135	Bob Montgomery	135	15	L (UD)
Lightweight Championship						
Jun. 21, 1943	Griffith Stadium, Washington, D.C.	135	Maxie Starr	130½	10	W (TKO rd. 6)
Jul. 19, 1943	Shibe Park, Philadelphia, PA	135¼	Johnny Hutchinson	134¼	10	W [TKO rd. 6)
Oct. 4, 1943	Madison Square Garden, New York, NY	140½	Bobby Ruffin	135½	10	L (UD)
Nov. 19, 1943	Madison Square Garden, New York, NY	132¾	Bob Montgomery	133¾	15	W (UD)
Lightweight Championship						
Jan. 7, 1944	Madison Square Garden, New York, NY	139	Lulu Costantino	136	10	W (SD)
Jan. 28, 1944	Madison Square Garden, New York, NY	138	Sammy Angott	140	10	D (pts)
Feb. 15, 1944	Public Hall, Cleveland, OH	138	Maxie Berger	143¾	10	W (UD)
Mar. 3, 1944	Madison Square Garden, New York, NY	134	Bob Montgomery	135	15	L (SD)
Lightweight Championship						
Mar. 17, 1944	Madison Square Garden, New York, NY	138	Al Bummy Davis	142½	10	W (UD)
Mar. 31, 1944	Madison Square Garden, New York, NY	136	Juan Zurita	133¼	10	W (UD)
Aug. 4, 1944	Madison Square Garden, New York, NY	138¾	Bob Montgomery	137	10	W (MD)
Dec. 14, 1945	Madison Square Garden, New York, NY	144	Willie Joyce	137½	10	W (UD)
Jan. 4, 1946	Madison Square Garden, New York, NY	143½	Morris Reif	146½	10	W (KO rd. 4)
Feb. 8, 1946	Madison Square Garden, New York, NY	142	Johnny Greco	145¼	10	D (pts)
May 31, 1946	Madison Square Garden, New York, NY	141½	Johnny Greco	146	10	W (UD)

Date	Venue	Wt.	Opponent	Wt.	Rd.	Outcome
Jul. 8, 1946	Griffith Stadium, Washington, D.C.	145	Sammy Angott	145	10	W (TKO rd. 7)
Aug 19, 1946	Griffith Stadium, Washington, D.C.	143¾	Danny Kapilow	145	10	W (UD)
Oct. 22, 1946	Armory, Elizabeth, NJ	142¾	Buster Tyler	142	10	L (pts)
Feb 21, 1947	Madison Square Garden, New York, NY	141	Tony Janiro	147¾	10	L (TKO rd. 4)
Nov. 3, 1947	Kiel Auditorium, Saint Louis, MO	141½	Humberto Zavala	139	10	W (KO rd. 4)
Dec 16, 1947	Auditorium, Hartford, CT	140	Frankie Vigeant	145½	10	W (pts)
Dec. 29, 1947	Rhode Island Auditorium, Providence, RI	140¾	Billy Kearns	144¼	10	W (pts)
Jan. 5, 1948	Arena, New Haven, CT	140	Jimmy Collins	143½	10	W (KO rd. 2)
Jan. 23, 1948	Chicago Stadium, Chicago, IL	139¼	Johnny Bratton	139	10	W (TKO rd. 8)
Feb. 20, 1948	Madison Square Garden, New York, NY	141¼	Terry Young	137½	10	L (SD)
Apr. 9, 1948	Forum, Montreal, Quebec	139¼	Johnny Greco	146	10	W (MD)
May 24, 1948	Griffith Stadium, Washington, D.C.	140½	Tony Janiro	147	10	W (UD)
Jul. 12, 1948	Shibe Park, Philadelphia, PA	134	Ike Williams	134	15	L (TKO rd. 6)

Lightweight Championship

Date	Venue	Wt.	Opponent	Wt.	Rd.	Outcome
Oct. 28, 1948	Uline Arena, Washington, D.C.	143½	Eric Boon	144	10	W (TKO rd. 3)
Nov. 23, 1948	Convention Hall, Philadelphia, PA	144	Chuck Taylor	145	10	W (TKO rd. 3)
Dec. 17, 1948	Olympia Stadium, Detroit, MI	139	Leroy Willis	136	10	W (UD)
Jan. 17, 1949	Boston Garden, Boston, MA	139½	Jackie Weber	136	10	W (UD)
Mar. 28, 1949	Forum, Montreal, Quebec	138	Johnny Greco	147	10	L (UD)
Jul. 13, 1949	Griffith Stadium, Washington, D.C.	139	Eddie Giosa	139	10	W (UD)
Aug. 31, 1949	Auditorium, Oakland, CA	138	Johnny Gonsalves	141½	10	W (SD)
Sep. 6, 1949	Olympic Auditorium, Los Angeles, CA	139	Tote Martinez	140¾	10	W (UD)
Sep. 30, 1949	Chicago Stadium, Chicago, IL	141	Livio Minelli	147	10	W (SD)
Oct. 14, 1949	Chicago Stadium, Chicago, IL	140	Kid Gavilan	148	10	L (UD)

Date	Venue	Wt.	Opponent	Wt.	Rd.	Outcome
Dec. 16, 1949	Madison Square Garden, New York, NY	142	Tuzo Portuguez	146½	10	L (SD)
Apr. 3, 1950	Auditorium, Hartford, CT	142	Joey Carkido	144½	10	L (pts)
Apr. 14, 1950	Uline Arena, Washington, D.C.	139½	Lew Jenkins	139	10	W (TKO rd. 4)
May 8, 1950	Rhode Island Auditorium, Providence, RI	142	Jackie Weber	135¾	10	W (TKO rd. 7)
May 22, 1950	Boston Garden, Boston, MA	141¼	Johnny Potenti	148¾	10	W (UD)
Jun. 28, 1950	Fairgrounds, Indianapolis, IN	141	Ronnie Harper	135½	10	W (TKO rd. 5)
Jul. 17, 1950	City Auditorium, Atlanta, GA	142	Bobby Timpson	138	10	W (TKO rd. 6)
Oct. 3, 1950	Honolulu Stadium, Honolulu, HI	141	Philip Kim	142½	10	W (pts)
Nov. 14, 1950	Honolulu Stadium, Honolulu, HI	144½	Frankie Fernandez	146¾	10	L (UD)
Jan. 1, 1951	Auditorium, Milwaukee, WI	141	Fitzie Pruden	144	10	L (SD)
Jan. 18, 1951	Auditorium, Minneapolis, MN	138	Del Flanagan	139¼	10	L (UD)
Jan. 31, 1951	Auditorium, Oakland, CA	140	Emil Barao	137	10	W (UD)
Mar. 5, 1951	Rhode Island Auditorium, Providence, RI	146	Ike Williams	142	10	L (SD)
Mar. 30, 1951	Coliseum Arena, New Orleans, LA	137	Leroy Willis	135	10	W (UD)
Apr. 16, 1951	Arena, Philadelphia, PA	142	Gil Turner	142½	10	L (UD)
May 21, 1951	Arena, Philadelphia, PA	145	Gil Turner	143	10	L (TKO rd. 8)
Jan. 20, 1955	Columbia, SC	147	Eddie Green	159	10	W (UD)
Apr. 9, 1955	Bell Auditorium, Augusta, GA	145	Ike Williams	155	10	D
Jul. 4, 1955	Beach Arena, Daytona Beach, FL		Willie Kid Johnson		10	W (SD)
Aug. 12, 1955	Bell Auditorium, Augusta, GA	146	Ike Williams	154	10	L (TKO rd. 8)

Chapter Notes

Note regarding newspaper citations: In most cases the page number is in accordance with newspapers.com and may not match the printed page number of the actual newspaper.

Introduction

1. Michael Hirsley, "Beau Jack: Heroic, Dignified," *Chicago Tribune*, April 20, 2000, 58.

Chapter 1

1. Mark Karlin, "'The Birth of a Nation' 100 Years Later: Why Woodrow Wilson's Embrace of the KKK Still Matters," Buzzflash, last modified July 23, 2015, accessed August 13, 2018, http://buzzflash.com/commentary/white-supremacists-have-always-baptized-their-perverted-cause-in-christianity.
2. Lillian Smith, *Killers of the Dream* (New York: W.W. Norton & Co., 1978).
3. Jack London, "Jack London Describes the Fight and Jack Johnson's Golden Smile," *San Francisco Call*, December 27, 1908, 33.
4. *Ibid.*
5. "Comment on Big Battle," *Buffalo Commercial*, December 28, 1908, 6.
6. "Greatest Tragedy of Ring History Was Enacted in Roped Arena in Reno Today," *Reno Gazette-Journal*, July 5, 1910, 2.
7. Frank Hall, "Sullivan's Manager Could See Nothing but Johnson from Sound of Gong," *Reno Gazette-Journal*, July 4, 1910, 3.

Chapter 2

1. "Georgia White Planter Holding Men in Peonage—Killed Eleven; Deaths of 11 Negroes Charged to Employer," *New York Age*, April 2, 1921, 1.
2. In other accounts, his grandmother is referred to as Evie Mixom.

3. Bill Plaschke, "After the Punch Is Gone," *Fort Lauderdale News*, June 28, 1982, 59.
4. "Watchman Shoots Negro Boy Here," *Augusta Chronicle*, February 16, 1931, 1.
5. Harry Gage, "The Sports Gage," *Augusta Chronicle*, April 5, 1946, 14.
6. *Ibid.*
7. Oscar Fraley, "Back to the 'Shine' Box for Ex-Champ," *Muncie Evening Press*, July 10, 1957, 19.

Chapter 3

1. James Brown, *James Brown: The Godfather of Soul.* (New York: Thunder's Mouth Press, 1997)
2. Ralph Ellison, *The Invisible Man* (New York: Vintage International, 1952), 25–26.
3. Bob Bloodworth, "A Beau for Clay, Frazier," *Palm-Beach Post*, February 6, 1970, 34.
4. Bill Plaschke, "After the Punch Is Gone," *Fort Lauderdale News*, June 28, 1982, 59.
5. Tom Archdeacon, "Battle Royal: A 'Fit of Blind Terror.'" *Miami News*, May 10, 1988, 15, 19.
6. *Ibid.*
7. Larry Guest, "Roberts Missing the Boat," *Orlando Sentinel*, June 30, 1976, 47.
8. Clifford Roberts, *The Story of the Augusta National Golf Club* (New York: Doubleday and Company, Inc., 1976), 68.

Chapter 4

1. "Lenox Theatre Finest Theatre Owned and Controlled by Colored People in the

United States," *Augusta Chronicle*, January 9, 1921, 6.

Chapter 5

1. Tom Wall, "Demaret Clinches Masters; 10,000 Follow Final Round," *Augusta Chronicle*, April 8, 1940, 1, 4–5.
2. "Beau Jack Credits Bobby Jones," *Augusta Chronicle*, January 28, 1979, 3B.
3. Patrick Kelly, "Monday's Mood," *News-Press*, July 8, 1968, 18.

Chapter 6

1. "Beau Jack Matched with Jackie Small," *Hartford Courant*, August 30, 1940, 14.

Chapter 7

1. Regis M. Welsh, "Zivic Rips Armstrong to Shreds in Winning Title," *Pittsburg Press*, October 5, 1940, 9.
2. Harold Parrott, "Both Sides," *Brooklyn Daily Eagle*, March 31, 1943, 17.
3. "Twin Headliners Mark Fight Card at Foot Guard Armory Tonight," *Hartford Courant*, April 22, 1941, 7.
4. W.J. Lee, "With Malice Toward None," *Hartford Courant*, April 26, 1941, 11.
5. "Twin Headliners Mark Fight Card at Foot Guard Armory Tonight," *Hartford Courant*, April 22, 1941, 17.
6. Jack Cuddy, "Beau Jack Latest Sensation Along Cauliflower Row," *Danville Morning News*, August 20, 1941, 7.
7. Bob Considine, "Old Hauts Are to See Beau Jack," *Cincinnati Enquirer*, November 4, 1941, 14.
8. "2 Georgians Indicted on Slave Charge," *Des Moines Register*, May 30, 1941, 1.
9. "Jack to Fight Spiegel Monday at Valley Arena," *Hartford Courant*, June 1, 1941, 45.
10. "Beau Jack Wins in Fistic Upset," *Arizona Republic*, June 3, 1941, 53.
11. "FDR Orders Negro Jobs in Defense," *Democrat and Chronicle*, June 16, 1941, 1.
12. *Ibid.*

Part III

1. Gary Smith, "Still Fighting Old Wars Former Lightweight Champ Beau Jack Lives Out His Legend," *Sports Illustrated*, February 15, 1988, http://www.si.com/vault/1988/02/15/117125/still-fighting-old-wars-former-lightweight-champ-beau-jack-lives-out-his-legend, accessed December 11, 2017.

Chapter 8

1. Edward J. Shugrue, "Between Ourselves," *Bridgeport Post*, April 8, 1962, 60.
2. "From Rags to Riches for Beau Jack," *Evening Standard*, December 23, 1942, 10.
3. Edward J. Shugrue, "Between Ourselves," *Bridgeport Post*, April 8, 1962, 60.
4. Dillon Graham started his journalism career at the *Gainesville Daily Sun* in Florida. He quickly worked his way up to the national feature sports editor of the Associated Press. He was well known for his colorful coverage of football and golf.
5. Dillon Graham, "Beau Jack Latest of Negro Fighters to Reach Big Time," *Green Bay Press-Gazette*, September 30, 1942, 14.
6. Whitney Martin, "Sports Trail," *Wilkes-Barre Record*, January 3, 1943, 15.
7. John Kieran, "Sports of the Times: Bubbling Over Beau Jack," *New York Times*, November 13, 1942, 30.
8. "Waikiki Crossroad," *Honolulu Star-Bulletin*, November 20, 1950, 4.
9. Edward J. Shugrue, "Between Ourselves," *Bridgeport Post*, April 8, 1963, 60.
10. Bob Considine, "On the Line," *Tampa Bay Times*, March 29, 1943, 9.
11. Conrad was one of the founders of the Boxing Writers Association. After his journalism career, he became a fight promoter.
12. Harold Conrad, "Ebbets Boxing Show Stars Crack Welters," *Brooklyn Daily Eagle*, August 5, 1941, 15.
13. Harold Parrott, "Both Sides," *Brooklyn Daily Eagle*, September 1, 1942, 11.
14. A. O. Edmonds, *Joe Louis, Boxing, and American Culture* (Grand Rapids, MI: Wm. B. Eerdmans Publishing Co. 1973), 137.
15. Marcus Norman, "Beau Jack: The Garden's Favorite," Boxing.com, July 9, 2012, Accessed December 3, 2017. http://www.boxing.com/beau_jack_the_gardens_favorite.html.
16. Robert Seltzer, "Fear in the Ring: A Second Opponent for Fighters," *Philadelphia Inquirer*, June 27, 1988, 19.
17. Leslie Matthews, "Leslies' Boxing Bits," *New York Age*, May 6, 1950, 19.
18. Jeffrey Sussman, "Lous Stillman's

Filthy Gym," *East Hampton Star*, October 6, 2016, accessed November 20, 2017, http://easthamptonstar.com/Opinion/20161006/Lou-Stillmans-Filthy-Gym-Jeffrey-Sussman.

19. Joe Rein, "Stillman's Gym: the Center of the Boxing Universe," Mr. Beller's Neighborhood, June 1, 2003, accessed November 3, 2017, https://mrbellersneighborhood.com/2003/06/stillmans-gym-the-center-of-the-boxing-universe.

20. Irving Rudd, "I Remember: Stillman's, Oiv, Benny," *New York Times*, April 7, 1974, 220.

21. Jack Troy, "All in the Game," *Atlanta Constitution*, July 25, 1941, 20.

22. Harold Parrott, "Both Sides," *Brooklyn Daily Eagle*, December 17, 1942, 17.

23. *Ibid.*

24. Murray Rose, "Lou Stillman Says Fight Racket Dying," *Daily Press*, June 7, 1953, 30.

Chapter 9

1. Raymond Johnson, "One Man's Opinion," *Tennessean*, August 20, 1941, 10.

2. *Ibid.*

3. Harold Conrad, "Roth Stopped by Beau Jack," *Brooklyn Daily Eagle*, August 15, 1941, 13.

4. *Ibid.*

5. Al Abrams, "Sidelights on Sports," *Pittsburgh Post-Gazette*, August 19, 1941, 13.

6. Jack Cuddy, "Beau Jack Latest Sensation Along Cauliflower Row," *Danville Morning News*, August 20, 1941, 7.

7. Harold C. Burr, "Broadway Arena Boro Institution," *Brooklyn Daily Eagle*, February 13, 1947, 16.

8. "Beau Jack Now Ready for Big Time," *Brooklyn Daily Eagle*, October 15, 1941, 19.

9. The Axis powers were comprised of Germany, Italy, Japan, Hungary, Romania, Slovakia, and Bulgaria.

10. Bob Considine, "Old Haunts Are to See Beau Jack," *Philadelphia Enquirer*, November 4, 1941, 14.

11. Billy Goodrich, "Rivers Doesn't Even Make Beau Breathe Hard," *Brooklyn Daily Eagle*, December 2, 1941, 16.

12. "Went Back to Sleep at Pearl Harbor, Says Wounded Vet," *Brooklyn Daily Eagle*, November 7, 1943, 13.

13. *Ibid.*

14. Hal Bock, "Continuing Games at a Time of Conflict," *Post-Star*, December 7, 2001, 24.

Chapter 10

1. Ralph Trost, "They Tell Me," *Brooklyn Daily Eagle*, April 25, 1942, 9.

2. Lawton Carver, "Fair or Foul," *Courier-Gazette*, February 24, 1948, 6.

3. Harry Markson joined the Twentieth Century Sporting Club in 1937 as publicity director. He soon became the general manager for boxing at Madison Square Garden. Subsequently, he served as a general manager for the International Boxing Club's New York Branch, from 1949 until it was dissolved ten years later.

4. Harold Parrott, "Both Sides," *Brooklyn Daily Eagle*, November 11, 1942, 17.

5. *Ibid.*, 11.

6. *Ibid.*

7. Dillon Graham, "On the Spot with Sports," *News Leader*, October 1, 1942, 10.

8. Harold Parrott, "Both Sides," *Brooklyn Daily Eagle*, September 1, 1942, 11.

9. Subsequently, Arcel trained Ezzard Charles (1949 heavyweight champion).

Chapter 11

1. Harold Parrott, "Both Sides," *Brooklyn Daily Eagle*, November 18, 1942, 17.

2. Grantland Rice, "The Sportlight," *Atlanta Constitution*, November 2, 1942, 15.

3. Grantland Rice, "Four Horsemen of Notre Dame Ride to Victory Over Army Team," *Courier-Journal*, October 19, 1924, 60.

4. Grantland Rice, "The Sportlight," *Asbury Park Press*, November 2, 1942, 11.

5. *Ibid.*

6. *Ibid.*

7. "Sammy Angott, 135-Pound Ring King, Quits Game," *Morning News*, November 14, 1942, 18.

8. "Sammy Angott to Quit Ring for War Job," *Altoona Tribune*, November 14, 1942, 6.

9. "Beau's Wallop Worries Odds Sharpshooter," *Brooklyn Daily Eagle*, November 12, 1942, 14.

10. Grantland Rice, "The Sportlight: Lightweight Beau Jack Windmill Type Fighter," *Valley Morning Star*, December 22, 1942, 19.

11. James P. Dawson, "Beau Jack Stops Stolz in Seventh When Referee Intervenes in Garden Bout," *New York Times*, November 14, 1942, 19.

12. Jack Cuddy, "Sports Parade," *News Journal*, November 14, 1942, 17.

13. Grantland Rice, "The Sportlight: Rise of Beau Jack Grabbing War's Waning Ring Spotlight," *Akron Beacon Journal*, November 23, 1942, 18.

14. *Ibid.*

15. Jack Cuddy, "Sports Parade," *News Journal*, November 14, 1942, 17.

16. James P. Dawson, "Beau Jack Stops Stolz in Seventh When Referee Intervenes in Garden Bout," *New York Times*, November 14, 1942, 19.

Chapter 12

1. Jack Mahon, "Stolz Stopped by Beau Jack in 7th Round," *News Journal*, November 14, 1942, 17.

2. *Ibid.*

3. "Peralta in Line for Garden Bout," *Brooklyn Daily Eagle*, December 15, 1942, 14.

4. Peter R. Hofstra, Op. Ed., "Divine Intervention," *Arizona Republic*, January 2, 1994, 28.

5. Bob Considine, "Beau Jack Flattens Larkin in third, Gains New York Version of Ring Toga," *Democrat and Chronicle*, December 19, 1942, 19.

6. Dick McCann, "Jack New 135 lb. King; KO's Larkin in 3d," *Daily News*, December 19, 1942, 320.

7. Jack Cuddy, "Beau Jack's Win Impressive," *Berkshire Eagle*, December 19, 1942, 7.

8. Bob Considine, "Beau Jack Flattens Larkin in third, Gains New York Version of Ring Toga," *Democrat and Chronicle*, December 19, 1942, 19.

9. *Ibid.*

10. "A New Champion," *Augusta Chronicle*, December 21, 1942, 4. Alvin McAuliffe was the Chairman of the Georgia Railroad Bank where the Syndicate was placing Beau's earnings in trust.

11. Jack Cuddy, "Beau Jack's Win Impressive," *Berkshire Eagle*, December 19, 1942, 7.

12. Harold Parrott, "Beau Jack's Title Celebration," *Brooklyn Daily Eagle*, December 19, 1942, 5.

13. *Ibid.*

14. Jack Cuddy, "Beau Jack, Human Blitz, Kayoes Larkin in 3rd to Win Title," *Star-Gazette*, December 19, 1942, 10.

15. Lawton Carver, "Husky Beau Jack Still Uses Battle Royal Style," *Lansing State Journal*, January 10, 1944, 9.

16. *Ibid.*

17. *Ibid.*

18. Stanley Woodward, "Masters Recalls a Little Champ," *Miami News*, April 5, 1954, 11.

19. "A New Champion," *Augusta Chronicle*, December 21, 1942, 4.

20. Whitney Martin, "The Sports Trail," *Times Record*, February 9, 1943, 26.

21. Jack Cuddy, "Beau Jack Symbolizes Era of Fast-Breaking Warfare," *Sheboygan Press*, December 28, 1942, 10.

Chapter 13

1. "Beau Jack Favored Over Fritzie Zivic in Garden Rematch," *New York Age*, February 6, 1943, 11.

2. Sid Feder, "Zivic Confident of Trimming Beau Jack," *Times Herald*, February 1, 1943, 16.

3. Joe Williams, "Joe Williams Says: Mr. Otto Did Not Do Good Ring Job," *Pittsburgh Press*, February 6, 1943, 10.

4. "Zivic Likely to Suffer as Beau Sizzles," *Brooklyn Daily Eagle*, March 4, 1943, 13.

5. Harold Parrott, "Both Sides," *Brooklyn Daily Eagle*, March 4, 1943, 13.

6. Joe Falls, "Beau Jack Shines Shoes … and Dreams," *Detroit Free Press*, December 5, 1965, 44.

7. *Ibid.*

8. John P. McFarlane, "The Sports Front," *Pittsburgh Post-Gazette*, February 8, 1943, 18.

9. Jack Cuddy, "Beau Jack Prepares for Rematch with Former Champ," *Ogden Standard-Examiner*, March 2, 1943, 6.

10. See https://www.salk.edu/; https://www.cdc.gov/polio/us/for more information.

11. "Armstong, Beau Jack Booked for Jan. 29 Bout," *Democrat and Columbia*, January 5, 1943, 14.

12. *Ibid.*

13. "The Sports Patrol," *Press Democrat*, January 6, 1943, 14.

14. Beau Jack, "Fighting Provides Jack His Thrills," *Pittsburgh Courier*, May 29, 1943, 19

15. Harold Parrott, "Both Sides," *Brooklyn Daily Eagle*, March 31, 1943, 17.

16. "The Gaudy Touch," *Time*, Vol. 41, Issue 15, 76.

17. Jack Cuddy, "Cuddy Says…," *Dunkirk Evening Observer*, April 3, 1943, 10.

18. "Armstrong's Ring Comeback Due to Need for Ready Cash," *St. Louis Post-Dispatch*, April 12, 1943, 14.

19. *Ibid.*

20. "Angott Champ, Manager Says," News Journal, May 7, 1943, 23.

21. Sandy Stiles, "'Orphaned' Beau Jack Here to Visit Mother," *Tampa Bay Times*, April 12, 1943, 9.

22. *Ibid.*

23. *Ibid.*

24. *Ibid.*

25. "Champion 'Beau Jack' Visits and Talks with Students," *Tampa Bay Times*, April 18, 1943, 27.

26. "Jordan Elementary Stresses War Loan," *Tampa Bay Times*, April 18, 1943, 27.

Chapter 14

1. Jack Cuddy, "Beau Jack Begins Training," *Republican and Herald*, May 4, 1943, 8.

2. Ted Meier, "Up-Again-Down-Again Bob Montgomery Figures Body Attack Will Lead to Victory in Championship Battle," *Indianapolis Star*, May 9, 1943, 41.

3. Jack Cuddy, "Montgomery Mauls Jack for Decision, Title," *Democrat and Chronicle*, May 22, 1943, 15.

4. *Ibid.*

5. Haskel Cole, "'Jack Easy to Hit'—Bob Says," *Pittsburgh Courier*, May 29, 1943, 18.

6. "Beau's Boss Is Hot Under Collar," *Cincinnati Enquirer*, May 27, 1943, 17.

7. Arthur Daley, "Sports of the Times," *New York Times*, November 19, 1943, 27.

8. Bill Westwick, "The Realm of Sport," *Ottawa Journal*, May 7, 1943, 20.

9. "Boxing," *Brooklyn Daily Eagle*, June 24, 1943, 14.

10. Harold Parrott, "Jack's Something New Added by Trainers," *Brooklyn Daily Eagle*, November 20, 1943, 6.

11. David Condon, "It Was a Much Too Quiet Farewell for Larry Amadee," *Chicago Tribune*, October 14, 1978, 3.

12. Richard Calisch, "Don't Smoke No Cigars; Don't Get in No fights," *Chicago Tribune* Magazine, November 13, 1977, 56–57.

13. *Ibid.*

14. "Beau Jack's 'Farm Fund' Held in Trust," *Dothan Eagle*, July 15, 1943, 10.

15. "Beau Jack Gambles in Bout with Ruffin," *Brooklyn Daily Eagle*, September 26, 1943, 25.

16. Hugh Fullerton, Jr., "Sports Roundup," *Freeport Journal-Standard*, October 5, 1943, 7.

Chapter 15

1. Harold Parrott, "Both Sides," *Brooklyn Daily Eagle*, November 15, 1943, 11. "Beau Jack Trains for Match," *Ithaca Journal*, November 17, 1943, 11.

2. Wendell Smith, "Smitty's Sports Spurts; a Champ's Life Before and After a Title Fight," *Pittsburgh Courier*, November 27, 1943, 14.

3. Beau Jack, "Eye-Poppers: Manager's Appetite Floors Boxer," *Ithaca Journal*, August 17, 1944, 13.

4. Wendell Smith, "Jack's 'Wild Man' Attack Baffles Bob Montgomery," *Pittsburgh Courier*, November 27, 1943, 16.

5. "Jack's Infighting Defeats Montgomery," *Press and Sun-Bulletin*, November 20, 1943, 13.

6. Lawton Carver, "Husky Beau Jack Still Uses Battle Royal Style," *Lansing State Journal*, January 10, 1944, 9.

7. Ted Yates, "I've Been Around," *New York Age*, February 5, 1944, 11.

8. "Beau Jack 3–1 Choice Over Berger," *Star-Gazette*, February 15, 1944, 9.

Chapter 16

1. "Clash Friday Night in Championship Bout at the Garden," *Pittsburgh Courier*, March 4, 1944, 12.

2. Jack Cuddy, "19,066 Fans See Montgomery Win," *Democrat and Chronicle*, March 4, 1944, 13.

3. Grantland Rice, "The Sportlight: Al Bummy Davis Has 10 Pounds and Left Hook on Beau Jack," *Harrisburg Telegraph*, March 15, 1944, 23.

4. Fritz Howell, "Beau Jack Easily Outpoints 'Bummy' Davis," *Wilkes-Barre Times Leader*, March 18, 1944, 11

5. Robert Seltzer, "Fear in the Ring: A Second Opponent for Fighters," *Philadelphia Inquirer*, June 27, 1988, 23.

6. Tom Archdeacon, "The Pugs' Day of Thanks," *Miami News*, November 23, 1984, 18, 25.

7. Grantland Rice, "The Sportlight," *Cumberland News*, March 20, 1944, 7.

8. *Ibid.*

9. *Ibid.*

Chapter 17

1. "Beau Jack Goes Into the Army," *Florence Morning News*, April 19, 1944, 5.

2. *Ibid.*

3. "Wells Declares Race Hate Must Vanish If War Has Meaning," *New York Age*, August 5, 1944, 2.

Chapter 18

1. David Condon, "In the Wake of the News," *Chicago Tribune*, March 22, 1969, 1.

2. Michael Hirsley, "Beau Jack: Heroic, Dignified," *Chicago Tribune*, April 20, 2000, 58.

3. Bob Considine, "On the Line," *Democrat and Chronicle*, July 14, 1944, 20.

4. Tommy Holmes, "Beau and Bob Make Real Match," *Brooklyn Daily Eagle*, August 3, 1944, 17.

5. Harold Conrad, "260 Wounded to See Bond Fight," *Brooklyn Daily Eagle*, August 3, 1944, 17.

6. Bob Considine, "Mangled Veterans Appear to Have No Hate in Hearts," *Cincinnati Enquirer*, August 6, 1944, 26.

7. *Ibid.*

8. Harold Conrad, "Jack and Monty Bout Nets $35,864,900," *Brooklyn Daily Eagle*, August 5, 1944, 6.

9. *Ibid.*

10. https://www.dollartimes.com/inflation/inflation.php?amount=15000&year=1944; accessed October 26, 2018, 12:16 pm.

11. http://www.golf.com/tour-and-news/boxer-beau-jack-got-his-start-augusta-national

12. Harold Conrad, "Jack and Monty Bout Nets $35,864,900," *Brooklyn Daily Eagle*, August 5, 1944, 6.

13. Tom Kenny, "Crack O' Dawn," *Augusta Chronicle*, August 20, 1944, 8.

14. David Condon, "In the Wake of the News," *Chicago Tribune*, March 22, 1969, 1.

15. Elliott Denman, "Beau Jack Fought for His Uncle Sam," *Asbury Park Press*, June 3, 1982, 43.

Chapter 19

1. "Three Champions Crowned, Attendance Hits New Peak During Banner Boxing Year," *Star-Gazette*, December 28, 1944, 18.

2. Jack Cuddy, "Beau Jack Selected as 'Boxer of the Year.'" Rochester *Democrat and Chronicle*, December 28, 1944, 19. the Ring, February 1945 (Vol. XXIII, No. 1), 3.

3. "Honor Beau Jack at Fete in Atlanta," *Pittsburgh Courier*, January 20, 1945, 12.

4. Roy Graham, "Graham's Sportsographs," *Florence Morning News*, January 14, 1945, 6.

5. *Ibid.*

Chapter 20

1. "'Beau Is Back' by Pap," *Argus-Leader*, December 17, 1945, 3.

2. *Ibid.*

3. Oscar Fraley, "Beau Jack Gains Weight and His Boss Loses Some Worrying About It," *Dunkirk Evening Observer*, January 2, 1946, 10.

4. "Bob Montgomery Favors Beau Jack as New Champion," *Wilkes-Barre Times Leader, the Evening News*, July 8, 1948, 23.

5. Tommy Holmes, "Beau Jack Figures but Could Be Hit," *Brooklyn Daily Eagle*, January 3, 1943, 13.

6. Tommy Holmes, "Scatter Shot at the Sports Scene," *Brooklyn Daily Eagle*, January 7, 1946, 13.

7. *Ibid.*

8. Tommy Holmes, "Garden Fight Good—But Not for $20," *Brooklyn Daily Eagle*, February 9, 1946, 6.

9. "Beau Jack to Rest Before Next Battle," *Augusta Chronicle*, February 10, 1946, B3.

10. "Nations Top Golfers Set for Opening in Augusta," *Florence Morning News*, April 4, 1946, 5.

11. *Ibid.*

12. Whitney Martin, "Sports Trail," *Daily Press*, July 2, 1946, 10.

13. "Angott Paid Off for Beau Jack Bout" *Harrisburg Telegraph*, July 10, 1946, 15.

14. Ned Mills, "Bonesetter Fixes Lamotta's Hand and Beau Jack's Leg to Be Miracle Man of Fighters," *News Herald*, August 1, 1946, 14.

15. *Ibid.*

16. "Beau Jack, Tippy Larkin Told to Fight Robinson," *Morning News*, September 27, 1946, 35.

17. "Jack Spurns Bout, Says Robinson Rightful Champ," *Post-Standard*, September 28, 1946, 10.

18. *Ibid.*

19. "Reilly's Oxygen for Tyler Gives Beau Jack the Air," *Brooklyn Daily Eagle*, October 23, 1946, 19.

20. "Newsmen Fume as Beau Jack Goes to Movie," *Chicago Tribune*, November 12, 1946, 26.

21. Frank Mastro, "Beau Jack Jars Spar Mates in 4 Round Drill," *Chicago Tribune*, November 13, 1946, 34.

22. "Beau Jack's Knee Operation Success," *Dunkirk Evening Observer*, November 27, 1946, 11.

Chapter 21

1. Jimmy Cannon, "The Old Garden Was for Fights," *Asbury Park Press*, March 6, 1968, 26.

2. *Ibid.*

3. Matt Schudel, "The Ballad of Beau Jack No Fighter Was Tougher Than the Man Who Went from Shoeshine Boy to Champion and Back Again," *South Florida Sun-Sentinel*, October 9, 1988, 6.

4. "Bouncing Beau About at the End of the Fight Game," *Index-Journal*, February 22, 1947, 2.

5. "Beau Jack Beaten; Ring Career Ends," *Marshfield News-Herald*, February 22, 1943, 8.

6. "Beau Jack Ends Fistic Career," *Daily Mail*, February 22, 1947, 5.

7. "Beau Jack's Career Seen Ended, Knee Gives Way, TKO Loser," *Miami News*, February 22, 1943, 3.

8. Claude Hammerston, "Beau Jack Meets Young," *Ottawa Citizen*, February 20, 1948, 25.

9. *Ibid.*

10. "Golden Goose," *Time*, March 3, 1947, Vol. 49, Issue 9, 53.

11. Oscar Fraley, "Beau Jack in the Sport Parade," *Daily Register*, April 8, 1964, 16.

12. "Beau Jack's Brother Killed by Policeman," *Palm Beach Post*, June 29, 1947, 19.

Chapter 22

1. "Beau Jack Kicks Up His Heels on Arrival Here, Says His Knee's Okay," *St. Louis Star and Times*, October 31, 1947, 28.

2. "Beau Jack's Knee Okay, X-Ray Shows," *St. Louis Post-Dispatch*, November 4, 1947, 14.

3. "Beau Jack Kicks Up His Heels on Arrival Here, Says His Knee's Okay," *St. Louis Star and Times*, October 31, 1947, 28.

4. W. J. McGoogan, "Beau Jack's Punch Is Snappier Than His Leg; Zavala Knocked Out," *St. Louis Post-Dispatch*, November 4, 1947, 28.

5. Lawton Carver, "Fair or Foul," *Courier-Gazette*, February 24, 1948, 6.

6. Eagan was a former boxer himself.

Before being appointed as the Chairman of the NYSAC in 1945, Eagan had won the National Amateur Heavyweight Championship and Olympic Gold in the 1920 Olympics in Antwerp, Belgium. He served as Chairman of the NYSAC for six years.

7. Tommy Holmes, "Scatter Shot at the Sport Scene," *Brooklyn Daily Eagle*, February 23, 1948, 11.

Chapter 23

1. "Beau Jack Adds New Fight Weapon," *Indiana Gazette*, July 7, 1948, 13.

2. "Bob Montgomery Favors Beau Jack as New Champion," *Wilkes-Barre Times Leader, the Evening News*, July 8, 1948, 23.

3. *Ibid.*

4. Jack Saunders, "The Sports Broadcast," *Pittsburgh Courier*, July 10, 1948, 10.

5. *Ibid.*

6. Jimmy Cannon, "Beau Jack's Shining Shoes Again," *Orlando Sentinel*, April 10, 1959, 3.

7. *Ibid.*

8. Mort Berry, "Williams' Story: 'Didn't Want to Hit Him Any More.'" *The Philadelphia Inquirer*, July 13, 1948, 32.

9. *Ibid.*

10. Jimmy Cannon, "Beau Was Real Man," *News-Herald*, March 7, 1964, 9.

11. Oscar Frailey, "Today's Sport Parade," *Daily Herald*, July 13, 1948, 8.

12. *Ibid.*

13. *Ibid.*

14. Mort Berry "Williams' Story: 'Didn't Want to Hit Him Any More,'" *Philadelphia Inquirer*, July 13, 1948, 32.

15. After Ike Williams took the New York-Pennsylvania title from Bob Montgomery on August 4, 1947, he also gave to charity, establishing two college scholarships for graduates of Trenton High School.

Chapter 24

1. "Beau Jack Scores 3rd Round TKO in Bout with Briton," *Arizona Daily Star*, October 29, 1948, 30.

2. Alan Ward, "On Second Thought," *Oakland Tribune*, August 28, 1949, 26.

3. *Ibid.*

4. "Jack Drills for Go Here," *Oakland Tribune*, August 27, 1949, 12.

5. Alan Ward, "On Second Thought," *Oakland Tribune*, August 29, 1949, 20.

6. "World Champion Becomes Promoter of Title Bout," *Press and Sun-Bulletin*, March 1, 1949, 1.

7. "Kid Gavilan Not to Delay Battle with Beau Jack," *Wilkes-Barre Record*, September 12, 1949, 22.

8. "Detectives Guard Chicago Fighter," *New Castle News*, September 20, 1949, 19.

9. Wendell Smith, "Sports Beat: Beau Jack's Fighting for Another Pile," *Pittsburgh Courier*, October 22, 1949, 22.

10. *Ibid.*

Chapter 25

1. "Many Sections of Country Are Feeling Water Shortage Pinch, *Green Bay Press-Gazette*, December 5, 1949, 2.

2. Joe Lee, "Jack Nears End of Boxing Trial," *Brooklyn Daily Eagle*, December 17, 1949, 6.

3. *Ibid.*

4. "Jenkins-Beau Jack Meeting Tops Week's Boxing Card," *Morning News*, April 10, 1950, 15.

5. Tom Archdeacon, "Beau Jack: At Age 61, the Spirit Is Still Strong," *Miami News*, May 24, 1982, 25, 28.

6. "Award Jack TKO Decision After Foul," *Star-Gazette*, April 15, 1950, 7.

7. "Beau Jack to Retire at Year's End, He Says," *Democrat and Chronicle*, July 14, 1950, 31.

8. "Beau Jack Arrives, First Concern Is Over Fishing," *Honolulu Star-Bulletin*, September 26, 1950, 6.

9. Andrew Mitsukado, "Beau Jack Fights Philip Lee," *Honolulu Advertiser*, October 3, 1950, 12.

10. Red McQueen, "Hoomalimali by Red McQueen," *Honolulu Advertiser*, October 1, 1950, 9.

11. Andrew Mitsukado, "Punching Duel Expected," *Honolulu Star-Advertiser*, October 1, 1950, 10.

12. Arthur Suehiro, *Honolulu Stadium: Where Hawaii Played* (China: Watermark Publishing, 1995).

13. Gene Wilhelm, "Beau Jack Decisions Kim," *Honolulu Star-Bulletin*, October 4, 1950, 21.

14. Andrew Mitsukado, "Jack Sees Tough Fight with Fernandez," *Honolulu Advertiser*, November 9, 1950, 29.

15. Andrew Mitsukado, "Frankie Fernandez Decisions Jack," *Honolulu Advertiser*, November 15, 1950, 18.

16. Gene Wilhelm, "Only 4,649 Pay to See Slugging Bee," *Honolulu Star-Bulletin*, November 15, 1950, 20.

17. *Ibid.*

18. "Trouble Brews as Jack-Davis Bout Cancelled," *Honolulu Advertiser*, November 21, 1950, 13.

19. Alan Ward, "On Second Thought," *Oakland Tribune*, November 21, 1950, 39.

20. "Del Vows He'll Knock Out Jack," *Minneapolis Star*, January 15, 1951, 24.

21. "'Del Fought Perfect Fight' Says Viscusi," *Star Tribune*, January 19, 1951, 18.

22. *Ibid.*

23. Dick Cullum, "Cullum's Column," *Star Tribune*, January 20, 1951, 13.

24. *Ibid.*

25. "Lecture Given Jack-Turner; Beau Impresses Gym Crowd," *Philadelphia Inquirer*, April 13, 1951, 48.

26. *Ibid.*

27. John Webster, "Turner Gains Decision Over Jack," *Philadelphia Inquirer*, April 17, 1951, 34.

28. *Ibid.*

29. John Webster, "Sportscope," *Philadelphia Inquirer*, May 13, 1951, 67.

30. "Gil Turner Beats Beau Jack on TKO," *Shamokin News-Dispatch*, May 22, 1951, 10.

Chapter 26

1. Will Grimsley, "Beau Jack Runs Gamut," *Ithaca Journal*, January 17, 1975, 12.

2. J. Suter Kegg, "Tapping on the Sports Keg," *Cumberland Evening Times*, June 1, 1951, 16.

3. Arthur Daley, "Larceny at Its Worst," *New York Times*, May 25, 1951, 39.

4. John Wheeler, "The Old Second Guesser," *Anderson Herald*, January 30, 1952, 3.

5. *Ibid.*

6. *Ibid.*

7. Scott Hochman, "Beau Jack Ponders Long Comeback Road," *Augusta Chronicle*, April 27, 1952, 1C.

8. Bill Ferguson, "Beau Jack Confident about Ring Comeback," *Times*, May 27, 1952, 21.

Chapter 27

1. "Maciano Stops Joe Louis on TKO in Eighth Round," *Kingston Daily Freeman*, October 27, 1951, 7.

2. Pat Robinson,"Beau Jack to Try

Comeback," *Arizona Republic*, January 3, 1955, 20.

3. *Ibid.*

4. "Wergeles Against Beau Jack Boxing," *Asbury Park Press*, December 30, 1954, 16. "Beau Jack Hoping to Stage Comeback," *Florence Morning News*, January 20, 1955, 8.

5. "Beau Jack Will Go on with Bout Against Greene," *Gastonia Gazette*, December 30, 1954, 3.

6. Fran Walosin, "Beau Jack Risking Injuries in Comeback Bid Thursday," *Elmira Advertiser*, January 19, 1955, 9

7. "'That Killer Felling' Has Beau Jack Cocky," *Press and Sun-Bulletin*, January 20, 1955, 24.

8. *Ibid.*

9. "Beau Jack Wants Ike Williams Next," *Press and Sun-Bulletin*, January 21, 1955, 17.

10. "Beau Jack Loses Bid for Another Crack at Boxing," *Index-Journal*, March 5, 1955, 3.

11. Promoter Ben Braunstein initiated the idea of a Commission in 1952. Mayor Hugh Hamilton appointed G.W. Lewis, Art Patchin, Jack Johannsen, Same Smoak and Herbert Herman to the commission.

12. Randy Russell, "All in the Game," *Augusta Chronicle*, March 4, 1955, 6B.

13. Art Grace, "Beau Wants Another Chance," *Miami News*, July 25, 1955, 6.

14. *Ibid.*

15. Johnny Hendrix, "Ike Williams Wins on TKO," *Augusta Chronicle*, August 13, 1955, 6.

16. Jimmy Cannon, "Beau Jack Victim of Sport He Loves," *New York Post*, May 27, 2001, 79.

17. Joe Falls, "Beau Jack Shines Shoes … and Dreams," *Detroit Free Press*, December 5, 1965, 44.

18. Art Grace, "Beau Won't Take Advice," *Miami News*, August 29, 1955, 14.

19. This overall record includes those bouts before his first bout at Valley Arena.

20. Art Grace, "Beau Won't Take Advice," *Miami News*, August 29, 1955, 14.

21. *Ibid.*

22. *Ibid.*

23. John Nogowski, "Still Champs After all this Time," *Times Herald*, June 16, 1991, 20.

24. *Ibid.*

Chapter 28

1. Roy Kerrison, "Beau Jack, a Happy Fallen Idol," *Age*, August 5, 1957, 14.

2. Oscar Fraley, "Today's Sport Parade," *Orlando Sentinel*, July 29, 1957, 4.

3. Dan Burley was the editor of numerous African American publications, such as the *New York Age*, *Amsterdam News*, *Jet*, and *Ebony*. He was also a well-known actor and pianist.

4. Dan Burley, "Dan Burley on Sports," *New York Age*, January 29, 1949, 12.

5. "Beau Jack Is 'Broke.'" *The Winnipeg Tribune*, March 30, 1949, 18.

6. Wendell Smith, "Sports Beat: Beau Jack's Fighting for Another Pile," *Pittsburgh Courier*, October 22, 1949, 22.

7. Arthur Daley, "Larceny at Its Worst," *New York Times*, May 25, 1951, 39.

8. Jack Lait, "Why Elizabeth Will Skip N.Y.; Queen Mary Back of Decision," *Akron-Beacon Journal*, August 28, 1951, 5.

9. Roy Kerrison, "Beau Jack, a Happy Fallen Idol," *Age*, August 5, 1957, 14.

10. Red McQueen, "Hoomalimali by Red McQueen," *Honolulu Advertiser*, October 3, 1950, 12.

11. Stanley Woodward, "Masters Recalls a Little Champ," *Miami News*, April 5, 1954, 11. Dan Parker, "Broadway Bugle," *Courier-Post*, February 27, 1956, 19.

12. Bill Plaschke, "After the Punch Is Gone," *Fort Lauderdale News*, June 28, 1982, 59.

13. "Beau Jack Is 'Broke.'" *The Winnipeg Tribune*, March 30, 1949, 18.

14. Pat Robinson, "Beau Jack to Try Comeback," *Arizona Republic*, January 3, 1955, 20.

15. Les Matthews, "Sports Train," *New York Age*, July 14, 1951, 9.

16. Bill Nunn, Jr., "Change of Pace," *Pittsburgh Courier*, January 29, 1955, 15.

17. Fred Young, "Young's Yarns," *Pantagraph*, June 17, 1951, 11.

18. Red McQueen, "Hoomalimali by Red McQueen," *Honolulu Advertiser*, October 3, 1950, 12.

19. Bill Nunn, Jr., "Change of Pace," *Pittsburgh Courier*, January 29, 1955, 15.

20. Stanley Woodward, "Masters Recalls a Little Champ," *Miami News*, April 5, 1954, 11.

21. Red McQueen, "Hoomalimali by Red McQueen," *Honolulu Advertiser*, October 3, 1950, 12.

22. Jack Cuddy, "Garden Prepares for Pep-Saddler Battle," *Honolulu Star-Advertiser*, February 4, 1951, 15.

23. Dan Parker, "Broadway Bugle," *Courier-Post*, February 27, 1956, 19.

24. J. Suter Kegg, "Tapping the Sports Keg: Is Beau Jack Broke?" *Cumberland Evening Times*, June 18, 1951, 7–8.

25. Dan Burley, "Dan Burley on Sports," *New York Age*, January 29, 1949, 12.

26. Arthur Daley, "Larceny at Its Worst," *New York Times*, May 25, 1951, 39.

27. "Beau Jack Gets Good Results from Bank's Handling of Funds," *Augusta Chronicle*, September 4, 1955, 12B.

28. Art Grace, "Beau Wants Another Chance," *Miami News*, July 25, 1955, 6.

29. Frank Colley, "The Colley See Um Sports," *Morning Herald*, March 6, 1961, 16.

30. Jimmy Cannon, "Beau Jack May Be Shine Boy to Tourists but Not Cannon," *Asheville Citizen-Times*, March 29, 1957, 29.

31. Dave Condon, "In the Wake of the News," *Chicago Tribune*, March 22, 1969, 1.

32. Jack Cuddy, "Garden Prepares for Pep-Saddler Battle," *Honolulu Star-Advertiser*, February 4, 1951, 15.

33. Jimmy Cannon, "Beau Jack's Shining Shoes Again," *Orlando Sentinel*, April 10, 1959, 3.

34. Gary Smith, "Still Fighting Old Wars Former Lightweight Champ Beau Jack Lives Out His Legend," *Sports Illustrated*, February 15, 1988, http://www.si.com/vault/1988/02/15/117125/still-fighting-old-wars-former-lightweight-champ-beau-jack-lives-out-his-legend, accessed December 11, 2017.

35. Gary Smith, "Still Fighting Old Wars Former Lightweight Champ Beau Jack Lives Out His Legend," *Sports Illustrated*, February 15, 1988, http://www.si.com/vault/1988/02/15/117125/still-fighting-old-wars-former-lightweight-champ-beau-jack-lives-out-his-legend, accessed December 11, 2017.

36. *Ibid.*

37. *Ibid.*

Chapter 29

1. The auditorium has since been renamed the "Fillmore Miami Beach at the Jackie Gleason,"

2. Ruth La Ferla, "Flamboyance Gets a Face-Lift," *New York Times*, October 31, 2008, 1.

3. *Ibid.*

4. Ronnie Joyce, "Chief Bootblack…" *The Pensacola News*, August 3, 1967, 13.

5. Jimmy Cannon, "Beau Jack May Be Shine Boy to Tourists but Not Cannon," *Asheville Citizen-Times*, March 29, 1957, 29.

6. Gary Smith, "Still Fighting Old Wars Former Lightweight Champ Beau Jack Lives Out His Legend," *Sports Illustrated*, February 15, 1988, http://www.si.com/vault/1988/02/15/117125/still-fighting-old-wars-former-lightweight-champ-beau-jack-lives-out-his-legend, accessed December 11, 2017.

7. David Condon, "In the Wake of the News," *Chicago Tribune*, March 22, 1969.

8. Fay Searcy, "For Old Warriors, a Worthy Salute," *Philadelphia Inquirer*, November 18, 1998, 62.

9. Johnny Hendrix, "A Friendly Visit," *Augusta Chronicle*, June 24, 1960, 12A.

10. Bill Corum, "Rocky Up, Beau Down at the Fontainebleau," *News Journal*, February 14, 1956, 36.

11. Samuel Ha, "Top 30 Greatest Cus D'Amato Quotes," *Mighty Fighter*, http://www.mightyfighter.com/top-30-greatest-cus-damato-quotes/, accessed November 22, 2018.

12. Jim Murray, "He Succeeded by the Seats of Fans' Pants," *Los Angeles Times*, July 10, 1990, 1.

13. Tony Consiglio & Franz Douskey, *Sinatra and Me: The Very Good Years* (Old Saybrook, CT: Tantor Media, Inc., 2012).

14. Gary Smith, "Still Fighting Old Wars Former Lightweight Champ Beau Jack Lives Out His Legend," *Sports Illustrated*, February 15, 1988, http://www.si.com/vault/1988/02/15/117125/still-fighting-old-wars-former-lightweight-champ-beau-jack-lives-out-his-legend, accessed December 11, 2017.

15. Bill Gallo, "Hard-Working Beau Jack Never Loafer," *New York Daily News*. December 22, 1996, http://www.nydailynews.com/archives/sports/hard-working-beau-jack-loafer-article-1.749907.

16. Dave Anderson, "Jimmy Cannon, Columnist, Dies; Sportswriter Ranged Far Afield," *New York Times*, December 6, 1973, 51.

17. *Ibid.*

18. Richard Goldstein, "Beau Jack, 78, Lightweight Boxing Champion in the 1940's," *New York Times*, February 12, 2000, 28.

19. Bill Plaschke, "After the Punch Is Gone," *Fort Lauderdale News*, June 28, 1982, 27.

20. Tom Archdeacon, "Beau Jack: At Age

61, the Spirit Is Still Strong," *Miami News*, May 24, 1982, 25, 28.

21. "Beau Jack: He's Miami's Favorite Shoeshine Boy," *Star-Gazette*, November 26, 1972, 25.

Chapter 30

1. After retiring from the ring, Beau trained numerous boxers in Augusta and at several gyms in Miami, most often the Fifth Street Gym. a partial list of people Beau Jack trained and/or worked with include: heavyweight Trevor Berbick, heavyweight Gerry Cooney, lightweight Freddie Pendleton, James Brown (The Godfather of Soul), Johnny Sellers, light heavyweight, Leroy Hester, junior middleweight Ricky Fisler, Jon Ruiz, middleweight Raymond Jones, middleweight Leon Stewart, welterweight Jerry Cayard, Bob Tumminia, Mark Sanford, super welterweight Angelo Gray, cruiserweight Richard Brown, super lightweight Aaron Pryor, Keith Kelly, and Mike Vaughan. He also trained female boxers, Bonnie Levin and Diana Sambuceti.

2. Tom Tiede, "Drug Culture Has Been Real Drag on Once Energetic Boxing World," *Lancaster Eagle-Gazette*, February 2, 1990, 16.

3. "One-Time Champion Now Broke," *Palm Beach Post*, April 1, 1980, 27.

4. Tom Archdeacon, "Beau Jack: At Age 61, the Spirit Is Still Strong," *Miami News*, May 24, 1982, 25, 28.

5. Charlie Nobles,"Buoniconti Leads the Keep-Fit Parade of Miami's Ex-Jocks," *Miami News*, July 8, 1981, 15–16.

6. Bob Hill, "Beau Jack: Legend Back Where He Belongs," *Fort Lauderdale News*, July 7, 1985, 38.

7. *Ibid.*

8. Matt Schudel, "The Ballad of Beau Jack No Fighter Was Tougher Than the Man Who Went from Shoeshine Boy to Champion and Back Again," *South Florida Sun-Sentinel*, October 9, 1988, 6.

9. Bob Hill, "Beau Jack: Legend Back Where He Belongs," *Fort Lauderdale News*, July 7, 1985, 38.

10. Matt Schudel, "The Ballad of Beau Jack No Fighter Was Tougher Than the Man Who Went from Shoeshine Boy to Champion and Back Again," *South Florida Sun-Sentinel*, October 9, 1988, 6.

11. Robert Seltzer, "Fear in the Ring: A Second Opponent for Fighters," *Philadelphia Inquirer*, June 27, 1988, 19, 22.

12. Matt Schudel, "The Ballad of Beau Jack No Fighter Was Tougher Than the Man Who Went from Shoeshine Boy to Champion and Back Again," *South Florida Sun-Sentinel*, October 9, 1988, 6.

13. Bob Hill, "Beau Jack: Legend back Where He Belongs," *Fort Lauderdale News*, July 7, 1985, 38.

14. The Dundee's last name was Mirena, but they adopted the name Dundee after their brother Joe chose it when he was a fighter so that their parents wouldn't know he was boxing. Both brothers were inducted into the Boxing Hall of Fame.

15. "Hall of Fame trainer Angelo Dundee dies," *ESPN.com News Service*; http://www.espn.com/boxing/story/_/id/7530790/muhammad-ali-legendary-trainer-angelo-dundee-dies-90; February 2, 2012, accessed Jan. 7, 2018, 1:11 pm.

16. *Ibid.*

17. Richard Goldstein, "Angelo Dundee, Trainer of Ali and Leonard, Dies at 90," *New York Times*; http://www.nytimes.com/2012/02/02/sports/angelo-dundee-trainer-of-boxing-champions-dies-at-90.html, February 1, 2012, accessed January 5, 2018.

18. Hal Habib, "Heaven on 5th St.: A Once Dank Gym, Where Boxing Legends Grew, Is Set to Reopen with a Flood of Memories," *Palm Beach Post*, September 16, 2010, 1C.

19. Matt Schudel, "The Final Bell for 40 Years, the Greatest Fighters in the World Came to Miami Beach to Ply Their Hard Craft," *South Florida Sun-Sentinel*, May 16, 1993, 16.

20. George Diaz, "Boxing's Basic Elements Remain the Same Across the State," *Orlando Sentinel*, July 8, 1990, 16, 36.

21. Hal Habib, "Heaven on 5th St.: A Once Dank Gym, Where Boxing Legends Grew, Is Set to Reopen with a Flood of Memories," *Palm Beach Post*, September 16, 2010, 1C.

22. Matt Schudel, "The Final Bell for 40 Years, the Greatest Fighters in the World Came to Miami Beach to Ply Their Hard Craft," *South Florida Sun-Sentinel*, May 16, 1993, 16.

23. Brian Doogan, "Prize Fight," *Sunday Times*, February 13, 2005, 25.

24. Hal Habib, "Heaven on 5th St.: A Once Dank Gym, Where Boxing Legends Grew, Is Set to Reopen with a Flood of Memories," *Palm Beach Post*, September 16, 2010, 1C.

25. *Ibid.*

26. Matt Schudel, "The Ballad of Beau Jack No Fighter Was Tougher Than the Man Who Went from Shoeshine Boy to Champion and Back Again," *South Florida Sun-Sentinel*, October 9, 1988, 6.

27. Hal Habib, "Heaven on 5th St.: A Once Dank Gym, Where Boxing Legends Grew, Is Set to Reopen with a Flood of Memories," *Palm Beach Post*, September 16, 2010, 1C.

28. Tom Tiede, "Drug Culture Has Been Real Drag on Once Energetic Boxing World," *Lancaster Eagle-Gazette*, February 2, 1990, 16.

Chapter 31

1. Christy was a tremendous female boxer who, at that time, had a record of 31–1-2, with 25 of her victories coming by way of knockout. Several months earlier, Martin had graced the cover of *Sports Illustrated* magazine.

2. Ed Schuyler, Jr. (1997, Mar. 9). "Former Champions Reminisce," *Albuquerque Journal*, March 9, 1997, 99.

3. Ian MacDonald, "Champ Escaped Fisherman's Hook: Morre, Durelle Reminisce About Their Fabulous 40-year-old Fight at the Forum," *Gazette*, April 6, 1998, 43. Inter-Box is quite a unique company. They seek out the best young boxers and bring to Montreal to be trained and managed. At the InterBox facility in Montreal, there are three full-time trainers, a strength coach, a sports psychologist, a physiotherapist, medical doctors and a 10,000-square-foot, modern training facility with two rings and 20 heavy bags. InterBox offers a complete package to its boxers. It covers each boxer's lodging costs, pays them an average salary of $1,000 per week, provides them $4,000 per year to further their education and offers them retirement pensions and investment counseling.

4. Ian MacDonald, "Champ Escaped Fisherman's Hook," *Gazette*, April 6, 1988, 43.

5. "Boxers Ball Will Salute a True Hero," *Philadelphia Daily News*, November 18, 1998, 77.

6. *Ibid.*

Chapter 32

1. Oscar Fraley, "Back to the Shine' Box for Ex-Champ," *Muncie Evening Press*, July 10, 1957, 19.

2. Joe Falls, "Beau Jack Shines Shoes … and Dreams," *Detroit Free Press*, December 5, 1965, 44.

3. "Beau Jack Victim of Sport He Loves," *New York Post*, May 27, 2001, 79. Opposing Viewpoints in context, link.galegroup.com/apps/doc/A75117006/OVIC?u=egc1&x-id=f27f452e. Accessed 14, Oct. 2017.

4. Bob Hill, "Beau Jack: Legend Back Where He Belongs," *Fort Lauderdale News*, July 7, 1985, 38. The *Ring* magazine established its Boxing Hall of Fame in 1954, which operated until 1988. Out of the 168 members inducted, 154 have been subsequently inducted into the International Boxing Hall of Fame.

5. Michael Hirsley, "Beau Jack: Heroic, Dignified," *Chicago Tribune*, April 20, 2000, 58.

6. Matt Schudel, "The Ballad of Beau Jack No Fighter Was Tougher Than the Man Who Went from Shoeshine Boy to Champion and Back Again," *South Florida Sun-Sentinel*, October 9, 1988, 6.

7. Earl Ruby, "Ruby's Report," *Courier-Journal*, December 28, 1963, 14.

8. *Ibid.*

9. Matt Schudel, "The Ballad of Beau Jack No Fighter Was Tougher Than the Man Who Went from Shoeshine Boy to Champion and Back Again," *South Florida Sun-Sentinel*, October 9, 1988, 6.

10. Richard Goldstein, "Beau Jack, 78, Lightweight Boxing Champion in the 1940s," *New York Times*, February 12, 2000, 24.

11. *Ibid.*

12. "Beau Jack Victim of Sport He Loves," New York Post, May 27, 2001, 79; Opposing Viewpoints in context, link.galegroup.com/apps/doc/A75117006/OVIC?u=egc1&xid=f27f452e. Accessed 14, October 2017.

Bibliography

Albright, J. S. "Whirlaway of Sports: From Rags to Riches for Beau Jack." *Evening Standard*, December 23, 1942.

Archdeacon, Tom. "Battle Royal: A 'Fit of Blind Terror.'" *The Miami News*, May 10, 1988.

Archdeacon, Tom. "Beau Jack: At Age 61, the Spirit Is Still Strong." *Miami News*, May 24, 1982.

"Beau Jack Credits Bobby Jones." *Augusta Chronicle*, January 28, 1979.

"Beau Jack Gets Good Results from Bank's Handling of Funds." *Augusta Chronicle*, September 4, 1955.

Berry, Mort. "Williams' Story: 'Didn't Want to Hit Him Any More.'" *The Philadelphia Inquirer*, July 13, 1948.

Bloodworth, Bob. "A Beau for Clay, Frazier." *Palm-Beach Post*, February 6, 1970.

"Boxer Beau Jack Got His Start at Augusta National." *Golf.com*, March 17, 2009. http://www.golf.com/tour-and-news/boxer-beau-jack-got-his-start-augusta-national.

Brown, James. *James Brown: The Godfather of Soul*. New York: Thunder's Mouth Press, 1997.

Calisch, Richard. "Don't Smoke No Cigars; Don't Get in No Fights." *Chicago Tribune Magazine*, November 13, 1977.

Cannon, Jimmy. "Beau Jack May Be Shine Boy to Tourists but Not Cannon." *Asheville Citizen-Times*, March 29, 1957.

Cannon, Jimmy. "Beau Jack Victim of Sport He Loves." *New York Post*, May 27, 2001.

Cannon, Jimmy. "Beau Jack's Shining Shoes Again." *Orlando Sentinel*, April 10, 1959.

Cannon, Jimmy. "Beau Was Real Man." *News-Herald*, March 7, 1964.

Cannon, Jimmy. "The Old Garden Was for Fights." *Asbury Park Press*, March 6, 1968.

Carver, Lawton. "Fair or Foul." *Courier-Gazette*, February 24, 1948.

Carver, Lawton. "Husky Beau Jack Still Uses Battle Royal Style." *Lansing State Journal*, January 10, 1944.

Cole, Haskel. "'Jack Easy to Hit'—Bob Says." *Pittsburgh Courier*, May 29, 1943.

Condon, David. "In the Wake of the News." *Chicago Tribune*, March 22, 1969.

Conrad, Harold. "Jack and Monty Bout Nets $35,864,900." *Brooklyn Daily Eagle*, August 5, 1944.

Conrad, Harold. "260 Wounded to See Bond Fight." *Brooklyn Daily Eagle*, August 3, 1944.

Considine, Bob. "Beau Jack Flattens Larkin in Third, Gains New York Version of Ring Toga." *Democrat and Chronicle*, December 19, 1942.

Considine, Bob. "Mangled Veterans Appear to Have No Hate in Hearts." *Cincinnati Enquirer*, August 6, 1944.

Considine, Bob. "Old Haunts Are to See Beau Jack." *Cincinnati Enquirer*, November 4, 1941.

Consigilo, Tony, and Franz Douskey. *Sinatra and Me: The Very Good Years*. Old Saybrook, CT: Tantor Media, Inc., 2012.

Corum, Bill. "Rocky Up, Beau Down at the Fontainebleau." *News Journal*, February 14, 1956.

Cuddy, Jack. "Beau Jack, Human Blitz, Kayoes Larkin in 3rd to Win Title." *Star-Gazette*, December 19, 1942.

Cuddy, Jack. "Beau Jack Latest Sensation Along Cauliflower Row." *Danville Morning News*, August 20, 1941.

Cuddy, Jack. "Beau Jack Selected as 'Boxer of the Year.'" *Rochester Democrat and Chronicle*, December 28, 1944.

Cuddy, Jack. "Beau Jack Symbolizes Era of Fast-Breaking Warfare." *Sheboygan Press*, December 28, 1942.

Cuddy, Jack. "Garden Prepares for Pep-Saddler Battle." *Honolulu Star-Advertiser*, February 4, 1951.

Daley, Arthur. "Larceny at Its Worst." *New York Times*, May 25, 1951.

Daley, Arthur. "Sports of the Times." *The New York Times*, November 19, 1943.

Dawson, James P. "Beau Jack Stops Stolz in Seventh When Referee Intervenes in Garden Bout." *New York Times*, November 14, 1942.

Denman, Elliott. "Beau Jack Fought for His Uncle Sam." *Asbury Park Press*, June 3, 1982.

Dollar Times. Accessed October 26, 2018. https://www.dollartimes.com/inflation/inflation.php?amount=15000&year=1944.

Drum, Bob. "Sports Stew—Served Hot." *Pittsburg Press*, July 3, 1950.

Edmonds, A. O. *Joe Louis, Boxing, and American Culture*. Grand Rapids, MI: Wm. B. Eerdmans Publishing Co., 1973.

Ellison, Ralph. *The Invisible Man*. New York: Vintage International, 1952.

Falls, Joe. "Beau Jack Shines Shoes. .. and Dreams." *Detroit Free Press*, December 5, 1965.

Feder, Sid. "Zivic Confident of Trimming Beau Jack." *Times Herald*, February 1, 1943.

Fleischer, Nat. "Beau Jack Named Boxer of the Year in 1944 Competition." *Ring*, February 1945 (vol. 23, no. 1).

Fraley, Oscar. "Back to the 'Shine' Box for Ex-Champ." *Muncie Evening Press*, July 10, 1957.

"The Gaudy Touch." *Time*, April 12, 1943, vol. 41, issue 15.

"Georgia White Planter Holding Men in Peonage—Killed Eleven; Deaths of 11 Negroes Charged to Employer." *New York Age*, April 2, 1921, 1.

"Golden Goose." *Time*, March 3, 1947, vol. 49, issue 9.

Goldstein, Richard. "Angelo Dundee, Trainer of Ali and Leonard, Dies at 90." *New York Times*, February 1, 2012. http://www.nytimes.com/2012/02/02/sports/angelo-dundee-trainer-of-boxing-champions-dies-at-90.html.

Grace, Art. "Beau Wants Another Chance." *Miami News*, July 25, 1955.

Grace, Art. "Beau Won't Take Advice." *Miami News*, August 29, 1955.

"Greatest Tragedy of Ring History Was Enacted in Roped Arena in Reno Today." *Reno Gazette-Journal*, July 5, 1910.

Habib, Hal. "Heaven on 5th St.: A Once Dank Gym, Where Boxing Legends Grew, Is Set to Reopen with a Flood of Memories." *Palm Beach Post*, September 16, 2010.

"Hall of Fame Trainer Angelo Dundee Dies." *ESPN*, February 2, 2012. http://www.espn.com/boxing/story/_/id/7530790/muhammad-ali-legendary-trainer-angelo-dundee-dies-90.

Hendrix, Johnny. "Ike Williams Wins on TKO." *Augusta Chronicle*, August 13, 1955.

Hill, Bob. "Beau Jack: Legend Back Where He Belongs." *Fort Lauderdale News*, July 7, 1985.

Hirsley, Michael. "Beau Jack: Heroic, Dignified." *Chicago Tribune*, April 20, 2000.

Hochman, Scott. "Beau Jack Ponders Long Comeback Road." *Augusta Chronicle*, April 27, 1952.

Jack, Beau. "Eye-Poppers: Manager's Appetite Floors Boxer." *Ithaca Journal*, August 17, 1944.

Johnson, Raymond. "One Man's Opinion: Beau Jack, Cotton-Picker, Looms as Next Lightweight Champ." *Tennessean*, August 20, 1941.

Karlin, Mark. "'The Birth of a Nation'100 Years Later: Why Woodrow Wilson's Embrace of the KKK Still Matters." *Buzzflash.com*, July 23, 2015. http://buzzflash.com/commentary/white-supremacists-have-always-baptized-their-perverted-cause-in-christianity.

Kegg, J. Suter. "Tapping on the Sports Keg." *Cumberland Evening Times*, June 1, 1951.

Kegg, J. Suter. "Tapping the Sports Keg: Is Beau Jack Broke." *Cumberland Evening Times*, June 18, 1951.

Kenny, Tom. "Crack O' Dawn." *Augusta Chronicle*, August 20, 1944.

Kerrison, Roy. "Beau Jack, a Happy Fallen Idol." *Age*, August 5, 1957.

Kieran, John. "Sports of the Times: Bubbling Over Beau Jack." *New York Times*, November 13, 1942.

Lee, W.J. "With Malice Toward None." *Hartford Courant*, April 26, 1941.

London, Jack. "Jack London Describes the Fight and Jack Johnson's Golden Smile." *San Francisco Call*, December 27, 1908.

Matthews, Leslie. "Leslies' Boxing Bits: Inside Closeup on Master Trainer Bill Miller." *New York Age*, May 6, 1950.

McCann, Dick. "Jack New 135 lb. King; KO's Larkin in 3d." *Daily News*, December 19, 1942.

McGoogan, W. J. "Beau Jack's Punch Is Snappier Than His Leg; Zavala Knocked Out." *St. Louis Post-Dispatch*, November 4, 1947.

McQueen, Red. "Hoomalimali by Red McQueen: Opportunity Knocks for Kim Tonight." *Honolulu Advertiser*, October 3, 1950.

McQueen, Red. "Hoomalimali by Red McQueen: Wergeles Says Charles Will Prove Popular Champ." *Honolulu Advertiser*, October 1, 1950.

Mills, Ned. "Bonesetter Fixes Lamotta's Hand and Beau Jack's Leg to be Miracle Man of Fighters." *News Herald*, August 1, 1946.

Murray, Jim. "He Succeeded by the Seats of Fans' Pants." *Los Angeles Times*, July 10, 1990.

Norman, Marcus. "Beau Jack: The Garden's Favorite." *Boxing.com*, July 9, 2012. http://www.boxing.com/beau_jack_the_gardens_favorite.html.

Nunn, Bill, Jr. "Change of Pace." *Pittsburgh Courier*, January 29, 1955.

Parker, Dan. "Broadway Bugle." *Courier-Post*, February 27, 1956.

Plaschke, Bill. "After the Punch Is Gone." *Fort Lauderdale News*, June 28, 1982.

Rein, Joe. "Stillman's Gym: The Center of the Boxing Universe." *Mr. Beller's Neighborhood*, June 1, 2003. https://mrbellersneighborhood.com/2003/06/stillmans-gym-the-center-of-the-boxing-universe.

Rice, Grantland. "The Sportlight: Lightweight Beau Jack Windmill Type Fighter." *Valley Morning Star*, December 22, 1942.

Roberts, Clifford. *The Story of the Augusta National Golf Club.* New York: Doubleday and Company, Inc, 1976.

Robinson, Pat. "Beau Jack to Try Comeback." *Arizona Republic*, January 3, 1955.

Rudd, Irving. "I Remember: Stillman's, Oiv, Benny." *New York Times*, April 7, 1974.

Russell, Randy. "All in the Game." *Augusta Chronicle*, March 4, 1955.

Schudel, Matt. "The Ballad of Beau Jack: No Fighter Was Tougher Than the Man Who Went from Shoeshine Boy to Champion and Back Again." *South Florida Sun-Sentinel*, October 9, 1988. https://www.sun-sentinel.com/news/fl-xpm-1988-10-09-8802280757-story.html.

Schudel, Matt. "The Final Bell for 40 Years: The Greatest Fighters in the World Came to Miami Beach to Ply Their Hard Craft." *South Florida Sun-Sentinel*, May 16, 1993. https://www.sun-sentinel.com/news/fl-xpm-1993-05-16-9302120238-story.html.

Seltzer, Robert. "Fear in the Ring: A Second Opponent for Fighters." *Philadelphia Inquirer*, June 27, 1988.

Shugrue, Edward J. "Between Ourselves." *Bridgeport Post*, April 8, 1962.

Smith, Gary. "Still Fighting Old Wars Former Lightweight Champ Beau Jack Lives

Out His Legend." *Sports Illustrated*, February 15, 1988. http://www.si.com/vault/ 1988/02/15/117125/still-fighting-old-wars-former-lightweight-champ-beau-jack-liv es-out-his-legend.

Smith, Lillian. *Killers of the Dream*. New York: W.W. Norton & Co., 1978.

Smith, Wendell. "Smitty's Sports Spurts: A Champ's Life Before and After a Title Fight." *Pittsburgh Courier*, November 27, 1943.

Smith, Wendell. "Sports Beat: Beau Jack's Fighting for Another Pile." *Pittsburgh Courier*, October 22, 1949.

Stiles, Sandy. "'Orphaned' Beau Jack Here to Visit Mother." *Tampa Bay Times*, April 12, 1943.

Sussman, Jeffrey. "Lous Stillman's Filthy Gym." *East Hampton Star*, October 6, 2016. http://easthamptonstar.com/Opinion/20161006/Lou-Stillmans-Filthy-Gym-Jeffrey-Sussman.

"Three Champions Crowned, Attendance Hits New Peak During Banner Boxing Year." *Star-Gazette*, December 28, 1944.

Troy, Jack. "All in the Game." *Atlanta Constitution*, July 25, 1941.

Walosin, Fran. "Beau Jack Risking Injuries in Comeback Bid Thursday." *Elmira Advertiser*, January 19, 1955.

"Watchman Shoots Negro Boy Here." *Augusta Chronicle*, February 16, 1931.

Woodward, Stanley. "Masters Recalls a Little Champ." *Miami News*, April 5, 1954.

Young, Fred. "Young's Yarns." *Pantagraph*, June 17, 1951.

Index

Numbers in **_bold italics_** indicate pages with illustrations